ALSO BY RICHARD A. CLARKE

FICTION

The Scorpion's Gate

Breakpoint

NONFICTION

Against All Enemies: Inside America's War on Terror

YOUR GOVERNMENT FAILED YOU

BREAKING THE CYCLE OF
NATIONAL SECURITY DISASTERS

RICHARD A. CLARKE

ecco

An Imprint of HarperCollinsPublishers

YOUR GOVERNMENT FAILED YOU. Copyright © 2008 by RAC Enterprises. All rights reserved. Printed in the United States of America. No part of this book may be used or reproduced in any manner whatsoever without written permission except in the case of brief quotations embodied in critical articles and reviews. For information, address HarperCollins Publishers, 10 East 53rd Street, New York, NY 10022.

HarperCollins books may be purchased for educational, business, or sales promotional use. For information, please write: Special Markets Department, HarperCollins Publishers, 10 East 53rd Street, New York, NY 10022.

FIRST EDITION

Library of Congress Cataloging-in-Publication Data is available upon request.

ISBN: 978-0-06-147462-0

08 09 10 11 12 DIX/RRD 10 9 8 7 6 5 4 3 2 1

www.RichardAClarke.net is not affiliated with HarperCollins

In Memory of Sam Hamrick
aka W. T. Tyler,
Dedicated public servant,
Talented author, iconoclast,
and friend

Contents

ONE

9/11 CHANGED EVERYTHING?

When I said "Your government failed you" to the families of the victims of 9/11, it seemed to me that I was merely stating the obvious: the government had failed the American people. And I had.

Three thousand people had been murdered in a morning, not on a battlefield, not in their battleships as had happened at Pearl Harbor, but in their offices. They had been killed by a terrorist group that had promised to attack us, and which we had been unable to stop. The CIA had been unable to assassinate its leadership. It had also been unable to tell anyone when the terrorists had shown up in this country, even though it knew they were here. The national leadership had been unwilling to focus on the threat for months, although repeatedly warned to do so. And I had been unable to get either the bureaucracy or the new national leadership to act toward the terrorist network before the big attack in the way they would want to respond after thousands of Americans had been murdered.

The American people had a right to know what the failures were that led to 9/11 and why they occurred. I tried to tell that story as I saw it, stretching over more than two decades, in *Against All Enemies,* a book I wrote two years after the attack. Then the 9/11 Commission was forced into existence by the victims' families. Its report and staff studies looked at what had happened from a number of perspectives and uncovered new information. Since then several authors and analysts have added further detail.

On that horrific day in September, while trying to make the machinery of government work in the minutes and hours after the attack, I suppressed my anger at al Qaeda, at the U.S. government, at myself. There was an urgent job to be done that day. But in one brief moment of catching my breath, I was consoled by my colleague Roger Cressey, who noted that now, finally, all of our plans to destroy al Qaeda and its network of organizations would be implemented. The nation would deal seriously and competently with the problem. I assumed he was right and got back to work. It turned out he was wrong. Incredibly, after 9/11 our government failed us even more, much more.

"9/11 changed everything." That was the remark we heard over and over again in the years that followed. It was only partially true. 9/11 did not change the Constitution, although some have acted as if it did. Nor did the government's response to the attacks make us more secure. Though a great deal of activity has taken place, al Qaeda the organization and al Qaeda the movement still threaten the United States. We still have significant vulnerabilities at home. And abroad, we have far fewer friends and far more enemies than on 9/12.

By the second anniversary of the attack on America, the United States had invaded and occupied two Islamic nations, created an Orwellian-sounding new bureaucracy, launched a spending spree of unprecedented proportions, and was systematically shredding international law and our own Constitution. Despite our frenzy, or in many cases because of it, the problem we sought to address, violent Islamist extremism, was getting worse. Much of what our government did after 9/11, at home and abroad, departed from our values and identity as a nation. It was also massively counterproductive. Our government failed us before and after 9/11, and it continues to do so today.

Indeed, as this book unfolds you will see how I believe that we have been failing at important national security missions for a long time. Sometimes, as perhaps proved by the end of the Cold War, we succeed despite ourselves, like a student who makes it by even with some failing grades and incompletes. But the failures are piling high and we are not correcting them; in some cases we are making them worse. And there are new challenges that, like al Qaeda before 9/11, we know are coming and are not addressing sufficiently or successfully. Though al Qaeda still exists and is growing stronger, there are new risks in cyberspace and from climate change. What is wrong that we cannot become sufficiently motivated and agreed as a nation to address known threats before they become disasters? Why do we accept costly chronic problems whose cumulative effects are far greater than those of the well-known disasters?

This book is my attempt to understand what happened after 9/11 and answer the larger question of why the U.S. government, despite all of its resources, performs so poorly at national security. The problems lie in how we as a nation have decided to conduct the process of national security, from problem identification and analysis, through policy development and implementation, to oversight and accountability. We have allowed the role of partisan politics to expand and that of professional public sector management to atrophy. As a result, we repeatedly misdiagnose the problems we face and prescribe the wrong cures. In this volume, to attempt to diagnose the problems accurately, we will sometimes go back in history before 9/11. We will sometimes go forward to see what effects changing technologies and continuing policies will have. I will attempt to suggest what we might do differently to address the unique and cross-cutting problems in a set of related and vital national security disciplines:

- The conduct of sustained, large-scale, complex operations, such as Iraq

- The collection and analysis of national security information by the "intelligence community"

- Dealing with violent Islamist extremism, or "the global war on terrorism"

- Domestic security risk management, or "homeland security"

- Global climate change and national energy policy including the security effects

- The migration of control systems and records into the unsafe environment of networked systems, or "cyberspace security"

This book is, as was *Against All Enemies,* a personal story, one told by reference to my experiences as I remember them and to the many personalities I have encountered along the way as a Pentagon analyst, a State Department manager, a White House national security official, and now as a private citizen. In the weeks before we invaded Iraq, I left government after thirty years in national security under five Republican and two Democratic presidents. I have since been teaching, writing, and traveling about the country and around the world consulting on security issues. My time in government and since provides me with a special perspective and, no doubt, distinct prejudices. One of those prejudices, which you will soon detect, is that I think that on issues of national security our government can and must work well. Before we begin this analysis of the systemic problems of U.S. national security management, perhaps I should reveal how that belief was shaped and formed.

As a child in the 1950s, I was aware from my parents that government had ended the Great Depression that they had struggled through and in doing so had built infrastructure across the nation. Government had mobilized the entire country, including my parents, to create and arm a military that had simultaneously liberated a captive Europe from Nazi rule and pushed back imperial Japan from its occupation of most of Asia and the Pacific. My father spent four years in the Army Air Corps in the Pacific, while my mother gave up an executive assistant job in the private sector to make artillery in the Watertown Arsenal. Along the way to wartime victory, government had organized the colossal effort that was the Manhattan Project and had given birth to the nuclear age.

In my own lifetime, government had sent the World War II veterans to school, financed their new homes, and linked the country with interstate highways. It had created an entirely new human endeavor, space flight, had laced the skies with satellites, placed humans on the moon, and sent probes to the planets. As an eight-year-old watching the Echo satellite move through the night sky and later following in detail the manned space flight missions, I was thrilled at what thousands of skilled and hardworking Americans, including my older cousins, were doing together, "to go to the moon and do the other things . . . not because they are easy, but because they are hard."

On that bitterly cold day when John F. Kennedy was sworn in, he appealed to us to "ask what you can do for your country." I was an impressionable ten-year-old who believed that government service was a high calling. The public school I was to attend a few months later led Kennedy's inaugural parade that day, its band tramping down Pennsylvania Avenue in the snow. When I did enroll in Boston Latin School later that year, the headmaster pointed to the names of alumni carved on the frieze above the auditorium: John Hancock, Paul Revere, Samuel Adams, Benjamin Franklin, and on through the years to more recent graduates such as President Kennedy's father, Joseph Kennedy. He told us that we followed in that tradition, to serve the nation. For six formative years in that school, the lesson was repeated that public service was both demanding and a duty.

My last semester at the Latin School, the Tet Offensive made many in my graduating class think that our government was somehow getting something wrong in Vietnam, but we did not know yet how wrong. We had seen the civil rights movement as a way in which government could do the right thing, undo the wrongs of the past. Then, weeks after Tet, Martin Luther King, Jr., was killed and every major American city went up in flames. Our hopes dimmed that America would soon judge people "not by the color of their skin but by the content of their character." At the hour that my class walked onstage to graduate several weeks later, Robert Kennedy succumbed to wounds from an assassin's gun. It was a bad year: Tet, Martin, Bobby. Our optimism was turning to anger.

As America's experience in Vietnam devolved into debacle and tragedy, my generation saw as none had before that the great resources of the U.S. government could be mismanaged with horrific effect. Good government was not self-executing. Badly run, our government did not just fail, it was a highly lethal weapon capable of spawning disaster on an immense scale, ruining the lives of millions.

But as I marched in the streets of Washington to protest that war, my desire to serve in government did not diminish, it grew. With the conceit and arrogance of youth, I thought that if those of us who had learned from the mistakes of Vietnam joined the government, we could prevent similar follies in the future. How much more effective could we be on the inside helping to shape decisions than on the streets protesting after they were made?

I went to work in the Pentagon in the latter days of Richard Nixon's presidency. There was no better place to see how government functioned. I saw how teams of analysts pored over data, trying to make complex decisions about budgets and weapons system procurements. Other analysts sifted through mountains of intelligence, trying to assess the threats to our nation and its forces. And there were real threats. Although it may now seem like a quaint and distant time, the Cold War brought real peril. The government of the Soviet Union worked hard to undermine the United States and our allies. Nuclear weapons flew through the air every day, only hours from their targets.

Within days of my assignment to the Pentagon's Middle East Task Force in 1973, the Soviet Union began moving nuclear weapons and troops in reaction to the ongoing Arab-Israeli War. Secretary of Defense James Schlesinger ordered American forces worldwide to go on full alert. Tens of thousands of nuclear weapons were ready to be used. I asked a Pentagon colleague what we would do if nuclear war began. The young Army major laughingly suggested that we go to Ground Zero, which was what the Pentagon staff called the courtyard hamburger stand, and look up to watch the missiles coming in. (Years later I would work again with that major when he was a four-star general. And later, a hijacked aircraft would turn part of the Pentagon a few feet away from the hamburger stand into a real Ground Zero.)

For much of the following twenty years, I worked on the Cold War, which, despite its seeming unimportance now, was a struggle far greater than what we face today. Many years after that struggle was over, on

the day Ronald Reagan died, I was driving into Berlin on the auto-
bahn. When I heard on the radio that he had passed, I changed my
destination from the hotel to the Brandenburger Tor, where Reagan
had famously said "Mr. Gorbachev, tear down this wall." (A few years
after that speech, the young people of Berlin tore it down—with their
hands.) Getting there just before midnight, I saw young couples walking together, apparently oblivious that a few years before this had been
no-man's-land, where once American and Soviet tanks had pointed
their cannon at one another, where East Germans had been gunned
down running for freedom. Ronald Reagan and eight other American
presidents, supported by tens of millions of American citizens, had prevailed. Our conduct of the Cold War was certainly imperfect and the
Soviets may have lost that struggle more than we won it. Nonetheless,
the U.S. government did both prevent nuclear war and contribute to
the collapse of the opposing Communist alliance. Doing so was complicated, expensive, and challenging. It required a sustained, multifac-
eted, and coordinated effort, equal in scale to what government did in
World War II. You can see the results today, not only there in Berlin on
Unter den Linden, but also on every street in America. Nuclear missiles
did not fall. Communism did not take away our freedoms. The American government had worked.

In the post–Cold War world, my government career gave me additional windows onto instances of government succeeding. George
H. W. Bush created an improbable diplomatic and military coalition of
more than sixty nations that liberated Kuwait and reestablished an international security system. When Bill Clinton was in office, the U.S.
government–created internet burst forth, creating cyberspace and forever changing the nature of society. His Vice President, Al Gore, sliced
through bureaucracies, "reinventing government" and bringing better
service with less cost and fewer government employees.

Just as my personal history taught me that government can work,
there are many people today whose formative experiences have produced a different conclusion. Few young people today think of government service as a high calling or as something they would want to do.
When they do think of government, they envision a wasteful, incom-

petent, muscle-bound behemoth, damaging all it touches. They envision the calamity we have made of Iraq, the images of Americans demeaned in the wake of Hurricane Katrina. They recall the repeated intelligence failures and botched law enforcement efforts. They may recall the ineffective "War on Drugs" or picture our porous borders. They know of the continued growth of the terrorist movement and the contempt with which America is held in much of the world.

Something has happened. Government has ceased to work well, not just in the well-known failures but almost across the board in the area of national security. There seems to be an inability to get anything done, to successfully tackle any major issue. Democrats attribute the problems to one cause, the presidency of George W. Bush. But the causes go well beyond the personalities of incumbent officials. There is a pattern of incompetence and a lack of achievement running throughout the components of national security: homeland security, intelligence, defense, foreign policy, federal law enforcement, energy policy, and the "war on terrorism." These failures are important because, despite the exaggeration and hype often used by government officials, there are serious threats and important issues that only the federal government can address. Failure to deal successfully with these issues can mean the deaths of thousands of people and the waste of trillions of dollars, as we have just tragically witnessed.

The United States spends more than a trillion dollars a year on national security, running up a national debt that could, combined with health care and retirement costs, burden the next generation and stifle economic growth in this country. For that amount of money—indeed, for less—the American people should get far better results. Moreover, the culture of mediocrity that is asserting itself in our national security apparatus increases the likelihood of further calamitous failures, with the personal pain and suffering that will mean for Americans and others.

I am not inherently a pessimist; quite the opposite. I know government has worked in these areas in the past, and I believe it can again, if we can identify what has gone wrong in each area and across the board and if we can devise initiatives and programs to overcome the entropy and decay that has set in. This book contains my contribution to thinking about those remedial initiatives and programs. I hope it will stimulate further contributions and debate, as well as increasing the basic recognition that there is a systemic problem in how America conducts national security.

For if we continue to operate as we do now, many more government officials will sit before investigatory panels. Many more will have to say to victims and their loved ones, "Your government failed you."

Two

NO MORE VIETNAMS

For no institution is the pain of failure more personal than for our military. When the military fails, their friends die and leave widows. Many of the living lose limbs or acquire post-traumatic stress disorder. And no institution has tried as hard as the U.S. military to understand why failure occurs or has worked as diligently to correct mistakes so that they do not recur. The formal Lessons Learned process is ingrained in the U.S. military's way of doing business. And yet there is Iraq.

The U.S. military is so richly deserving of our thanks and respect that few civilians have been willing to suggest that the Iraq disaster is at all the military's fault. Clearly the elected civilian commander in chief, his seasoned Vice President, the two-time Secretary of Defense, Congress, and others should bear most of the blame. But the military, more precisely the officer corps, and specifically many general officers over the course of thirty years, deserve some culpability. I say that not to add to the chorus of scapegoating and finger-pointing, but so that we as a nation can follow in the military's tradition of lessons learned, so that we can avoid Santayana's condemnation. And I believe the trail leads back to the military's own reactions to the national failure that was the Vietnam War. To understand Iraq, we need to remember Vietnam and what happened in the U.S. military after that war.

Most of America tried to forget Vietnam after the fall of Saigon. It took years for the veterans to be honored. The officer corps, however, could not forget. They had been there. Their friends had died or been maimed there. Their Army, their beloved military, was now for many Americans an object of distrust, discredited and ridiculed. The officer corps also knew that in a democracy like America, one that was then still challenged by its Cold War enemies, a rift between the military and the people could be fatal for the republic. If the Congress did not appropriate enough defense funding to deter the Soviet Union, if smart young people did not join the ranks, the downward spiral of the military would continue. They had to do something.

What the officer corps did, over many years, was to bring about changes designed to prevent another Vietnam. Ironically, the unintended consequences of those changes brought us the kind of Iraq war that developed thirty years after Vietnam.

The changes were at the military, political-military, and purely political levels. On the military level, the new Army the post-Vietnam officers built was designed to "fight and win" quickly, overwhelming an enemy on the battlefield. It was also designed with one capability intentionally omitted: the ability to take the lead in fighting an insurgency such as Vietnam had initially been. When some civilians and renegade military tried to build and use a robust counterinsurgency Special Forces, the officer corps tried to block them.

On the political-military level, the officer corps remade the Army's organizational structure with the explicit goal of creating a political reality: they created an Army designed to be unable to fight a prolonged major war without the support of Congress and, more important, of the American people.

Politically, the corps abandoned a century-long tradition that the officer corps did not register in either political party and did not vote in elections. Officers and enlisted personnel were now actively encouraged both to register and to vote. Systems were put into place to connect military voters to the local election authorities in their home cities and counties. The military and their extended families became a voting bloc.[1] They voted overwhelmingly for one party, which embraced them and sought to use its "support of the military" as a differentiator among voters.[2]

These changes were not brought about by some secret cabal of officers or any form of conspiracy. The changes were legitimate policy choices made openly by honorable people, people whose goals were to avoid another failure, to defend America, and to maintain its traditions of civil-military relations. They are also changes that had a profound impact on the Iraq War.

My professional relationship with the U.S. military, coincidentally, spans exactly the same period, from the end of fighting in Vietnam to the Iraq War. So for me, this is not just an academic inquiry into how the U.S. military deals with failures; it is the story of my friends and colleagues, and of the crises and wars that filled my thirty years in the national security departments. And it is the story of how the military that so many of us love and value has again found itself misused and in an unsuccessful war.

So you will know my prejudices, let me briefly sketch my relations with the military. I started working in the Pentagon in 1973, as the American military was still reeling from the Vietnam War. I had decided, after graduation from college, to find a career in government, specifically in national security, because I, too, was powerfully motivated by a desire to contribute however I could to ensure that there would be "no more Vietnams." I acted not because I was antimilitary, but because I revered the U.S. military and thought it had been misused. Moreover, I believed the costs to America had been enormous and we had been weakened by the war.

My respect for and interest in the military were undoubtedly a product of the home in which I grew up. My grandfather, after immigrating from Scotland, served in the U.S. Navy in World War I and the Coast Guard in World War II. As I noted earlier, my father served in the National Guard before Pearl Harbor and in the Army Air Corps in World War II, in the jungles of New Guinea. My mother gave up a job as a corporate executive's secretary to make artillery during that war. Anytime during my youth that a nearby military base had an open house or a Navy ship allowed civilians on board, my family went. I began following events in Vietnam closely while in junior high school but by the time of the Tet Offensive in February of my senior year in high school, I thought we were hopelessly off track. I did not understand how we thought we could be successful with the strategy and tactics we were employing. Nor did I think the war justified the cost to the United States. One of those costs was to my cousin, who had grown up with me in an extended Scottish family. Ripped from the University of Massachusetts by a draft board, Billy soon found himself leading a squad of troops in the jungle of Vietnam. Wounded twice and almost killed the second time, he came home with what we now call post-traumatic stress disorder (PTSD).

Thus, while in college and enjoying a student deferment from the draft, I joined antiwar protests. And after college, with the arrogance of youth, I applied to work in the Pentagon in the hope that someday I might rise to a position where I could help to stop stupid wars. Amazingly, I got a management trainee job in the office of the Secretary of Defense. As a civil servant in the Pentagon, I had jobs where I reported to military officers. In later years at the State Department and the White House, I would have many military officers on my staff, reporting to me. During thirty years in national security, I worked closely with generals and admirals. So long was my professional relationship with military officers that some of my friends, such as John Gordon and the late Wayne Downing, went from major to four-star general and into retirement while I served with them as a civilian. The years of watching our top officers created a deep respect in me for our military leaders, but I also know that they are like civilians in one important respect: they are not infallible.

In 1973 I suspected that working in the Pentagon would bring surprises, but I had no idea how different a world I was entering when I first walked into the five-sided home of the Defense Department. More like a city, the fictional space station Deep Space Nine, or a giant creature than a building, the Pentagon's sheer physical scale was the most immediately obvious thing to which I had to adjust. It took twenty minutes to walk from my office to where the parking lot began. Late at night, the sense of being inside a beast was unavoidable. I heard the pumps thumping in the basement, preventing the Potomac from flooding in, and cleaning crews singing, unseen down a maze of interconnected corridors.

Understanding the language was, however, my most difficult adjustment to the Pentagon. Words that I thought I knew had different meanings inside the building. Told by a major to "burn" a document, I was about to light it on fire when he explained that I was to copy it. Thus alerted to the linguistic anomalies, when told to "chop" another document, I guessed that no one really expected me to cut it into pieces. But it took a while for me to realize that the intent of the instruction was that I was to "sign off" on the memo.

Then there were words I did not know at all and were not in any dictionary I consulted. "Reclama," for example, turned out to be both a noun and a verb, meaning an appeal and to appeal a decision. Sometimes asking for a translation only led to more questions. When I was told that "Reforger" was to occur in a month, I asked if that was some kind of holiday. "No," a colonel shot back as though I should have known. "Reforger is when we break out the POMCUS." Not having any POMCUS to break out, I silently wondered what I would do when Reforger happened. Eventually I learned that we were discussing an annual exercise (REturn of FORces to GERmany), in which a U.S. Army division stationed in the United States quickly flew its personnel to Germany, where they unboxed a second set of tanks and all the division's other equipment (PrepOsitioned Materiel Configured to Unit Sets) that they kept stored there.

Working long hours alongside majors and lieutenant commanders, colonels and captains, I learned about the Defense budget system and the amazing weapons and capabilities it bought. But it slowly became obvious to me that the real gems of the Defense Department, the secret strengths that set the U.S. military apart, were my colleagues in uniform themselves. Their individual dedication, selflessness, energy, and character were extraordinary. When one realized that there were hundreds of thousands of them, who could at times be organized effectively to combine all of those individual strengths into a single effort, the immense power available to our nation became clear and stunning. The U.S. military is, I learned then and saw many times in crises over three decades, a remarkably capable organization when used effectively, when it can channel the strength of its great people.

The officers who patiently taught me how to speak militarese (and so much more) had all joined up before Vietnam and had all fought in that war. They had all lost friends there, and they were more than just upset about the results. My buddies were bitter that, despite their sacrifices, we had "lost" the Vietnam War. Some of the bitterness came from the way they had been treated by their fellow Americans when they returned home from the war, as though it had been the troops' own idea to suffer in the jungles and destroy three or four countries in Indochina. When their fathers had come home from World War II, they had been treated as heroes. For the Vietnam veterans, there had often been a hostile reception, or no reception at all.

Over beers after work, I listened as they debated whether we could ever have "won," whether it would have required invading and occupying North Vietnam, or whether even that would have resulted only in a prolonged guerrilla war without victory. Many believed that the goal of preserving an independent South Vietnam could have been accomplished with more time, but the public and Congress had refused to give them more time after six years and 58,000 American dead.

Others disagreed and thought that the public had been right, that the mission was not one that could ever have been accomplished, or at least not at a price that the American people were willing to pay. The majority of the public eventually thought 58,000 American dead was too great a sacrifice for a goal that seemed vague. Like the public, many in uniform had come to doubt that the reasons we were in Vietnam were valid.

For men raised in the "can-do" hero culture of the U.S. military, where anything was possible, it was difficult for them to come to the conclusion that they had been asked to do something that was both impossible and unpopular. But many of them did come to that conclusion. And they resented both the "politicians" (civilians) who had asked them to do it, for being so uninformed and so willing to expend the lives of American soldiers, and the "brass" (generals and admirals) who had readily obeyed, for being overly compliant and so badly prepared. Over time, the military's resentment at Congress and the American public declined and a view developed that the military in a democracy should do only what the people genuinely want it to do and what the public is willing to support, even in tough times.

What surprised me was the extent to which the bitterness of these midcareer officers was directed at the military itself, at the generals who had poured hundreds of thousands of U.S. fighting men into a war for which the U.S. armed forces were so badly prepared. These young officers complained that their commanders had agreed to send them off to a war for which the generals had not created doctrine or tactics, had not procured the appropriate weapons, and had not trained the force.

In the Officers' Club bars and in the seminar rooms of the various war colleges where midcareer officers recharged their batteries and had a chance to think about their institutions, the conversations turned that bitterness over Vietnam into a determination to reform. These officers in their thirties and early forties were determined to bring a new professionalism to the officer corps, one based on analysis, rigor, and a better understanding of the system of systems of which weapons were just one part.

They came to the conclusion that structural changes were necessary in how the military was organized, how it planned, how it promoted officers, and how it interacted with the rest of the government. Procedures had to be instituted so that the right questions were always asked and the necessary planning, training, and equipping accompanied a decision to use force. The military needed to say when a task given to it was beyond its current capabilities or could not be accomplished at a cost the public would support. Some of these changes had to be written into law in a way that they could not be easily altered or ignored, so that the military officer corps could be sure that there would be "no more Vietnams."

THE CORPORATE MEMORY OF VIETNAM

There are, of course, important differences between Iraq and Vietnam, most importantly the U.S. fatality level. (Over the period of involvement of U.S. combat units in Vietnam, America averaged more than 6,000 dead annually. In Iraq, thankfully, the number of dead U.S. soldiers has averaged about 14 percent of the annual Vietnam War fatality rate.) The most obvious connection between the two wars is the people, the senior U.S. military officers serving now who were youngsters in Vietnam. Even those who are generals now who did not serve in Vietnam learned about it, as I did, from officers who had suffered there. Vietnam is part of the institutional memory of the senior officers of the U.S. military.

The U.S. military officer corps is, for those who rise to the most senior command levels, a thirty-year or longer dedication. You do not become a four-star general by starting out as a one-star general transferring in from being a senior vice president in an investment bank or technology firm. You get to be a "flag officer" (a general or an admiral) by entering the military as a second lieutenant around age twenty-one and serving in each of the intervening six grades over the course of three decades. The military is your life. You may complain about its shortcomings, but you are more dedicated to the institution of your service (Army, Navy, Air Force, or Marines) and to the U.S. military in general than you are to almost anything else. Although they will not admit it readily, for most general officers the military has been and is more important to them than their religion, their favorite sports team, or their hometown. For many, it was more important to them than their first spouse. Even when they retire from active duty, much of their life will be taken up by their interaction with their service.

The absence of lateral entry of senior managers is also true for some civilian federal agencies, including most of the CIA and FBI. The military, however, is more of a closed society. Its members' medical care and that of their families will usually be at military hospitals. Often their children's schools and the stores they shop in will be for the military only. For much of their careers, military officers will live on military bases and their off-duty hours will be spent in a military environment. More important, over the course of a thirty-year career, most U.S. military officers will have been personally involved in "real-world" operations, and many will have been in combat. Their jobs will at some point involve death—that of their colleagues or other military personnel connected to them in some way. They have a clear sense that what they do matters greatly, even if the importance of their jobs is not reflected in their pay.

Thus, most senior military managers, the "flag officers," have an enormous emotional investment in their service and in the U.S. military. They do not want to see the institution hurt. Although they recognize that members of the military can be called upon to risk their lives, they do not want to see their colleagues wounded or killed if that can reasonably be avoided. They want that kind of sacrifice to occur only for very worthy causes. Thus, early in my thirty-year civilian career of working closely with the military and with flag officers, I learned what seems counterintuitive to most civilians: that the military are the least likely of any group in government or even in American society to want to employ military power, to engage in the use of force.

It is not just that military managers do not want to see their people wounded or killed, they also do not want to see their institution damaged. They want the thing to which they gave their lives to be effective and respected. Without a reputation of effectiveness and respect from the civilian community, they will not be as able to recruit personnel or gain support for the funding they need for training, weapons, salary, and working conditions. The U.S. military, unlike armed forces in many other nations, is by design subservient to civilian control, as exercised by elected officials and by the civilians the elected officials appoint and approve.[3] In nations as diverse as China and Iran, the military own giant companies that provide civilian goods and services, generating profits. Even in democracies as different as Turkey and Thailand, the military has a standing in the national system that has effectively given it an ultimate veto over the activities of their elected civilian governments.[4] In the United States there is civilian control of the military. The military wants it that way, and the officer corps is taught about civilian control from day one of their careers.

This fact, obvious to most educated Americans, is nonetheless essential to understanding the military. The size, missions, and overall health of the U.S. military as an organization are highly dependent upon its relationship with America's civilian society and its democratic institutions. Even though the military sometimes seems to live somewhat apart from the rest of society, it is the strength and nature of its relationship with that society that determines much about it.

Although Vietnam was traumatic to America as a whole, it was devastating and earthshaking to the U.S. military as an institution. For the first time in the republic's two-hundred-year history, the U.S. military had lost a war, or at least had not won it. The conduct of that war had not just divided opinion, it had ripped apart the society, pitting Americans against one another, emotionally and often violently. Moreover, unlike the near-national mobilization of World War II, which had involved the majority of Americans in the war effort in one way or another, the burden of fighting the Vietnam War seemed to fall disproportionately on two groups: the career military and the poor, including disadvantaged racial and ethnic groups.[5] Media, congressional, and public criticism of the war and the way in which it was fought often portrayed the U.S. military as ineffective, drug-abusing, sadistic, and even immoral. A wide gap developed between the American military as an institution and the nation that employed it.

Returning from Vietnam, most American military personnel wondered how they could have been sacrificing so much in a cause that most of their fellow citizens did not appear to want them to pursue. Far from thanking them for their sacrifices, often the people of the United States seemed to resent the institution and individual military personnel for having been involved in Vietnam. For career military officers, who understood that it was the civilian leadership and the civilian Congress that had sent them into war, the cognitive dissonance was stark and deeply disturbing. They feared for the future of the U.S. military. That fear was not selfish protection of their job and their lifestyle. The career military officers of the 1970s knew that however unimportant Vietnam might have been to the security of the United States, there were very real national security threats for which we needed a strong military. The Cold War was still under way, and the Soviet Union was still a very real threat and a highly capable enemy.

The collapse of the Soviet Communist nation and its military alliance was not something that anyone could then envision. Quite the opposite, it seemed to many as though the enemy was winning the Cold War.

Two views emerged as dominant among the military professional class. Both were written by Army colonels, many years after the war. Harry Summers, in his book *On Strategy*, concluded that the Army in particular had become too focused on the technical issues of getting things done at the cost of looking at the big picture. If the Army had focused on strategy, Summers concluded, it either would not have gone into Vietnam in the first place (because doing so would have meant a war with China, which might have better been fought elsewhere) or would have realized that the war was not really a counterinsurgency but an invasion by North Vietnam (requiring a conventional response against the North Vietnamese Army). Summers concluded that the Army had done well what it was good at, tactical victories and massive logistics, but had failed to see the big picture. He was dismissive of counterinsurgency as a President Kennedy–inspired fad. Had the Army fought the real enemy, the North Vietnamese divisions, it would have succeeded, Summers believed.[6]

Much later H. R. McMaster wrote *Dereliction of Duty*, charging that the generals who had made up the Joint Chiefs of Staff in the Vietnam era had made a fundamental error in not standing up to the Secretary of Defense and the President, not insisting that many more troops were needed early in the war, not opposing the "graduated response."[7] Ironically, McMaster later fought in Iraq and paid the price of generals who did not push hard enough, or at all prior to the start of the war to make the case that more troops were needed, or alternatively, that the war might best be avoided.

The thoughtful among the young officer corps realized that they needed to understand what had happened in Vietnam. They needed to repair the damage in their relations with the rest of American society. They set about, with the help of civilians and of members of Congress, to put into place changes built on their perception of what had gone wrong in Vietnam.

THE MILITARY CHANGES

The military leadership made the first major changes quickly after Vietnam. The changes were structural and focused on the Army. They were designed to achieve two goals: (1) to make the military more professional and (2) to prevent the civilian leadership from being able to order the military into another war that did not really have the backing of the people.

Creighton Abrams (for whom the M-1 tank is named) was the head of the U.S. Army in 1973. He had come to the job directly from being the commander in Vietnam who had overseen the withdrawal of half a million U.S. troops from that country. As Army Chief of Staff, Abrams began the implementation of structural changes designed to prevent a recurrence of the war he had inherited and that had been terminated so ingloriously.

The Army leadership hated the draft (compulsory military service) as much as the draftees. The conscription system filled the Army with disgruntled, often pot-smoking, young men who really did not want to be there. The result was often insubordination and ineffectiveness.

Richard Nixon realized that the draft was the chief motivator of the massive antiwar protests sweeping the country. Although much of the public still objected to the war, when the draft was slowed and then stopped, the big protests almost disappeared. Thus both the President and the Army leadership found common cause in ending the draft and creating a smaller "all-volunteer force" (AVF). But there were other, less publicly discussed, motivations among the Army generals. The Army leadership thought that without a draft it would be almost impossible to have another Vietnam, another big war.

There simply would not be enough men in the AVF to fight a war that was simultaneously big and long-lasting. Any future President who wanted again to put half a million Americans into a long war would have to get Congress to reinstitute the draft. Given the attitude of the voters toward the draft in 1973, the Russians would have to be landing on the New Jersey shore before Congress would approve involuntary conscription again. Indeed, for some in the early 1970s, the Russians taking over New Jersey would not have been motivation enough to re-institute the draft.

The problem was, however, that, there was a risk that came with the AVF: The public might not really care too much if there were a smaller war. After all, the people forced to fight it would have willingly signed up for that sort of thing. For the post–Vietnam War military, fighting another war without popular support and approval seemed like a bad idea. Vietnam had made the Army an unpopular institution in the United States, unable to recruit the best people and unlikely to get the funds needed for modernization from Congress. An AVF could become a small mercenary army, fighting wars without the political support of the American people. So Abrams believed that the creation of the AVF had to be accompanied by another set of organizational and structural changes.

Thus, Abrams reorganized the smaller Army that resulted from ending the draft. He chose to do so not by eliminating a lot of divisions, with both their combat and support units being eliminated, but instead by keeping as many combat units as possible. Volunteers liked being in combat units. Support units essential to sustained, large-scale combat were reassigned to reserve and National Guard units.[8] Abrams called the shift of the less sexy but essential units required for major military action into the National Guard and reserve the "Total Force" concept.[9] Like the move to end the draft, this reorganization came from an understanding of American politics. Unlike the termination of conscription, however, the reorganization was not ordered by the civilian leadership. This move was the Army leadership's idea, and most civilian leaders outside the Pentagon did not notice it or understand the significance of what was being done.

What the Army believed was that mobilizing the National Guard and reserve to go off to a war would be far more wrenching than ordering an AVF to fight and even more alarming to society than drafting eighteen-year-olds into the service.[10] National Guard and reserve personnel were often in their late twenties and thirties, sometimes older. They had families who needed them. They had jobs as policemen, firefighters, and supervisors in corporations. Sending them off to war would affect communities throughout the country, just as in World War II.

Everyone involved would want to think twice before starting a war that necessitated that kind of mobilization. So while units like tank battalions stayed in the active-duty Army, units like the transportation battalions (the big trucks that haul in the supplies), military police, and military intelligence began moving into the part-time force.

The dirty little secret was that the Army now, quite intentionally, could not fight a big or long war without calling up reserves. Calling up the reserves would pull people out of workplaces all over the country, people with families. If the war were not popular, such a mobilization would be politically hard to do. If civilian leaders wanted to fight a future war, it would have to be well thought out because those leaders would have to sell it to Congress and to the American people.

Abrams died in office in 1974, but his reforms went ahead. The Army became an AVF and eventually recruited a higher standard of soldiers by offering good pay, benefits, skills training, and reenlistment bonuses. The peacetime force worked well enough in exercises, supported by National Guard and reserve units when needed, and by civilian contractors, which increasingly took on the work previously done by draftees and other active-duty personnel.

The second wave of "no more Vietnam" changes was more difficult to achieve. Before they could be justified and institutionalized, there were three lesser disasters that drove home two points to the military: that civilian leaders must be forced to be more thoughtful about using the military, and the military must be more effective when it was called upon.

The first of these three debacles was in 1980. The nation was humiliated by having its embassy in Tehran seized in November 1979 and its embassy staff paraded in blindfolds. Months went by with the staff being held by Iranian "students." ABC News began a nightly television program Ted Koppel titled "America Held Hostage, Day __." President Carter looked at military options, such as bombing Iran to pressure it into releasing the hostages. Most of his advisers thought that such attacks would have the opposite result and urged a diplomatic solution. Carter's approval ratings plummeted.

Frustrated with the failure of diplomacy, President Carter secretly authorized military force to rescue the U.S. Embassy hostages in early

1980. Before the rescue team could even reach Tehran, the operation was aborted when an accident caused aircraft to explode at a makeshift en route refueling base ("Desert One") in the Iranian desert.[11] Iran trumpeted the failed mission, giving media access to the charred hulks of the American aircraft. Carter was defeated for reelection.

Three years later came the twin disasters of Beirut and Grenada. Many in the Reagan administration had wanted to dispel the notion that the U.S. military was a "paper tiger" and to overcome the Vietnam Syndrome. Lebanon, which had been embroiled in a civil war since 1975, achieved a veneer of stability in 1982 through negotiations organized by the U.S. Reagan was persuaded by his Deputy National Security Advisor (a recently retired admiral), Robert McFarlane (a retired Marine who became National Security Advisor in 1983), and Secretary of State George Shultz (a former Marine), to intervene militarily in Lebanon, as President Eisenhower had done there more than twenty-five years earlier.[12]

A U.S. Marine force was landed with an unclear mission, imprecise rules of engagement, and no clear strategy. It operated as part of a multinational force that also included Italian, French, and British forces. The Secretary of Defense, Caspar Weinberger, objected on behalf of the Pentagon, but was overruled by the President. There was little national debate over what seemed likely to be a small, quick peacekeeping operation.

Through 1983, the Marines came to be seen as allies of the Lebanese Christian faction fighting Lebanese Muslims. Despite receiving mortar fire and sniping attacks, the Marines weren't allowed to respond aggressively because of the rules of engagement they operated under while participating in a peacekeeping mission.[13] The operation drew an Iranian-backed Hezbollah terrorist attack on the Marine base in Beirut in October 1983. The truck bomb killed 241 Marines and wounded 60. Reagan was forced to explain to the American people what U.S. forces were doing in Lebanon in the first place. In a prime-time television address he mentioned, among other reasons, the oil in the region. (Lebanon and the countries it borders in the Levant region in fact have little or no oil.)

As a small fleet of amphibious assault ships loaded with Marines was getting under way in Virginia to relieve the beleaguered force in Beirut in 1983, infighting boiled over between factions of a pro-Communist government that had seized control in 1979 of Grenada, a small Caribbean island that had become independent of Great Britain nine years before. The links of the group that seized power to Fidel Castro's Cuba troubled the Reagan White House. Looking into the Grenada issue, Reagan's advisers became aware that there were scores of U.S. students at a medical school on the island. "Saving" those students from an Iranian-style hostage situation and diverting people's attention from the U.S. disaster in Beirut seemed like a good idea to Reagan's advisers. (There was in fact little or no reason to believe that the students would be taken hostage.)[14]

With little debate and almost no preparation, Marines and paratroopers assaulted the island nation. The attack on Grenada came as a surprise to the U.S. forces involved, as well as to the Cuban and Grenadan forces and the U.S. students. In what should have been a cakewalk, 19 Americans were killed and 116 wounded in a confused ad hoc operation.[15]

I had moved to the State Department in 1979 and by 1983 was working closely with the military from the department's "Little Pentagon," the Bureau of Political-Military Affairs. Thrown into both the Beirut and Grenada operations to plan and coordinate, I was amazed at the ease with which the decision was made to deploy our military and what little precision there was on what it was to do. More frightening was the obvious lack of planning for the kind of operation the forces were being asked to conduct.

At one point well into the Grenada operation, the allegedly threatened medical students called in to the command center where I was operating to tell us where they were and to ask where the U.S. military was. The students could hear gunfire, but no one had tried to "rescue" them. Learning from radio broadcasts that Reagan had acted to save them, the students were growing concerned that they had not yet been rescued and at how easy it would be for the Cuban military advisers to take them hostage. The military commanders to whom I passed that information told me they had no orders to rescue the American students, despite the fact that the President had been on television that morning justifying the intervention in part by the need to save the medical students. That incident was typical of that day of confused fighting in Grenada. U.S. units were cut off, could not communicate with other U.S. forces, underestimated the opposing force's strength, and suffered more than 130 casualties in one day.

Although it was obvious even then that the reasons for being in Beirut and Grenada were questionable, both operations should have been easy for the giant U.S. military to accomplish. Those interventions, like Desert One, raised the issue of who in the military was to blame when things went wrong, as they seemed to do whenever we used force. Putting aside for the moment the issue of whether the recent military missions had been wise to conduct, there was clearly the question of why the U.S. military was not performing them better.

In seeking to answer that question, two Air Force generals took on the difficult task of challenging the existing power relationships within the military. They came to believe that the long-standing arrangements left over from the 1947 reorganization of the U.S. military had fragmented authority, prevented professionalization of the officer corps, and made the military unable to respond well when ordered to use force by civilian authority. The two men were unlikely rebels. The first was the Chairman of the Joint Chiefs of Staff under both Carter and Reagan, David Jones.

But Jones was not impressed by his own position or power; quite the opposite. Jones thought the Chairman was little more than someone who ran a committee of peers consisting of the heads of the Army, Navy, Air Force, and Marines. The heads of those services had the real power. The committee process produced least-common-denominator results. More important, though, Jones thought that by preserving the Army, Navy, and Air Force as separate power centers, the sum was less than the parts. There was no single U.S. military; there were three very separate organizations, duplicating capabilities and often not coordinating. And some important missions and capabilities fell through the cracks, being done well by none of the services.

No one could ensure that the overall U.S. military had the doctrine, tactics, training, planning, and equipment to address all of the kinds of threats that a President might call upon the military to address. There was no one in uniform who could think about or command the overall U.S. military. Jones was hardly alone in his thinking. Even those of us in the State Department joked that "the Navy is in a loose alliance with the United States."

Jones proposed that there should be a single, overall U.S. military commander, with a deputy, and that the U.S. forces in each region of the world, regardless of their service, should be integrated under a single commander reporting directly to the Chairman in Washington. With this "unity of command" would come accountability and responsibility. The top military commander would report to the President through the Secretary of Defense, but would give the President military advice independently from the Secretary. Naturally, the Army and Navy both opposed the plan as a threat to their independence.

But the Jones plan eventually gained the support of a key one-star general in the Air Force Reserve. He was key because his day job was U.S. Senator from Arizona, and in 1986 he became the Chairman of the Senate Armed Services Committee. Although he was soundly defeated for President in 1964, Barry Goldwater was highly respected in the Senate for his straight-talking style, honesty, independence, and military expertise (the man who would later replace him in that Arizona seat, John McCain, would gain a similar reputation). Teaming with House members William Nichols, Ike Skelton, and Les Aspin, Goldwater narrowly and without White House help forced through a landmark piece of legislation that essentially made the Jones Plan into law.[16] Congress codified the concept of "joint forces" over the independent Army, Navy, Air Force, and Marines by:

- Making the Chairman of the Joint Chiefs the senior military adviser to the Secretary of Defense and, separately, to the President

- Placing all U.S. forces in a region under a single regional commander in chief (CinC, pronounced "sink"), who would in turn report to the Secretary of Defense and the President through the Chairman

- Giving each regional commander clear authority over all units in his Area of Responsibility in peacetime and in war, for planning and for operations

- Requiring all senior officers to be trained in "joint operations" and "joint doctrine"

- Establishing a "joint assignment" (a two-year job in some organization that was an integrated Army, Navy, and Air Force unit) as a prerequisite for promotion to senior ranks

- Allowing the creation of new joint commands that were functionally, not regionally, focused; beginning with one that Congress created to take charge of all military transportation assets worldwide (Transcom)

The Goldwater-Nichols revolution addressed the issue of accountability and responsibility within the military, empowering the new joint organizations to determine what the possible contingencies were in their areas, figure out what forces and equipment they would need to deal with them, plan operations in detail, and train forces to carry out the missions. The Chairman and the Joint Staff (which now clearly worked for him) had oversight over the process.

Although many in the military were opposed to the various interventions, some civilian and military analysts thought that there was a legitimate need for quick, surgical military operations from time to time, such as to rescue a captured U.S. ship (like the *Mayaguez* in 1975[17]) or to rescue U.S. Embassy personnel (as in the Iran hostage crisis in 1980) or possibly even Americans in a country in turmoil (such as Grenada might have been in 1983). Recent rescue attempts had proved disastrous, in part because of the lack of a centralized center of excellence for training commandos or Special Forces to work together across service boundaries.

An integrated Special Operations commando capability was something that fell between the cracks, not only of the three services, but also of the newly created regional CinCs. The heads of the three services and the CinCs generally thought that Special Operations officers were cowboys who were difficult to control. The thought of giving them any authority was anathema even to reformist generals and admirals. But the memory of Desert One and its charred wreckage lingered. Special Forces officers convinced their friends in the Congress that something had to be done.

In 1987, a year after the Goldwater-Nichols Act, the Congress again overrode the objections of the Army, Navy, and Air Force to create a joint command. The new Special Operations Command would develop tactics and doctrine, as well as train and exercise all U.S. commando units, including what became known as Delta Force and the SEALs.[18] The head of the new Special Operations Command would have real power. He would have his own budget to develop and procure specialized weapons and would have a guardian angel in the form of a new civilian Assistant Secretary of Defense for Special Operations to fight his battles in the Pentagon. That civilian would also provide oversight over what most of the military still thought of as a bunch of "snake eaters" and wild men.

The new joint structure set about more rigorously creating and reviewing contingency plans for wars and other scenarios that could develop. The military leaders began joint exercises to test the plans and the units involved. They institutionalized the process of "After Action Reports" (AAR) and "Lessons Learned" so that there was a system to ensure that weaknesses identified in exercises were fixed. The AAR process also identified questions that emerged in the conduct of the exercises for civilian policy makers to provide guidance.

Having thoroughly changed the military through the "jointness" revolution, members of Congress who knew the military well, both its strengths and its weaknesses, continued both official and unofficial dialogues with some of the generals and admirals who were increasingly seeking to impose professional systems on their organizations, making decision processes more explicit, transparent, and participatory among the military leadership.

Thus, Congress required the regular preparation of a military strategy as a component of a higher-level National Security Strategy.[19] This would make clear what threats the military should be preparing for, what capabilities it had, and what it was developing. The strategies would make a connection between explicit statements of national security policy and the forces needed to support them.

A strategy could, however, still result in a military that was "prepared to fight the last war." In the 1930s neither of the two services had wanted an air force. The Navy leadership had clung to its battleships and refused to see the new threat to ships from aircraft. Similarly, the Army had not built a powerful air component. (When Pearl Harbor was struck, my father was in a horse cavalry unit in Massachusetts. A year later he was in the Air Corps and in New Guinea.) Seeking to ensure that similar misalignments did not occur in the latter part of the twentieth century, Congress required periodic reviews by "Roles and Missions" panels. These studies looked at what the likely missions in the future would be and whether some element of the U.S. military was building the needed capabilities.

Later, Congress also required that the civilian and military leaders of the Pentagon conduct an even more detailed and rigorous analysis of priorities every four years, a Quadrennial Defense Review (QDR) to be submitted to the Congress. The first was produced in 1997.[20] The most recent QDR was released in early 2006.

These changes were intended to make the military more effective and to minimize the possibility that it would not be ready for the kind of missions it might be asked to do.

THE POLITICAL-MILITARY CHANGES

Just as improving the military's effectiveness needed civilian champions in the Congress to overcome the disagreements within the military and within the executive branch, so too the question of how to restrain civilians from using force needed a civilian champion. The spokesman for that cause was, perhaps surprisingly, the civilian given the legal authority to supervise the military, Secretary of Defense Caspar Weinberger. And just as the Goldwater-Nichols reforms were legislated without any prior agreement within the executive branch, Weinberger acted without gaining the approval of his colleagues such as the Secretary of State or his boss, the President.

Weinberger, who had opposed the intervention in Lebanon and blocked a retaliatory strike on Iranian and Hezbollah elements there after the Beirut barracks attack, went public in 1984 with what he proposed as guidelines for the use of force:[21]

- U.S. vital interests must be at stake.

- We must be committed to winning decisively.

- The political and military objectives must be clear and obtainable.

- The forces necessary to win decisively and achieve the goals should be made available and the appropriate force size should be regularly reviewed.

- There should be reasonable grounds to suppose that the American people would support the operation.

- Force should be used only as a last resort, after all other alternatives are exhausted or proven unworkable.

Weinberger rejected using our forces "as a regular and customary part of our diplomatic efforts" because doing so would generate "domestic turmoil" and "tear at the fabric of our society." At the State Department, where I was working, the leadership saw Weinberger's speech as an attempt to make it impossible to use military force at all, except in responding to some kind of Pearl Harbor–like attack. Some critics asked how the Reagan administration could simultaneously call for the doubling of the defense budget[22] in peacetime and then adopt guidelines that would mean that expensive force could be used only in the event of the Apocalypse.

But the Weinberger Doctrine was widely hailed in the military as a much-needed antidote to the civilian adventurism that had thrown the military into "no-win" or embarrassing situations for which it was not prepared. Among the generals cheering was a two-star Army aide to Weinberger, Colin Powell. (Weinberger's reluctance to use force may not have extended to covert operations by the CIA. He was indicted for perjury about the Iran-contra scandal but received a presidential pardon from President George H. W. Bush in the last days of the latter's administration. There was speculation that Weinberger knew of and kept quiet about Bush's role in the scandal.)

Although the Weinberger doctrine did not restrain the next three presidents (Reagan, Bush, and Clinton), the uniformed military leaders who were reluctant to use force and understandably hesitant to incur casualties did not give up. Indeed, they fought rearguard actions to limit military action, sometimes even after a decision had been made to intervene or use force. Military leaders, often including Colin Powell, drew on the many arrows in the Weinberger Doctrine quiver. Often they were justified and the plans for the operations were improved. Sometimes their risk aversion seemed excessive and counterproductive.

The military leaders often argued that the force needed to do anything had to be "overwhelming." While originally aimed at ensuring quick and decisive victories against an enemy, the supersizing requirement was sometimes employed to deter civilians from acting. The case of the U.S. victory in the Persian Gulf War (1990–1991) is instructive. When Iraq invaded and occupied Kuwait in 1990, President George H. W. Bush decided, after a few days of consideration, that U.S. troops should be deployed in Saudi Arabia to deter Iraq from continuing to collect Arab oil fields. The then Chairman of the Joint Chiefs, Colin Powell, argued against using U.S. forces to evict the Iraqis from Kuwait, favoring instead using economic and political sanctions and keeping the U.S. forces sitting in the Saudi desert.

Bush's National Security Advisor, Brent Scowcroft (a retired Air Force general), urged an invasion to liberate Kuwait and convinced the President to ask for a plan to do so. Powell responded by asking the President to double the size of the U.S. forces from 250,000 to half a million to ensure overwhelming force. Doing so, he knew, would require stripping U.S. combat forces from Europe, something that at the time seemed very unlikely. The request for more forces moved quickly to the President, who, to the shock of many involved, ordered the needed U.S. forces out of Europe.

When the war came, however, the U.S. ground forces sat idle for a month while air forces destroyed much of the Iraqi military. When the U.S. ground forces did get under way, they moved to liberate Kuwait and, in conjunction with continuing air strikes, to destroy the last of the elite Iraqi Republican Guard troops. It was then that Powell invoked the sixth test of the Weinberger Doctrine, public support. Despite the fact that the war was extremely popular and its popularity was growing with the apparent ease with which we were winning, Powell argued that the images of the U.S. forces devastating the Iraqi Republican Guard would produce a public backlash. He asked the CinC, General Norman Schwarzkopf, to cease hostilities just as General Barry McCaffrey was racing his 24th Mechanized Infantry Division to destroy the Republican Guard. Initially, Schwarzkopf disagreed and urged that he be allowed to complete his plan for the destruction of the Iraqi Army. When Powell persisted, Schwarzkopf reluctantly agreed.[23] Powell told the President that the military wanted to stop the war, and Bush agreed.

The Iraqi Republican Guard divisions, which were thus spared their planned fate, then went on to slaughter Shiites in the south and Kurds in the north, both of whom had risen up in response to President Bush's public urging. Using those divisions, Saddam Hussein stayed in power in 1991 and for another dozen years. President Bush (41) was defeated in his bid for reelection.

General Powell became a national hero for his victory over Iraq, but he was concerned that the victory might rekindle a desire to use the U.S. military to solve the world's problems. Thus, in 1992 he publicly suggested additional tests for the use of military power. Like his old boss Weinberger, Powell laid out his doctrine without gaining prior consensus or approval in the government. Repeating Weinberger's six criteria, Powell added even more hurdles:[24]

- Have all of the risks and costs been fully and frankly analyzed?

- Is there a plausible exit strategy to avoid endless entanglement?

- Have the consequences of our action been fully considered?

- Do we have genuine and broad international support?

Powell was still in office as the senior U.S. military officer when Bill Clinton moved into the White House. Clinton's national security team quickly focused on three issues they had inherited from the outgoing Bush administration. First, there was Yugoslavia, which had dissolved into a civil war. Powell had argued successfully during the Bush administration that the United States should not interfere militarily, despite the urgings of many NATO allies that wanted to end the bloodshed but believed that they could not operate there without us. The general urged the Clinton team to stay out and leave the peacekeeping to the Europeans.[25] Peacekeeping was not appropriate for U.S. military forces, Powell contended. He is said to have estimated that even a 250,000-strong U.S. intervention force might not be sufficient to enforce a peace in Bosnia. Based on his doctrine, he saw in the Bosnian civil war the potential beginnings of a quagmire in which U.S. forces would inevitably have to choose sides and be drawn into a Vietnam-like scenario.

Second was Haiti, where a military coup had deposed the elected President and caused an outpouring of refugees trying to get into the United States. Powell saw no role for the U.S. military, other than helping the Coast Guard, if necessary, to keep the refugees out. The U.S. military should not be engaged in refugee affairs, contended Powell. After Powell left office, Clinton authorized an invasion of Haiti that successfully reinstalled the elected President, stopped the refugee flow, and replaced the Haitian military with a newly created police. There was one U.S. combat fatality in the three-year operation.[26]

Third, Somalia had already represented a defeat for the Powell Doctrine. Bush had intervened against Powell's advice and allowed the operation combining humanitarian activity and peacekeeping, two things that the U.S. military was allegedly not designed to do. The intervention, which came after Bush's defeat in the polls, was designed to protect U.N. food relief organizations from warlords and their gangs.

Powell's advice to the Clinton team was to get out fast. When the head of the U.N. operation in Somalia (a retired U.S. Navy four-star admiral) sought U.S. tanks and Special Operations forces to deal with a warlord whose thugs had killed U.N. troops, Powell rejected the request and got the Secretary of Defense to back him up. When the use of AC-130 gunships to attack the warlord was criticized in the media, Powell ordered the gunships to be returned to the United States. Without notifying the White House, Powell approved the withdrawal of some of the U.S. forces from Somalia.

Shortly before Powell's tenure as Chairman expired, he acquiesced to the use of Special Operations forces to deal with the warlord, whose forces had now killed American troops, but he still did not agree to send tanks or AC-130 gunships.[27] Less than a month after he left office, U.S. Special Operations forces became trapped in a shoot-out. There were no U.S. tanks or AC-130 gunships to run to their rescue. In the "Black Hawk down" incident, eighteen American troops died.[28] The Secretary of Defense, Les Aspin, resigned. Clinton ordered in more U.S. forces, including tanks and AC-130 gunships, and kept them there six months more until sufficient U.N. forces arrived to take over the mission, as originally planned. He instructed me to work with the military to ensure that the operation was successful and that there would be no more U.S. combat deaths. In the six months that it took to bring the U.N. forces up to full strength, the reinforced U.S. forces suffered no fatalities.

Powell's foot-dragging caused the Clinton administration to look carefully at who would take his place. The Secretary of Defense was the official charged with nominating a general or an admiral to the President for approval. In practice, the Secretary developed a list of candidates and shared it with the White House prior to narrowing in on one nominee. One name stood out on the list developed by Secretary of Defense Aspin. The general in question had distinguished himself by leading a humanitarian relief mission, Operation Provide Comfort, which had saved thousands of Kurds who were being attacked by Iraqi forces in 1991. It seemed that John Shalikashvili might be more flexible than Powell had been on the use of the U.S. military in less than apocalyptic situations. As a European refugee, he might also have a different attitude toward getting involved in the civil wars of the former Yugoslavia.

Those judgments proved to be accurate. Chairman Shalikashvili agreed to support a gradual and limited U.S. military role in Bosnia.[29] Starting in 1994, he supported U.S. Air Force involvement in enforcing a NATO no-fly zone in the former Yugoslavia. In 1994 and 1995, he supported air strikes by U.S. warplanes against Serb military forces that attacked U.N. "safe areas" in Bosnia. He fully supported the 1995 Dayton peace accords, which effectively ended the civil war, sending approximately 20,000 U.S. ground forces to Bosnia as part of a NATO force, along with about 5,000 troops to Croatia and other countries near Bosnia.

With the Bosnia operation under way, the Clinton White House turned to Haiti, where the flow of attempted refugees to the United States was overwhelming our ability to intercept and detain them. After giving the coup leaders ample opportunity to strike a deal to restore the elected President, the NSC Principals Committee asked General Shalikashvili for an invasion plan.[30] Shali balked.

He asked for a private meeting with National Security Advisor Anthony Lake and me. The general explained his fear that the U.S. Army forces that would invade the country would then be called upon to police the island nation "since we will have destroyed their Army and they have no police force." The U.S. Army units, Shali explained, were not trained or equipped to be police. Even the few military police units were not trained for urban police work. We would have a choice after invasion of either permitting widespread looting and disorder or imposing martial law and shooting the Haitians we were supposed to be liberating. Looking stern, the general said that unless this problem were fixed he would recommend, as the President's senior military adviser under the Goldwater-Nichols reform, that the President not order the U.S. military to invade Haiti.

"How do we fix it, Shali?" Lake asked.

The Chairman of the Joint Chiefs shrugged as if the answer were obvious. "Get some police."

Within days, the once and future New York City Police Commissioner Ray Kelly was in command of a multinational police force for

Haiti including, among others, Israelis and Jordanians, Indians and Pakistanis, and some Haitian-speaking New York cops.[31]

But Shali was not the only one who had a precondition for using the U.S. military in Haiti. When the proposal went to the President, he too demurred. He was uninterested in the details of the military plan, which his advisers had already vetted. "If we can't invade Haiti successfully, somebody has been wasting a heck of a lot of money," he said. Clinton wanted a "civilian plan" that would show what the State Department, the United Nations, international aid organizations, and others would do to put Haiti back together again. The "Haiti Political-Military Plan" took us two weeks to create, although it evolved continually after its approval by the President.

Clinton was so pleased by the Pol-Mil Plan that he later asked us to consider institutionalizing the process of creating "civilian plans" with the sophistication and complexity of the military's contingency plans. That instruction culminated in NSC Presidential Decision Directive 56, "Managing Complex Contingency Operations," issued in May 1997. These contingency operations were defined as either peace operations, such as NATO's peace accord implementation in Bosnia from 1995 to 1997, or foreign humanitarian assistance operations, such as Operation Support Hope in central Africa in 1994. PDD-56 was put into practice in 1998–1999, when the State Department's Bureau of Political-Military Affairs coordinated U.S. planning for non-military activities in Kosovo. Its report identified essential tasks for the U.S. government in four areas, including humanitarian assistance, institutional development and reconstruction, war crimes, policing, and holding elections.[32]

Although the PDD was signed with the enthusiastic support of then–JCS Chairman Hugh Shelton, I always thought of it as Shali's corollary: If you are going to use military force, be sure first that you have all the other instruments of government ready for when the shooting stops.

Despite Shali's greater willingness to use force, a risk aversion deriving from the Weinberger-Powell Doctrine continued. That attitude was taken to its illogical extreme in dealing with terrorism. Before 9/11, as the President's head of counterterrorism, I came to the reluctant but inescapable conclusion that the U.S. military leadership did not want to be part of offensive operations against terrorists. On several occasions the National Security Advisor and his cabinet colleagues in the NSC Principals Committee asked the Chairman of the Joint Chiefs to plan operations to go after terrorists. Sometimes the targets involved were just one man—a lone al Qaeda operative in a hotel room in Khartoum in 1998 or in 1995 a single terrorist working in the Water Department in Qatar. Every time the military came back, recommending against the operations and presenting plans intentionally oversized, involving enormously outsized forces that would have blown any chance of surprise and would have looked as if we were invading.

The man working in the Qatar Water Department was reported to be the uncle of 1993 World Trade Center bomber Ramzi Yousef, whom we had hunted down in Pakistan in 1995.[33] The man in Qatar had been secretly indicted in New York, and evidence suggested that he had had a hand in other operations and would probably plan more. We wanted him badly, but we knew that if we approached the Qatari government to arrest him and hand him over, someone would probably tip him off and he would escape. The CIA correctly said it had no capability to stage covert snatches in Qatar, nor did the FBI. So, remembering that there were small Special Operations Command units trained to do just such things, I urged that the military be ordered to go in with a small team. The Chairman came back not with a small covert unit of Special Operations forces but with an enormous force package and a recommendation against using it. The principals decided not to overrule the military and instructed us to ask the Qataris to arrest the terrorist. We did, but then the Qatari police went to do so, our terrorist had, predictably, just fled the country.

The man in the Qatar Water Department did, as we suspected, go on to plan other terrorist strikes. His name was Khalid Sheik Mohammed. He went on to mastermind the 9/11 attacks on the United States.

Even when al Qaeda directly attacked U.S. military assets, as it did in October 2000 by striking the U.S.S. *Cole*, the military was reluctant to employ its assets to respond offensively. Secretary of Defense William Cohen supported that view, telling the NSC Principals Committee that there would "have to be many more body bags" before we could justify a military operation against al Qaeda in Afghanistan.

President Clinton's desire to destroy al Qaeda before it could do significant damage led him to personally ask the Chairman of the Joint Chiefs, Hugh Shelton, to consider whether we could launch a special operations strike against al Qaeda camps in Afghanistan, or, as the President put it, "commandos, guys in black ninja suits jumping out of helicopters." Luckily for Osama bin Laden, the Chairman demurred. It would be too difficult, too risky, too likely to involve an unacceptable level of U.S. military casualties. Of course, not doing so ultimately resulted in an unacceptable level of U.S. civilian casualties.

THE POLITICAL CHANGES

The third type of significant change affecting the military after and because of Vietnam was political. Two types of things happened: the increasing use of the military as a political issue and the growth of the number of military voters.

Throughout American political history, military-related issues had been political fodder. But in the post–Vietnam War era, one party consistently labeled itself the champion of the military and its opponents antimilitary.

The Vietnam War, although it had been started by a Democratic President, became the policy of Republican Richard Nixon. The Democratic Party, abandoning its earlier position, became increasingly vocal against the war and ultimately used its control of Congress to cut off funds for the war. The leading antiwar figures in the nation and Congress were Democrats. Naturally, the Republicans, defending their President's policies, attacked the Democrats, calling them "soft on Communism," defeatist, and ultimately antimilitary. Republicans accused Democrats of dishonoring the sacrifice of those who had fought in Vietnam. Some claimed that the war could have been "won" had it not been for the Democratic Congress.

For many military families and veterans (of earlier wars and Vietnam), that labeling of the Democrats as antimilitary took hold. When another Democrat was elected President in 1976, Republicans in the Congress were soon accusing him of failing to fund the military adequately. They recounted anecdotes about military units with inadequate equipment or parts as evidence of a "hollow Army."[34] Carter's policy of seeking arms limitations in negotiations with the Soviet Union was also portrayed as weakness on national security. When the Soviet Union then invaded Afghanistan, Carter was forced to put arms control on hold. When the Shah of Iran fell and Iranian students seized the U.S. Embassy and its staff, Carter's reluctance to use force in response seemed to indicate further weakness. The failure of the military rescue mission Carter launched effectively ended his chances of reelection.

Carter was a graduate of the U.S. Naval Academy at Annapolis, a submarine officer, and the only American President who had ever personally worked with nuclear weapons and nuclear reactors. He launched a major program of rebuilding U.S. and NATO forces in Europe, including the program I worked on, placing nuclear cruise missiles in five European nations. Yet the partisan attacks on him shaped an image of an antimilitary Democrat.

It was twelve years before another Democrat became President. This time it was someone who not only had no military service record, he had opposed the Vietnam War and found deferments that kept him from being drafted during that war. Early in the Clinton administration, the President advocated ending discrimination against gays and lesbians in the military. A story spread that an unidentified young White House staffer had made antimilitary remarks to my friend General Barry McCaffrey while he was waiting at the Southwest Gate of the White House to be cleared into the complex for a meeting.

Clinton continued the plan of his Republican predecessor to contract the size of the U.S. military in the wake of the collapse of the Soviet Union and the end of the fifty-year-long Cold War. But the cuts came during the Clinton administration. It was the largest contraction of the U.S. military since the end of the Vietnam War. The end of the Cold War had also opened an opportunity to end many of the proxy wars that the Soviet Union and the United States had been engaged in.

The first President Bush, a former Ambassador to the United Nations, had set into motion a series of U.N. peacekeeping operations to deal with proxy wars in Angola, Cambodia, and elsewhere. The staggering U.N. bills began arriving during the Clinton administration, quickly putting the United States in arrears of its U.N. financial obligations.[35]

With the advent of the Clinton administration, I was asked to examine the burgeoning U.N. post–Cold War peacekeeping programs. What my team found was that U.S. and U.N. decisions on peacekeeping had been made with little planning, rigor, or evaluative criteria. Deploying troops from other countries under U.N. authority was certainly cheaper than employing American troops, but the forces were often ineffective because the United Nations lacked the command control, logistics, intelligence, transportation, and planning capabilities. With President Clinton's approval, we set out to meet those deficiencies by providing U.S. military support. U.S. Air Force planes flew other countries' troops to operations. U.S. officers were placed on U.N. peacekeeping staffs. Nonsensitive intelligence information was provided, with the sources and methods of the materials' origin fully protected.

An American U-2 spy plane was painted in U.N. colors for flights over Iraq in support of the U.N. Special Commission (UNSCOM) that was destroying Iraq's remaining chemical weapons and missiles.[36] To encourage other nations such as Germany and Japan to send troop units to U.N. peacekeeping, a single American battalion was assigned to the U.N. forces and assigned to Macedonia.[37] Although the United States owed the United Nations hundreds of millions of dollars in U.N. peacekeeping assessments, the United States billed the United Nations and was paid for most of the support operations it conducted.

The Republican Congress, which came into power in the 1994 midterm elections, still stunned that Clinton had defeated an incumbent Republican President, saw in the expanding support for U.N. peacekeeping a way of further attacking the Democrats as being antimilitary. They accused the Clinton administration of putting U.S. troops in foreign uniforms and under foreign command, ceding U.S. sovereignty to some odd collection of third-world socialists in New York.

Republican members of Congress and Republican commentators accused the administration of weakening the U.S. military by draining its resources with spurious missions. They suggested that U.S. troops working with the United Nations would be captured or killed by terrorists (as Marine Colonel William Buckley had been while on a U.N. mission in Lebanon during the Reagan administration).

In 1994, Republicans in the House ran on a platform called the "Contract with America," pledging to pass laws that would keep U.S. troops out of foreign uniforms, foreign command, and peacekeeping.[38] Colin Powell suggested that U.S. forces should be used only for offensive operations, like the Desert Storm war against Iraq, not peacekeeping or other postwar "nation-building" roles. The not-too-subtle implication was that American troops were real soldiers and should not have to do the kinds of lesser missions that Indians, Bangladeshis, and Pakistanis did for the United Nations.

None of this anti–United Nations sentiment had been apparent to me months earlier when I was a Bush White House staffer, as President Bush pushed the United Nations into a leading role in his "New World Order." The sudden Republican opposition to U.S. support for U.N. peacekeeping, the vehement opposition to nation building, seemed to me disingenuous.

The fact is that U.S. troops had been placed under foreign commanders' tactical control in the Revolutionary War, World Wars I and II, and Desert Storm. U.S. troops in Korea had been under U.N. command for half a century. In all of those conflicts, as in U.N. peacekeeping missions, the units operated under U.S. laws, rules, security, and overall command. No American troops had been asked to wear foreign uniforms during the Clinton administration, and none had been captured or killed while on U.N. peacekeeping missions.

The eighteen American troops killed in Somalia during the "Black Hawk down" incident had not been operating as part of the U.N. force there, but as a unilateral force under the command and control of American generals. Ironically, had the Americans involved in the "Black Hawk down" operation been willing to work with the U.N. forces, the United Nations' Malaysian armored unit could have been ready to move in quickly to support and rescue them. Clinton's Secretary of Defense, Les Aspin, had resigned over the eighteen deaths in one day. Sensing that the Republicans were increasingly using military affairs as a wedge issue, Clinton appointed a Republican senator, Bill Cohen, to replace Aspin. The move did nothing to stop the attacks on Clinton for nation building, humanitarian interventionism, and putting U.S. troops under U.N. command.

Other nations, including such "first-world" forces as Canada and Australia, and nuclear powers such as France and the United Kingdom, did not think it was beneath their dignity or regard it as strength-sapping to engage in peacekeeping and nation-building operations. They had been doing it for decades. Of course, Americans had, too. In addition to the American troops in Korea, U.S. peacekeepers had previously been deployed to the Sinai Peninsula between Egypt and Israel. Indeed, American forces had pioneered modern postwar nation building in Germany and Japan.

As Clinton used the U.S. military against Iraq, Somalia, Haiti, and Serbia, it was clear that Republicans could not accuse him of being reluctant to use force. Instead, they argued in the 2000 election that he was weakening the military by—well—using it. The Republican platform noted with horror that two Army divisions were not fully ready (elements of the divisions had been deployed in the Balkans).[39] Candidate George W. Bush decried "nation building" with U.S. forces and promised it would not happen under his administration. He depicted the U.S. military as abused and unappreciated by its commander in chief. Here is an example of his stump speech, so well known at the time that the partisan audience delivers his applause line before he does.

BUSH: We'll be realists when it comes to the state of readiness of today's United States military. I want you all . . .
(APPLAUSE)
Oh, I heard the words about how supposedly prepared we are, but that's not what the facts say. We're having trouble meeting recruiting goals, we're having trouble retaining captains in the United States military.
But don't ask me. Ask your friends and neighbors what morale is like in the United States military, who may be wear-

ing the uniform. Ask the people who wear today's United States—wear the uniform of the military, morale is dangerously low.

In order to keep the peace, this administration will rebuild the military power of the United States of America.
(APPLAUSE)
AUDIENCE: Help is on the way. Help is on the way. Help is on the way. Help is on the way. Help is on the way.
BUSH: Help is on the way.

Of course, there was no crisis in the U.S. military in 2000, but there is now an acute problem, perhaps a crisis, of readiness and morale because of the ways in which President Bush used the military, including largely unsuccessful nation-building operations.[40] Of forty-four Army combat brigades in March 2007, nearly half had served two tours in Iraq or Afghanistan and a quarter had served three or four tours. Tours have been extended significantly, cutting down on time at home with family, training with new equipment, and repairs of existing equipment. Cases of post-traumatic stress disorder jump when soldiers serve repeat deployments in Iraq. Suicide rates peaked above previous records in 2006. The National Guard and reservists have been deployed to help shoulder the burden of the Iraq War, with more than 410,000 deploying for an average of eighteen months per mobilization. Along with the fundamental human element is the burden created on the military's budget and on equipment that is being repaired in theater rather than in depot. Evidence is mounting that the Republican Party has been no friend to the armed services in the last eight years.

In my personal experience working in both Republican and Democratic administrations, neither party respects the U.S. military more or less than the other does. Both parties' leaders have been aware of the strengths of the military and have honored those who wear the uniform. Of the post–Vietnam War presidential nominees, two Democrats and two Republicans were veterans of foreign wars (Al Gore and John Kerry in Vietnam, the first President Bush and Bob Dole in World War II). Two presidents had no military experience: Reagan and Clinton, one a Republican and one a Democrat; both were popular and both were reelected.

Despite the Republicans attempting to paint themselves as the only party that understands the military, both parties are filled with veterans, including Democrats like Senators Jack Reed (Army Airborne) and Jim Webb (Marines). In 2006, my friend Joe Sestak (D-Pa.) who had served with me in the White House and had been a Navy admiral, became the highest-ranking former officer ever to serve in the House of Representatives.[41]

But that was 2006, after the failure in Iraq was evident. In the 1970s, '80s, and '90s, the U.S. military was changing profoundly. It was more professionalized, did more planning, had better technology and leadership, and had become more aware of the need to interact with the civilian policy community to "shape the environment." Those efforts had proven spectacularly successful in fighting Iraq in 1990–1991. Now they were about to be tested there again, in a different way. And in the decade since Desert Storm, the Iraqis had also engaged in Lessons Learned.

THREE

NO MORE IRAQS

Some of the post–Vietnam War changes in the U.S. military and its relationships with civilian authorities should have prevented the Iraq War from happening in the way that it did. Obviously, they didn't.

POST-VIETNAM FIXES DIDN'T WORK

The changes in the structure and roles of the military were the least successful. The restructuring of the Army to rely upon volunteers and reserves (especially the National Guard) did not deter the President, his advisers, or Congress from going along with the Iraq War. In 1973 Creighton Abrams and his colleagues assumed that to fight a large and long war, a future administration would need to reinstate the draft and mobilize the Guard, thereby testing popular and congressional support.[1] Only a clearly "just" war could generate such support, they thought. What they could not imagine, however, was that thirty years later:

- Jobs done by draftees for subminimum wage in the Vietnam War era were performed in the Iraq War by civilians sometimes paid twice what the same work would earn in the United States. While there was civilian contractor support in Vietnam, it amounted to only a tiny fraction of the half-million U.S. military personnel there. In Iraq there has been roughly one contractor for every U.S. soldier. These well-paid civilians, many of them armed, are doing jobs that in the Vietnam War era were done by draftees and professional military personnel.[2]

- The administration would intentionally send fewer forces into war than were needed, as I will discuss more below, in large part to avoid a potentially unpopular, large-scale National Guard mobilization.

- The President, Vice President, and other senior officials would intentionally distort information in the prewar period to generate popular support for the war and ensure congressional authorization. The administration correctly assumed that if the people and Congress believed that Iraq had a hand in the worst foreign attack ever on the U.S. mainland, there would be little chance of serious opposition to the war. It would be like Roosevelt going to Congress after Pearl Harbor. When Congress authorized action, nearly seven in ten Americans were persuaded that Iraq had had a role in 9/11.[3] Unlike the distortions about WMD, in which the intelligence community played some role,[4] administration officials cleverly linked Iraq to the attacks despite the intelligence community unambiguously telling them that there had been no Iraqi role.[5]

- Army and Marine units and individual personnel would be sent on multiple deployments to Iraq. In Vietnam, a draftee served a year in that country and was then deployed elsewhere or released from service. As the Iraq War dragged on, the one-year deployment period was extended. In addition, units that had already been in combat and returned to the United States were reassigned to Iraq, sometimes without the requisite training for new personnel.[6] If the Pentagon were forced to deploy individuals to Iraq for only twelve months, as was the practice with draftees in Vietnam, it would have gone through the all-volunteer force and run out of active-duty troops.

- National Guard units were mobilized in increasing numbers in the third and fourth years of the war. Soldiers older than the average eighteen- to twenty-year-old recruit were ordered to leave their jobs in the economy and separate from their spouses and children. Although these mobilizations probably did contribute to the steadily increasing opposition to the war, they did not cause the instantaneous and widespread political reaction that military planners in 1973 had imagined.

- Although a majority of the members of Congress were opposed to the war, they would be unable to stop it. Congress went along with the Iraq War in 2003 because most members did little analysis of the issue. Many also wanted to avoid the mistake that some had made in opposing the 1991 Iraq War (which had turned out to be quick, decisive, and therefore popular). When the second Iraq War turned out to be long, casualty-generating, and unpopular, the voters elected an anti-war majority to Congress in 2006. Just two months before that election, less than half of the people, about 46 percent, still believed that Iraq had been involved in 9/11, and only 36 percent of Americans felt the war in Iraq had been worth the loss of American lives.[7] Yet the antiwar majority could not agree upon a legislative means of stopping the war. Congressional rules of procedure required more than a simple majority of 51 senators to adopt a measure, such as setting a specific date to initiate withdrawals or imposing a limit on troops in Iraq. Such a law would need a "supermajority" of 60 senators to pass and 66 to overcome a presidential veto. Though 51 senators could have defeated bills that funded the war, such a majority never emerged. The administration successfully (if erroneously) characterized supporting a funding cutoff as voting to leave the troops without food, fuel, or ammunition.[8]

The Goldwater-Nichols changes that had created a strong Chairman of the Joint Chiefs and powerful regional commanders did not work well to prevent failure in Iraq. Nor was the force structure created appropriate for the war. So did the U.S. military really fail in Iraq? Certainly not the soldiers and Marines who have given it their all, who bear the burden of combat, heat, dust, and deprivation. They have performed heroically and in a vastly more disciplined and professional manner than did much of the draftee Army in Vietnam.

Nor can you find many senior members of the military among the chorus who called for invading Iraq after, or indeed even before, 9/11. Dick Cheney, Donald Rumsfeld, Paul Wolfowitz, and the "create-a-war" crew had no active-duty general prominent in their ranks.

GENERAL FAILURE

Yet the war came, and when it did, the generals, not the troops, failed. They failed when called upon to start the war and they failed in its prosecution. Moreover, their failures in the years before the war were revealed.

Not all "flag officers" touched by Iraq are culpable; indeed only a few were in a position to affect the key decisions that might have changed the outcome. Some tried to resist the mistaken strategy of the civilian leadership. A few resigned—a very few. Members of the general officer corps failed in some key respects.

What were their failures? Over the next several pages I identify six distinct failures by the military leadership.

The first and most obvious failure of the senior military was that neither the Chairman of the Joint Chiefs nor the regional commander at CENTCOM dissented from the initial war plan, even though they knew that it did not have the forces in the standing CENTCOM invasion plan and did not provide for a posthostilities stability operation, as required by the JCS deliberate planning guidelines.

As envisioned by the reformers of the 1980s, the empowered Chairman of the Joint Chiefs should have compared the civilian leadership's goals for the war with the capabilities of the forces available and advised against going to war, or at least not doing so as proposed. He should have given military advice independent of the Secretary of Defense. He did not.

Some civilian leaders of the Bush administration national security apparatus are said to have thought that the Clinton administration did not rein in the military leadership adequately. If so, they never said so publicly. They did, however, act to bring the military under tighter control. They sought a Chairman who would be easily guided by the White House and Pentagon civilians. In Air Force General Richard Myers they intentionally chose a man who was not a forceful or independent thinker and leader.[9] But even if he did not speak up, the Goldwater-Nichols reforms provided for a backup; the regional commander could do so.

The regional commander at the time of the war's inception was General Tommy Franks, who was also not known as a detail-oriented or intellectual commander, not a man familiar with the history and cultures of the region he was assigned. After 9/11 Tommy Franks had hurriedly prepared a plan for invading Afghanistan[10] (there had not been one at the ready despite President Clinton's expressing his desire to use U.S. forces there to JCS Chairman Hugh Shelton). At the same time as Franks began planning for Afghanistan, the National Security Advisor, Condoleezza Rice, appointed me cochair of something called the Campaign Coordination Committee, a new interagency group charged with bringing together all of the necessary elements of a campaign to destroy al Qaeda. I asked that the committee be briefed on the military plan for Afghanistan. In the past, as a senior civilian at the State Department and the White House, I had participated in reviews of military plans prior to several interventions. These reviews were vital to ensuring that the military plans would actually accomplish what the policy makers wanted without creating new problems. The reviews also provided an opportunity for the military to tell civilian agencies what they needed from them in the way of support. This time, however, I was told that "the Pentagon" did not want any "outside review." The Secretary of Defense would tell the President about the plan directly. No President, and certainly not one who could not be bothered with details, could know all of the pitfalls to look for in a military plan. No single individual could. No hourlong PowerPoint briefing would reveal all of the serious potential flaws in a military plan.

Franks's plan for Afghanistan, which we learned about as it unfolded, focused not on seizing bin Laden and the al Qaeda leadership, but on taking down the Taliban government of Afghanistan.[11] Franks and his supporters excuse bin Laden's escape by citing the difficult terrain of the Afghan-Pakistani border. They tend to gloss over the fact that bin Laden was not on the border, but in Kandahar for almost two months following 9/11.

When Franks was then asked to prepare for an intervention in Iraq, he pulled off the shelf a plan that had been developed after the first Iraq War and updated frequently. It was highly detailed and called for the use of a large force. Secretary Rumsfeld rejected that plan. Not only did Franks not insist on CENTCOM's plan, he was complicit in actually removing the needed forces from the standing war plan for Iraq. The plan to invade Iraq that had been on the shelf ever since the end of the first Gulf War called for a force of about 400,000, most of whom would be needed for the postcombat phase.[12] CENTCOM regularly reviewed and updated the plan over the decade. Civilians in the Office of the Secretary of Defense also ensured that the plan was ready and acceptable during that time. Franks, working with Secretary Rumsfeld, stripped most of the forces out of that plan and approved a slimmed-down invasion and occupation force.[13] Because the resulting force was too small, the insurgency was able to get under way, stealing arms from unguarded Iraqi Army facilities, planting roadside bombs, ambushing convoys.

The opportunity for the Chairman or regional commander to recommend to the President that the war not go ahead until there were sufficient forces available was lost by the reticence of Myers and Franks.

Although Shalikashvili had, a decade earlier, told the National Security Advisor and me that he declined to recommend an invasion of Haiti until there were adequate civilian police to quell postinvasion instability, Franks approved of a plan for Iraq that actually had the forces needed for postinvasion stability explicitly removed. Central Command, under General Tommy Franks, did not insist on the standard operating procedure for a major operational war plan; he did not include a detailed plan for postcombat operations.[14] Troops arriving in Baghdad and elsewhere had no instructions as to what to do once they had taken over. Even with the downsized force CENTCOM employed in the invasion, it could have achieved initial stability if they had acted to stop the anarchy and theft of weapons that began soon after the Americans' arrival. Franks, however, did not attempt to develop the kind of post-combat operations plan that might have prevented the slide of Iraq into complete disorder.[15] In fact, he had his eye on the door; shortly after the invasion, he retired.

The result was the disorder in Baghdad that immediately followed the arrival of U.S. forces, the absence of U.S. security for Iraqi weapons dumps,[16] and the United States' inability to secure supply roads against improvised explosive devices. Thousands of U.S. troops died as a direct result of the original war plan's being abandoned by General Franks.

If Myers and Franks were silent or complicit, where were the other generals? Under the Goldwater-Nichols reforms, the head of the Army was no longer in the chain of command for conducting operations. That chain went from the regional commander through the chairman to the Secretary of Defense and the President. Nonetheless, as a member of the Joint Chiefs of Staff, the Army commander could advise the operational officials. Army Chief Eric Shinseki apparently tried to do so. Having had his staff review the war plans, Shinseki came to the conclusion that the full-size force of the original plan was needed. In answer to a congressman's question, he said as much publicly,[17] only to be publicly rebuked by the civilian leadership of the Pentagon.[18] His replacement was soon announced. In retirement, however, Shinseki refused repeated calls for him to publicly criticize the war and the civilian leadership.

Four years into the Iraq War, the nation saw something unusual in its history of civil-military relations: not only did several recently retired general officers criticize the President's conduct of the war, but many appeared in antiwar television commercials before the 2006 congressional election. Some of them indicated that they reflected the views of many colleagues still on active duty. Much of their criticism focused on the Secretary of Defense, Donald Rumsfeld, whom they said had ignored military advice about the war. Generals told reporters that Rumsfeld had "bullied" and intimidated them. They called upon the President to fire his defense secretary.

Instead President Bush gave Rumsfeld his unqualified support publicly,[19] but when his party lost control of both houses of Congress in the 2006 election, he fired him the next day.[20] Many defeated Republicans wondered aloud what might have happened if Rumsfeld had been fired a week earlier.

To the best of my knowledge, only one senior officer resigned before the Iraq invasion because he disagreed with the plan to conduct the war. My colleague in several interagency committees, Marine Major General Gregory Newbold, was the Director of Operations for the Joint Chiefs of Staff, or, as it is known in Pentagonese, the J-3. He was soft-spoken and thoughtful. Seen in civilian clothes, he might have been mistaken for a Lutheran cleric rather than a top leatherneck. Had he stayed in the Marines, Greg would almost certainly have become a four-star general running either the Marines or a regional command. After thirty years of seeking such a position, he walked away from the Corps he loved rather than be a part of what he considered a needless war that would be conducted in a way likely to cause the equally needless deaths of Marines and Army troops. Newbold publicly voiced his criticism in 2006,[21] only to have his honesty rewarded by being fired as a military analyst for CBS News.

Commenting on what the media dubbed the "Revolt of the Generals" in 2006, Secretary Rumsfeld noted that the seven retired general officers who had called for his resignation were a small number of the hundreds of retired flag-level officers (generals and admirals). He contended that none of the Joint Chiefs of Staff or other active-duty generals involved in Iraq had objected to the war or the war plan, despite having been given the opportunity to do so. But as Michael C. Desch has pointed out, "the fact that Rumsfeld and his team were, through a year and a half of 'probing and questioning,' . . . able to whittle the final troop number to less than half of the 380,000 the original war plans called for does not alter the fact that civilian views on force levels prevailed over the military consensus—with disastrous results after the fall of Baghdad."[22]

Dissenting publicly with Bush and Rumsfeld would have meant resigning and then being criticized by the administration's media machine. Resigning a lifelong career you love is hard. You wonder if perhaps you are wrong, whether perhaps the policy makers you disagree with are right after all. You want to give them a chance, free of former colleagues sniping at them. When, in June 2001, I became convinced that the Bush administration was hopelessly naive and deaf on the terrorism issue, I resigned the senior U.S. counterterrorism job effective October 1. But I decided to stay on in the government to work on another issue that was important to me, cyberspace security. Only in February 2003, convinced that the unnecessary Iraq War would happen and would make progress in counterterrorism impossible, did I resign altogether from government. I then publicly criticized the war, but I understand the generals' reluctance to do so. They had been taught that military officers obey orders. They had been taught that in a democracy, the civilian leaders tell the military what to do. However, they also had direct responsibility for the lives of the troops under their command. That responsibility makes their decision different. The words of Winslow T. Wheeler and Lawrence J. Korb ring particularly true here: "In the profession of arms, a profession that involves life and death decisions, competence, not cronyism, must be king."[23]

The case of Lieutenant General Ricardo S. Sanchez, the top commander in Iraq for roughly a year during the early stages of the war, is telling. Now retired, Sanchez has criticized the "catastrophically flawed, unrealistically optimistic war plan" and the "glaring and unfortunate display of incompetent strategic leadership within our national leaders."[24] But Sanchez did not speak out during his time in Iraq, saying that active-duty officers should not challenge lawful orders. He could, however, have resigned his command. The difference between generals who implement policies in which they do not believe and civilians who do is that generals have a responsibility for the safety and security of their troops. The policies they implement in wartime by definition involve the troops' lives. Had Sanchez spoken out earlier, he might have helped hold the Pentagon's leadership to account. And he was not alone.

In the case of the Chairman, each of the service chiefs on the Joint Chiefs, and the CENTCOM commander, the law had been rewritten after Vietnam explicitly to authorize them to provide military judgment independent of the Secretary of Defense. A considered dissent by General Myers or General Franks could have postponed or stopped the Iraq invasion. Republican legislators such as Senator John Warner (R-Va.) and others who understood military affairs could have forced the administration to slow down and answer the kinds of questions that the generals could have asked about the abandonment of the original CENTCOM plan, the need to attack just then, the lack of planning for the postinvasion period. As Retired Army Lieutenant Colonel Ralph Peters wrote, "the generals' greatest shortcoming though, is that they failed in their duty to inform decision-makers as to what war means and requires, to give honest advice—and to keep on giving it, even at the cost of their careers."[25]

The second failure of the generals involved their attitude toward counterinsurgency. After the initial combat phase and the seizure of Baghdad, the war became almost exclusively the job of the ground forces, the Army and Marines. It was less of a "joint" or multiservice operation than anything the U.S. military had done in more than a decade. Although Pentagon leaders Rumsfeld and Wolfowitz were predicting that the Iraqi people would welcome and cooperate with the invaders,[26] the CIA and the State Department had forecast the likelihood of an insurgency. The Joint Chiefs, CENTCOM, and the commander in Iraq were aware of those predictions, but did not initiate plans for a counterinsurgency effort.

One reason given for this omission is that the Secretary of Defense did not want anyone to use the word "insurgency." In one press conference, he chided General Peter Pace, who was standing next to him, for saying "insurgents." They should instead, he said, be called "enemies of the legitimate government of Iraq."[27] Although it seemed almost comic at the time, Rumsfeld's idiosyncracy apparently actually deterred some military leaders from initiating a comprehensive counterinsurgency effort.

Beyond Rumsfeld's apparent ability to intimidate the military, there was a more substantive reason that the military did not commence counterinsurgency operation as soon as it became apparent that there would be armed opposition. No one had a counterinsurgency (COIN) game plan. The COIN preparations and capabilities that were needed were not regarded as something that any particular command should have developed. Thus, despite the empowering of the regional commands and the development of multiservice "jointness," neither the Joint Chiefs of Staff nor Central Command had apparently noticed, or at least did anything about, the fact that the U.S. Army, the operation's major force provider, had not trained or equipped its forces for counterinsurgency. Once the fact that there was an insurgency going on became undeniable, some divisions used their own counterinsurgency techniques, others did not. One who did work to develop a COIN strategy was Marine Major General James Mattis, who led Marine forces during the invasion in 2003. He ordered members of his 1st Marine Division to read about past counterinsurgencies prior to its deployment to Anbar province in early 2004. He also emphasized the importance of respecting Arab cultural sensitivies, including ensuring that Iraqi men not see themselves as being treated in a humiliating way—especially in front of their families—by Marines during searches. By contrast, Major General Ray Odierno and his 4th Infantry Division in the Tigris River Valley north of Baghdad in 2003 and early 2004[28] were criticized by other U.S. commanders for heavy-handed tactics, including indiscriminately rounding up populations of Iraqi men in sweeps and using howitzers to respond to mortar attacks from villages.[29] During the same time frame, Colonel David Hogg in Baqubah would comment that his forces were there to "kill the enemy, not to win their hearts or minds," as he gave civil affairs activities a low priority.[30]

Well into the insurgency, the Army reassigned General David Petraeus from Iraq to Kansas to develop a counterinsurgency program.

He later returned to Iraq to attempt to implement it, four years into the fighting.

Unfortunately, the absence of a counterinsurgency doctrine and capability was no accident or mistake that can be blamed on civilians. I believe the leadership of the Army intentionally failed for thirty years to develop counterinsurgency capability. Not wanting to fight another insurgency because they believed the U.S. Army had no advantage in such wars and indeed was disadvantaged by an impatient U.S. public, the Army leaders developed no counterinsurgency doctrine, trained few forces in counterinsurgency tactics, and procured little of the equipment needed to fight an insurgency. It was the generals' way of saying "no more Vietnams."

Part of this attitude manifested itself in the struggle within the Army between what in Vietnam were called the "Green Berets" and the traditional infantry and armor officers. In the language of the Pentagon, this was a fight between SOF (Special Operations Forces) and "Big Army." The modern-day SOF had been created by President Kennedy, over the objections of Big Army, because he thought that future conflicts would be counterinsurgencies. SOF had taken on two roles: "Black SOF," which did stealthy commando missions using elite units like the Special Forces company that has become known as "Delta Force"; and "White SOF," which conducted civic actions with villagers and trained indigenous troops using small Special Forces units called "A Teams." Big Army consistently tried over the years to limit SOF's size and budget. It fought against there being a multiservice, unified Special Operations Command (SOCOM), which came into existence only when Congress took the unprecedented initiative of creating it and giving SOCOM its own budget.

When opportunities came along for Black SOF to operate, the regional commanders, who were all from Big Army, tried to prevent them from doing so. I recall General Norman Schwarzkopf telling me in his Saudi Arabian command bunker in 1990 that he did not trust the "snake eaters" and would not let them operate behind the lines in Iraq. He changed his mind when Washington ordered him to find and destroy the SCUD missile launchers that were raining destruction on Israel. When opportunities arose to use Black SOF to go after al Qaeda

in the 1990s in Sudan, Qatar, and Afghanistan, Big Army commanders insisted that Black SOF could not do the missions alone and added
so many other troops to the plans that the missions resembled invasions and became undoable. Even after 9/11, when al Qaeda leaders
were discovered inside Pakistan, Big Army leaders would not approve a
mission by a small Black SOF unit. Once again, they added so many
units to the plan that even Donald Rumsfeld thought it would look
like an invasion of Pakistan and canceled the operation.[31] The underlying opposition to SOF came from a fear in Big Army that SOF would
be used in counterinsurgencies, that counterinsurgencies would drag in
the rest of the military, and that the United States was not good at such
politically controversial and long-lasting fights.

Instead, the Army leaders wanted to concentrate on the "AirLand
Battle," a high-tech war of maneuver, the modern equivalent of the
German blitzkreig. AirLand Battle was initially designed to deal with
the massed tanks and artillery of the Soviet Union and Warsaw Pact, a
battle on the plains of Germany. The doctrine was used successfully in
1990 to destroy Iraq's tanks and artillery in the open desert. AirLand
Battle played to the strength of U.S. forces: speed, logistics, intelligence support, and "smart" bombs. It was designed to get the job done
quickly, before support back home might dry up.

Grudgingly, after the interventions of the post–Cold War era (including in Bosnia and Haiti), the Army recognized in its formal manual on operations, "the bible," that there were things other than
blitzkreig. In 2001, it listed ten such Stability Operations missions.

None of the ten missions, including foreign internal defense, or
FID, involved postconquest occupation. FID, as the Army saw it,
meant helping a friendly government. The emphasis was on helping,
not taking on the leading responsibility:

"The U.S. provides military support to counterinsurgency efforts,
recognizing that military power alone cannot achieve lasting success. U.S. military power cannot, and will not, ensure the survival
of regimes that fail to meet their people's basic needs. Military programs and U.S. actions promote a secure environment in which
to implement programs that eliminate causes of insurgencies and

encourage insurgents to rejoin civil society. As with other FID actions, support to a counterinsurgency balances security with economic development to enhance or reestablish stability.

Army forces conduct support to counterinsurgencies within the context of the U.S. Ambassador's country plan and the host nation's internal defense and development strategy. The goal is to integrate all resources—civilian and military, public and private—so that host nation combat operations and development efforts complement each other. The intended result is measurable improvement in the economic, social, and political well-being of those supported. Army forces can also assist in development programs by helping governmental and private agencies provide essential supplies and services.

Support to counterinsurgencies helps host governments deal with two principal groups: the insurgents and the people. Army forces help host governments protect the people from insurgent violence and separate them from insurgent control. These actions require persuasion, prosecution, and destruction to attack insurgent leadership and organization. The goal is to deny insurgent organizations sources of personnel, materiel, funds, and intelligence. The fundamental cause of insurgent activities is widespread dissatisfaction with standing ethnic, religious, political, social, or economic conditions by some sizable portion of the population. For U.S. military power to be effective in supporting a counterinsurgency, the host government must address or revise its policies toward the disaffected portions of the population. *There are few immediate, decisive results in military operations against insurgent forces.* When results occur, they are short lived unless the host government acts just as decisively to address the problems that underlie the insurgency."

But what if the problem underlying the insurgency is the very presence of the U.S. Army? What if there is no host government to support and no host nation forces to take the lead? Army doctrine did not envision situations like that, where the United States would be the only counterinsurgency force operating in a war, where the host nation forces either would be nonexistent or would include large numbers of units covertly supporting the insurgency. They did not plan for such a case because it reminded them too much of Vietnam. To make its view on Vietnam emphatically, the Army inserted a "Lesson Learned" case study in the FID subsection of its bible:

VIETNAM—A CASE STUDY IN
U.S. MILITARY INVOLVEMENT

Direct US involvement in Vietnam began in 1954, when the US military assistance advisory group there received French permission to assist in training South Vietnamese soldiers. Over time, US advisors gradually increased their training role. The Americans assumed fuller control over Vietnamese military affairs, transforming the Army of the Republic of Vietnam (ARVN) into a US-style force. Vietnamese exercises ended with regimental and division maneuvers, training that removed soldiers from fighting the insurgency. In 1956 the French left Vietnam, and the US continued to emphasize conventional warfighting methods. Special Forces worked with the local populace while conventional US forces increased their influence over the ARVN with the creation of Military Assistance Command–Vietnam. In 1965, the war escalated and US forces assumed greater responsibility for military operations. The majority of South Vietnamese people came to rely on US forces for their protection, eroding their confidence in their own government to provide for their security. US forces intended to support the South Vietnamese, but by significantly increasing their role in defending Vietnam, they undermined Vietnamese government authority and ARVN credibility.

In short, the theme of the "bible" and the explicit message of leading generals over many years (including Colin Powell) was "We don't do windows," we do AirLand Battle; if you want somebody to do Stability Operations, call the United Nations or just stay out.

The Army leadership's arrogance was to believe that because they did not wish to fight an insurgency ever again after Vietnam, that the nation would never need them to do so, or the nation's leaders would never order them into such a war. Not wanting to do it, they did not prepare for it.

The third failure happened when it became clear that the President and his advisers were intent on invading Iraq, and those generals empowered to give professional military advice to the civilian commander in chief (and the Congress) failed to point out that the U.S. military was not prepared for what was a foreseeable—indeed, I would argue a likely—scenario: insurgency.

CIA analyses at the time made clear that insurgency was a possible postinvasion outcome. In January 2003, two intelligence assessments, "Principal Challenges in Post-Saddam Iraq" and "Regional Consequences of Regime Change in Iraq," predicted that internal violence and a surge in Islamist extremist violence might follow an overthrow of Saddam Hussein and an occupation.[32]

It is one thing not to prepare for counterinsurgency in the hope that America will never have to fight one. It is quite another thing not to tell the President that you have little or no counterinsurgency capability when he directs you to conduct a war where an insurgency is likely. The point of not having a counterinsurgency capability was, presumably, so we would never have to fight one again. However, the strategy works only if you tell the Secretary of Defense or the President or the Congress the dirty little secret that you are not prepared for such a war. Then, if you are lucky, they will decide not to run the risk of going into a war that could result in a counterinsurgency. That strategy does not work if you remain silent. I am reminded of the scene in the 1960s movie *Dr. Strangelove*, in which the Soviet Ambassador reveals that any U.S. nuclear attack on the USSR will automatically trigger a world-ending response. Incensed, Dr. Strangelove yells at him, "the . . . whole point of the doomsday machine . . . is lost . . . if you keep it a secret! Why didn't you tell the world, eh?"

The military leadership, therefore, had an obligation to tell the Defense Secretary, the President, and the Congress that they should shift to a different strategy that would not put U.S. forces at such a high risk. With body armor, anti-IED systems, and explosive-protected vehicles in short supply, most U.S. forces should have been deployed into their large, protected bases. Inside these vast spaces, they could have trained the new Iraqi Army and police. The new CENTCOM Commander, John Abizaid, and his deputy in Iraq, George Casey, "feeling that the large U.S. military presence in Iraq provoked more resistance than it suppressed, advocated turning combat operations over to Iraqi forces as quickly as possible."[33] Abizaid told Congress that he did not need additional troops.

As 2006 ended, American commanders in Iraq, including General George Casey and General Peter Chiarelli, had finished their plan to move most U.S. forces into large, secure camps where they could train the new Iraqi Army. The virtue of the plan was that it would have dramatically reduced U.S. casualties by taking American troops out of the streets and towns where they were being killed by increasingly sophisticated roadside bombs and snipers. It would also accelerate the training of the Iraqi Army, to which the U.S. would hand off missions when U.S. forces left.

After the Democrats took control of the House and narrowly gained the majority in the Senate in November 2006, the Bush administration faced the prospect of the new Congress voting to withdraw troops from Iraq faster than the Pentagon had planned. All of 2006 could have been a debate about the rate of withdrawal. Bush administration officials were clear what they thought about withdrawal: if U.S. forces left after four or five long years in Iraq, chaos would ensue. By that they meant a level of chaos that was noticeably worse than the living hell that much of Iraq had already become. How much worse it would actually get and how long that violence would last can be debated, but the point is the Bush administration feared presiding over a scene similar to the inglorious departure of the last American troops from Saigon. There would be no way that they could spin that kind of rout into a positive legacy for George W. Bush.

The Bush White House, searching for an alternative, found a proposal bubbling up in places like the American Enterprise Institute, a right-wing think tank in Washington. The idea was simple: the situation in Iraq had gotten out of hand because the U.S. had failed to send in enough troops in 2003; so send them now. To get to the full 300,000 that the original plans had required would mean adding another

170,000 troops, more than doubling the U.S. presence. To do that, the President would have to activate most of the National Guard simultaneously. (Guard units were being used in Iraq, but only a few major units at a time.) Doubling the force would have meant ripping people out of civilian jobs and families across the country, right after the nation had just voted in a way that made clear it wanted to end the war. That full mobilization option was not politically feasible. Instead, the President could turn to the active-duty Army and wring out more troops from its already badly worn-out units. If units that had just come back were returned to Iraq before they fully recovered from their last deployment, if units in Iraq were delayed in their scheduled departures, the number of brigades there could be raised from 15 to 20 for six months, but only at great cost to the Army's readiness and the welfare of the troops and their families.

Thus, in January 2007 President Bush announced a "surge," ordered in five more brigades, and extended the units already in Iraq, saying he was adding 20,000 troops. The number of U.S. troops in Iraq actually rose from 132,000 in January 2007 to 168,000 in September, an increase of 36,000.

The U.S. had the full 20 brigades in country from June until December 2007. During that time General Petraeus returned to Iraq, but this time as the overall U.S. commander. Casey and Chiarelli were out. President Bush, who had said he did not make the decisions, he only took the advice of his commanders, decided to change the commanders because he did not like their advice. Petraeus had previously been in charge of training the new Iraqi Army, something at which he had not proven too successful. While back in the U.S. he had supervised an effort to rewrite the Army's counterinsurgency manual. Now, he wanted to try out his theories. With the added forces, he flooded the zone around Baghdad from which the Iraqi resistance had staged its attacks in the city. Not surprisingly, when these neighborhoods had U.S. troops on every major corner, resistance activity diminished.

Other factors were also at work. Sectarian fighting had declined because over four million Iraqis had fled the country into refugee camps in Syria, Jordan, and elsewhere. Ethnic cleansing of neighborhoods was almost complete. Over the objections of the Baghdad government, Petraeus also armed Sunni militia who had pledged to fight al Qaeda in Iraq. The Shi'a-dominated government worked to get the largest Shi'a militia to declare a cease-fire and to persuade Iran to halt the flow of sophisticated roadside bombs to insurgents. The levels of violence decreased.

Nonetheless, more American troops died in Iraq in 2007 than in any previous year. There were 957 American forces killed, bringing the total U.S. military dead to almost 4,000 as 2008 opened. Also in the year of the surge, 6,084 U.S. troops were wounded (using DOD's definition of "wounded"), bringing the cumulative total to almost 29,000 at year's end. There is no doubt that the casualties would have been fewer if the Casey-Chiarelli plan had been followed and the forces placed in secure garrisons where they would have trained the Iraqi Army. The surge plan had, however, accomplished at least five things.

First, it allowed the Bush administration to point to at least one period in the five years of U.S. military occupation when there was relative stability in some areas for several months. Second, the surge allowed General Petraeus to personally prove his new counterinsurgency doctrine. Third, it converted the U.S. military into what commanders from the Chairman of the Joint Chiefs down called a "fragile force," with the extended and repeated tours in Iraq causing high levels of suicides, divorces, family violence, post-traumatic stress disorders, worn-out equipment, and low-readiness-level units. Fourth, the surge delayed the withdrawal of U.S. forces and the potential ensuing chaos in Iraq until after George W. Bush left office. Fifth, as Steven Simon has elaborated, it armed local units not controlled by the Iraqi government, planting the seeds of future civil conflict.

By April 2008 the Pentagon was admitting that after the "surge" brigades were fully withdrawn in the summer of 2008, there would be a "pause" in withdrawals because the "surge" had not created a lasting reduction in violence. Thus, as the U.S. went into an election campaign to replace George W. Bush, the number of U.S. troops deployed in Iraq would be about the same as it was when the Democrats took control of Congress two years earlier. Moreover, the Pentagon was planning to stay. The Bush Administration was negotiating an agreement with Iraq for a long-term U.S. military presence. Supporters of the U.S. presence in Iraq compared it to Korea, where U.S. forces have been present sixty years. Sen. John McCain suggested the U.S. might be present militarily in Iraq for one hundred years. A different U.S. President might withdraw the U.S. troops, but if that happened and there was chaos after the U.S. troops left, it would be somebody else's fault, not Bush's. By executing the "surge," or "the delay" as it might have been more truthfully labeled, Bush had obtained relative stability in Iraq for his legacy, if only for a few months of the five years he supervised the occupation of Iraq.

During the Korean War, two men who had risen to the rare rank of five-star general, Dwight D. Eisenhower and Douglas MacArthur, considered running for President. One succeeded and is remembered for, among other things, warning Americans about the defense industrial complex. The other, who is remembered in part for resisting presidential authority and therefore being fired, did not succeed in gaining the nomination of his party to run for President. Thus, we have had generals involved in politics and disagreeing with presidents within the lifetime of many Americans.

What we saw in 2007 was, however, something new. The President quietly relieved his two senior commanders in Iraq because they advocated a strategy to reduce U.S. casualties by concentrating on training Iraqis inside safe bases. He replaced Casey with Petraeus. Over the course of several months, the President deflected criticism of his handling of the war by saying that he was following his generals' advice. He repeatedly mentioned Petraeus's scheduled return to report to him and to Congress as a reason to defer congressional consideration of a troop drawdown.[34]

When Petraeus did report, he called for keeping as many troops as possible in Iraq for as long as possible.[35] The only forces he thought could be withdrawn were ones that, coincidentally, were scheduled for return anyway when their extended tours were over. He was attacked in full-page newspaper ads ("General Betray Us?")[36] by antiwar groups, and they, in turn, were attacked by members of Congress for impugning the general's integrity. Although Petraeus did not resist the President as MacArthur had, he was in the middle of political controversy because he was seen as supporting the President and the President was seen as using him, hiding behind the man in uniform to defend a policy widely recognized to have failed.

In answer to a question from the senior Republican on the Senate Armed Services Committee, John Warner, on whether Petreaus felt the Iraq War "is making America safer," the general said, "I don't know, actually. I have not sat down and sorted in my own mind."[37] His answer implied that he was just trying to make the best of the mission in Iraq, whether or not it was a good idea to be there. Earlier the general and the U.S. Ambassador to Iraq, Ryan Crocker, had both said publicly that there could be no military victory in Iraq, that military activity was designed only to provide a window within which the Iraqis could seek a political solution to the factional fighting that was tearing the country apart. Crocker had said that we were buying that window for Iraqi political activity "with the lives of our troops."[38] When there was no political movement by the Iraqis, however, Petraeus changed his rationale for the large U.S. troop presence. Now, he argued, we should be there because where there were more U.S. troops, there was greater security. It began to seem as if the reason for the surge, in Petraeus's mind, was to prove that his new counterinsurgency strategy could work.

One cannot fault David Petraeus for doing what earlier generals had failed to do, create and implement a counterinsurgency strategy. Nor can one complain that a general wanted to retrieve something of the reputation of the U.S. Army by appearing, however briefly, to have gained control of the situation in Iraq. The reputation of the U.S. Army is part of our national deterrent.

But by keeping the U.S. Army engaged at a high tempo in Iraq for longer than his predecessors would have, Petraeus's strategy cost the lives of American forces and ran the equipment and readiness of the Army into the ground. That might have been justified if it had been, as Senator Warner asked, good for the overall security of the United States, but it was not. It was counterproductive. By defending a policy that in the larger sense was injurious to the United States and the Army, by arguing for staying on when he admitted that his own condition for the U.S. presence (real progress toward Iraqi unity) was not being met, Petraeus raised new questions about what makes a general political.

As unusual as the Petraeus episode was, even more unprecedented has been the honorable and valuable decision by numerous junior officers to voice their criticisms of the war's implementation. One of the first to speak out was Lieutenant Colonel Paul Yingling, who published "A Failure in Generalship" in May 2007.[39] Yingling had served in Iraq under Colonel H. R. McMaster, whose 1997 book, *Dereliction of Duty*, had excoriated Vietnam War–era generals. (McMaster's book documented how in the 1960s U.S. Army generals had failed to tell the civilian leadership that they could not succeed in Vietnam. The Chairman of the Joint Chiefs of Staff, General Hugh Shelton, urged officers to read the book, but McMaster was repeatedly passed over for promotion to general.)

Now Yingling charged that "America's generals have repeated the mistakes of Vietnam in Iraq." Yingling outlined the generals' key failures in being "checked by a form of war that they did not prepare for and do not understand." He argued that the generals should have told the civilian leaders that there was a gap between what the civilians wanted and what the Army could do. His article stirred debate in the Army, discussion between the low-level officers and their generals about responsibility and accountability. Is it a general's responsibility to tell a civilian leader that there is a mismatch between the civilian's goals and the Army's capabilities? Should there be accountability if a general adopts a strategy or tactics that result in unnecessary casualties or even mission failure?[40]

Yingling was the pioneering tip of the iceberg. In August 2007, seven junior officers published a *New York Times* op-ed, "The War as We Saw It." "To believe that Americans," they wrote, "with an occupying force that long ago outlived its reluctant welcome, can win over a recalcitrant local population and win this counterinsurgency is farfetched." They told the truth about the situation in Iraq as they saw it, but they did not call into question their loyalty to the military: "We need not talk about our morale. As committed soldiers, we will see this mission through."[41] These were not armchair commentators like me. One of the seven authors was subsequently killed in combat.

More recently, twelve captains wrote about "The Real Iraq We Knew." "Even with the surge," they said, "we simply do not have enough soldiers and Marines to meet the professed goals . . . the sad inevitability of a protracted draw-down is further escalation of attacks—on U.S. troops, civilian leaders and advisory teams." In closing, the twelve captains captured the spirit of many of the junior officers who have spoken out: "This is Operation Iraqi Freedom and the reality we experienced. This is what we tried to communicate up the chain of command. This is either what did not get passed on to our civilian leadership or what our civilian leaders chose to ignore."[42]

The fourth failure was the inadequate training and inadequate equipment given to American military personnel sent into combat in Iraq. In many ways the U.S. force in Iraq in 2003 was as inappropriately trained and equipped for its mission as the Americans in Vietnam had been in 1968. This failure built on past mistakes—the systematic reviews and preparations that had been instituted after Vietnam, including Goldwater-Nichols, had failed to create a force ready for the next war—but was exacerbated by a military leadership that failed to recognize and respond to critical shortcomings on the ground.

In addition to the absence of a doctrine or training for counterinsurgency, the forces were not equipped for the mission. Within months of the occupation of Iraq, it became clear that in the years before the war, the U.S. military had not procured anywhere near sufficient personal body armor protection or vehicle armor plating. Families were forced to buy body armor and send it to their soldiers in Iraq.[43] Almost all of the ubiquitous Humvees, the modern-day military Jeeps, that went into Iraq had canvas or fiberglass side doors. They were badly shot up by insurgents. Patch-on armor plate kits for Humvees were ordered to be produced rapidly. The number of armored Humvees in Iraq rose from 235 in 2003 to more than 5,000, but only four years later. Some Humvees were assigned to convoy protection duty, even though in 1997 the Army had ordered an armored security vehicle called the Guardian for such missions. When the Iraq War started, there were only 53 Guardians in the Army. More than 1,700 have now been ordered.[44]

But the patch-on armor and the Guardian's armor were insufficient to deal with improvised explosive devices (IEDs), which by 2006 were responsible for 70 percent of troop deaths.[45] Jammers were deployed to prevent radio-controlled IEDs from firing, but the insurgents began to use frequencies the jammers could not cover and employed non–radio command detonation techniques. The Pentagon hurriedly created a task force and then an office to figure out ways to stop IEDs, allocating the program more than $10 billion.[46] Then insurgents began using explosively formed projectiles (EFPs) and placing mines under paved roads. The Pentagon procured a handful of MRAP (mine resistant ambush protected) vehicles modeled on a South African armored vehicle and designed to deal with IEDs and EFPs. Although the new vehicles could not survive all the insurgents' weapons and attacks, they were better than anything else in the U.S. inventory. Their V-shaped hulls and heavy armor gave a soldier a four-to-five-times-greater chance of surviving an IED than in a Humvee.[47] Said Senator Joseph Biden, "the Pentagon should have moved faster. . . . You cannot tell me that this country is incapable in the next six months of building every single damn one of these vehicles that needs to be built."[48]

Body armor, IED jammers, MRAPs, and similar equipment were not unknown before the war in Iraq. The U.S. Army concluded in 1994 that the body armor it had used in Somalia was insufficient and ordered some new equipment sets. I worked with the U.S. Secret Service on the need for IED jammers in the mid-1990s. MRAPs were developed in the 1970s, and South Africa, Israel, even Germany, were producing these vehicles in the 1990s. The Pentagon tested MRAPs in 2000 and knew they worked[49]: They were provided to Marine explosives disposal units in Iraq. When finally deployed they endured 300 bomb attacks without a fatality.[50] The Pentagon also knew that MRAPs were in demand from commanders on the ground: Marine commanders in 2005 requested nearly 1,200 MRAPs, but were told to wait for procurement of an even newer vehicle—to be ready in 2012. In February 2005, then–Brigadier General Dennis Hejlik was one of the commanders in Anbar province to protest the lack of MRAP. Marines, he said, "cannot continue to lose . . . serious and grave casualties to IED . . . at current rates when a commercial off the shelf capability exists to mitigate" them.[51]

But General Hejlik's urgent plea was lost in the bureaucracy and then initially rejected because the funds it would take would delay future procurement of systems the Marine Corps had already planned on, according to Franz Gayl, a former Marine who went to work as a civilian in Marine Corps procurement. Gayl's scathing report on the MRAP delay says "hundreds of deaths and injuries could have been prevented." He was right about the ability of MRAPs to save lives. Twenty-five months after General Hejlik's plea from Iraq, the Marine Corps Commandant wrote to the Chairman of the Joint Chiefs saying that the vehicle could have reduced casualties from roadside bombs and other improvised explosive devices by eighty percent. Franz Gayl claims he has been harassed by superiors for having the courage to write his report on the Marines' failure to procure MRAPs when they were first requested. He has sought protection under the Whistle Blower Act.

IEDs and even the more lethal explosively formed projectiles were not invented by Iraqi insurgents after the U.S. invasion. They had been used in some version in Lebanon, the Palestinian territories, and by American-supplied fighters in Afghanistan. But the Army, the Marines, and military's Joint Requirements Oversight Council, chaired by the Vice Chairman of the JCS as part of the Goldwater-Nichols reforms, did not think that these counterinsurgency weapons were needed except in the handfuls in which they were being procured. Throughout the 1990s analysts had written widely about the coming problem of asymmetrical war, where a small number of technologically unsophisticated terrorists could fight and even defeat a modern army. But the U.S. military had not acted on that analysis to procure the defensive equipment or weapons needed to fight such a war. Then–Defense Secretary Rumsfeld also played a role in slowing procurement of the MRAPs: he "famously fought any plan that conflicted with his vision of a lighter, faster military. The heavy, slow, expensive MRAPs would not have conformed to that vision. Nor would a huge order for MRAPs have been consistent with the administration's insistence at the time that the insurgency was entering its 'last throes.'" [52] Ironically, the Pentagon was pushing forward procurement of MRAPs in 2004, but not for U.S. Marines and Army troops. They were going to buy some for the Iraqis.[53] Four years after the U.S. invasion of Iraq, the Pentagon ordered 17,000 of the new MRAP vehicles for $20 billion. The order was expected to be filled sometime in 2009, if the schedule held—six years after the war began.[54]

A fifth failure of some generals crossed a line that had long been defended by the leadership of the U.S. military. For generations, the U.S. military's leaders had held fast to observing international law with regard to prisoners. They believed that only if we upheld international standards did we have any chance of convincing others to do so. In short, if we tortured and abused prisoners, it increased the chances that our own troops would be abused when they were captured. Yet the record seems clear that generals, perhaps including the top U.S. commander in Iraq, Rick Sanchez, knew about, condoned, and authorized the kind of despicable treatment that the world saw in the pictures from Abu Ghraib. There may even have been daily reports to Secretary of Defense Donald Rumsfeld on the progress of abusive interrogations and torture. Beyond the effect on what others might do to future U.S. prisoners, the Abu Ghraib phenomenon had an immediate effect on Arabs' and Muslims' perceptions of the United States of America. It was like rocket fuel for the al Qaeda movement worldwide. While generals failed in their legal, moral, and strategic mission by permitting such activity, at least one general did his duty. Major General Antonio Taguba was asked to investigate what had happened and write a report. He was encouraged to sweep as much as possible under the rug, make it look as if a "few bad apples," low-ranking personnel, had run amok. Instead, Taguba told the truth.

For doing so, he was asked to retire early. He knew that he was sacrificing his two-decade-long career, but he also knew he had to do the honorable thing. After retiring, he told the reporter Seymour Hersh, "We inculcate duty, honor, integrity . . . and yet when we get to senior officer level we forget those values. I know the Army will be mad at me . . . but the fact is that we violated the laws of land warfare, . . . our own principles, . . . and the core of our military values. . . . Those civilian and military leaders responsible should be held accountable." In any hall of American military heroes, there should be a special place for Antonio Taguba, for he demonstrated a form of courage rarer than battlefield valor, and he gave real meaning to the word *honor*.

The sixth failure of the generals was not to ensure fully that their wounded soldiers were properly and respectfully treated after they were returned to the United States. The U.S. military had created the best imaginable battlefield medical system but dropped the ball when it came to long-term care. Dana Priest's insistent and meticulous journalism about the conditions at Walter Reed Army Medical Center cast in a flashlight's beam the dishonorable treatment that had been widespread, but in the dark.[55] More than twenty thousand soldiers were dismissed from the military with post-traumatic stress disorder and told that it was "not service-related," informed with no proof that they had the condition before they entered the military. Congress had to intervene to stop that shameful practice. Other veterans were told that because they had not completed their tour of duty, they owed the Army money, would have to pay back some of their enlistment bonus. They had not completed their tour of duty because they had been wounded! Thousands of soldiers were rushed out of the Army medical system, discharged from the service, and told to get support from a Department of Veterans Affairs medical system. That system was woefully unprepared and underfunded, lacked the needed specialists in brain injuries and other war-related conditions, and often refused to let the veterans go to nearby civilian medical centers that could have helped them.[56] When Veterans Affairs staff assisted wounded soldiers at Fort Drum in filling out forms to document their need for continuing help after they left the service, Army personnel told the VA to stop because it was getting too costly. The responsibility of the generals who run the Army to care for their wounded does not end when they are medevaced out of the theater. Nor does dealing with those who, in Lincoln's words, "shall have borne the battle" mean passing them on like a hot potato to some other bureaucracy that is known to be incapable of adequately caring for them. In the case of our wounded, we cannot apply the old Pentagon saying that "an action transferred is an action completed." We have also ignored veterans who were not wounded, by failing to enforce laws protecting National Guard personnel from being fired when they are called up. One officer told me recently that his company had fired him as soon as he put on the uniform because "they know nobody will do anything about it." The way we have treated our Iraq and Afghanistan veterans makes my blood boil. We need to make a promise to ourselves that as a nation we will go above and beyond what is required to respect, honor, care for, and reward those who have served, no matter what it costs, no matter how long it takes. And we need to have watchdogs who ensure that we live up to that promise.

THE DOCTRINE THAT DID NOT BARK

If the generals failed to stop or adequately prepare for the war, so too did the civilians in the national security agencies and Congress. The third change in the post–Vietnam War military affairs, the one intended to stop presidents from ill-considered wars like the one in Vietnam, was also ineffective when it came to Iraq. Indeed, the Weinberger-Powell Doctrine and its attempt to constrain presidents never successfully restrained any President from using military force. The flaw in the doctrine was that Colin Powell and his supporters sought to apply it to all U.S. military uses of force, instead of just to major combat operations that ran the risk of being both large-scale and long in duration. Presidents Reagan, Bush 41, and Clinton could not see a compelling logic behind the doctrine's being applied to smaller contingencies. These operations could not result in large casualties that would erode public support sufficiently to damage the place of the military in American society, as Vietnam had.

Thus, they conducted a series of military operations that probably would not have fully passed the Powell Doctrine tests. The costs in terms of U.S. fatalities of their using the military were few. Ronald Reagan put U.S. forces into civil wars in El Salvador and Lebanon. He also bombed Libya and attacked both its navy and that of Iran, in addition to invading and occupying Grenada. His successor, George H. W. Bush, started by invading and occupying Panama, then put more than half a million U.S. forces into war on the Arabian Peninsula and ended his four years by intervening in Somalia. Clinton followed by using the U.S. forces he found in Somalia, invading and occupying Haiti, repeatedly bombing Iraq and Serbia, and putting ground forces into Bosnia, Kosovo, and Macedonia.[57] (He also considered military operations against Iran and Korea and placed naval forces between China and Taiwan during tensions there.)

In all of those dozen military operations combined, there were fewer than 700 U.S. military combat fatalities, many of them from "friendly fire" and a third of them from one terrorist attack (in Beirut). Fewer than 35 of the U.S. military combat deaths came in the eight years of the Clinton administration.[58]

I participated in the planning and coordination of nine of those military operations while working in the State Department and then the White House, for more than a decade in each. What was clear about the three presidents who ordered them was that they had overcome the supposed "Vietnam Syndrome" and, with varying degrees of doubt, disregarded the military's call for restraint in the use of force. Although each of the three presidents experienced controversy over their actions, the opposition was limited and did not, as Weinberger predicted, create "domestic turmoil" or "tear the fabric of society."

Moreover, many of the casualties took place in the Reagan administration before the military reforms and "Jointness" were instituted. As the reforms kicked in, the military performed with increasing skill and success, often with amazingly low casualties, prior to the second Iraq War.

Of all of those operations, only the first Gulf War (1990–1991) ran the risk of being large-scale, sustained, and accompanied by high casualties. Although the first Gulf War seemed to meet the doctrine's criteria for use of force, then-General Powell was reluctant to see the military employed and recommended a prolonged period of sanctions. When, more than a decade later, the second President Bush wanted a second war with Iraq, General Powell was Secretary of State, a member of the National Security Council, and one of the most admired people in America. What if he had presented the National Security Council and the President with an attempt to apply the Powell Doctrine[59] to the Iraqi situation; what would it have said?

The Iraq War failed to meet almost all criteria of the Powell Doctrine. The doctrine requires that for force to be used, U.S. vital interests must be at stake. The Bush administration argued that U.S. vital interests were threatened by Iraqi weapons of mass destruction (WMDs) and by the connection between Iraq and al Qaeda. Because of these threats, it said, the United States had to act preemptively against Iraq. These clear and present threats to U.S. vital interests would have satisfied the Powell Doctrine's first criterion, except that they were neither as clear nor as present as the administration claimed they were. We know that now, of course, but senior administration officials knew it in 2003, too. The information contradicting the administration's argument that became available to the public later was distributed inside the government before the war.[60] Secretary Powell must have known, and the senior U.S. military commanders could have known, should have known.

Would Iraq's having WMDs have been a challenge to our vital interests? It had had WMDs—chemical weapons, at least—for almost twenty years. They had not transferred them to terrorists. They had not even used them on an army that invaded Iraqi territory, the U.S. Army in 1991. Nuclear weapons, of course, were a different matter. A nascent Iraqi nuclear weapons capability would have been cause for appropriate U.S. action. The evidence presented in 2002 of a renewed Iraqi nuclear program was scant and unconvincing to many nuclear weapons proliferation intelligence analysts. Some of the evidence was known even at the time to be forgeries.[61]

Would Iraq's helping al Qaeda be a threat to our vital interests? Of course, and it would have required a response. But there was even less evidence about such a link than there was about WMDs. The administration—particularly Vice President Cheney—pointed to a meeting in Prague between 9/11 hijacker Mohammed Atta and Iraq's consul at the Iraqi Embassy in the Czech Republic, Ahmad Khalil Ibrahim Samir al-Ani.[62] But Vice President Cheney had been told that the CIA and FBI had both discounted that report as early as 2001.[63] Nonetheless, his aide Scooter Libby confronted me outside the West Wing, saying "I understand you are going around saying that the report on Atta in Prague isn't true. We believe it. You need to take another look at it." His message was clear: "We believe it" meant "You need to believe it." I told him what I believed was that day Atta had been in Norfolk, Virginia, a town where we kept much of our Navy, and he ought to look into that. Scooter was not pleased. The CIA intelligence on Iraqi training of al Qaeda operatives in chemical and biological weapons was similarly dubious, based on one report extracted from a prisoner being tortured by Egyptian intelligence, and again administration officials knew it.[64] Despite its mistakes about Iraqi WMDs, the intelligence community clearly and unequivocally stated well before the war that there was no operational or in any way significant relationship between Iraq and al Qaeda.

There were many U.S. vital interests in the region, but they weren't at risk. Containment was working to keep Saddam Hussein in check, and the situation, though not ideal, was stable. Secretary Powell had told Congress in 2001 that containment was working.[65] It had not ceased to work a year later. Without the WMDs and the al Qaeda connection, there was no clear and present danger and no urgent need for a U.S. military campaign. The intelligence debunking the administration's claims about nuclear weapons and about al Qaeda was briefed to senior U.S. military officers.

Second, the Powell doctrine says that force should be used only as a last resort, after all other alternatives are exhausted or proven unworkable. Iraq had agreed in 2002 to the most intrusive international weapons inspections yet conducted. The inspectors had found nothing, but the inspections were continuing. Both the International Atomic Energy Agency (IAEA) and a renewed U.N. special commission (then called UNMOVIC) reported that they needed more time to complete their assessment. As the man who had led both organizations at different times, Hans Blix, makes clear in his book *Disarming Iraq,*[66] the inspectors' work was not complete, and, given more time, they could have collected the evidence necessary to prove that Iraq did not have the WMDs that the Bush administration alleged.

The Bush doctrine of preemption also turned the question of "last resort" on its head, since it advocates striking against an emergent threat before it is fully formed. In the words of the 2002 National Security Strategy of the United States of America,[67] the United States "will not hesitate to act alone, if necessary, to exercise our right of self-defense by acting preemptively." Ultimately, the basic tenet of the preemption doctrine makes it fundamentally incompatible with the Powell Doctrine's idea of waiting and playing out the alternatives.

Third, the Powell Doctrine says that all consequences should be fully considered and risks and costs should be "fully and frankly" analyzed. Inherent in this criterion is the idea of looking at the possibility that things will not go as planned. Rumsfeld reportedly drew up an exhaustive list of things that could go wrong, but the list was so long that it looked more like an ass-covering operation than serious analysis. There was no attempt to focus on a manageable set of risks that were most likely to go wrong and then look at whether the overall operation would still be worth conducting. The intelligence community did suggest that an insurgency was possible. Many people wrote before the war that the invasion and occupation would strengthen terrorism and anti-Americanism.

The fourth Powell doctrinal requirement is that the political and military objectives must be clear and obtainable. Arguably, the military objectives—the elimination of the Iraqi government and the unconditional surrender of its military—were clear and obtainable. The political goal was the establishment of some sort of democratic national government. Almost no expert on Iraq thought that was obtainable. Indeed, the reason the United States had not marched on Baghdad in 1991 was that people like Colin Powell, Dick Cheney, Secretary of State James Baker, and Brent Scowcroft knew that putting together a national government, let alone a democratic one, after Saddam would be extremely difficult, if not impossible. Nothing had changed the basic facts affecting that outcome in the next decade.

Fifth, when applying the Powell Doctrine there should be a plausible exit strategy to avoid endless entanglement. There *was* an exit strategy: General Franks told his commanders to plan on pulling all troops out in a matter of months, except for a small residual force of 30,000. Had that strategy been reviewed seriously, it would never have been thought to be plausible. There was no plan on who or what would replace the U.S. forces, no plan for U.N. replacements, no notion of how the Iraqi Army would reestablish security.

Sixth, Powell says, we must be committed to winning decisively. The forces necessary to win decisively and obtain the goals should be made available, and the appropriate force size should be reviewed regularly. As I discussed earlier, there was actually an effort by Rumsfeld and Franks to strip out units that were in the standing contingency plan for Iraq. They did the exact opposite of what this Powell criterion calls for. Inadequate troop levels are one leading example of a broader pattern: the Bush administration repeatedly failed to commit the resources necessary to win, including body armor; armored vehicles; noncombat personnel trained in crowd control, reconstruction, and law enforcement; and funding for reconstruction. Rumsfeld "wanted to fight this war on the cheap," said one colonel roughly ten days into the fighting. "He got what he wanted." [68]

Seventh, to conform with the Powell doctrine, there should be genuine and broad international support. The 1990 military coalition that went to war with Iraq included significant forces from Egypt, Syria, Saudi Arabia, and France. All four of those nations opposed the new war, as did Russia, Germany, and every Arab country. No international organization endorsed the war, not the United Nations, the Arab League, NATO, or the Gulf Cooperation Council. [69]

Eighth, if force is to be used, there should be reasonable grounds to suppose the American people will support the operation. Here the war in Iraq seems to have satisfied the Powell Doctrine, at least superficially. In the days before the war, only one-third of the country disapproved of taking military action against Iraq. Although nearly two-thirds believed that the U.N. inspectors should be given more time and that the United States should not act without its allies' support, a majority of Americans were not against the war itself. [70]

Further, it is reasonable for the Bush administration to have expected that even more Americans would come to support the operation once it began. Americans have historically rallied 'round the flag even for operations they did not originally support. To really assess Americans' support of the war, though, we have to look deeper. We need to ask *why* they supported the war. We also need to ask whether Americans had other priorities that they deemed more important, even as they supported the war in Iraq when viewed on its own. In the lead-up to the war, 42 percent believed that Saddam had been involved in the September 11, 2001, attacks.[71] Fifty-one percent saw al Qaeda as a greater "threat to peace and stability" than Iraq,[72] even as many believed that the war in Iraq went in tandem with an attack against al Qaeda.

The fact that so many Americans misunderstood the war provides an important explanation for the public support of the war. Technically, Americans supported the war when it began. But the fact that their understanding was based on bad information helps explain why, as the war dragged on and more truths came to light, support fell away and left U.S. forces once again putting themselves in harm's way for a war that a majority of their compatriots don't support.

LESSONS RELEARNED

After reviewing the concerted efforts of the U.S. military to prevent a recurrence of Vietnam and the smaller military failures of the 1980s, I am reluctant to suggest that there are now ways of putting systems or other reforms in place to prevent another Iraq. In fact, the United States is more likely to suffer from an "Iraq Syndrome," an overreluctance to use force again, than it is to have another President who wants to start a disastrous war. Nonetheless, war colleges, think tanks, and Lessons Learned centers in the military will be poring over the details of the operations in Iraq for years. They will try to find what went wrong by examining the many After Action Reports and oral histories that will be produced. They will make proposals and suggestions for change, as their predecessors did after Vietnam.

I would urge them, in addition to looking at the tactical issues and the purely military concerns, to begin as I have in these two chapters and look at the effects of the earlier post–Vietnam War changes. Some of them need to be abandoned or heavily modified. Specifically, the officer corps needs to design, in conjunction with civilians and retired officers, a post–Iraq War strategy that I believe must include the following seven changes in its approach to military, political-military, and political issues.

1. *Reliance on the National Guard:* The idea of the active-duty force relying on the reserves, especially the National Guard, to conduct major operations should be dropped. The Abrams restructuring did not prevent presidents from going to war or waging unpopular wars; it only disrupted families and sent units overseas that were needed at home. The National Guard is required in the U.S. territory to deal with natural and terrorist disasters, pandemic diseases, and other domestic concerns. In February 2008 the congressionally chartered Commission on the National Guard and Reserves found that the Guard had "an appalling gap" of ability to deal with catastrophic situations such as nuclear, chemical, or biological attack "that places the nation and its citizens at greater risk." Retired Marine General Arnold Punaro said, "We don't have the forces we need, we don't have them trained, and we don't have the equipment."[73] The Guard's force structure should be adjusted to deal better with those problems, including the establishment of field hospitals, military police, and communications units.

   The active-duty force should also be structured differently, without political considerations. We should not have to take a state trooper off the roads in America to put an MP on the streets of another country when a U.S. intervention is required. The Army should be able to operate a large force in combat without significant National Guard activations. That may mean adding military police, civil affairs, and other units to the active force. Having such units in the active force would also mean that there could be better peacetime planning and training for their utilization.

2. *Special operations:* The President, as commander in chief, needs to state explicitly whether he/she wants significant

commando capabilities (black SOF) and, if so, direct the leaders of the U.S. military to strengthen them and employ them. If the President concludes that the traditional Big Army view is correct, that the Army should not conduct such missions, the Special Operations Command and black SOF should be eliminated and the funds for these units be reduced. The white SOF capabilities should be assigned to the regional commanders. Because the United States would still need a commando capability, the President would also need to direct the CIA to significantly enhance its paramilitary mission. I would prefer to see such missions carried out by the Army because I believe it could do them far better than any other organization, including the CIA. But even a CIA paramilitary capability is better than none and the current situation, in which the Pentagon will never use the black SOF units, is like having none. One way or another, the President needs to make an explicit decision and the NSC staff needs to enforce it. The President should not have to address this issue for the first time when the Army and Pentagon refuse to let a small commando unit stage a stealthy raid to capture a terrorist leader.

3. *Counterinsurgency:* Related to the Special Operations decision is the need for a policy on how far we are willing to go in having the two related capabilities to fight counterinsurgencies and to engage in the security aspects of nation building (including peacekeeping).

On counterinsurgency, President Kennedy seems to have thought that we should have a large, robust counterinsurgency program to help friendly nations threatened by insurgents but should not supplement such operations with the introduction of U.S. conventional ground forces, such as infantry brigades. After the Vietnam War of Presidents Johnson and Nixon, the Army tried to have nothing to do with counterinsurgency and then reluctantly developed a policy that we would help friendly nations with "foreign internal defense." The Army policy, however, made it clear that U.S. conventional ground forces should not be used in such missions because their presence would be counterproductive to the goal of strengthening the friendly government. The history of counterinsurgency suggests that the Army policy is usually the right choice, but that policy requires three things: (1) explicitly informing the President of that policy and obtaining approval for it, (2) conducting large-scale training and assistance capability in Special Forces and elsewhere in the Army, and (3) developing and integrating CIA and State Department capabilities to train and assist friendly nations that are combatting insurgencies. Someone, ideally on the White House National Security Council staff, should have the clear responsibility of ensuring that the DOD, CIA, and State Department counterinsurgency capabilities are adequate and coordinated.

Because there will continue to be regional wars and failed states creating instability that threatens our interests, a similar decision needs to be made explicitly on the related issue of nation building and peacekeeping. What capabilities do we want to have, and what parts of the U.S. government should provide them? What are we willing to do as part of a U.N. operation, and what conditions need to be satisfied before we participate (e.g., that U.S. and other U.N. forces will proactively use force in self-defense and disarm those who seek to subvert the peacekeeping mission)? What do we want the United Nations to be able to do, with or without U.S. units involved? What capabilities do we want other organizations, such as NATO and the African Union, to have for peacekeeping and more robust stability operations in support of nation building? Rather than pretending that we will never undertake such missions or that international organizations are capable of doing so without us, I would suggest that the U.S. military have an active program to train, assist, and, if directed, participate in or even lead peacekeeping and stability operations. This program, in close coordination with the State Department, would have detailed joint civilian-military contingency plans, training, and doctrine, a joint civilian-military headquarters unit, and on-call forces. It would also actively support the growth of similar capabilities at the United Nations and in regional organizations. Again, the NSC staff should perform oversight to ensure that both the military and the State Department provide the required contributions and work well together, as outlined in Clinton directive PDD-56.

To ensure that the inadequacy of civilian agencies in this area is highlighted and addressed, in addition to NSC oversight, there ought to be an annual report by the Chairman of the Joint Chiefs to the Secretary of State, describing both (1) what the military needs from State (and other civilian agencies) to conduct counterinsurgencies, peacekeeping, and aid to failed states and (2) any perceived shortfalls in those capabilities. The secretary should be required to respond with what, if anything, will be done to address those shortfalls, and by when.

4. *The Powell Doctrine:* It must disturb Colin Powell that the doctrine that bears his name has had such limited success in restraining presidents from using force, sometimes with unfortunate results. The motivation behind the doctrine was sensible enough after Vietnam, and Iraq has proved its value even further. So what went wrong, and can the doctrine be resurrected and adapted for the future? The first thing that went wrong was that the doctrine was so broadly drawn as to cover (and recommend against) every use of the U.S. military, no matter how small or safe. Presidents therefore ignored it, and the doctrine was discredited and fell into disuse. The second problem was, obviously, that it was not used by anyone in judging the Iraq War decision. Nothing required its use: no law, no executive order, no DoD directive.

The Powell Doctrine (or the Weinberger Doctrine if you prefer the original version) should be modified to address only those uses of the U.S. military that might involve both large-scale and long-term combat operations. For such operations, the President should be required by law to submit a report to the Congress analyzing the proposed operation in light of the Powell (or Weinberger) criteria.

Congress should be required to empanel a bipartisan/nonpartisan expert review group to do a similar analysis in parallel. In conjunction with that report and review, the intelligence community should also report to the President and Congress on the basis for the war and the possible outcomes. A bipartisan/nonpartisan expert review of that report should then be conducted for Congress. If that had been done in the case of Iraq, some of the dangers of intervening might have emerged. Although the President might not have been stopped, some of the shortcomings in the plan (or lack thereof) and some of the pitfalls might have been highlighted and avoided. There is the risk that this law would make it more difficult for the United States to launch a major war, but that risk is preferable to beginning an ill-thought-out war with not even a credible plan for an endgame. A major war almost always unleashes unexpected consequences, horror, and widespread personal suffering. It should be a last alternative. It should be difficult to start one.

5. *Independent military advice:* Thinking of remedies in the wake of the Iraq War, I am tempted to suggest that the leaders of the U.S. military should be able to provide the President and Congress with independent military advice, but we made that change with the Goldwater-Nichols legislation after Vietnam. It did not work because the two military leaders at the initiation of the Iraq War, the Chairman of the Joint Chiefs of Staff and the Commander of CENTCOM, the regional command, were compliant officers without strategic vision. Moreover, even if they had given the President solid military advice, there is little reason to believe that he would have been swayed by it. Congress, however, might

have been. Even if the generals had given their testimony in closed (secret) session of the Senate Armed Services Committee, their doubts would have had an effect. Congress might have passed resolutions setting prerequisites for the war. The war might have been avoided or, if it went ahead anyway, it might have been performed with a larger, better-equipped force. There might have been a plan for postcombat security.

While it is likely that Bush administration officials picked General Myers as Chairman of the Joint Chiefs precisely because he was viewed as someone likely to be compliant, even if they had sought a thoughtful leader, there might have been difficulties in selecting one under the current law and practices. The law restricts the pool of applicants to the heads of the four military services and the major joint commands. Although that creates a pool of fourteen officers, it has often been the case that few of them had the experience and background necessary to lead the U.S. military. Often those who did have the qualifications failed to pass the new personal ethics standards that implicitly became criteria during the 1990s. Those unwritten standards meant that the only officers considered were the few who were thought to have been completely faithful to their spouse.

The same law that specifies which officers can be considered as candidates for the Chairman's position also allows the President to waive the requirements and appoint any officer. That could mean calling back to active duty a retired general (as President Kennedy did when he appointed Maxwell Taylor as Chairman and President Bush did when he appointed Peter Schoomaker to head the Army). To enhance the pool from which a Chairman can be chosen, the law ought to be changed to remove the criteria and the possibility of a presidential waiver. At the same time, the law could be changed to extend the tenure from two years to four. (Peter Pace was not reappointed in 2007 and served only two years as Chairman, the first with such a short tenure.) Knowing that one has to be renominated by the President almost as soon as one enters the job must be a deterrent to providing truly independent military advice. Future presidents should also tell those sifting for nominees as chairman that they will consider a general or admiral even if the candidate nominee has had a messy divorce or an extramarital affair. Few of our greatest Commanders in Chief would have passed the new personal ethics standards.

Congress should then hold semiannual, closed-door hearings with the Chairman to obtain his independent military advice. Rarely will JCS chairmen use this opportunity to highlight a difference within the Pentagon any more than a civilian agency head would, but on matters of great principle they will. This process may drive future secretaries of defense mad, but if we truly value independent military advice we ought to have a way of getting it. Secretaries of defense should have to justify their policy differences with the military. If the civilian leaders are right in their disputes with senior military officers, as often they will be, their arguments ought to carry the day.

6. *Planning:* No part of the government does planning more systematically and professionally than the military. Civilian agencies would do well to adopt their Deliberate Planning processes and Lessons Learned procedures. The every-four-year review of the military that Congress requires, the Quadrennial Defense Review (QDR to Washingtonians), has also been supplemented by the occasional blue-ribbon panel to study what tasks the military will be called upon to do in the future and what branch of the military should do them, a Roles and Missions Commission.

Nonetheless, the absence of counterinsurgency doctrine, training, and equipment in the Army was either not noticed or not acted upon by the Army, the Joint Staff, the regional commanders, the QDR, or the last Roles and Missions Commission. The American military still looks a lot like the force that was around at the end of the Cold War in 1990, only somewhat smaller. The Navy is still built around aircraft carrier battle groups, the Air Force is deploying more and more advanced manned fighter aircraft, the Marines are still designed as a beach-taking amphibious force, and the Army is still dominated by divisions with tanks. The Air Force and the Navy still have significant strategic nuclear missile forces.

There was a time in the twentieth century when one service would create analyses proving that it was more deserving of funds than another service was. That kind of competition sometimes found the flaws in Army, Navy, or Air Force planning. The Army famously demonstrated that its Air Corps could sink Navy battleships. The Navy argued strenuously that its missile submarines were more survivable than the Air Force's missiles in silos. The Air Force was always trying to see if there was a way the Soviets could uncover the location of the Navy missile submarines. In more recent years, there has been an implicit bargain that the services would all support one another, or at least not reveal the others' flaws. One Pentagon civilian called it "You scratch my back, I'll support your budget."

When a civilian agency (the Office of Program Analysis and Evaluation) regularly challenged service planning assumptions and weapons claims with its own analyses, members of Congress railed against it and demanded that it be eliminated. It still exists, but more quietly than before. Nonetheless, contention and debate, competing analyses and challenges to assumptions are necessary checks on the tendency of all military organizations to prepare for the previous war. In an Air Force run by fighter pilots, how many generals with wings on their shirts will give up new manned fighter aircraft for remotely piloted vehicles (RPVs) or cyberwarfare units?

To minimize the chances of another rude awakening when we find out that our troops are in vehicles with canvas sides and the enemy has made roadside bombs that slice through them like swords through cardboard, we need to try harder to make the force structure reviews serious exercises. Rather than waiting four years and then conducting complex reviews in which many issues are buried and compromises are traded around like baseball cards, there should be an annual review of a handful of alternative force structure issues. That review should give the same standing and resources to a team advocating change as it does to the service advocating more of the same. The ultimate decisions should be made annually by the commander in chief, in consultation with the Defense Secretary, with input not just from the Pentagon but also from all of the national security departments and other concerned experts. Congress should be fully briefed on the reviews.

7. *Political partisanship:* I reject the idea of going back to the old days when the military officer corps was told by their military superiors that they should not vote. That would take the idea of civilian control of the military to a ridiculous conclusion. If any group has earned the right to have a say in choosing our leaders, it is those who pay the price of military service to our country.

Nonetheless, I am troubled by the effect on military-related policies of having the officer corps vote overwhelmingly and consistently for one political party. Moreover, it is not just the officers; the military voting bloc includes active-duty, reserve, and retired personnel and their extended families.[74]

The blind loyalty to the Republican Party that most officers appear to have internalized has made it difficult for military families, including the retired, to criticize the Bush administration and vote against it and its supporters, even when it repeatedly does things inimical to the military. If a Democratic administration had cut in half the number of troops in a military war plan, sent a force into battle without a postcombat plan, failed to provide troops needed body armor and protected vehicles, and topped it all off by providing poor medical care to the wounded, there would have been a protest march on the Pentagon and White House led by military families. The families would have become active in congressional elections, sweeping all Democrats from office. All of this would have been followed by an impeachment. Moreover, those steps would have been justified.

Instead, what we see too often is military families repeating the slogans developed by the Republican Party strategists: "We have to fight in Iraq so we don't have to fight them here" and "We are fighting in Iraq to preserve our freedom." It has become so routine for many military families to repeat Republican mantras that some do not appear to notice when those slogans make no sense and put our military at great and unnecessary risk.

President Bush's treatment of the military and the readiness crisis created by the Iraq War are finally shifting long-standing political terrain in how the military and promilitary civilians vote. In the middle of President Clinton's tenure, there was a remarkable gap between civilian and military voters, with only a third of civilians identifying as Republican but roughly 70 percent of officers doing so. That was a much more stark difference than had existed in the mid-1970s, when a quarter of civilians and a third of military officers self-identified as Republicans.[75]

The Iraq War is weakening that bond. A *Military Times* annual poll of active-duty service members showed that by the end of 2006, only 46 percent of respondents self-identified as Republicans, down from 60 percent in 2004.[76] Only 35 percent of respondents approved of President Bush's handling of the war, and nearly three-quarters said the military was "stretched too thin to be effective." The Republican Party still has an edge with servicemen and -women, with their families, and possibly even with national security voters writ large, but the advantage has diminished and many more military votes are up for grabs.

I would hope that after the Iraq fiasco military families will in the future be less attached to one party, but old traditions die hard. Or I could think that perhaps the Democratic Party could stage a successful effort to draw a significant number of military families to its banner, but the Democratic Party does not exactly have the marketing skills of Apple with its iPod or Sony with its *Spider-Man* movies.

The reason that military families should become more independent of the Republican Party is not that the GOP will necessarily bring forth another President who will hurt the military. Indeed, in the future Republicans may be more supportive of military families than Democrats are or vice versa; we cannot know. What we can know is that as long as one party can take a huge voting bloc like military families for granted, that voting bloc is likely to be ill served. Moreover, the nation is likely to be harmed if a patriotic voting bloc blindly or reflexively supports one party and is largely silent or supportive when an administration of that party makes huge mistakes that damage the country.

It would be better for the welfare of the military families and the security of the nation if there were an active, nonpartisan political organization that advocated for those families, provided them with information, and educated both parties and Congress on their needs and views. Such an entity could have the two parties compete for support. Would that mean that there would be undue military influence on elections? I doubt that many more military family members would vote than do now, but their votes would mean more. The lives of our men and women in uniform might matter more in the thinking and the voting of Congress, as indeed they should.

Would these changes prevent another Iraq or some other failure of the military system? I don't know; the changes made in the three decades after Vietnam should have prevented another such war. The impressive professionalization of the U.S. military should have made the force better capable of handling the mission or altering it. What I do know is that the system did not work well enough and our soldiers and marines have paid the price, as have the Iraqis. We need not and should not overreact to the failures in the Iraq War by ignoring the great work that the military has done to increase its professionalization. Nor should we blame the soldiers for the failures of some generals, nor the generals for the failures of cabinet members and elected leaders. Worse than all of those possibilities is that we might as a nation recoil from using force again when it is necessary or fail to fund needed military programs.

But the very worst thing we can do is to ignore the failures that have occurred in the Iraq War, including in the military, and do nothing to correct them.

CAN WE REDUCE
INTELLIGENCE FAILURES?

Our black Mercedes moved slowly on the snowy back roads of the Vienna Woods. Few cars had been down the streets of the forest before us that day. The Wienerwald was busy only on weekends, when Viennese hiked paths to remote, rustic wine or beer halls and a few nice restaurants hidden in the clearings. We were headed to one such restaurant that weekday. There would only be four customers for lunch: a KGB officer and his assistant, my boss, and his assistant, me. It was 1975. I was twenty-four and on my first overseas assignment.

My introduction to the world of intelligence came in Vienna, a Graham Greene setting, on the streets where his classic spy story, *The Third Man,* had been filmed. The Austrian capital was nestled at the edge of the Iron Curtain and surrounded by it, well east of Prague. Red Army tanks were a short drive away. The capital of neutral Austria had been a den of spies since the city had fallen to American and Russian troops in 1945. I was there in support of talks between the two armed alliances that faced each other with massed armor and nuclear missiles: NATO and the Warsaw Pact. The Cold War was not just a concept then, especially not there. Each alliance had managed to squeeze about a million troops into the narrow space that was central Europe. Both sides believed another devastating war was possible, even though the ruins of the last war were still in evidence. The talks were designed to find a way for both sides to move back from the brink gradually, lower troop levels, withdraw tanks. And the talks were deadlocked.

Our lunch with the KGB was also unproductive, even disappointing. It reminded me of a time, slightly more than a year before, when I had been "read in" to the special intelligence programs that produced satellite photography. I had been expecting to be surprised, amazed, or awestruck. Instead, what I found was pedestrian, plebeian, prosaic. The satellite pictures had looked like any other aerial photography. At the lunch in the woods, the senior KGB man turned out to be just a gray bureaucrat. The food and wine, however, were far above my young standards for a midday repast.

Over the next three decades I would serve in jobs in which I performed and managed intelligence analysis, tasked intelligence collection, provided oversight to covert action, and tried as a policy maker to utilize intelligence analysis as an aid in decision making. Unlike that Viennese lunch, working with the U.S. intelligence community often left a bitter taste. After thirty years I learned that intelligence work has nothing in common with the fictional image of spies, and most of the time the good guys have not seemed to have much positive effect.

But back in Vienna in 1975, it was easy to see how intelligence officers could become preoccupied with their world of spy versus spy. Even for a member of the arms talks delegation, espionage was in the air. Being tailed around the medieval streets of Vienna by Bulgarian agents, we routinely tried to lose them. When we discovered an active listening device in our conference room, we gamed out what false information we could feed to those listening. A courageous source inside the Warsaw Pact volunteered information proving that the Soviet Union was lying significantly in the talks. But for all the cloak and dagger around them, the talks took fifteen years. I left after three and was an Assistant Secretary of State by the time agreement was reached. And shortly after the arms limits and modest reductions were agreed, it no longer mattered. Far greater troop reductions were about to happen: the entire Warsaw Pact military alliance collapsed over a few days in 1991. The Red Army tank divisions, which we had negotiated about for so long, creaked slowly back to the Soviet Union, where most of them demobilized. They left not because they were required to by the treaty we had struck but because, to our surprise, the Soviet Union and the Warsaw Pact were both about to go out of existence.

The fact that the end of the Cold War came as a surprise was widely viewed as a devastating indictment of U.S. intelligence. We had spent more than forty years and untold billions of dollars focusing our intelligence collection and analysis on one main target, the Soviet Union. Yet when the Cold War enemy fell over like a tree that had been dead for years crashing down in a high wind, it came as a shock to U.S. intelligence and, therefore, as an unanticipated crisis to the stunned U.S. and NATO policy makers.

Surprises owing to intelligence failures did not always bring such happy results. On the day I was born in October 1950, the CIA told President Harry Truman that China would not invade Korea to fight U.S. forces.[1] In fact, the forward elements of the massive Chinese invasion had already crossed into Korea a few days before, and as a result the U.S. Army was about to suffer the worst series of defeats in its history. Forty years later, less a few weeks, the CIA assured me that Iraq would not invade Kuwait ("It's far too hot in August, Dick, don't worry about it"). Within hours of that intelligence briefing, the Iraqis swept over Kuwait.

The phrase "U.S. intelligence failure" runs like a leitmotif throughout the last sixty years of American national security activities. Presidents seem always to be passing blame off onto the intelligence agencies. Congress and blue-ribbon commissions seem regularly to conclude investigations by being shocked at our lack of intelligence information. Are the charges fair, or are the intelligence agencies just the whipping boys, the scapegoats for policy failures? What should we expect intelligence to do, and, whatever that is, has U.S. intelligence really failed to do it? If so, why?

WHAT WE SHOULD EXPECT
OF THE INTELLIGENCE COMMUNITY

For many, including Washington policy makers, the U.S. intelligence bureaucracy (which likes to call itself the intelligence community) is a large and confusing array of secret agencies whose purposes are not always clear. Far from transparent, they are intentionally opaque to most of Washington. Thus, it is sometimes difficult to judge what it is they are meant to do and what we should expect of them.

The output we should expect from intelligence is partially a function of the input, the resources we give to the function. There are sixteen U.S. intelligence agencies. Their budgets are secret but are widely thought to now be in excess of $50 billion a year. (The total was $44 billion in 2005, according to Mary Margaret Graham, the deputy director of national intelligence for collection, who inadvertently let that little fact slip out in a public setting in Texas.)[2] The number of people employed in the agencies is also secret, but is in the tens of thousands, supported by many more in private sector companies on contract to the government. In short, although they may complain about needing more resources, the leaders of U.S. intelligence seem to have substantial resources to carry out their main two missions.

Broadly speaking, those two missions are collection and analysis. (Two other functions, covert action and counterintelligence, are small in terms of their budgets and human resources. Nonetheless, they have played important roles in the history of intelligence failures, and I will discuss them later in this chapter.) Most of the funds are devoted to the collection of intelligence, and most of that money goes to satellites and computers. There are four big boys in the field of intelligence collection. Somewhat simplified, this is what they do: The National Reconnaissance Office (NRO), widely thought to be the most expensive of the agencies, builds and runs satellites that collect intelligence from space. The National Security Agency (NSA) processes the electronic signals collected in outer space, in cyberspace, and on the ground. The National Geospatial-Intelligence Agency (NGA) analyzes the photographs the satellites take. Finally, the National Clandestine Service (NCS) deploys people to secretly collect information from other people—i.e., they are the spies. Of those four agencies, only the NCS is a part of the Central Intelligence Agency (CIA); the others are independent agencies within the Defense Department. The Defense Department has also fielded the Defense HUMINT Service (DHS) since 1993; it is smaller than the NCS and does its own clandestine human collection.

All of that collection of intelligence (the signals, the pictures, the spies) is designed to give the other side of the intelligence community the raw material to do its job. The other side, which is far smaller in terms of people and budget, is analysis.

The analytical process is the sifting through of information to tell policy makers what is going on, what is likely to happen, and why and how these events take place. Analysis is meant to answer questions that decision makers ask—or should ask. The questions usually do not have readily available or obvious answers; otherwise the policy makers would not need the intelligence community to provide them. Some of the questions are purely factual, but usually the facts are not readily available to the public (How many ships are there in the Chinese Navy?). Others require an interpretation or opinion (How much political discontent is there in Iran?). Policy makers also ask for predictions of the future (Who will win the election in Ukraine?). And they expect to be warned when something important they have not asked about is going to happen. (Excuse me, but . . . ah . . . India is about to invade Pakistan. Thought you might like to know.)

That is what intelligence is all about: answering important questions, often based on hard-to-get information, and providing warnings to policy makers.

Many of the analysts are employed by the Directorate of Intelligence (DI) of the CIA. Many others are in the Defense Intelligence Agency (DIA) and other military organizations. Small, specialized units are in the Departments of State (INR) and Energy. Law enforcement–related intelligence units are in the FBI and Drug Enforcement Administration. Since 2003, the new Department of Homeland Security (DHS) has also created an intelligence analysis capability. On terrorism, the National Counterterrorism Center (NCTC) was officially created in 2004 after Congress passed a law making it the primary terrorism analysis center in the government; President Bush separately authorized its creation in an Executive Order earlier that year. The NCTC succeeded the Terrorist Threat Integration Center (TTIC), which President Bush created in 2003 to place the FBI's, CIA's, and other agencies' terrorism analysts in the same physical space to try to break down institutional barriers (this has succeeded only partially).[3] To some extent these agencies overlap in what they analyze, intentionally creating duplication and perhaps competition. For the most part, the analysts in each of the agencies all have access to the same raw information from the four big boys of collection (NRO, NSA, NGA, and NCS) and other sources. Both of these efforts, collection and analysis, are supposed to be orchestrated by the Office of the Director of National Intelligence (ODNI), which was created in 2005.[4]

So how well do we collect? How well do we analyze?

COLLECTING SECRETS,
AND OTHER THINGS WE NEED TO KNOW

Every morning when I walked into my office in the Bureau of Intelligence and Research (INR) at the State Department in the mid-1980s, there was a stack of raw intelligence that I could not have read completely, even if I had spent the entire twelve-hour day plowing through it. Every day a new stack arrived. Some years later at the White House, I began every day by looking at a computer monitor (the information technology revolution having intervened) with hundreds of new intelligence reports, scanning down the subject lines to see which ones had to be read right away. There was never any shortage of intelligence reports. There was, however, a shortage of needed information. To understand that seeming contradiction, think about the nature of the two types of information collected, technical intelligence (e.g., from satellites) and human intelligence (e.g., from spies).

TECHNICAL COLLECTION: ELECTRONS AND PHOTONS

If it involves photons or electrons, if it can be photographed from space or collected in the spectrum of electromagnetic radio signals, U.S. intelligence can get it. The barrier to success for such technical collection is usually not whether we have sufficient collection systems or whether they have the needed capabilities; rather, the opportunities for collection are so numerous that the major difficulties with technical collection are prioritization and sorting, knowing when and where to look and then processing all of the data collected. In the jargon of the intelligence world, the first of those problems is called "cueing," having information that leads us to point the collection systems in the right direction. My favorite example of the cueing problem is the case of the Iraqi nuclear weapons development facilities in 1991. It tells us a lot about the limitations of technical collection (and it had an unfortunate effect on Dick Cheney).

There is no dispute now that the Iraqis had a significant nuclear weapons development program through 1991, but U.S. intelligence did not really believe that prior to or during the first Iraq War. Israeli intelligence analysts had come to Washington and sat in my office in 1989, adamant that Iraq was well along in making a nuclear bomb. The CIA analysts sitting opposite them were equally convinced that the Iraqis had only the beginnings of a program, an aspiration. The Israelis could not, or would not, prove it. Perhaps they feared that the proof, floating around Washington, would leak into the newspapers and get their spies killed.

When the war came in 1991, the first phase was a sustained U.S. strategic bombing campaign. More than two thousand aircraft sorties were launched every day, supplemented by hundreds of pilotless cruise missiles. Toward the end of the bombing campaign, it grew difficult for the Air Force officers who developed the daily Air Tasking Order (ATO), or hit list. They were running out of things to bomb and were going back for restrikes on targets that had already been badly damaged. My friends in CENTCOM even asked me if there was anything I would like to put on the ATO. (They declined my suggestion of the giant statue of Saddam in Baghdad, but didn't say why.)

While that bombing was going on, I was working with my British counterparts to develop something we called the U.N. Special Commission on Iraq (UNSCOM). Although the first President Bush had hardly mentioned Iraqi weapons of mass destruction as a rationale for his war, we thought that we would take advantage of the war victory by having something like UNSCOM find and destroy Iraqi chemical and other special weapons. We planned to make Saddam Hussein agree to our UNSCOM plan as a condition for ending the war. He did.

Thus, after the war, the new UNSCOM and the U.N. International Atomic Energy Agency (IAEA) went around Iraq destroying weapons of mass destruction, mainly bombs and artillery shells filled with lethal gas.[5] They also, shockingly, found evidence that Iraq had a full-scale nuclear weapons development program that was only months away from creating its first nuclear weapon.[6] The Israelis had been right. The CIA had been wrong.

An Iraqi report that the U.N. inspectors found specified the location of the facilities. Only two of twenty sites had been known and attacked during the war. After the U.N. report, U.S. satellites were ordered to take a look at the newly disclosed locations. Within hours, images appeared on my desk of an enormous campus with scores of buildings, none of which we had bombed. Some of the facilities were on the same scale as the sprawling campuses that had been built in the 1940s for the U.S. Manhattan Project to make the first nuclear weapon. There had been no cueing of satellites to these sites prior to or during the war. The stunning conclusion we came to was that a nuclear weapons development program involving thousands of Iraqis and billions of dollars in procurement (mainly from outside Iraq) had been largely missed by U.S. intelligence. Maybe the United States can take pictures from space better than anyone else, with the highest resolution imaginable, but unless you know where to look, the picture-taking spy satellites don't tell you what you need to know.

Dick Cheney, then Secretary of Defense, learned a lesson from this incident. He concluded two things: first, that Saddam wanted a nuclear bomb and second, that the CIA would probably have known about Iraq getting a nuclear weapon only after the first Iraqi nuke exploded somewhere. Intelligence failures cause policy makers to doubt the intelligence community later on.

About the same time as the first Iraq War ended and the UNSCOM inspections began, a Soviet scientist defected.[7] He claimed to be the deputy director of a secret nationwide program to research and build biological weapons in the Soviet Union. The program he described employed tens of thousands of people at more than forty locations. He claimed that hundreds of tons of anthrax, smallpox, and other germs had been made by the USSR and many had been placed in weapons, ranging from artillery shells and bombs to intercontinental ballistic missiles (ICBMs) pointed at the United States. Enough lethal biological material had been made to wipe out the entire U.S. population many times over. Furthermore, the defector claimed, the Soviets were engaged in advanced recombinant DNA work, creating entirely new and highly lethal biological agents. It all sounded incredible and exaggerated.

It was also not something that American Secretary of State James Baker wanted to hear. Baker had just negotiated agreements on a series of arms control treaties that had been hung up for years. Baker had developed close personal relations with the Mikhail Gorbachev–Eduard Shevardnadze team in the Kremlin and convinced them with his hard-driving, "let's make a deal" style. I recall landing in Moscow with Baker one cold night. Our team, including Robert Gates (later Secretary of Defense), Condi Rice (later Secretary of State), and Stephen Hadley (later national security advisor), searched for something to eat. Most of us ended up eating hot dogs from a truck. Baker went immediately to Foreign Minister Shevardnadze's residence for a sumptuous one-on-one meal. The two men bonded. But if the defector was right, "Eddie" had been lying to "Jim," claiming that the Soviet Union was in compliance with the Biological Weapons Convention (BWC).[8] It was hard to imagine how it could be any more out of compliance than what the defector claimed.

The State Department had been sending annual reports to Congress on Soviet compliance with arms control agreements. Those reports had said for years that the Soviets were not violating the BWC. I had been one of the people approving the reports to Congress. Every year, Fred Eimer, an arms control verification specialist in the U.S.

Arms Control and Disarmament Agency (later merged with the State Department), had claimed that the Soviets were violating the BWC. We would hear him out and then turn to the CIA's experts, who mocked Eimer's paranoia. There was no convincing evidence of a Soviet BW program, the CIA contended. And then came the defector.

The problem went beyond the Biological Weapons Convention. If the Soviets were lying about that, what other lies were they telling us? President Reagan had famously made up a Russian proverb, "Trust but verify." Reagan notwithstanding, the truth was that arms control was based mainly on trust because verification procedures were limited and if the Soviets really wanted to cheat and worked hard at it, we assumed they could get away with it. We also assumed that they would not run the political risk of violating a treaty because there was always the risk of getting caught. If the defector was right, that assumption now looked badly wrong and Baker would look naive, used, betrayed. Arms control would be dead if the Congress found out about the massive violation of the BWC.

So for a while, the defector's story was kept very secret. New collection efforts were targeted on what he suggested were the bioweapons plants. It soon became clear that much of his story, and perhaps all of it, was true. Baker secretly confronted the Soviet leadership, seeking their agreement to destroy the illegal weapons. He hoped to tell Congress about this little problem and at the same time tell them that the Soviets were getting rid of all the nasty bugs and germs that they had mistakenly made. Unfortunately, the Soviets did not agree. Instead, they said that they assumed we were cheating, too. It gave us a chilling insight into what they really thought about arms control agreements.

The Soviets did eventually fess up to lying about the BW, but by then the Soviet Union was collapsing, so the issue did not become the scandal that it would have earlier. Today Russia assures us that the Soviet BWs have now been destroyed.

In the case of the biological weapons, the Soviets had not even worked hard at hiding their weapons plants. We had taken satellite pictures of the sites many times. They had told us that the facilities were pharmaceutical labs or fertilizer plants. From space, we could not tell that the Soviets were lying and were actually cooking up enough germs to wipe out a continent. The Soviets were adept at hiding in plain sight and using other deception techniques to fool U.S. intelligence. (During the Cold War, one of the most famous pictures taken by a U.S. satellite showed what was obviously a phony nuclear missile–carrying submarine. You could tell from the picture that it was a decoy, an inflatable fake, because it had sprung a leak and was bent at a right angle.)

The Soviets claimed to have no nuclear warheads in Germany and derided America for having put several thousand atomic warheads on German soil. Nonetheless, U.S. photography revealed that the Soviets had built well-guarded nuclear weapons bunkers in Germany. If a war started, we planned to destroy the bunkers quickly. My friend Dennis Gormley reminded me recently of what had happened in the late 1980s when he was was running a small consulting firm. A young Russian soldier swam across the Oder River and defected. His captain, he said, had driven over the motorbike for which he had saved for years. It was more than the youth could take. So he defected and was quickly debriefed by U.S. intelligence and found to know nothing of value. The report on him said little but noted that he had worked in some sort of transportation unit called a PRTB.

Gormley had just explained to me his own work on trying to find PRTBs, the Russian acronym for Mobile Technical Rocket Base. Gormley believed that PRTBs actually placed the nuclear warheads on top of the Soviets' mobile missiles in Europe. The warheads were stored separately to prevent some renegade officer from starting a nuclear war. In the event of an authorized war, the missiles would meet up with the warheads in predesignated clearings in the German woods. Along would come the PRTB and mate the warhead to the missile. Destroy the PRTB, and you would stop the nuclear missiles. I told Gormley about the defector, and with Dennis's help, the defector was debriefed again. His explanation of what a PRTB did was exactly what Gormley had guessed. And he was happy to locate his PRTB for us. He also noted that, of course, the nuclear warheads were not in the nuclear warhead storage areas. The storage sites were empty. They were just there for the Americans to bomb and think they had destroyed the threat. The real storage areas were hidden.

Years later, after the fall of the Berlin Wall, Professor Gormley went to the East German site where the defector said the weapons had been. He found an abandoned base with "Keep Out" signs noting a radioactive hazard. Police chased him away. The "hazard" was caused from weapons that the Soviets and now the Russians, the East Germans and now unified Germany, claim were never there.

With the Iraqi nuclear facilities, we had not known they existed and therefore did not photograph them or bomb them. As in the case of the Soviet biological plants, we had photographed them and not known what they were. And as in the case of the Soviet nuclear warhead storage facilities, we had found them on photographs and properly identified them for what they were but could not look inside to realize that they were empty and were there to be found. Photography from space has its limitations.

There are similar problems with the other class of technical collection, Signals Intelligence (SIGINT). The problem is not usually a matter of our ability to collect electrons; it is sometimes a question of recognizing the importance of what has been collected. In 1988 a young State Department INR analyst reported to me that he had found, in the many reports sent to him, a one-line item about a signal normally associated with Chinese long-range nuclear missiles. The problem was that the analyst covered Saudi Arabia, not China, and the report was about Saudi Arabia.

No one else seemed to have noticed the routine report, nor did anyone seem to care when he raised a question about the aberrant signal. The report of that electronic bleep made no sense to me at first. Saudi Arabia was a close U.S. ally and got its weapons from us and from the Europeans. Neither we nor the Europeans would ever have sold it long-range nuclear-capable missiles. But wait, that was the point. Of course, we would not have sold it such a missile. Maybe the Saudis, therefore, had not asked us. Maybe they were crazy enough to have wanted such a weapon and bought them from the Chinese. Surely, however, we would have detected the negotiation of such a deal, or at least the delivery of such a big weapons system. As I said those words to the analyst, I realized that they were probably not accurate. I had already learned never to assume that U.S. intelligence had detected something, no matter how big and obvious. We asked for satellite photography and promptly found an extremely large base in the Saudi desert, complete with Chinese troops and long-range nuclear-capable missiles. The base was almost completed and the missiles were not yet operational.[9]

Conveniently, the Chinese foreign minister was a floor above me at the time, meeting with Secretary of State George Shultz. Shultz was less than delighted with the prospect of having to confront his guest and the Saudis about their secret activities. However, he quickly understood that the Saudis appeared to be pulling their own version of the Cuban Missile Crisis. It looked as if the Saudis were trying to sneak nuclear missiles into their country and have them operational before anyone knew about them. China, which in the 1980s was not rich and had little respect for the Nuclear Non-Proliferation Treaty, had readily agreed to sell the old missiles for a small fortune. Had it also agreed to sell the nuclear warheads without which the inaccurate missiles were worthless? Shultz did not ask that question of his guest. Instead, he asked the Saudi king to agree that no nuclear warheads would be introduced into Saudi Arabia and that the Chinese base would be open for inspection. The Saudis agreed. Had they not, it is likely they would soon have seen heavily laden fighter-bombers marked with the Star of David streaking overhead well before their missile base was completed.

Having collected the random bleep in the ether had not been enough to avert the crisis. What was needed was for it to be reported. Only a small fraction of the signals collected and recorded are ever reported. And then someone had to understand its significance and, in a timely manner, tell somebody who could do something about it. The day after 9/11, NSA issued a report made the day before the terrorist attacks, indicating that something big was imminent.[10] It is not clear what good that information would have done me or others had we received it before the attack, because it lacked actionable information (such as where the attack was going to be, what kind of attack it was, and who the attackers were). Nonetheless, it highlights the fact that information is virtually worthless unless you recognize the significance of what has been collected and get it to the right people in time for them to use it.

While technical collection is often described as a vacuum cleaner collecting all that exists, what we collect can, of course, be ambiguous. At one point the intelligence community decided that al Qaeda used the word "wedding" to describe an attack. That sounded like a break-through, until you realized how often people talk about real weddings on the phone. People who suspect they are being monitored can also say things that are not true, in order to throw off intelligence agencies. Or they can communicate only through couriers. Osama bin Laden once routinely communicated over a satellite telephone. The conversations gave us great insight into him and what he was doing (and, interestingly, into his relations with his mother). Then one day someone, who obviously was not thinking, revealed that fact to a newspaper that, exercising no discretion, published it. The calls stopped almost immediately.[11] Bin Laden is now thought to use only face-to-face communication to avoid interception and tracking. I sometimes wonder if we could have learned enough about the 9/11 plot to stop it had bin Laden continued to use his satellite phone, had the newspaper not published the story, had the leaker been more observant of the law.

An Israeli intelligence officer once told me a colorful tale that crystallized the differences among some well-known international intelligence agencies: "So there was a contest among the CIA, the Soviet KGB, the British SIS, and us, the Mossad. To see who was best, they let loose a fox into the woods four times. Each agency had an hour to find the fox and bring it to the judges. The CIA dropped tiny little cameras and listening devices from an airplane into the woods. They got great pictures of the fox and even tape-recorded the fox in the act of making love with another fox, but they could not catch the fox. The Soviet KGB then lined up a hundred guys shoulder to shoulder and they walked through the woods beating the ground with sticks. The fox heard them coming and ran into a hole. No fox. The British SIS dressed a guy up in a rented fox suit, but it could afford to rent it for only half an hour, during which time, he could not find the fox. At the end of their hour, the Mossad guys didn't appear. So the judges went looking for them in the woods. They found the Israelis with a bunny strapped to a tree. They were slapping the bunny and yelling at it, 'Admit it! Admit you're a fox!'"

The Israeli was unnecessarily self-deprecating, but he did make a point. Technical collection is what most of the U.S. intelligence budget goes to. It's what we Americans are good at: satellites, cyberspace, and computers to sift through what is collected. There is good reason to believe that the United States is far better overall at technical collection than any other nation. We may spend more on it than we need to (most pictures we need taken from space, for example, do not require high resolution; a lot of what you need from space photography, you can now get relatively cheaply from commercial space satellites; look at Google Earth, which is free), but nations, like individuals, have personalities. Intelligence agencies do, too. For America's intelligence community, it's all about gizmos.

HUMAN COLLECTION: SPIES LIKE US

Human collection—spying—has not proved to be our forte. As *New York Times* intelligence reporter Timothy Weiner made clear in his tour de force history of the CIA, *Legacy of Ashes,* at every point in its history the CIA failed to place spies inside the main target country of that day in positions where they could report on the intentions, plans, or thinking of the opponent.[12] Weiner does not simply make that claim; he reveals declassified documents in which the CIA itself or investigating committees show the paucity of successful U.S. spying. We had no major source inside the USSR during the Cold War, no major source inside Iraq prior to the U.S. invasion in 2003, no major source inside North Vietnam during that long war or in North Korea during that war or now. And, of course, we had no major source inside al Qaeda before 9/11 and probably do not have one now.

How can that be? One reason often given is that these are what the CIA calls "hard targets." If they were easy targets, of course, we would not need to spend billions of dollars on them every year and employ thousands of spies. A hard target, CIA notes, is one in which the typical American would stand out. How can it be expected to get an American into Central Committee meetings in Hanoi or Pyongyang? Or into the al Qaeda shura council?

When I asked for efforts to penetrate al Qaeda in the late 1990s, the CIA thought that a direct approach would not work. An American would not be accepted into al Qaeda, he would stand out. (Of course an American would stand out in al Qaeda, but that had not stopped al Qaeda from accepting Americans into its ranks, where they presumably did stand out. Several American members of al Qaeda were even allowed to meet with Osama bin Laden.[13]) Even an American posing as a Moroccan (assuming the CIA even had someone who could pass for a Moroccan) might be uncovered and then tortured and killed (as the CIA's Beirut station chief had been when kidnapped by Hezbollah in 1984).[14]

Typically, the CIA does not insert one of its own staff into a target organization using a false identity. Instead, it often has a CIA officer approach someone who already works in the target organization. The officer tries to persuade that person to report on what is going on inside. Not only had the CIA not tried to put a CIA officer posing as an American (or Moroccan or anything else) inside al Qaeda, in 1999 the new director of the Counterterrorism Center (CTC), Cofer Black, told me he had been shocked to learn on taking the job that no attempts had been made by the CIA to develop useful sources inside al Qaeda. "Hell, just because it's hard, that's no excuse for our not even trying." The CIA had been so risk-averse that when Black took over CTC it not only had no source in al Qaeda, it did not even have a single CIA employee in all of Afghanistan. Black had to get permission each time he wanted to insert someone briefly to visit the northern areas held by friendly tribesmen fighting al Qaeda.

Imagine, however, that a CIA officer had walked up and knocked on the gate of Derunta (as then–*New York Times* reporter Judith Miller did in 2000) or some other al Qaeda camp. What if he had been admitted to al Qaeda, pretending to be an American convert or a Moroccan convert. Perhaps to test the convert's seriousness, maybe to see if he were an American spy, his al Qaeda trainer could have asked him to go on a mission with him into nearby Pakistan to kill an American. If that had happened, the CIA officer would have tried to escape the terrorist organization. There is not the slightest chance that the CIA would have permitted him to kill an American. Indeed, had the officer failed to ask permission and actually shot a U.S. citizen dead, the CIA officer would have been charged with murder as soon as CIA headquarters learned of his indiscretion. We would not want it any other way, we would not condone for a second a CIA officer killing an innocent U.S. citizen just to prove himself to al Qaeda and gain its confidence.

And yet that is exactly what British Intelligence allegedly did when infiltrating the Irish terrorist network. A British agent who won his spurs killing fellow Brits eventually rose to a position within the terrorist network where he knew so much about the secretive cells that the British could break up terrorist attacks, could destroy the organization.[15] That kind of "end justifies the means" thinking is not something that any American intelligence organization can do. It's not in our ethos as a country. If every nation and every intelligence organization has a personality, ours was one with a set of scruples that rules out some things that others might do. One can argue about whether that is bad or good, but there is little dispute that it is a given, a limitation, one we accept.

Other limitations are more questionable. Throughout the Cold War and well into the decade that followed, CIA officers abroad were almost always assigned to well-protected, overt U.S. government facilities overseas. No protected facility, no CIA officers. When the U.S. Marines hit the beaches of Somalia in 1992, ordered into that chaotic land by the first President Bush, the U.S. Embassy had been closed for years. There were no CIA officers in country to welcome the Marine landing force.[16] The Marines were, instead, met on the beach by CNN and a former U.S. Ambassador to Somalia, Robert Oakley. Bob had managed to get into Mogadishu a day earlier, talk to the warlords, and urge them to behave. "CIA grudgingly agreed to send some personnel into the country after the Marines went in," recalls Michael Sheehan, who was a U.S. Army officer assigned to the U.N. team that went to Somalia. "They didn't stay long. They rotated new guys in every few weeks. None of them knew anything about Somalia or even Africa. They were just guys willing to get the 'danger pay bonus.' And they pretty much stayed in their trailers on the beach, well inside U.S. lines."

CIA directors have assured Congress that they are now placing officers in jobs in which they never go to the U.S. Embassy in the country to which they are assigned. These officers have a cover story that they are something other than a U.S. government employee. In the jargon, they are called NOC, for "not official cover." It's hard to know how many NOCs there are, but it is a safe assumption that they still represent only a small percentage of CIA officers stationed abroad. Building their cover story is expensive. If they are arrested by the local police, they cannot claim diplomatic immunity and leave the country. Moreover, to have credibility with potential sources and to develop a deep understanding of the culture and country, they need to live their fake life for several years. If they ever show up as CIA officers in some future assignment, the front organizations they had been using while NOCs will be known for what they actually are. Given all of these difficulties, former CIA officer Reuel Marc Gerecht has proposed that the CIA pay NOCs as much as $250,000 a year (most of it placed in a bank account they can access only after they finish the assignment) and allow them to retire at age forty with a full pension.[17] Gerecht thinks that kind of pay will attract the very special kind of people that being a NOC requires. He thinks using twenty-year career CIA personnel is both risky (their identity will eventually be learned and their front companies fingered as CIA covers) and unlikely to produce the special talent needed for the job. One limitation under which the CIA is operating, we can be pretty sure, is that it is not yet paying any of its NOCs an annual salary of $250,000.

Each CIA Director seems to say that prior to him, efforts at building a robust NOC program had failed, but he will build one in five years or so. Even after five years on the job CIA Director George Tenet was saying the NOC program would not be good for another five years. In February 2008, *The Los Angeles Times* reported that the post 9/11 push to create a new NOC program had largely failed and was being abandoned.[18]

Thus, the average CIA officer sent overseas to collect information is probably still a young person who is openly a U.S. government employee. I assume most are young because, after 9/11, the Bush administration more than doubled the number of CIA officers in the National Clandestine Service. The Agency recruited heavily on college campuses, put its new officers through a training program, and shipped many of them overseas. A disproportionate percentage of the new CIA officers are from Utah, clean-cut types who have learned an unusual foreign language to do their religious missionary work abroad. (One CIA friend of mine had learned the almost impossible language of Finnish in order to do his religion's mission there. He later amazed a senior official from Finland in my office by answering his question in what was apparently fluent Finnish. I, of course, had no idea what he said.) Those who believe in the Angel Moroni seem to have few problems with those who believe in the CIA entry-level polygraph.

One effect of this rapid and large increase in CIA officers after 9/11 is a significant reduction in the experience level of the average U.S. spy. Inexperienced junior officers quickly became supervisors to the newly minted spies who began arriving at CIA stations around the world. Plopped down in a new country, these young CIA officers do not have a "James Bond" job. Their task is usually to find someone who has access to a target organization, either in the country's government or perhaps in a terrorist movement. Once they have identified someone with access, their task is to persuade them to give the United States (or somebody else whom the CIA agents are pretending to be) information. The very best intelligence officers in such roles are seducers, who must spend their time in disreputable places, persuading unsavory people to do illegal acts, i.e., turn over confidential information. The Americans we send abroad, fresh from their polygraphs, are not always cut out for that line of work.

To understand "human intelligence," try thinking how you might spend your day as a young American spy based in some overseas U.S. facility. Perhaps someone has contacted the embassy and said he has valuable information available, but, as Rick Blaine said in *Casablanca,* "For a price, Ugarte, for a price." One can imagine how delighted a CIA officer must be when he or she finally finds someone who offers to give him or her information. Then he or she has to determine whether the information is real. The world is filled with con men trying to peddle secrets to the CIA or other intelligence organizations. One now well-known example of bogus information is the document allegedly from the government of Niger, describing the sale of uranium to Iraq.[19] The document appears to be on real Niger government stationery, and it probably is. The Niger Embassy in Rome had suffered a break-in.

Unfortunately, the Niger officials who allegedly signed the letters were no longer in their jobs on the dates described in the document. Experts back in Washington quickly noticed that mistake and other slipups when the Italian intelligence service provided the CIA with material bought from a con man with the unlikely name of Rocco Martino.

One way to ensure that a source is not a con man is to slip him off to a safe house somewhere and strap him to a lie detector—assuming he agrees to cooperate with such a test. The CIA places great stock in lie detector tests, even though U.S. courts do not allow the admission of polygraph data as reliable evidence. Unfortunately, foreign intelligence agencies know of the CIA's fondness for "fluttering" sources. Thus, it is possible that a foreign intelligence agency trying to sell us false information will train its personnel in methods to deceive the polygraph, such as with biofeedback exercises. (It has been reported that the CIA's entire network of polygraphed sources in Cuba at one time were all actually working for the Cuban intelligence service, passing false information to Washington.[20]) Even CIA officers sometimes admit that the polygraph does not work on pathological liars or people with "certain cultural and ethnic backgrounds." It is harder for CIA to polygraph a source, of course, when the source is talking not to them but to another country's intelligence agency. Often a young CIA officer overseas gets her information not from her own sources, but from the intelligence agencies of friendly nations, so-called liaison services: the local intelligence service calls and suggests you drop by, as it has something it thinks you will find most interesting.

Other nations' intelligence agencies are often thought to be better at spying than the CIA is, perhaps because they are forced to be because they cannot afford the expensive technical collection sources available to the United States. Perhaps people who do not look or act American (because they aren't) have an easier time getting certain people to share information with them. Whether this belief that others are better at spying is true or not, other nations' intelligence agencies do often offer to help the United States by sharing what their spies have collected. Why? Sometimes they share because they want something in return, maybe money, maybe access to that fancy technical collection that the Americans are so good at. Sometimes they tell us what they think we want to hear. Sometimes they tell us what they want us to hear. Seldom do they let us have access to their primary sources, the guy their officers are getting the information from. This reliance on liaison services was well on display in Colin Powell's regrettable briefing to the U.N. Security Council on Iraq before the U.S. invasion.

The colorful Rocco Martino had provided his forgeries to the Italian intelligence agency, not to the CIA. Another infamous agent whom the CIA appropriately (but apparently without ironic intent) code-named "Curveball" was a source of German intelligence.[21] He had entirely invented the story about Iraq having mobile bioweapons factories, leading Secretary of State Colin Powell to tell the U.N. Security Council that "we have a source who is an Iraqi engineer who is an eyewitness" to the BW trucks.[22] As Powell was speaking, his staff was showing off a giant drawing of the imaginary bioweapons factory on wheels, a drawing based on Curveball's fabrications. Powell had been assured that the source of the information was German intelligence. Perhaps Powell never asked how the German source knew, who the source was, or whether the CIA had vetted the source. Some in the CIA say that they knew then that the source was a fabricator associated with the Iraqi exile movement trying to get the United States to invade Iraq. If they did know, no one told Powell.

Nor did anyone apparently tell him everything about the claim that he made to the Security Council that Iraq was training al Qaeda terrorists in the use of weapons of mass destruction, an allegation that some in the intelligence community questioned in early 2002.[23] The source was Ibn al-Shaykh al-Libi, an admitted al Qaeda member. Unfortunately for both al-Libi and Powell, the al Qaeda terrorist had told his story to the Egyptian intelligence service, the Mukhabarat.[24] Al-Libi had told the Egyptians what he assumed they wanted to hear, something about Iraq, something about weapons of mass destruction, something linking al Qaeda to Saddam. He was right, that was what his inquistors wanted to hear. Until he came up with a story that the Egyptians assumed the Americans would love to hear, Egyptians had been torturing him. When he invented that story, they stopped. They had what they needed, even though it was all a lie. Most people will say whatever it takes to get torture to stop. Often what they say is untrue, as in this case. The CIA later confirmed that there had never been any Iraqis training al Qaeda in WMD.[25]

It was not that the Italian, German, and Egyptian intelligence agencies were conspiring to get America into a disastrous war by intentionally ginning up phony information. The CIA had simply told them that there was a real demand in Washington for information on Iraq and weapons of mass destruction. Being good friends hoping to curry favor with CIA, they did what they do. The Italians and Germans probably put out the word that they would pay for information proving an Iraqi WMD program. Not surprisingly, people sold it to them. The Egyptians did what they do: they beat a prisoner almost to death until he answered some leading questions the way they wanted him to. One can easily picture what happened then. The Mukhabarat then happily told the CIA, which sent the word flying back to CIA headquarters in a highly encrypted, high-precedence message. Within hours, "senior White House officials" were told and later senators were briefed in a closed-door session.

While our young CIA officers are sitting around in their U.S. government building overseas, trying to think of how to find a good source, good sources often find them. These helpful and often courageous people are known in the jargon as "walk-ins." The deputy director of the Soviet BW program and the Red Army soldier with the broken motorcycle discussed earlier were walk-ins of a sort; they were defectors. They had come out of their homeland and were not going back. The best walk-ins, however, are those who are willing to stay in place, doing the job that gives them access to current information.

Walk-ins do not always come from inside the "enemy" camp. One of the most valuable was Chang Hsien-yi from Taiwan. He revealed that his nation, with which we were very closely associated, was building a nuclear bomb.[26] Despite the extensive and intimate defense and intelligence cooperation between our two nations, the CIA had not noticed the large-scale nuclear weapons infrastructure. As soon as we learned of the program, some of us at the State Department began drafting a very frank letter from Ronald Reagan to the Taiwanese leadership. There were, however, two problems that prevented us from sending the letter. First, Chang was still in place and might be identified as the source of our information and punished. He refused to leave unless he could take his extended family with him, and any trip abroad by that large a group would raise suspicions. We had to wait until they could all travel together on a long-planned Chinese New Year vacation. The second problem was that by then the President of Taiwan to whom our frank letter was addressed had grown old and died. The new President, who ultimately did receive the letter demanding that the weapon program be destroyed, said that he had never known of the nuclear weapons effort, that he was like Harry Truman, the U.S. Vice President, whom Franklin Roosevelt had never told about the U.S. nuclear weapons development effort.

In the Cold War the most famous walk-ins were Oleg Penkovsky, a colonel in the Soviet Military Intelligence, and Oleg Gordievsky, who ran Soviet intelligence operations in the United Kingdom. Both men continued in their jobs after making contact with and providing intelligence to the West. Penkovsky provided proof that the Soviets did not have a strategic rocket force of any size, despite John Kennedy's campaign claims of a "missile gap." Later, as President and using data from Penkovsky, Kennedy was able to calculate how great a risk he was running in the Cuban Missile Crisis.[27] Gordievsky told the British that the geriatric Soviet leadership thought that Ronald Reagan was a cowboy bent on nuclear annihilation of the "evil empire" and that the Soviets were, thus, on a hair trigger.[28] Washington then sent out signals that calmed things down.

But such valuable walk-ins are rare. Most are fabricators or people with little access to anything we need to know. They want money and a visa to the United States. A young CIA officer meets with such people every week. They are routinely sent away from the U.S. door. Other walk-ins are what in the jargon of the spy world are known as "dangles," or double agents. They are sent by one intelligence service to pretend to defect to the enemy intelligence service. Then they provide confusing, misleading, or false information. Or they simply meet with CIA personnel and note who they are, where their safe houses are, what they want to know. Despite this risk, if the walk-in can prove that he or she works for Russian, Cuban, North Korean, Iranian, or Chinese intelligence, he or she will likely be welcomed in for a chat.

No matter where a young CIA officer is stationed around the world, he or she probably has a mandate to recruit targeted personnel in certain other nations' embassies. During the Cold War, CIA officers in Africa, Asia, and Latin America often did not spend much of their time infiltrating the nation to which they were posted. Most of those nations had nothing we needed to know. Instead, the CIA spent its time in places like Zaire or Malaysia or Peru trying to recruit the KGB officers in the Soviet Embassy across town. A KGB officer in Africa would someday be posted back home to Moscow, where he might have access to important information. Or not.

For much of the Cold War, the KGB and CIA wasted their time trying to penetrate each other's ranks. Seldom did any valuable information come from this "spy-versus-spy" activity. The most famous example of this phenomenon was the case of Yuri Nosenko, a KGB officer who defected to the CIA shortly after the John F. Kennedy assassination. Conveniently, he had access to the KGB file on Kennedy's assassin. That file proved that neither the KGB nor Cuban intelligence had been running the assassin. The CIA's counterintelligence chief, the storied James Jesus Angleton, was not so sure and kept him under interrogation in a secret location in the United States for three years.[29] To this day the issue is debated. In 2007, Angleton's deputy published a detailed book, *Spy Wars: Moles, Mysteries, and Deadly Games,* which made the case that Nosenko (who had defected four decades earlier) was a double agent of the KGB.[30]

The paranoia and second-guessing about who could be trusted grew so bad under Angleton that the CIA could not trust anything that any of its Soviet sources told it. Everything was assumed to be a plant, misleading information intentionally given over. The purpose of CIA and KGB human intelligence officers in the Cold War might originally have been to find valuable information about the other nation, but it soon descended into placing spies in each other's intelligence agencies and trying to find the spies in their own agency. Spy agencies became the target of spy agencies; spying against the other side's spies became an end in itself, or what the Pentagon staff calls "a self-licking ice-cream cone."

While this sort of activity declined after the fall of the Soviet Union, a young CIA officer in a U.S. facility in Africa today is more likely to be seducing a Chinese embassy officer than meeting with someone in the local al Qaeda cell.

As I noted earlier, every morning my computer screen was filled with intelligence reports. The human intelligence reports were almost all from liaison services or walk-ins. Young CIA officers are very busy with wannabe walk-ins, fabricators with false documents, meetings with liaison services. They file reports on all of these activities. A very large proportion of what they file turns out to be inaccurate or untrue, or at least information that cannot be corroborated. A small amount is valuable information that was unknown before. To repeat myself, there was never any shortage of intelligence reports. There was a shortage of needed information.

The National Security Advisor repeatedly asked the CIA four questions about al Qaeda in the late 1990s: What was the size of its budget (how much did it cost to be al Qaeda)? Where did it get its money? Where did it keep its money? How did it move its money? The CIA was unable to answer any of those questions.

There were, however, scores of intelligence reports about al Qaeda seeking to acquire weapons of mass destruction. Reading the messages that floated in every week, one would have thought that bin Laden had a WMD stockpile as big as Russia's. Not one report provided information we could act on. Did it really have chemical weapons, or bio or radioactive, what kind, where? No one knew. Frustrated, in 2000 the indefatigable Charles Allen (who then coordinated collection efforts by all the U.S. intelligence agencies) and I held an all-day off-site meeting with more than six dozen intelligence officers from ten agencies. Although they were all working on the same issue, many had never met before. None had any real proof of al Qaeda's having WMD, nor any good ideas about how to get clear, actionable intelligence.

One useful thought did emerge, however, at that off-site meeting. We had the U.S. WMD experts role-play al Qaeda WMD experts. Where would they hide their program? What was the safest place, most easily defended, least likely for Americans to show up? The answer was a mountainous place in Afghanistan called Tora Bora. When American soldiers finally showed up near Osama bin Laden's Kandahar villa in 2001, he fled to Tora Bora. Yet CENTCOM had only sent a force made up of Afghans and a few U.S. liaison officers to Tora Bora. Bin Laden, not surprisingly, escaped.[31]

So how well do we do at collection? What does our $40 billion–plus a year buy? In my more cynical moments, when intelligence officers could provide me with no useful answers, I would reply to the "What are we getting for our money?" question this way: lots of pictures; an almost indigestible mountain of signals, most of which are ambiguous; and reports from CIA officers scattered around the globe, mainly about their talking to walk-ins and intelligence officers from other countries. Maybe we could save a lot of money, I would fume, if we just bought our pictures from Spot (a French commercial photo satellite company) and set up a desk for the walk-ins in the lobby of every embassy. Friendly intelligence services could deliver their reports to us in Washington.

Then, every once in a while, NSA would produce a hot lead that we could use to locate a terrorist. The CIA would go into the friendly host country police or intelligence agency and have the terrorist arrested. Lives would be saved. The CIA would cite it as another example of how its failures were well-known, but its successes were unheralded. Perhaps. But in my experience, the CIA almost always managed to let people know about its successes, and they were few relative to their failures. Michael Turner, a former CIA officer, provided a list of major CIA intelligence failures in his 2005 book *Why Secret Intelligence Fails*.[32] It omits the failure to properly estimate the state of Iraqi WMDs in 2002.

Professional career intelligence officers will quibble with their colleague Michael Turner's list. Tim Weiner's impressive study of sixty years of the CIA adds many other failures to the list, many of which were covert action operations. Richard Russell added to the enumeration of the failures with his 2007 work *Sharpening Strategic Intelligence: Why the CIA Gets it Wrong and What Needs to Be Done to Get It Right*.

What is a failure sometimes depends on what you think an intelligence agency should be capable of doing. Was 9/11 an intelligence

MICHAEL TURNER: NOTABLE U.S. INTELLIGENCE FAILURES SINCE 1950	
North Korea's invasion of South Korea	1950
China's entry into the Korean conflict	1950
The defeat of the French in Vietnam	1954
The British-French-Israeli invasion of Egypt	1956
The Bay of Pigs invasion	1961
The Vietnam War	1960s
The toughness of the Vietnamese guerrillas	1960s
The Tet Offensive	1967
The Soviet invasion of Afghanistan	1979
The fall of the Iranian shah	1979
The United States' support for the Contras	1980s
The breakup of the Soviet Union	1989–91
Developments in Somalia	1993
Ethnic cleansing in Bosnia	1990s
Genocide in Rwanda	1990s
Indian nuclear tests	1998
Serbian actions in Kosovo	1999
Terrorist attacks on September 11	2001

failure? I was asked that question by the 9/11 Commission.[33] I replied that it had not been a failure to provide strategic warning that al Qaeda existed and was intent on attacking us. That message had loudly and repeatedly been given to the leadership of the Bush administration, who, for all practical purposes, had ignored it. But 9/11 was clearly an intelligence failure at the tactical level, since the intelligence agencies were unable to tell us when, where, how, or who was going to attack us. In short, they provided me with no actionable intelligence, nothing to utilize to preempt the attack.

CIA officials explained to the commission that getting that kind of information was very difficult, if not impossible, and implied that no one should expect them to be that good. At the same time, CIA officials claim to have stopped many other attacks. And, as we now know, CIA did actually have some of the who, what, and where answers. They knew that al Qaeda terrorists had entered the United States. They knew their names. They just didn't tell anybody for months, until it was too late. That was a failure.

WHERE ALL THE COLLECTION ENDS UP: THE ANALYSTS

Are the failures a matter of too little collection and too little information, or is the problem lots of collection but little of it useful? My admittedly prejudiced view is that, while Americans seem to be genetically incapable of being or recruiting good spies, the larger problem is usually one of analysis. When there has been an "intelligence failure" and a team is assembled after the fact to figure out what happened, they almost always find that the key information either was in the system or easily could have been. Sometimes the analysts have just not thought to task the collection systems to get the precise data they need. Often it is the analysts who fail to recognize the significance of the data that are collected. Or they have, as in the case of 9/11, inexplicably decided not to tell anyone who could do something with the information. (This collecting and not distributing phenomenon is what I call the philately school of intelligence, wherein information is collected and stored almost for the sake of collecting. For me, the purpose of buying postage stamps is to mail letters.)

A small portion of the intelligence budget goes to the analysts, who sit usually in and around Washington, D.C. The average analyst is far cheaper than a U.S. spy living overseas, and all of the analysts together are almost infinitely less expensive than our technical collection systems. Yet all of the collection is done to provide analysts with the grist for their reports. Just as the CIA doubled the number of U.S. spies after 9/11, it also doubled the number of analysts. As a result, the average CIA analyst today has, according to General Michael Hayden (the CIA director), fewer than five years' experience.[34] Many have less.

Was there really a need for twice as many analysts? The idea of doubling the staff seems unlikely to have been derived from a precise human resources requirements study. Some analytical supervisors were told that they would be getting new staff and created jobs for them by assigning a new full-time analyst to a job that really required only 20 percent of an analyst's time. Assigning bright and eager new staff from good graduate schools to study second-order capillaries creates poor morale and eventually produces an organizational reputation that makes recruiting other good staff more difficult.

In the wake of 9/11 and the consequent infusion of new funds into the intelligence community, the leadership of U.S. intelligence turned to two other ways of enhancing analysis: open sourcing and outsourcing.

OPEN SECRETS AND SECRETS IN THE OPEN

Open-source information was given a major push by the 9/11 Commission. Others, like former Assistant Director of Central Intelligence Mark Lowenthal, had been trying to encourage its use for years.[35] Lowenthal, a bald and bearded fast talker, had been staff director for the House Intelligence Committee, a manager of analysts at the State Department, and a winner of TV's *Jeopardy* Tournament of Champions. A master of trivia and history, he was a walking open-source encyclopedia. After the 9/11 Commission recommendation, as if to prove it endorsed the idea, the intelligence community began referring to open-source information in jargon as OSINT. What is it?

Again, my Israeli storyteller provides the clearest answer in the form of a parable. In his undoubtedly apocryphal story, my friend told of an Israeli concern about knowing when a ship would dock in Tripoli delivering to Libya a new North Korean missile system. The leaders of Israel's intelligence agencies all met and devised strategies. Air Force intelligence planned to fly aircraft over the port every day to take pictures, but the Libyans shot at the aircraft. Navy intelligence slipped a submarine into the port to look through its periscope, but the sub bumped into an oil tanker. The Mossad placed a listening device in a flashy suit that Moammar Qadhafi had had made in Rome, but it picked up only the loud music of the leader's partying. Only the Israeli Foreign Ministry guy, however, found out when the delivery had occurred. He had simply phoned up the Tripoli harbormaster and asked him. Today the Israeli would have gone to the Tripoli harbormaster's web site.

In its simplest form, open-source intelligence is information that is unprotected, available to anyone who knows how to access it. The revolutionary thought involved in the renewed push behind open-source intelligence is that the intelligence community might actually pay attention to something that it did not steal or buy. For generations the intelligence community distrusted any information unless it had acquired it surreptitiously. David Ignatius tells the story in his "fictional" account of the CIA, *Agents of Innocence,*[36] that the CIA refused further information from a good source in the PLO because the source would not accept money in return. Shortly thereafter in the novel, the U.S. Embassy is blown up and much of the CIA's leadership in the Middle East is killed. The source we refused could have told us about the attack in advance. (Much of Ignatius's story is the true account of the career and death of CIA officer Robert Ames.) So the CIA's starting to use open-source information is a major change.

Unfortunately, the embrace of the freely available information is far from complete. Many analysts still sit in front of computer screens that are not connected to the internet. They can search only the closed-loop network known as Intel Link, a intranet with secret level information. Security officials fear that a rogue intelligence officer might download classified information from an internal network and then upload it onto the internet, or that "the enemy" could tell that it was a CIA officer browsing a web site and in the process the enemy might learn about the CIA's interests. Maybe a web site would have a secret Trojan horse program on it that would download itself onto the CIA officer's computer. All of those fears can be easily addressed using existing and proven IT security procedures, but such fears still keep many intelligence analysts from being able easily to "use the Google," as President Bush once said.

Open-source information on the internet may not always be accurate, but then neither is what a spy says or what NSA hears in the ether. New search engines, automated web crawlers, data-mining correlation tools, and language translation software all offer the possibility of maximizing the potential of finding and understanding what is freely available in cyberspace. Moreover, software can repeat the query on a regular basis, automatically updating the answer for the analyst. Other forms of open-source information include such things as simply asking an expert, whether a professor or someone in a relevant industry. Working as a talking head for ABC News, teaching at Harvard, and writing books have taught me to use open-source material. My conclusion is that much of what one needs to know in order to do sensible policy analysis is available in the open, and often available only in open source.[37]

IS IT INTELLIGENT TO OUTSOURCE INTELLIGENCE?

Another reality in the post-9/11 growth of intelligence analysis capability is outsourcing. We have outsourced the management of billion-dollar technical collection programs, and we have contracted for intelligence analysts.

The National Reconnaissance Office is a lot more than an office; it may have the largest budget of all the U.S. intelligence agencies. It may also be the best example of how U.S. government contractors, i.e., private industry, are taking over the government and costing us needless billions of dollars. The NRO buys spy satellites. Over the course of the last ten years, much of its government employee expertise has largely been eliminated by swapping career experts out for military personnel rotated in for a few years. Instead of having an Air Force officer who worked on satellites for ten or fifteen years making decisions, the NRO began bringing in officers on two- and three-year assignments. Someone who was procuring tires last year would be procuring satellite component systems this year. The result was that the big aerospace contractors gained greater influence in the decision making, not only because they were the only ones left with expertise, but also because the NRO decided to transfer much of its own program management responsibility to a single, big contractor.

Simultaneously with handing off management responsibility to the contractor, in the late 1990s and the first five years of this decade, the NRO and the aerospace industry were planning to spend scores of billions of dollars on a new generation of spy satellites with even more marvelous capabilities. The winning contractor was Boeing, which set about to build billions of dollars' worth of new spy satellites with incremental capabilities under the project named Future Imagery Architecture, or FIA. The costs escalated, the delivery dates slipped by years, but the NRO kept going. Eventually, presented with ever bigger bills and ever later schedules, the NRO canceled FIA under congressional pressure. Billions of dollars had been wasted.[38]

These costly new spacecraft were to be built not so much because we needed to use their capabilities, but rather because if we spent the money, we would keep the industrial base alive by ordering newer and better satellites. It became a perpetual motion machine: constantly building slightly more capable satellites at ever-increasing cost, spending more on research to develop more capabilities, even though those capabilities did not address important intelligence collection needs. I was part of that cycle thirty years ago when, during my one year as an employee at a defense contractor, I was told by the NRO that it had developed a new capability that could lead to a new satellite. My job, at the NRO's request, was to come up with some problem on which we could use the new technology. In other words, I was to figure out the need that the new satellite would meet, the requirement. This same backwards process (first developing the technology and then figuring out why we need it) has been going on for decades.

After you can see really small objects, after you have a synthetic aperture radar satellite that can take pictures at night, after you can pick up any signal released in the radio spectrum, what more do you really need? When most of the world's communication is moving from electrons passing through the air to photons in fiber-optic cables, when commercial imaging satellites allow private companies to sell reconnaissance imagery, should we perhaps consider spending less on satellites, rather than more? Maybe what we do need is more numerous, less expensive spy satellites, capable of being quickly launched in a crisis to augment existing satellites or to replace satellites that may fail or be destroyed. Although the nation's spy satellite agency is not planning to do that, another part of the Defense Department is. In addition to the costly satellites of NRO, the Air Force is planning to build the cheaper, more quickly launched birds as part of an additional program.

We do need to maintain an industrial base with the expertise to innovate intelligence platforms in space, but what we have done is destroy career government expertise and hand the keys to an agency over to giant contractors. These companies have so much congressional influence that feeding the beast becomes the requirement, rather than collecting intelligence we need at a reasonable cost, so that available funds can also be spent on other needs.

In the area of analysis, the number of contractors also grew. Not satisfied with doubling the number of analysts at the CIA, the intelligence community wanted access to even more staff. The intelligence community turned to the private sector, or at least privately owned companies. Many of the companies involved, such as Lockheed Martin, earn almost all of their money by selling to governments. Others, such as Booz Allen Hamilton, also have a commercial line of business. The companies are consultancies, weapons manufacturers, software developers, and IT support firms. What they now have in common is that they have established intelligence analysis staffs that are on contract to support various intelligence agencies.

A drive around northern Virginia reveals the many newly constructed high-rises in which private companies employ intelligence analysts to do the work that was formerly done only by government employees. Inside the buildings, in highly secured suites, analysts with top secret clearances write intelligence analyses for the CIA, DIA, and other agencies. Often the analyses are only slightly edited by government employees before being sent off to policy makers. A former government official told me that the initial draft of one National Intelligence Estimate was reportedly written by an analyst who was not a government employee; it was allegedly revised only slightly by the government. When an analysis is done by a contractor, the corporate logo is usually replaced by CIA letterhead and the policy maker is often unaware that the CIA did not really produce the analysis; a for-profit corporation did.

The private intelligence officers are not just in the corporate high-rises. Many work "on site," meaning they go to the intelligence agencies and work alongside government counterparts doing similar work. As Sebastian Abbot, a former student of mine at Harvard and now with the Associated Press, reported, "That has led to a phenomenon known as 'butts in seats'—contractors literally sit beside their public sector counterparts and perform equivalent tasks. According to [former CIA official John] Gannon, 'Butts in seats within the analytic community . . . is really a post-9/11 phenomenon, for the most part.' John Brennan, former acting Director of the National Counterterrorism Center (NCTC) and currently President and CEO of TAC, says that more than half of the 200 analysts at the NCTC were from the private sector while he was there . . . the vast majority of Booz Allen's intelligence work is not classic management consulting, but simply providing 'butts in seats' to the intelligence community."[39]

One colleague of mine being given a tour of the National Counterterrorism Center (NCTC) expressed surprise at the number of people working there and was told that "most of them are contractors." He could have been told the same at the intelligence analysis division at

Homeland Security or many other agencies in and around Washington. R. J. Hillhouse has made it her preoccupation to track intelligence outsourcing. She writes, "For all practical purposes, effective control of the NSA is with private corporations, which run its support and management functions . . . more than 70 percent of the staff of the Pentagon's newest intelligence unit, CIFA (Counterintelligence Field Activity), is made up of corporate contractors. Defense Intelligence Agency (DIA) lawyers revealed at a conference in May that contractors make up 51 percent of the staff in DIA offices. At the CIA, the situation is similar. Between 50 and 60 percent of the workforce of the CIA's most important directorate, the National Clandestine Service (NCS), responsible for the gathering of human intelligence, is composed of employees of for-profit corporations."[40]

The head of one private intelligence analysis program proudly told me that the hundreds of analysts in his division average many more years of experience than do the young analysts now at CIA. Why have these experienced staff left the government to do essentially the same jobs in a privately owned company? The popular assumption is that the pay is better. For the corporate vice presidents and partners, that is the case. They have almost all been senior officials in intelligence agencies for twenty years or more, "retired" to collect their federal pension, and are now also being paid by their new private sector employer, often more than twice their previous federal salary. For the typical analyst, however, the private salary is about the same as what he or she would be paid "on the inside." The analysts I have spoken with say they prefer the corporate environment because "it's just run better" or "there is less bureaucratic chickenshit." Their supervisors all seem to agree that they have "more time to focus on the issues" and "more ability to select only really good staff and an easier time getting rid of the ones who don't work out."

But does it cost more money than if the government's work were done by government employees? Some studies show that a contract for a given number of analysts' time is more expensive than paying a similar number of government employees. The contractors, however, cry foul and note that in an "all-in" comparison including the support costs (IT systems, buildings, and other overhead), the cost of private analysts is about the same. There is, however, a profit margin associated with the contracts. The hefty bonuses given senior officials in the contractor firms, along with the publicly reported profitability, are costs that would not have been accrued had the jobs been done in-house, in the government agencies. Cost, however, is not the determining factor in the outsourcing boom. Ease of execution is probably the driving consideration. After 9/11, when money flowed quickly and in large sums to intelligence agencies, it was the path of least resistance to simply sign contracts rather than to rebuild the intelligence community in a thoughtful way with a long-term strategic plan.[41]

Senior intelligence managers have found it easier and quicker to turn to private companies to hire and house staff than to fix their own agencies' hiring systems. The problems of hiring and firing civil servants that are often given as a justification for outsourcing really do not hold. Intelligence agency personnel are exempted from normal civil service personnel rules. They could be paid more than other government employees. They can quickly be fired without cause anytime an agency believes they are doing substandard work or their expertise is no longer in demand. The government could easily rent office space for more analysts. It was just easier for an intelligence agency manager to have a contractor do it all.

The result of all those many decisions to take the easy way out and sign contracts is that we have created a two-tier system for intelligence analysis. For now, at least, the more experienced analysts are often in profit-making firms, aspiring to be among the ranks of their highly paid bosses someday. And their highly paid bosses are motivated to persuade the intelligence agencies, where they once worked, of the continued need for their contracts. And many of the bosses in the intelligence agencies are thinking about what they will do when they have worked twenty years and can begin pulling down a government pension. Given those dynamics, it is unlikely that the post-9/11 boom in intelligence analysis outsourcing will be reversed anytime soon. The CIA did, however, promise in 2007 that there would be a 10 percent cut in outsourcing soon.[42] It will, of course, be difficult to know if that really happens.

What is more likely to happen is that the dramatic growth in the intelligence community budget will slow and the budget may even have to retract, given overall federal fiscal realities. When cuts have to be made, based on past tendencies, the agency managers will cut their contracts before they reduce their own staffs and other activities. What we may then discover is that many of the best analysts we had, those with institutional memories, are no longer working on the important problems.

THE LIFE OF A GOVERNMENT INTEL ANALYST

Just as we tried to imagine the life of a young spy, think about what a new analyst goes through. The new analyst is often pressured by a supervisor into conforming to the desired outcome. Alex Rossmiller details such experiences recently at the Defense Intelligence Agency in *Still Broken: A Recruit's Inside Account of Intelligence Failures from Baghdad to the Pentagon* (Ballantine Books, 2008). It is very easy for new analysts to make mistakes. Their computer screens are filled every morning with reports from the intelligence collection agencies, just as my monitor was. The last thing on their mind as they sit with their coffee at eight in the morning is that they need more information. But they probably do.

Mark Lowenthal, the intelligence veteran and *Jeopardy* champion, and I taught classes for our analysts at State's INR bureau in the 1980s. Meeting in classrooms atop Mount Weather in rural Virginia, we asked our analysts to begin thinking about a question with a blank slate and then to list all of the sources they would wish to have in a perfect world. Be realistic, though, we would suggest. Don't say you would want Saddam Hussein as a source, he's the collection target. But maybe you want his Foreign Minister (CIA did, but would not believe him because he said there was no WMD), his personal secretary, or his secretary's sister, or his telephone, or his photocopier. List what information that human and technical collection would give you in that perfect world. And then compare it with what you actually have. Then all of those reports on the screen suddenly look like not enough. Then you realize on what limited basis you are making your estimates. The problem is not that you are deluged with reports, it's that you have too little valuable information.

"But we don't live in that perfect world," the INR analysts would protest to me. "We have tough bosses, you two guys, who want us to produce analyses; we have to write based on the information we have, not what we would dream about having." From my perspective, that attitude is the most frequent mistake in intelligence analysis.

Rather than jumping into the drafting of analyses based on what is at hand, the analysts should first attempt to increase the quality of the information available to them. Analysts should meet regularly with the collection managers from the NSA, NGA, NCS, and the other agencies and engage in a two-way dialogue about the lack of availability of the information needed to answer analytical questions. Too often, for example, the analysts never even know much about the identities of the human sources. The spies usually do not trust the analysts to know. Or perhaps the spies do not want to reveal that they are spending so much of their time on other things than the analysts' concerns. At best, most analysts have an annual opportunity to fill out forms that are summarized and provided as "collection guidance." Few have any real idea about the size or priority of the collection resources devoted to their issue. Joan Dempsey, formerly the Deputy Director of Central Intelligence, told me that "the procedures for communicating the analysts' needs to the collectors do not work. Most analysts do not understand how collection systems work or how to drive the requirements process." If there were more transparency, a good analyst could help direct collection.

In the absence of most of the information that analysts would want to know, it is their obligation to say that they have an insufficient basis on which to make a judgment, not cover up for the collection failures. Yet most plow ahead and answer the question they have been asked. The most publicly well-known example of that behavior is what is known in Washington acronym jargon as the WMD NIE.

For most Americans who have heard the term "National Intelligence Estimate," or NIE, their first experience with it was the now-infamous NIE on Iraqi weapons of mass destruction written in 2002.[43] It was an analysis approved by all sixteen U.S. intelligence agencies and written by the CIA. Some of that NIE has been declassified. The NIE was also the source of the most thorough ex post facto congressional oversight of an intelligence analysis in the history of U.S. intelligence. The Senate Select Committee on Intelligence (SSCI) issued a damning report, which is worth summarizing because the mistakes it found in that NIE are often repeated in intelligence analysis. The SSCI noted that the analysis had concluded:

Iraq is reconstituting its nuclear program;

Iraq has chemical and biological weapons;

Iraq has developed an unmanned aerial vehicle (UAV), probably intended to deliver biological warfare agents;

And all key aspects—research and development and production—of Iraq's offensive biological weapons program are active and that most elements are larger and more advanced than they were before the (first) gulf war.[44]

All of those conclusions were, of course, completely wrong. What is important here is to understand why, according to the SSCI, these important judgments were so in error. The committee looked at the same information that the CIA had used to come to those conclusions and, admittedly with the benefit of hindsight, said that the conclusions "were not supported by the intelligence." There were no good, recent sources, yet the CIA "did not accurately or adequately explain the uncertainties behind the judgments." It did not admit that there was insufficient data to answer the questions they were asked. "Analysts," the committee continued, must "clearly convey . . . the difference between what they know, what they don't know, what they think . . . and making sure that policy makers understand the difference."

Why did this sloppiness happen? The SSCI suggested a few possibilities. "Groupthink" was one. Now officially anathema at the CIA, groupthink is the phenomenon wherein all analysts involved assume an answer at the outset of an investigation and then fit the facts they find to support that answer, suppressing the rest. It is something that most readers of police detective novels understand well. A bad detective decides who is guilty and then sets about to prove it, unjustly accusing an innocent man. Yet in criminal cases, the prosecution is legally required to provide the defense with any exculpatory evidence it turns up. The cops have to give the defense counsel anything they have that could prove the accused to be innocent. Not so in bad intelligence analysis. The Iraq WMD NIE failed to note that the man who ran the Iraqi WMD program, Saddam's son-in-law, had briefly escaped to freedom in Jordan and been interviewed by UNSCOM. Hussein Kamal had told UNSCOM that the WMD had been destroyed on Saddam's orders.[45] (Kamal was later lured back to Iraq and killed.) That kind of information was discarded by CIA because it did not fit the groupthink conclusion.

In my experience, groupthink was a regular part of NIEs. During the Reagan administration, I often attended the meetings of sixteen intelligence agency heads that approve the NIEs. (My boss at the INR at the time found the meetings dreadful and often sent me.) I would sit at the large table to the left of CIA Director William Casey. The placement was symbolic. Casey would begin by asking for a brief—actually, very brief—summary of the draft National Intelligence Estimate. He would then go around the table counterclockwise, and each agency representative would repetitively say "We support the NIE." Then, when fifteen agencies had made the consensus clear, Casey would nod at me. Typically, I would then launch into a dissent and distribute a summary of our reasoning. There was never any real discussion of our opposing view; the NIE had already been passed by a 15-1 vote. Instead, someone would move to note the INR's dissent in a footnote and publish the report.

The INR did not, contrary to Casey's belief, dissent frequently just to be obstinate or different. We did not dissent because the Secretary of State wanted a different policy outcome than Casey; the secretary seldom knew in advance that the INR was dissenting. We dissented because we encouraged original thinking and had taught analysts way back in the 1980s to be suspect of groupthink. Often, given that encouragement, the handful of analysts in the INR (then 5 percent of the number in the CIA) would find holes in the consensus analysis. One of those analysts at the INR during the Reagan administration was a very young Foreign Service officer named Greg Theilmann. I was delighted to learn that Theilmann drafted an INR dissent from the 2002 Iraqi WMD estimate. Carl Ford, a bearded straight talker with a slight southern drawl who had served a tour of duty in Vietnam and had worked in the DOD and CIA and as an East Asia expert on the Senate Foreign Relations Committee staff, led the INR at the time of the estimate. Later, in describing the NIE to PBS's *Frontline,* he called it "garbage" and added, "If you read the footnotes of INR very closely, the ones that are made public, you will find that. . . . We said: 'You don't have the evidence for that. It may be true, but if it is, there ought to be a way to show that that's the truth. And based on what you've shown us, we don't buy it.' "[46]

Another reason for the erroneous analysis was what the committee called "layering." That phenomenon occurs when an analyst assigned to draft a report begins by finding the last report on the same subject and then basically updates and repackages it. Layering compounds initial errors. It is an understandable phenomenon, however, because the analyst is probably working for a supervisor who wrote the previous report when he had the job the analyst now holds. It would hardly be ingratiating to begin by challenging the boss's product. Analyses of important questions should be performed de novo. They seldom are.

Perhaps more important than groupthink or layering was that analysts failed "to adequately characterize intelligence" collection. Nowhere in the NIE, for example, did it say what the committee later discovered: that "CIA had no human intelligence sources inside Iraq who were collecting against the WMD target." In short, the CIA had no spies who knew anything about Iraq's WMD but the Agency did not bother to say so when providing their conclusions about that program. Analysts cannot be blamed for the failure to collect intelligence if they have made it clear what they need, but they can and should be blamed for not admitting that there is insufficient information to make a judgment.

In the absence of information and having admitted that there is insufficient direct data, analysts can attempt to discover what I call "secondary indicators." Analysts are regularly reminded that "the absence of evidence is not the evidence of absence." Just because we cannot prove something exists, that does not necessarily mean that it is nonexistent. In the case of a possibly hidden WMD effort, analysts could try to find the kinds of things that would exist if there had been a secret weapons development program—ask what would be the signs of a country trying to pretend it was not doing something when in fact it was.

In Iran's case, for example, nongovernment analysts have pointed out tunneling into mountains near known nuclear facilities, clearly visible on commercially available satellite photography. Could one say on the basis of this and other evidence that Iran has a covert nuclear weapons program? No, but one could say that it is a possibility and that the evidence is not inconsistent with that option. Policy makers are thereby put on notice that the evidence is not conclusive either way. It is then the policy makers' job to deal with ambiguity. They won't like that, but it is a far better outcome than coming to a conclusion without sufficient evidence to support it.

THE POLICY MAKER–INTELLIGENCE ANALYST INTERACTION

Policy makers, of course, see such "wishy-washy" analysis as the intelligence community's punting. As George W. Bush described a pre-9/11 CIA warning about al Qaeda, "it was their guess." Policy makers deride "on the one hand . . . on the other hand" analysis as not telling them anything that they did not already know. They see conditional analysis as offering no value added. That attitude of policy makers often drives intelligence analysts into false certainty. As a result, some intelligence managers like to keep analysts hidden in their Dilbert cubicles at the CIA or other intelligence community headquarters. This tendency is reinforced by the allegation that Vice President Cheney, visiting CIA headquarters numerous times, may have bullied analysts into adopting his conclusion.

As much as I disagree with Cheney on Iraq policy and other issues, I doubt that he bullied any analyst at the CIA. What is more likely is that he demonstrated a detailed knowledge about the subject, asked questions that stumped analysts, and introduced information that his staff had acquired from nontraditional (and sometimes erroneous) sources. If that amounts to bullying intelligence analysts, I must admit to being a serial bullier, too. I also went frequently to the CIA and met with frontline analysts, the junior staffers who were often the only people who were working full-time on some narrow aspect of an issue. For example, in the mid-1990s I learned from a nongovernmental source that al Qaeda had used a front organization to support the travel of terrorists, Makhtab Al Khidamat (MAK). I pressed CIA analysts on why they did not know that, why they had not targeted the network for collection. The director of the Counterterrorism Center insisted that MAK was nothing more than a travelers' aid organization. We proved to CIA that it had been founded by Osama bin Laden and had offices around the world, including in New York and Arizona.[47]

Later, when I learned from another nongovernment source that al Qaeda was moving money around using the hawallah system, I wanted to know why no one working on al Qaeda even knew that there was such a system.[48] (Hawallahs are men throughout the world who maintain a ledger system with their counterparts in other countries. If Imad, for example, shows up in Yemen and needs money, he goes to Ahmed in the back of Ahmed's carpet store. Imad's cousin in Karachi previously dropped off $500 with a hawallah man there and told him to make that money available to Imad in Yemen. At the end of the year Ahmed will see how much he owes his counterpart in Karachi and how much the Karachi man owes him. The balance will be moved from one to the other, perhaps by Ahmed's shipping the cousin rugs, perhaps by the cousin's overpaying for the rugs. The CIA was not alone in its ignorance of this widespread phenomenon; even though there were hawallahs in New York City, the FBI did not know what the word meant either.)

Steven Emerson's Investigative Project on Terrorism,[49] a not-for-profit research group, repeatedly told me things about terrorists on the web and terrorists in the United States that neither the CIA nor the FBI knew. Often he was right. I am sure that some analysts saw my interventions, wanting to know why they did not know things, as bullying, just as they saw Cheney's efforts to draw their attention to "intelligence" as problematic. Cheney's information was often provided by an office established in the Pentagon by Undersecretary of Defense Douglas Feith to find information about Iraq that the regular channels of intelligence reporting were not finding.[50] Feith has been roundly criticized for that office. The idea of looking for information from nontraditional sources is commendable. What Feith's office seemed to do, however, was look only for information that supported its policy, and not to care very much about the quality of the source. Policy makers should have nongovernment sources who provide them with data, which they should pass along to the intelligence community for evaluation.

Experienced policy makers often know more about a subject than the young intelligence community analysts who write about their subject and whose writing may make it into the President's Daily Briefing or an NIE. The experienced policy maker has probably spent more time working the issue, repeatedly been to the parts of the world in question, met privately with foreign officials involved in the issue, and acquired a network of academic or corporate experts who trust him and will tell him things they would never confide to an intelligence officer. Who is likely to know more about the North Korean nuclear weapons program: Christopher Hill, the career Foreign Service officer who has led American negotiations on the subject for years, or a newly minted CIA analyst who has seen North Korea only through the lens of a satellite that flies by a hundred miles above?

The analysts' supervisors should protect them from political or policy-level interference but not from tough questioning about how well they have done their work. During my two decades with the State Department, it was tradition that five days a week the assistant secretaries of state heading the bureaus for Europe, Latin America, Asia, the Middle East, and other portfolios began their days by getting an intelligence briefing from an INR analyst specializing in their region or issue. Often the assistant secretaries, the policy makers, would disagree with the analysts. Sometimes the policy makers would call me to complain. If their complaint was that the analyst was using supporting intelligence in a biased manner, overlooking material to support a preconceived notion, I would review the matter and have a little chat with the analyst. If the policy maker simply did not like the legitimate conclusions of an analyst because it undercut his policy or made him look bad, I would encourage the analyst to keep up the good work and tell the Assistant Secretary to route further complaints to me, not the analyst. Analysts have to know that, if they are doing a good job, they have "top cover" from senior management against policy makers who do not like the bad news. An example of this is when Undersecretary of State for Arms Control John Bolton in 2002 tried to get an INR analyst reassigned for disagreeing with a planned Bolton speech that asserted that Cuba had an offensive biological weapons program. INR Assistant Secretary Carl Ford backed the analyst up then and recounted the incident during Bolton's Senate confirmation hearings to be appointed Ambassador to the United Nations in 2005.[51]

Thus, I believe strongly in the need for direct give-and-take between policy makers and analysts, even though there is a built-in grade disparity between a senior official and a young junior analyst. The daily meetings between the INR officers and the assistant secretaries gave the analysts a great insight into what the policy makers needed, what was current and useful. It also encouraged them to do a better job on their analyses because they knew they were going to be challenged to defend them. Many times the policy maker also passed on information available only to him, from sources he had developed in other governments. That kind of interaction was not regularly available to the CIA analysts sitting ten miles away in a secure wooded campus. It gave the INR a real competitive analytical advantage. Such interaction works, however, only if the rules of the road are clear: mutual respect and no political pressure on the analysts, only criticism based on the quality of their work. If analysts do not feel that they can count on their supervisors to protect them from policy makers' trying to slant their work, the interaction becomes poisonous. Sadly, it appears that in the case of intelligence about Iraq before the U.S. invasion, some intelligence community analysts did not think they had "top cover" to tell the truth as they saw it. The only way many analysts will believe that they have the protection to provide unpopular news is if they are repeatedly told by senior officials that they can.

Whether CIA Director George Tenet had told his analyst that loudly enough is debated. What is clear is that he personally clashed with policy makers, notably Vice President Cheney, whom he saw as trying to blame him for intelligence failures. Despite the controversies about politicized intelligence analysis, when Tenet departed, the White House chose a politician to replace him. Florida Congressman Porter Goss had served fifteen years in the House. As chairman of the House committee charged with oversight of the CIA, he had held few oversight hearings but issued a scathing report of the CIA shortly before being announced as the new head of the Agency. Upon arriving at the CIA, he swept out longtime career officers and announced to the staff that it was their mission to support President Bush's policies. The voluntary exodus of senior officers that followed left the Agency weakened.[52] Goss's chief aide was then arrested by the FBI for government fraud amid reports of poker games and hookers at, of all places, the Watergate complex.

REORGANIZATION:
MOVING HALF THE DECK CHAIRS AFTER 9/11

For years many senior officials in Washington had known that the job of running the CIA and all of the other intelligence agencies as well was too much for one person. Yet the law made the Director of the CIA dual-hatted as Director of Central Intelligence (DCI). Legally, the DCI had the authority to provide some direction to the heads of the NSA, the NRO, and the other agencies. James Woolsey spent much of his time at the CIA working on the future of NRO's capabilities. The law also gave the DCI the ability to move a certain amount of money around among the intelligence agencies, but whenever that possibility arose, the heads of the other agencies went running to the Pentagon for protection. Technically, most of the other intelligence agencies were part of the Defense Department, and their chiefs would at times complain to the Secretary of Defense that the mean old DCI was trying to give them directions. Despite the fact that independent observers saw how dysfunctional the system was, there was no opportunity to change things. Until 9/11.

The tragedy of 9/11 was sufficiently wrapped up in the intelligence issue that "fixing the intelligence community" seemed like one of the appropriate responses. Thus, the 9/11 Commission recommended an idea that had been kicking around for years: splitting the DCI's job into two: one official to run all of the intelligence agencies and another to run one of them, the CIA.[53] It made sense. The new top official would be called the Director of National Intelligence (DNI) and would create standards, priorities, and resource allocations for all of the agencies. The DNI would ensure coordination among them, so that all sixteen oarsmen were pulling together. The small Community Management Staff that had supported the DCI would now become the staff of the DNI. Just to make sure everyone understood this was a new world, the DNI would not sit in the CIA headquarters complex in the Langley woods.

Then came two seasoned bureaucratic players, one short and one tall. The short one, Donald Rumsfeld, was once again the Secretary of Defense. He wanted control of the intelligence agencies that were administratively assigned to the Pentagon (the NSA, NRO, NGA, DIA, etc.). He had clashed with George Tenet when Tenet, as Director of Central Intelligence, had tried to assert his authority over the intelligence agencies. Rumsfeld opposed giving the proposed new DNI authority over what he saw as DOD agencies; but he could not openly oppose the recommendations of the 9/11 Commission, which President Bush had supported. To reinforce his control over the agencies, Rumsfeld placed his personal staffer in the position of Undersecretary of Defense for Intelligence and issued new directives giving that job greater control over the agencies. Then Rumsfeld worked behind the scenes. His obedient Chairman of the Joint Chiefs of Staff, General Richard Myers, wrote to Congress with concerns about the role of the proposed DNI. One concern that the defense committees in Congress got right away was that nothing should happen that would reduce the DOD's control over the $50 billion intelligence budget, because that could mean reducing the defense committees' control, too. When the legislation creating the DNI finally passed Congress, it gave little new authority to the DNI above what the DCI had previously. It also left the Secretary of Defense in charge of most of the intelligence community.[54]

The tall one was John Negroponte, a seasoned bureaucrat who had served as Ambassador several times, including at the United Nations. Negroponte, who had barely unpacked his bags as Ambassador in Baghdad, was the consensus choice to be the new DNI. Negroponte had never worked in the CIA, NSA, NRO, DIA, or NGIA. He was given an office in a Defense Intelligence Agency building in the depressed Anacostia neighborhood of Washington, not far from the sewer treatment plant. Press reports soon surfaced claiming that he was regularly spending long lunch hours at the Metropolitan Club in downtown D.C. Hopes faded that the DNI would seize control of the U.S. intelligence community and provide it with dynamic leadership. A year into the new job, *The New York Times* reported on bipartisan criticism of Negroponte:

> "I don't think we have a lot to show yet for the intelligence reform," said Mark M. Lowenthal, a former top C.I.A. official. "What's their vision for running the intelligence community? My sense is there's a huge hunger for leadership that's not being met." Mr. Lowenthal said he spoke regularly with intelligence officers about Mr. Negroponte's office, and heard little praise. "At the agencies, officers are telling me, 'All we got is another layer,'" he said. Ms. [Jane] Harman, the ranking Democrat on the House committee, said the success of the Intelligence Reform Act, which created Mr. Negroponte's office and was passed in December 2004, would depend "50 percent on leadership." "I'm not seeing the leadership," she said in an interview, adding that Mr. Negroponte, who had a long career as a diplomat, is now a "commander" and must act like one. "The title is director, not Ambassador," Ms. Harman said. "The skill sets are very different. The goal is not to grow a bureaucracy."
>
> Senator Susan Collins, [R-Maine] said "I remain concerned about the balance of power with the Pentagon," . . . Mr. Negroponte should have responded more assertively to a Pentagon directive last November that appeared to assert control over (NSA, NRO, and NGIA).[55]

After fewer than two years in the new DNI job, Negroponte stepped down and was given the lower-level job of Deputy Secretary of State, which had been vacant for an extended period.

The creation of the DNI position had not been a mistake, although perhaps Negroponte's selection had. New jobs are often defined by the first person to hold them. The hope of those behind the 9/11 Commission's recommendation had been to put one person clearly in charge, who would ultimately be responsible for U.S. intelligence priorities and operations. Congress had failed to deliver that outcome by watering down the legislation and giving the Pentagon significant continued control over almost all of the intelligence community. The Defense Department claims the need for that control on three grounds: (1) the money for the agencies is part of the Defense budget, (2) many of the agencies' staffs are military personnel, and (3) the military needs those intelligence agencies to support military operations. None of those rationales requires that the U.S. intelligence community continue in the hybrid, schizophrenic dual-control model. The intelligence budget should be separated out from the Pentagon's and authorized by the intelligence committees of Congress. The Defense Department can be repaid for the cost of its personnel on loan to the intelligence agencies. Military requirements for intelligence can and should compete with other requirements. In time of war or when needed to support operations, the military's needs would obviously be given priority. Moreover, the Defense Intelligence Agency and the intelligence branches of the military services exist to support the uniformed forces.

To achieve the goal of strengthening the intelligence community by creating a DNI, Congress must finish the job it started. It should formally move all of the collection organizations (NSA, NRO, and NGIA) out of the Pentagon and have them report, along with the National Clandestine Service (currently part of CIA), to the DNI. The DNI should control their budgets as part of one integrated intelligence program, just as the Secretary of Defense annually decides budgetary priorities among the Army, Navy, and Air Force. No longer an intelligence collection agency, the CIA would then be free to do all source analysis without the prejudice for human intelligence that now comes from the spies' and the analysts' being part of the same organization.

Because I believe that frequent bureaucratic reorganization is disruptive of the agencies' doing their missions, I am reluctant to propose further changes in intelligence structures, but I do believe that the problems with intelligence analysis require one small modification. My experience with INR, with Australia's Office of National Assessments (ONA), and with the British Joint Intelligence Committee (JIC) have persuaded me that in the world of intelligence analysis, small is good. The large analytical staffs of the CIA and DIA are less likely to produce thoughtful work than a smaller team with more scope per person. Therefore, I suggest that the DNI be supported by a team of no more than one hundred of the best analysts available from the military, State Department, CIA, law enforcement, private contractors, and other nongovernment experts. They would be an Intelligence Assessments Staff for the new DNI.

Analysts would compete for the honor of being named to the elite Intelligence Assessments Staff, which would identify problems where groupthink, layering, mirror imaging, or simply lack of attention or understanding were impeding good analysis. They would encourage competition, create high analytical standards, and serve as a watchdog for the politicization of analysis.

UNCOVERT ACTIONS

When most of the public think about spies, they think of agents blowing things up or shooting people in some exotic foreign locale. As discussed earlier, U.S. spies actually typically work in the open and they deal in information and rumor. No U.S. spy can cross the line from collecting information to doing something that will affect the real world without first getting a presidential authorization, called a Finding, that specifically creates a covert action program. So, in the jargon of the intelligence community, most of the time U.S. spies are only engaged in *clandestine* activity, meaning secretly gathering information. When authorized to intervene to alter events, they are performing *covert action*. My guess is that more than 90 percent of the work hours of U.S. spies are in clandestine activity and less than 10 percent in covert action. For the United States, intelligence work is collection and analysis; covert action is a sideline—often a messy one.

It was not always that way. During the early days of the Cold War, throughout the 1950s and 1960s, the CIA engaged in many and sometimes large-scale covert actions. The emphasis was not on intelligence collection and analysis, it was on action. The CIA organized anti-Communist "armies" and tried to send them into the Soviet Union, China, Eastern Europe, parts of Indochina, and, famously, Cuba. These attempts to send men behind the Iron Curtain to engage in sabotage were complete disasters, with thousands of CIA-trained personnel being captured and killed. If the outcomes of these misadventures had been known to the American people, there would have been public scandals.

The CIA did somewhat better at affecting elections in the 1950s and 1960s, notably in Italy and Japan, by funding political parties and leaders. In Asia, Latin America, Africa, and the Middle East, U.S. intelligence also organized, assisted, or acquiesced in numerous military coups d'état, some of which overthrew elected officials. The resulting military governments were often repressive and violated human rights, were corrupt, and sometimes engaged in drug running. They were not, however, Communist, which was all that really mattered to the short-sighted U.S. government during the Cold War. Because it became widely known that the CIA was engaged in engineering coups and supporting repressive governments, leaders throughout the world whipped up anti-American sentiment by charging that CIA was trying to interfere in their countries. Antigovernment movements charged that the CIA was propping up the unpopular regimes they opposed.

In Vietnam, the CIA conducted a covert action program in conjunction with the U.S. military that resulted in killing thousands of suspected Viet Cong political and military personnel.[56] It may also have created a backlash that generated support for the antigovernment forces.

By the 1980s, the Soviet Union had successfully supported insurgencies and political parties that had installed new pro-Communist regimes in Africa, Latin America, Asia, and the Middle East. There was a perception in many capitals that communism was on the march again and that the United States, humiliated by the Iran hostage situation and the earlier Arab oil boycott, was on the losing side of history. The Reagan administration sought to reverse the tide. Then–CIA Director Bill Casey had worked in the predecessor of the CIA, the Office of Strategic Services (OSS), during World War II. The OSS had carried out extensive covert action, with mixed results. Casey, in the 1980s, wanted to get the CIA back into the covert action business. He obtained presidential approval for several operations designed to turn the tables on the Soviet Union. Now that the Soviets had new pro-Communist regimes in many third-world countries, the United States would create or support insurgencies against those governments. For once, it would be the Soviet Union that would have to fund and train governments to fight counterinsurgencies.[57]

The whispered theory behind the United States' covert actions was that we would make it too expensive for the Soviet Union to support all of its newly friendly third-world regimes. We were hoping to roll back the gains the Soviets had made. At first, that theory seemed unlikely. I commissioned a series of analyses by INR experts, drawing in economists, military intelligence officers, and political experts. They examined the economic price to the Soviet Union of fighting the counterinsurgencies in Angola, Afghanistan, Nicaragua, Cambodia, and elsewhere. The resulting "Cost of Empire" series showed that the Soviets were paying a high price, but how significant the burden was depended upon assumptions about the state of the Soviet economy. We later learned that the Soviet economy was much smaller than we had thought.

Clearly the United States' covert action in Afghanistan demoralized the Red Army, which was suffering high casualties at the hands of U.S.-backed insurgents. That war also undermined popular support for the government back in the USSR. The resistance to the Communist regime in Poland was not an armed insurgency, but the political action measures taken there did severely undermine the Moscow-backed government. The Polish resistance inspired anti-Communists throughout the Soviet-dominated nations in Eastern Europe and, surprisingly, also affected nationalism inside the republics of the USSR.

Usually the covertness of the programs did not hide the United States' hand from those who were being targeted. Eventually, most of those covert action programs were discussed in the U.S. press. The only real effects of the programs' being covert were that (a) the U.S. government could refuse to discuss them with other governments when that would have been uncomfortable and (b) congressional oversight was restricted.

Thus, the CIA's covert action record in the twentieth century is mixed. Sometimes it worked, but covert action was also used in ways that created scandals for a series of U.S. presidents: the Bay of Pigs, the Iran-contra affair, the mining of Nicaraguan ports in violation of international law, the assassination of several foreign leaders. Retired CIA covert action staff were at the heart of the Watergate scandal.[58] The lesson that many younger career CIA officers learned from the covert actions of the 1950s through 1980s was that such activity usually becomes politically contentious in the United States, that the CIA (not the White House people who dreamed up the covert actions) is made the scapegoat when the operations fail, and that the people the covert actions support are often unsavory and incompetent.

Robert Gates, now Secretary of Defense, was a career CIA analyst. He had risen through the ranks to be the Deputy Director of the CIA under Bill Casey, one of the greatest advocates of covert action in CIA history. Somehow Gates managed to avoid being tainted by some of the scandalous and illegal activities Casey directed, but Gates's views of covert action were affected. I recall Gates in an unguarded moment in the Situation Room during his time as Deputy National Security Advisor. He shook his head and said, "My view of covert actions is pretty straightforward. On balance, they are not worth doing." Later, as CIA Director, Gates put his emphasis on collection and analysis. His attitude affected many CIA officers who wanted to move up in the organization.

One such protégé was James Pavitt, who eventually became the head of the Clandestine Service in the Clinton administration, with the title of Deputy Director for Operations (DDO) of the CIA. Pavitt dressed and acted like a salesman. He was the polished antithesis of the new head of the Counterterrorism Center, the aptly named Cofer Black. Black had personally run operations in dark alleys of places like Khartoum. For Cofer, being a CIA officer meant occasionally using "a little muscle." When in 1999 Black proposed sending CIA officers into Afghanistan to go after al Qaeda and bin Laden, Pavitt resisted.[59] Despite the fact that President Clinton signed several directives ordering that the CIA use force against bin Laden and other leaders of al Qaeda, little or nothing happened. When in 2000 I proposed using an unmanned aircraft, the Predator, to go after bin Laden, Pavitt told an internal CIA staff meeting that al Qaeda would figure out that the CIA was involved and "every CIA officer around the world would be at risk." I had thought, in fact, that every CIA officer was already at risk from al Qaeda. I had thought that being a CIA officer abroad met running some risk to eliminate terrorists threatening the United States.

Immediately after 9/11, George Tenet overcame the DDO's traditional opposition to covert action. CIA officers with paramilitary training were quickly sent in to support the Afghan Northern Alliance, as I had been proposing. With arms provided by the CIA and air support from the U.S. Air Force, the Afghan Northern Alliance swept the Taliban from power. Predator drones found and attacked al Qaeda leaders. Although none of these actions was at all secret, they had been done under the President's covert action authority. Because it had finally been tried and had worked in Afghanistan, covert action was back in good graces.

The pendulum seems to swing from one extreme to the other when it comes to covert actions; either it is the center of CIA activity or it is in disrepute. Covert actions are neither inherently good nor innately evil. Their worth depends upon the value of their goal. They have failed under certain circumstances: when they were a substitute for an overt program that could not garner congressional support, when they sought to support unpopular governments or movements, or when they were the only real activity the U.S. government was engaged in to achieve an objective (i.e., there was no overt diplomatic or other activity). Although some large-scale covert actions have worked (e.g., driving the Soviets out of Afghanistan), it is also generally true that the smaller the program, the more likely that it will remain secret and succeed. As one student of covert action observed, "In the modern era, the role of covert action will be to control, influence, and counter threats such as nuclear proliferation, global organized crime, information warfare, and openly hostile foreign governments."[60] And terrorism.

As with so much of the government's work on national security, covert action is less likely to go wrong if it is subjected to active oversight, in the first instance by the National Security Council staff, as required by presidential directives, and by the congressional intelligence committees, as required by law. As someone who carried out NSC staff oversight of some covert action programs, I would caution those doing oversight in the future to ask detailed questions and get written answers. Oddly enough, people who are paid to engage in deception abroad sometimes find it hard to break that habit even within their own government.

COUNTERINTUITIVE COUNTERINTELLIGENCE

Counterintelligence specialists will not find it surprising that the discussion of their field is the last part of the chapter on intelligence. Counterintelligence is often neglected by intelligence officials. The normally employed definition of the term *counterintelligence* is the prevention of other nations' spies' penetrating our government, chiefly our intelligence community. It should be more broadly defined.

The United States has repeatedly been the victim of other nations' spies from the time of our revolution to today. (Remember that Benedict Arnold was one of George Washington's chief deputies.) As a democracy with a tradition of privacy rights and civil liberties, we are at a certain disadvantage in ferreting out spies, when compared with paranoid totalitarian governments that might not care whether they investigate or punish the innocent. Such American inefficiency is a small price to pay for liberty. Nonetheless, we could probably do a much better job of protecting ourselves from the real damage spies can do to us, while still remaining true to our national values.

If every major espionage case should be considered a failure to prevent spies from doing serious damage to our government, we have had a lot of failures. Spies have provided other nations with our secret military communications codes, laying bare many other secrets and making our forces vulnerable to attack. They have revealed our own sources inside other nations, with the result that our sources were killed. Spies have stolen the plans for a wide variety of weapons, developed at the cost of billions of dollars in research. Career personnel in the American foreign ministry (State Department), intelligence service (CIA), national police (FBI), military (Army, Navy, Air Force, Defense Department), and signals intelligence organization (NSA) have been spies for other countries. Between 1974 and 2005, 118 people were indicted for espionage.[61] And those are only the ones we discovered.

The Americans who spied on the United States were often motivated by money and often by very little money. One CIA employee sold the top secret handbook to a new U.S. intelligence satellite for three thousand dollars.[62] Others were paid hundreds of thousands of dollars for years of spying. A smaller number of spies seem to have been motivated by ideology. At least one who worked in the State Department bureau that I led at the time was apparently romantically involved with a foreign agent.[63] A camera installed covertly above her desk filmed her stuffing her clothes with classified communications, which she then gave to an African rebel group. She served time in federal prison, but a surprising number of alleged spies have not.

Indeed, the failures of U.S. counterintelligence go well beyond preventing spies from doing major damage. Even when they are identified as spies, the FBI has often been unable to arrest them. One spy who was an FBI agent flew to Moscow while under suspicion and then defected. The FBI had staked out his house, but only the front door. Who would have thought that he might leave by the back? Not the FBI, evidently. Other "spies" were never prosecuted because the FBI lacked sufficient evidence, but they were publicly accused anyway. One who falls into that category is Felix Bloch, a career Foreign Service officer. His office in the State Department was literally one floor below mine. (We found no evidence that he had been listening to the politically incorrect dialogues above him.) He had allegedly been passing secrets to the Soviets for years, but U.S. counterintelligence agents could not prove that. He was dismissed from the State Department, his pension was denied, and he was then followed around Washington for weeks by the FBI, who in turn were followed by a gaggle of press.[64] There was never a trial. Wen Ho Lee was a nuclear physicist at Los Alamos National Laboratory who the FBI believed had passed secrets to China. Arrested, he was held in solitary confinement for nine months before the spying charges were dropped for lack of evidence.[65]

The quality of U.S. counterintelligence was demonstrated again in 2007, when an investigation into a Homeland Security official selling immigration documents in Detroit revealed that the official was cooperating with a Lebanese American, Talal Chahine, who was allegedly linked to the Hezbollah terrorist group and its leader, Hassan Nasrallah. When the investigation turned to Chahine, the FBI discovered that his sister-in-law, who was also his former employee, had actually been an FBI special agent and had then become a CIA employee. She had fraudulently become a U.S. citizen, applied to the FBI and passed through its background check, then later applied to the CIA and passed *its* background check. Although she was polygraphed by the FBI and CIA, no one discovered that she was an illegal alien. Nor did the FBI notice when she began accessing sensitive information about investigations into Hezbollah in Detroit, despite the fact that her job had nothing to do with that subject. Nada Prouty fooled both agencies and may very well have been passing information to Hezbollah.[66]

Many of the problems with U.S. counterintelligence are well-known, as are some of their causes. There has been a fragmentation in responsibility. Every agency is supposed to police itself, but few really believe their colleagues could be traitors. Often counterintelligence has been given such a low priority that the impression has built up that CI is staffed by those who could not find a better job in the CIA, DOD, or FBI. Moreover, the general notion of what the counterintelligence mission is, finding the "bad apples" among the staff, is no longer appropriate to the current challenge.

Although insiders in U.S. national security departments did significant damage in the Cold War, the greatest threat now is from nation-states' stealing information from American companies, including defense contractors making such things as the new F-22 fighter aircraft, and companies that have little to do with the government, such as the biotech firms surrounding MIT and the University of California–San Diego. Lost data from the defense contractors could allow China or Russia to cheaply leapfrog a generation in their own technological development or could reveal weaknesses in our new weapons systems. Even if hostilities with Russia or China seem remote, the prospect of their selling arms to Iran and similar nations is not. Losing data from high-tech companies could eliminate one of the few advantages our economy still enjoys over international competition.

There has been a long-standing debate about whether U.S. intelligence should help U.S. companies obtain a competitive advantage, and the consensus has been, rightly, that it should not. But U.S. counterintelligence should be aggressive in protecting U.S. companies from industrial espionage. Corporate security officials have repeatedly told me of their fears of Chinese industrial espionage, including both stealthy cyberattacks and the insertion of Chinese nationals as employees in U.S. firms. Their concerns seem to be well placed. Recasting the current interagency Office of the National Counterintelligence Executive[67] into a larger Office of Special Information Protection (SIP) could refocus the counterintelligence field and give it the cachet necessary to attract the needed resources, both human and fiscal. The SIP could be staffed jointly by government and industry and report to the Director of National Intelligence and a senior interagency group involving both the DOD and the Commerce Department. Our vital national interests include both those pieces of information marked "Secret" at the Pentagon and those marked "Proprietary" in places like Cambridge, San Diego, and San Jose.

FUTURE INTELLIGENCE

It will take a strong Director of National Intelligence with experience in the intelligence community to shift the emphasis from the fiefdoms of expensive intelligence collection technologies to an integrated, analyst-driven structure. I do not envy that person, for he or she will meet with mighty resistance in the Pentagon, from the Pentagon's friends in Congress, and from the intelligence agencies themselves. But the new DNI must energetically pursue at least the following dozen initiatives to derive the maximum possible benefit to our country from the billions of dollars we spend every year and the thousands of people we employ in the intelligence agencies:

1. For the new DNI to be responsible and accountable for U.S. intelligence, he or she needs to control all of the U.S. intelligence agencies and their budgets. Today most of their money is buried in the Pentagon's budget and the roles of the Secretary of Defense and the DNI are overlapping. There should be a single, independent, integrated intelligence budget, and most of the intelligence agencies now in the DOD need to be shifted to the DNI, specifically the National Security Agency, the National Reconnaissance Office, and the National Geospatial-Intelligence Agency.

2. Within that integrated budget, we need to further shift resources from traditional, costly satellite collection systems run by NRO to fund other programs using cyberspace and using human intelligence (spies). Once we had achieved high-resolution photographic and radar satellites many years ago, we had most of what we needed from such satellites. Nonetheless, the companies that make satellites, and some in the intelligence community, have pressed for the creation of satellites that can do more advanced sensing, at a high financial cost. Intelligence funds can be more usefully spent in other ways than launching billion-dollar satellites with ever newer capabilities.

3. The National Clandestine Service (NCS), our human spy agency, should continue its slow efforts to expand the use of nonofficial cover (NOC) programs (spies based outside U.S. government facilities), but it should also recast our spying effort to reflect the reality that most information will continue to come from open sources, walk-ins, and liaison services. Americans are not likely to become good at spying anytime soon, and therefore the NCS should probably be downsized and focus its efforts at enhancing what we can do.

4. The NCS also needs an understanding with the White House, Congress, and the American people that it will from time to time need to engage in risky actions, either to collect information or to effect outcomes. If such activities are well justified, Americans will accept casualties among their spies. They should not, however, accept excessive risk aversion from their spy agency.

5. The Director of National Intelligence must rationalize the roles, missions, and capabilities of the various U.S. intelligence agencies when it comes to operating in cyberspace. Increasingly, the information spy agencies want to collect is in cyberspace, as are the controls for vital systems. I will discuss this issue in detail in chapter 7, but the key point here is that the highly skilled personnel and sophisticated systems we need to operate in cyberspace are in such short supply that we cannot spread them out over dozens of military, defense, and intelligence agencies.

6. A relatively small, elite, highly trained and experienced, professional intelligence analysis organization should serve the DNI and the President. This Intelligence Assessment Staff must be institutionally insulated from political pressures, and it must be able to control intelligence collection to support its analysis efforts.

7. Counterintelligence programs need to be given greater importance, respect, resources, and professionalization. In addition to looking for spies in our ranks, however, the counterintelligence programs need increasingly to protect U.S. corporations and research facilities from theft of intellectual property by foreign governments. Counterintelligence officers are not usually highly skilled at operating in cyberspace, but they need to become so quickly because that is where our secrets are being stolen.

8. Congress should enact and enforce, through active oversight, a new Code of Intelligence Ethics covering such issues as politicization of analysis, human rights abuses, and specifically torture. America's intelligence activities can and should be consistent with its political and moral values, without putting us at risk. Electronic intelligence can be given active judicial and congressional oversight. Valuable information can be and has been obtained from detainees without torture, which often produces inaccurate "intelligence."

9. The Director of National Intelligence needs to reach out to civil liberties and human rights groups in the United States to restore trust in the intelligence community. The release in 2007 by NSA of the true history of the Gulf of Tonkin incident (a 1964 event in which intelligence was doctored to justify starting a war against North Vietnam) was a step toward restoring credibility. The CIA's release later that year of the so-called "family jewels" (documents about CIA abuses in the 1960s) may in the short term have reinforced impressions about the misuse of intelligence agencies, but in the long term it was a necessary step toward reestablishing moral and legal standards within the American government.

10. CIA Director Mike Hayden announced that he will reduce reliance upon outsourcing firms. The DNI should do that across all agencies by creating a resource management pro-

gram that can utilize streamlined and flexible personnel procedures to hire, fire, train, support, and compensate intelligence community staff. Outsourcing should be used for administrative support activities, not for writing intelligence analyses.

11. For intelligence agencies to be trusted by the citizenry, there must be a program in which somebody actively keeps an eye on them to ensure that there is no abuse of our laws or policies. Thus, the National Security Advisor and the DNI should create an active executive branch oversight program for all intelligence community efforts, especially the restricted covert action programs. The existing National Security Council staff mechanisms for that oversight are weak, underresourced, and actually run by the CIA itself.

12. Congress, too, must perform its role of active oversight of intelligence agencies. It is an understatement to say that Congress failed to do that activity very well for most of the last decade. The congressional leadership should explicitly set standards to ensure that the House and Senate Intelligence Committees are carrying out their oversight missions. These efforts may not prevent all intelligence failures, for that is an impossible goal given the nature of intelligence. But I believe that the Congress could reduce the frequency and gravity of these failures. Having timely, accurate, and insightful intelligence analysis supported by effective collection may not prevent bad policy choices by our nation's leaders, but it should make intelligent policy choices more frequent.

TERRORISM

When a nation fails to do something, it is not the failure of a building (the White House, the Pentagon), an institution, a party, or an administration; it is the failure of people, of individuals. Standing in the White House Situation Room on the morning of 9/11, just having been given the job of national crisis manager and more responsibility than I had ever had in thirty years of government, I knew that I had failed. In the days and years leading up to that awful moment I had failed to persuade two administrations to do enough to prevent the attacks that were now happening around me. Unfortunately, failures continued and most security experts agree that we face a threat at least as significant today as we did then.

There are now and there have often been in modern history many terrorist groups in the world. This chapter is not about the phenomenon of terrorism. It is about defeating the movement behind both the tragedy of 9/11 and so many other acts of violence around the world.

Those who attacked us that day did not come from or have the backing of Iraq. The attackers were funded and organized by al Qaeda, a transnational terrorist group then in its fourteenth year. It served as the hub for a network of other regional terrorist groups. These terrorist groups are the fighting forces of a larger ideological movement that has tapped into a spiritual discontent and identity crisis in a stratum of the Muslim world. This "revival" movement preaches the overthrow of existing governments in favor of a "purified" theocracy that will enforce a deviant, minority form of Islam, extreme and intolerant. There have been such zealots off and on for seven hundred years, going back to Muslim theologians like Ibn Taymiyyah and twentieth-century activists like Sayyid Qutb (both of whom died in jail, seven hundred years apart, both placed there on orders of governments in Cairo).

One would like to think that a debate over doctrine within a religion would not be a national security issue in the twenty-first century (although it clearly was in European nations in the sixteenth century). Yet this debate within Islam is a vitally important issue to us because the al Qaeda network wants to do two things inimical to the United States. First, it wants to inflict such pain on America ("the Far Enemy") that we will withdraw our interest and presence in majority Muslim countries such as Egypt, Saudi Arabia, Pakistan, and Indonesia. The movement believes that we somehow have invented or at least prop up the "apostate" governments ("the Near Enemy") that exist today in some three dozen Muslim majority countries. We do this, they believe, to rob those nations of their resources, to ensure that Islamic nations are badly governed, and to prevent Islamic culture from rising up again to enjoy world leadership.[1]

Second, the movement wants violently to overthrow both moderate governments and modern societies in majority Muslim countries and regions. Once in power in any nation, it would use it as a sanctuary for terrorists and a base for operations to gain further power through violence elsewhere. The movement would eliminate most human rights, creating brutal regimes, as the Taliban did in Afghanistan. Its ultimate goal is to re-create an Islamic caliphate stretching from Spain to Indonesia. They believe that could take centuries to accomplish.[2] While they are not similar to the Communist ideological movement, which actually took over a dozen countries and had tens of thousands of nuclear weapons, the threat this movement poses to the United States and to the world in general should not be underestimated. Despite what it would do if in power, its call is resonating with many discontented Muslims who want change. More and more people in the Muslim world buy al Qaeda's propaganda about America and the West suppressing and being at war with Islam. The movement's strength is growing, in part because of what America has and has not done.

Both "al Qaeda the organization" and "al Qaeda the network of terrorist groups and individuals" have been engaged in violence against the United States for more than a decade. Yet despite the fact that counterterrorism and defeating al Qaeda were the nation's number one priority for much of that decade, the United States failed to:

- Recognize fully the seriousness of the al Qaeda threat prior to the 1998 attacks on two U.S. African embassies

- Damage al Qaeda significantly in the period between the 1998 attacks and 2001

- Prevent the 9/11 attacks

- Capture or kill the al Qaeda leadership of bin Laden and Ayman al-Zawahiri after the 9/11 attacks

- Destroy the al Qaeda movement in the years after 9/11

- Halt the regeneration of al Qaeda and the Taliban in Afghanistan and Pakistan in the last three years

Few national security failures have been as persistent or pernicious as our inability to deal with the threat from this movement.

THE POST–COLD WAR WORLD

I discussed the first three of these six failures in *Against All Enemies*. We may not want to relive those mistakes in detail, but we have to understand them or we will add to that list in the future. So before looking ahead, we have to look back, at least briefly. Then we need to see what the common threads are among these failures and how we can begin to eliminate this threat. Let's take the last ten years and look at them as five phases.

BEFORE THE EMBASSIES: ANOTHER THREAT (1988–1998)

We know now that an organization by the name of al Qaeda emerged from bin Laden's Afghan Services Bureau network in 1988–1989. It took seven years, until 1996, for the U.S. government to learn definitively from a walk-in that there was such a group and what its name was.

Before that 1996 revelation, al Qaeda or people already related to it had a role in the 1993 truck bomb attack on the World Trade Center in New York, the planned bombings of tunnels and other landmark buildings in New York in 1993, the planned bombings of U.S. aircraft over the Pacific in 1995, the training of Somalis to fight U.S. and U.N. peacekeepers in 1993, and the bombing of a U.S. military training mission in Saudi Arabia in late 1995.[3] National Security Advisor Tony Lake and I had believed from 1993 that some new confederation of terrorists had taken shape and that Osama bin Laden was a key player in it. Lake had urged the CIA to create a special team to investigate, leading to CIA's creating of a "virtual station" in 1996.[4]

Academics and journalists are often the first to identify changes in the international environment, before governments do, but not in this case. Lake had recognized early on that in the new post–Cold War world, transnational groups engaged in terrorism and international crime cartels were the new threat.

While it had taken the CIA an amazingly long time to learn that al Qaeda existed, U.S. intelligence did set about trying to counter it once it had evidence of the group's reach and goals. We had already been working against bin Laden as an individual, influential troublemaker based in Sudan. By 1998, the CIA had identified numerous al Qaeda cells and was working with friendly nations to disrupt them. Al Qaeda's efforts to take over in Bosnia had been successfully stymied.[5] CIA had thought that the cell in Kenya had been broken up, only to learn when the U.S. Embassy there was attacked that al Qaeda was still operational in Nairobi. But neither the CIA nor I thought then that al Qaeda was the most significant terrorist threat to the United States.

After the Tokyo subway nerve gas attack and the Oklahoma City truck bomb attack, both in 1995, I became increasingly concerned with our vulnerability to domestic terrorism and to terrorists using nerve gas or other weapons of mass destruction. We increased the counterterrorism budget of the FBI and initiated a WMD protection program.[6] The greatest foreign terrorist threat, I thought, was Iran.

Iran, working through its Revolutionary Guard's Qods Force (Jerusalem Force) and through its Lebanese creation called Hezbollah (Party of God), had killed 260 Americans in three attacks in Lebanon (the Marine barracks, the embassy, and the embassy annex) in 1983–1984.[7] The Qods Force and Hezbollah had kidnapped, tortured, and killed the CIA's Beirut station chief, William Buckley, as well as Richard Higgins, a U.S. marine colonel assigned to a U.N. operation in Lebanon.[8] The two organizations had worked together on the 1985 hijacking of TWA flight 847, which involved the beating death of a U.S. Navy diver, Robert Stethem.[9] A decade passed without a major Iranian attack against the United States. Then in 1996 the Qods Force had organized the truck bombing of a U.S. Air Force barracks at Khobar, Saudi Arabia, killing 19 Americans and a Saudi, and wounding 372 from many countries.[10] Also in 1996, in nearby Bahrain, where the U.S. Navy had a major base, the government was convinced that Iran was attempting to stir up an insurrection among the majority Shia population.[11]

A small group of us in the White House and the Pentagon developed plans for a major military strike on Iran if the Tehran government did not heed our warnings to stop its terrorist attacks. For those of us secretly contemplating the prospect, the possibility of another war in the gulf was chilling. It focused our thoughts and filled us with a sense of seriousness and gravity. We could not foresee a way in which there could be a beneficial "endgame." (In 2008 it is again not obvious how we could successfully end hostilities that could begin with a U.S. air strike on Iran's nuclear infrastructure.) In 1996 we thought that if we bombed Iran, it would let loose more terrorist attacks against us and our friends in the region. As it did in the Eight-Year War with Iraq, Tehran could disrupt the shipment of oil and gas from the gulf and damage the world economy. We would then be forced into further bombings, but our attacks would only unify Iranians' support for their government and solidify the nation's opposition to America.

We struggled in 1996–1997 to find an alternative to bombing Iran. The warnings to Tehran, reinforced by U.S. intelligence activity, may have worked. In any event, the Iranian aggressive actions toward the United States ceased in 1997 and stayed contained until we invaded the countries to the east and west of them in 2001 and 2003.

Thus, the U.S. government's mistakes in handling al Qaeda terrorism prior to the attacks on the U.S. embassies in East Africa in 1998 fall into two categories: (1) For the first seven years of al Qaeda's existence, there was an intelligence failure to detect and diagnose the group. (2) For the three years prior to the embassy attacks, although we did begin an aggressive effort against al Qaeda, I thought in the mid-1990s that the greatest threat of foreign terrorism was that of Iran and its front groups. Both mistakes were failures to identify the problem properly, one of the recurring patterns noted throughout this book.

THE FIRST "WAR ON AL QAEDA" (1998–2001)

Emerging from an emergency meeting in the West Wing on August 7, 1998, Clinton cabinet members promised a "war on al Qaeda" in response to the attacks on two U.S. embassies in East Africa earlier in the day. The CIA Director issued a memo to his own agency saying that it was now "at war with al Qaeda" and that all of the CIA's resources would be devoted to that struggle.[12] In the two and a half years left in that administration, the United States:

- Bombed al Qaeda camps in Afghanistan once and then kept cruise missile submarines off Baluchistan for further attacks to be launched as soon as the CIA Director was satisfied that he had determined bin Laden's location

- Authorized the CIA to engage in lethal covert action against bin Laden and the al Qaeda leadership, breaking with a long tradition against actions that could be characterized as "assassinations" or the use of "hit lists"

- Successfully captured al Qaeda operatives and prevented several terrorist attacks

- Obtained U.N. Security Council sanctions against Afghanistan as part of an intense diplomatic effort to persuade the Taliban regime to surrender or evict bin Laden and the al Qaeda leaders [13]

After the embassy attacks both senior administration officials and the U.S. media focused on the fascinating face of the new militant, deviant strain of Islam, the Saudi millionaire named Osama bin Laden. The National Security Council principals refused to recommend further U.S. military strikes on the extensive al Qaeda facilities in Afghanistan unless the CIA Director could assure them that bin Laden would be in one of the facilities when the attacks occurred. He never could. The principals did, however, agree to warn the regime in Afghanistan that any further attacks on the United States by al Qaeda would result in U.S. retaliation against both al Qaeda and its Taliban hosts.[14]

That next al Qaeda attack came at the height of the presidential campaign in October 2000. A U.S. Navy destroyer was, amazingly, visiting a port in Yemen, which was a hotbed of terrorist groups. U.S. Navy ships had apparently been docking there for more than a year to refuel when the U.S.S. *Cole* was attacked by a boat bomb and nearly blown in half. Only a remarkable damage control operation by the crew kept the *Cole* afloat. Seventeen sailors died.[15] Terrorism as an issue had never emerged in the campaigns of George Bush and Al Gore before the *Cole* was attacked. It didn't become an issue for discussion after the attack, either.

Our retaliation against the Taliban, providers of al Qaeda's Afghan sanctuary, also never happened. Remarkably, neither the CIA Director nor the FBI Director would assert that it had been al Qaeda that had attacked the *Cole*. (I say "remarkably" because the intelligence evidence was clear within twenty-four hours.) Stung by charges of poor intelligence in the U.S. attack on a Sudanese chemical plant in 1998 and the mistaken bombing of the Chinese Embassy in Belgrade in 1999, the CIA was apparently being cautious so as to avoid somebody complaining if the United States tried to kill al Qaeda terrorists in Afghanistan. In the absence of an assertion that al Qaeda had done it (by someone in addition to me), the principals felt stymied and accepted inaction. They were also concerned that a military strike might somehow look like a political move meant to support Vice President Gore's image in the weeks before the election. The United States had bombed Afghanistan the first time at a key point in President Clinton's "Monica-gate" problem. Now the principals worried that they would once again be charged with "wagging the dog," using a military strike to divert attention and affect domestic politics. (Clinton had, in fact, ordered that strike despite the potential for his enemies' charging it was a diversion, which they predictably did. He ordered it because the CIA asserted that it knew where bin Laden would be on that date. It was wrong.)

In the weeks left in the Clinton administration, the President's top national security goal was obtaining an agreement between Israel and Palestine. On al Qaeda, the principals agreed to redraft the existing strategy to include options for more aggressive steps and to present that strategy to the new President, once somebody figured out who he was. Had Clinton succeeded in his last-ditch attempt at Middle East peace, much of the al Qaeda rhetoric about America being at war with Islam would have been proven false. Unfortunately, due to the intransigence and stupidity of Yasir Arafat, Clinton failed to bring peace to Palestine and Israel.

The failures in this phase of America's dealing with al Qaeda terrorism were three:

- Once again misdiagnosing the problem, the United States focused on one man, bin Laden. His death, however, desirable, would not have meant that al Qaeda would go away. By then it was a large, well-funded network with many capable leaders such as Ayman al-Zawahiri (who had merged his Egyptian group into al Qaeda) and Khalid Sheik Mohammed (who had escaped capture years earlier in Qatar). Rather than worrying about where bin Laden was and conditioning any attack upon his being located, the United States should have used military force against the extensive al Qaeda camp system so that no wannabe terrorist would even think of going to one for training.

- The United States failed to be proactive and waited for forcing functions such as further attacks, rather than making a determination about the seriousness of the threat based on the attacks that had already occurred. The Secretary of Defense had worried after the U.S.S. *Cole* was attacked that the American people would not understand our attacking Afghanistan unless there had been an incident with many more U.S. casualties. No other member of the Principals Committee ever agreed with my proposals to take the initiative, without waiting for further terrorism, to eliminate the al Qaeda camps. President Clinton told me years later that he might have approved further attacks on the camps, but he said he was never informed that my idea had come up in the Principals Committee discussions. (He had once asked JCS Chairman Hugh Shelton to evaluate the idea of a commando raid on the camps. Shelton had advised against it.)

- The issue became politicized. The Clinton administration had not politicized terrorism and security, but it reacted with great sensitivity when the opposition used those issues for political gain. Republican legislators such as Orrin Hatch had criticized Clinton's tough antiterrorism legislation and blocked some of its provisions (only to propose them themselves after 9/11).[16] Leading Republicans such as Dick Cheney had opposed some of the antiterrorism sanctions on Iran because the sanctions hurt U.S. businesses, particularly his own.[17] As if on cue, Republicans had charged "wag the dog" when Clinton had attacked Afghanistan at the CIA's urging during the Monica Lewinsky investigation. The CIA Director had been stung by the Agency's being ridiculed for the attacks on the chemical plant and Chinese Embassy. Often when they were uncomfortable with acting, the principals would see potential political connections that were not there, such as the possibility that bombing Afghanistan would hurt Gore's election or derail peace talks with the PLO (which actually hated al Qaeda).

As the clock ran down on the administration, the principals were concerned not to take new steps that would present the President-elect (who the Supreme Court finally decided was Bush) with new problems. They recalled how George H. W. Bush had invaded Somalia after Clinton had won election, thus leaving Clinton a mess. The al Qaeda mess, however, was already there, even if it was not on the new Bush administration's to-do list.

BUSH BEGINS: VULCAN GROUPTHINK (PRE-9/11)

There is little need for me to repeat the details that the 9/11 Commission documented about the Bush administration's willful refusal to focus on al Qaeda despite what, in retrospect, was an unprecedentedly blunt and repeated series of warnings by both the CIA and me. The commission has been accused of blunting its criticism in order to achieve a unanimous Republican/Democratic report. Philip Shenor has documented how White House partisans such as Karl Rove attempted to manipulate the commission.[18] I could also quibble with parts of the report, but the facts about the Bush administration's inaction are clearly recorded.[19] The administration had attempted to limit the commission's access to White House documents, such as my own e-mails, and to White House officials, such as National Security Advisor Condi Rice. We can thank the diligence of the 9/11 families for creating the public pressure that forced the administration into turning over the documents and witnesses.

The unanswered question is *why* the Bush administration ignored the warnings about an impending attack and the urgent need for action. I have now had a lot of time to try to understand what happened in those months. My best guess is that what I was seeing was a form of "political groupthink," not unlike the groupthink that can be so disastrous when done by intelligence analysts.

The group in this case was the President and the self-named Vulcans (ironically named after a race of wise people from the planet Vulcan in the *Star Trek* television series): Cheney, Rumsfeld, and Rice. They had a preconceived agenda, developed before the election. High on the list was to do something about Iraq. Then there was the Vulcans' desire to reenergize Ronald Reagan's Star Wars program to defend against enemy ballistic missiles by changing the treaty with Russia. China's new strengths were also a concern. Iraq, Russia, and China were all problems of state-to-state relations, problems that had been on the agenda in 1992 when the anticipated eight-year administration of the man they called "Bush 41" was unexpectedly reduced to four years. Transnational threats and nonstate actors had not been important issues on their agenda then, and they were not in 2001, either.

The other key aspect of the Vulcans' political groupthink was a visceral dislike and disdain for Bill Clinton and his administration. They had so demonized it publicly that they had come to internalize that attitude. When during the transition Clinton and his national security advisor, Sandy Berger, urged attention to al Qaeda, the Bush team either did not pay sufficient attention to remember later on or intentionally disregarded the warnings because of the source. Their political groupthink betrayed an unthinking arrogance, dripping hubris.

People have asked me how I reconcile my analysis of the political groupthink with the fact Bush kept on two Clinton national security officials, George Tenet and me. Tenet played on the fact that the new President's father had tried to stay in the job of CIA Director after Jimmy Carter was elected. The elder Bush had argued that the CIA Director should not be political (although he had been the head of the Republican Party) and should not change with administrations. Carter had not been persuaded. In my case, Rice told me that they had no one in mind for the job I held (they had not thought about the issue, let alone anyone to handle it) and they knew me from when we had worked together in the Reagan and Bush 41 administrations. Moreover, I was a career Senior Executive Service officer, not a political appointee. I did

not want to walk away from dealing with al Qaeda without having gotten the U.S. government to do more to stop it. So I agreed to stay on.
In retrospect, that too was a mistake. If the Bush administration had
been forced to find "one of their own" to coordinate counterterrorism,
it might have believed him when he came running to them with his
"hair on fire," if he said in January that there was an urgent need for a
cabinet-level meeting to approve an offensive strategy, if he said there
would be "Americans lying dead in the streets."

STRAINING CREDULITY:
NAWAZ AL-HAMZI AND KHALID AL-MIDHAR (1999–2001)

Before leaving this period, I want to make a slight diversion to go into
detail on one of the more incredible parts of the 9/11 tragedy, the fact
that the CIA did not tell the FBI, Immigration, the State Department,
or the National Coordinator for Security and Counterterrorism (me)
that two known al Qaeda terrorists had made it to America and were
running around somewhere in this country. A year and a half later
those two terrorists participated in the 9/11 attacks.

As jaded and cynical as I am about government failures, I still find
this one mind-boggling and inexplicable. The 9/11 Commission Report does not tell us very much about how or why it happened, and
their explanations, while they could be correct, strain credulity and
leave many questions unanswered. Here are the facts as we now know
them:[20]

In 1998 the United States discovered that al Qaeda was using a
telephone number in Yemen. Monitoring the Yemen number, NSA and
CIA obtained names of al Qaeda operatives, including Khalid al-
Midhar. Link analysis connected him and others to the U.S. embassy
bombings.

In late 1999 al Qaeda planners used this telephone to place calls
discussing a meeting to be held in Kuala Lumpur, Malaysia, for just
after the millennium rollover at the beginning of 2000. (Al Qaeda
anticipated that several attacks would take place in Jordan, Yemen, and
the United States around New Year's Day, but the plots were foiled or

failed.) Khalid al-Midhar was among those traveling to Malaysia. Alerted to his travel and his planned change of planes in Dubai, the CIA arranged to obtain and photograph his passport. In that passport, CIA discovered a visa for entry into the United States. It had been issued by the U.S. Consulate in Jeddah, Saudi Arabia, several months before.

The CIA and NSA had not placed his name on the "don't give this guy a visa" list before his July 1999 application, even though they had known he was an al Qaeda operative from the Yemen intercepts (mistake number 1). Moreover, the Saudis had reportedly told the CIA that al-Midhar and al-Hamzi were al Qaeda members. Yet no one told that to the visa section in the U.S. Embassy in Riyadh (mistake number 2). When the CIA learned in Dubai that al-Midhar had a valid U.S. visa (by looking at it), they did not ask the State Department to revoke the visa, nor did they place his name on Immigration's "do not enter the United States" list (mistake number 3), even though there was a CIA program to do that kind of notification and CIA had done so hundreds of times before with other terrorist names.

Al-Midhar and al-Hamzi met in Kuala Lumpur with known al Qaeda operatives at a swank golf club condo. The CIA requested the local security service to photograph people entering the meeting, which it did. A few days later al-Midhar and al-Hamzi traveled to Thailand. No one followed them, but the CIA assumed for some reason that they would remain in Thailand for a while. Instead, the two men got on a United Airlines flight (not for the last time) and flew to Los Angeles, where they waltzed through Immigration. Two months later, the Thai intelligence service got around to telling the CIA that the two had gone to the United States.

To ensure that the CIA and FBI exchanged needed information and stopped keeping secrets from each other, we had created a system of exchange officers. There were several CIA officers at the FBI terrorism office and a number of FBI agents at the CIA's Counterterrorism Center. Some exchange officers even supervised the other agency's personnel. After Midhar and Hamzi showed up in Los Angeles, an FBI agent at CIA headquarters asked permission to tell FBI headquarters that terrorists were at large in California. The exchange program was working.

The FBI agent had seen something that he needed to tell his parent agency, something that had not yet been shared with the Bureau for some inexplicable reason. His request was denied by his CIA supervisor (mistake number 4). At that point, the failure to tell the FBI went from being a sloppy oversight to being a conscious decision.

Meanwhile, the two terrorists were trying to figure out how to cope in L.A., when one day they met a nice man in a restaurant. Omar al-Bayoumi was also from Saudi Arabia and, according to him, he just happened to hear some Saudi accents and befriended his fellow countrymen. Shortly thereafter, al-Bayoumi arranged for the two terrorists to move across the street from him in San Diego and then began receiving monthly stipends from his employer to take care of the boys. His employer was a Saudi company that had contracts with the Saudi government. Omar, however, did not actually work at the company. He spent his time roaming around among Saudis in Southern California. Many people, including the local FBI office at the time, assumed he was a Saudi intelligence officer.

The two terrorists signed up for flight school, did badly, and dropped out. Bored, al-Midhar went back to Yemen and may have been involved in the October 2000 attack on the U.S.S. *Cole*. The FBI investigators in Yemen working on the *Cole* case then found evidence of the earlier Malaysia meeting, where it seems the attack on the *Cole* had been on the agenda. The FBI provided the CIA with pictures of people who they believed had gone to the meeting and telephone numbers associated with them, asking for anything the CIA knew about them. Even though they knew about Midhar, the CIA said nothing (mistake number 5). Al-Midhar, meanwhile, went underground for a while, showing up again in Saudi Arabia in June 2001 to get yet another U.S. entry visa from the State Department (mistake number 6). He landed at John F. Kennedy International Airport on July 4, 2001, and again cleared Immigration (mistake number 7).

A little earlier, CIA officers had also flown to New York to meet with the FBI there. The New York FBI office had the lead in the Bureau's investigating al Qaeda and by then had indicted bin Laden and others. The visiting CIA officers showed pictures of al-Midhar and al-Hamzi and asked what the FBI knew about them. They seemed to be fishing. They offered the FBI no information. Sometime later in July, a CIA officer assigned to FBI headquarters sent a message back to the CIA expressing his concerns about the terrorists. He seems to have learned at CIA that al-Midhar and al-Hamzi were in the United States, but apparently had been instructed not to tell any of his FBI analysts or superiors (mistake number 8). He got no answer from CIA headquarters. Then an FBI agent in New York stumbled upon the fact that the CIA knew the two were in the United States, but was told by a CIA officer to "stand down" and do nothing about it (mistake number 9).

Finally, on August 23, 2001, the CIA alerted the FBI and Immigration that the two were in the United States. It did so in a way that attracted little attention. It did not mention it in the interagency Threat Committee, chaired twice a week by Roger Cressey of the NSC. It did not mention it in the Counterterrorism Security Group I chaired at least weekly. It did not call Dale Watson, the FBI's top counterterrorism official. In fact, it was so low-key that the FBI did not immediately grasp how important the information was and, therefore, did none of the obvious steps that would have located the two (such as checking if they had credit cards in their real names—they did—and where they had recently used them).

The names resurfaced on the day of the attack, 9/11. The CIA Director recalled the fact that the two al Qaeda terrorists were in the United States as soon as he heard about the attacks. Dale Watson, then the number two person in the FBI, was told by his staff that two of the names on the passenger manifests of the hijacked aircraft were those of known al Qaeda terrorists. That's how Dale found out that the U.S. government had already known about the two terrorists prior to the hijackings. Watson placed a call to me at the Situation Room, pulling me out of the crisis group to tell me. That's how and when I found out about al-Hamzi and al-Midhar.

The human brain is designed to take disparate data and order them, make sense of them, place them into a context we can understand from past experience. Sometimes it mistakenly forces data into a pattern, trying to cause things to make sense when they are purely random. This human tendency leads to conspiracy theories, which are attempts to order data that otherwise seem chaotic and improbable. Working in national security, intelligence, and terrorism, I have had to deal with a lot of conspiracy theories, such as: the queen of England is a narcotics trafficker, the U.S. Navy shot down TWA flight 800, the feds blew up the Alfred P. Murrah Federal Building in Oklahoma City, Y2K was a conspiracy by the software industry to make money, Israel blew up the World Trade Center on 9/11, there was no airplane that hit the Pentagon, Iraq had a role in 9/11. As an investigator you suspend disbelief. You check the theories out. You run them to ground. Ninety percent of the time or more, you debunk them. Once in a while, you keep the jury out.

I know that highly trained, independent investigators with the 9/11 Commission and with the Justice Department's inspector general examined the record of this amazing series of breakdowns surrounding Midhar and Hamzi. The CIA inspector general, John Helgerson, also did an extensive investigation into this and other alleged lapses of the CIA's performance related to al Qaeda.[21] The Helgerson Report notes that not one or two, but sixty (60) CIA personnel knew about the presence in the United States of al-Hamzi and al-Midhar and did nothing to tell the FBI. Maybe they thought it was someone else's job among the group of five dozen, but if they thought someone else had told FBI, did none of them ever think to ask what the FBI had done with the information, not once during a year and a half?

The Senate and House Intelligence Committees investigated 9/11-related intelligence in a rare joint committee. Senate Intelligence Committee Chairman Bob Graham came to the conclusion that Omar al-Bayoumi, the nice man in the L.A. restaurant, was a Saudi intelligence agent.[22]

The reason that there may be doubts about all of this is that there is an ordering explanation, a way of making these seemingly unbelievable facts fit a pattern. The 9/11 Commission's own staff report and the Helgerson Report both unintentionally provide a beginning. What if, they ask, the U.S. government had not been a bumbling giant unaware of what it already knew? Well, then, the reports posit, we would have had the option of intentionally letting Hamzi and Midhar into the United States and trying to flip them to become our first real sources inside al Qaeda, or we might just have followed them around to see where they went, who they talked to. But, the Commission staff reports note, that was probably not something the pre-9/11 FBI was up to. Quite right. Had the FBI known about the location in the United States of two known al Qaeda terrorists, it would have arrested them before the coffee cooled. Unlike some other police intelligence agencies around the world, the FBI does not usually believe in giving people a chance to slip surveillance when they know that the people being surveilled are likely to go out and kill.

The CIA would not try such a dangerous ploy as trying to flip al Qaeda terrorists in the United States into becoming CIA sources because that would violate laws prohibiting CIA operations inside the United States. The CIA would not ask Saudi intelligence to approach al-Midhar and al-Hamzi in Los Angeles, because foreign intelligence agencies are legally barred from running intelligence missions in the United States. Right?

There was a conspiracy theory that said in 1990 the "Blind Sheik," Omar Abdul-Rahman, had received a visa to enter the United States at a time when he was a known terrorist because the State Department visa officer was actually a CIA officer, who let Abdul-Rahman into the country so that Egyptian intelligence could keep an eye on him here.[23] If that had been true, the CIA would have lived to regret it because the Blind Sheik was later found to be behind terror plots in New York City (and was given a life sentence). Moreover, if CIA or the Saudis had attempted and failed to turn one or both terrorists into a source, the Agency would then have turned to the FBI when the terrorists rejected the approach to work for the United States. Or they would have finally told the FBI when it became clear that al-Hamzi and al-Midhar were really still working for al Qaeda.

The human mind rejects the randomness and chaos represented by the theory that the repeated mistakes made about al-Midhar and al-Hamzi were just routine, compounded incompetence. But incompetence happens. Often it is other people who pay for it.

So we prefer to think that repeated incompetence is what happened because we disdain conspiracy theories and would rather not confront the alternative.

THE POST-9/11 WORLD

By the day the planes flew into the World Trade Center and the Pentagon, al Qaeda had long since grown from an idea for unifying radical Sunni groups into a well-funded organization that had trained tens of thousands of terrorists and established cells or affiliated groups in fifty or sixty countries. By the end of that day, it had become, in the eyes of many in the Muslim world, the first organization to deal a crushing blow on the Westerners who had colonized and abused them. For the many Muslims who believed that their ethnicity and religion had been disrespected by other cultures, who thought that they had been the victims of injustice and oppression by regimes supported by the West, something new was happening.

A well-crafted program created with moderate Arabs might have been able to cast al Qaeda as a brief, deviant aberration. But al Qaeda was not crushed, just briefly damaged. The fact that bin Laden, the man who attacked America, whom Bush promised to get "dead or alive," is still free and defying the United States is a powerful symbol. It means to many disaffected Muslims that you can stand up against the authorities and survive, that al Qaeda was right about some things, and that the United States is weaker than they had thought. Far from crushing the terrorist organization that attacked us, the Bush administration since 9/11 has repeatedly approached the fight against al Qaeda from the wrong angle, frequently militarily. As Ambassador James Dobbins noted in a *Foreign Affairs* article, "[M]ost of the tangible successes in the 'war on terror' have come as a result of police, intelligence, and diplomatic activity. Not until U.S. leaders rebalance their rhetoric will it be possible to redirect the government's funding priorities toward the nonmilitary instruments on which the suppression of violent extremist movements is most likely to depend."[24]

SUCKING THEM IN (2001–2003)

As victory has a thousand fathers, bin Laden probably believes that he and the mujahedeen fighters had defeated the Red Army in Afghanistan in the 1980s. He dreamed of defeating the U.S. Army on the same battlefield. In fact, of course, the Red Army had done much to defeat itself by using poorly trained draftees. It was not bin Laden, but the various Afghan tribes who had fought tenaciously, with some special weapons from their Pakistani friends by way of America. The Arabs had contributed funds and a small group of them had fought in a few areas, including bin Laden's stand near Jalalabad.

There were reports that bin Laden's motivation for bombing a U.S. destroyer in Yemen (first, a botched attempt on the U.S.S. *The Sullivans* in January 2000 and then a repeat operation done properly on the *Cole* in October 2000) was to lure the U.S. military into fighting him and his Taliban hosts in Afghanistan.[25] When the United States did nothing in response, he was apparently as flabbergasted as I was. No doubt to provoke us and claim culpability, he wrote a poem about the attack and read it to video cameras at his son's wedding. He then had the video released to television networks immediately.

Following 9/11, al Qaeda undoubtedly expected another rain of cruise missiles followed by a quick U.S. invasion. The way in which the United States responded probably came as a surprise. Like Donald Rumsfeld, bin Laden probably thought that the U.S. Central Command had an invasion plan for Afghanistan on the shelf. It did not. In the weeks and months following 9/11, as General Tommy Franks tried to figure out how to insert U.S. troops inside Afghanistan, the CIA implemented the plan that it did have on the shelf, a plan to provide cash, military assistance, intelligence support, and U.S. advisers to the Uzbek ethnic northern Afghan tribes called the Northern Alliance.[26] The Uzbeks hated the Pashtun tribes in the south, the Taliban alliance, and had been fighting them for years. The Northern Alliance, supported by U.S. air strikes, moved with incredible speed to oust the Taliban. Support for the Taliban, even in the south, turned out to be tepid at best. Its religious zealotry had alienated much of the Pashtun population.

Bin Laden had left his well-known compound of Tarnak farms outside of the Taliban's capital of Kandahar shortly after 9/11. It was blown up early in the U.S. air strikes that began on October 7, 2001. The head of al Qaeda's military unit, Mohammed Atef, had gone north to the old capital, Kabul, to coordinate a defense against the Northern Alliance and the Americans. One can imagine bin Laden and Atef exchanging assessments near the end of October. They would have been surprised at how quickly the Taliban forces were folding and how slow the Americans were to come looking for bin Laden. Perhaps they would have puzzled over the fact that U.S. paratroopers had flown in to an abandoned al Qaeda training base far to the west of Kandahar, seized it briefly, and then flown back out of the country. The failure of the Taliban, the strength of the Northern Alliance, and the unexpected magnitude of the U.S. air strikes could have caused the two men to discuss the possibility of abandoning conventional resistance and going into a guerrilla phase in their war with America.

Two weeks later, the Northern Alliance seized the old capital at Kabul.[27] A Predator, the unmanned aircraft, identified a building that appeared to be a Taliban or al Qaeda headquarters. Nine weeks earlier the leaders of the CIA and DOD had sat in the White House Situation Room and argued against arming the Predator and using it in Afghanistan to hunt al Qaeda leaders. On November 16, a Predator fired its Hellfire missile into the building in Kabul and Mohammed Atef was killed.[28]

A little over a week later, the Taliban city of Kunduz was assaulted by the Northern Alliance. Pakistani Army transport planes evacuated Pakistani intelligence officers, Taliban officials, and perhaps al Qaeda personnel before the city fell.[29] Pakistan, which had helped to create the Taliban to bring order to Afghanistan, which had provided the Taliban with arms and advisers in its earlier fighting with the Northern Alliance, had now declared itself an ally of the United States in the fight against al Qaeda.[30] (Deputy Secretary of State Richard Armitage had made Pakistani President Pervez Musharraf an offer he could not refuse.) But Pakistan had not washed its hands of the Taliban, a problem that would resurface in a few years.

Still the Americans had not yet come for bin Laden or for the Taliban capital of Kandahar. Finally, in early December, U.S. Marines and Northern Alliance troops entered Kandahar. Bin Laden had by now realized that the conventional war with the Americans would soon be over and the guerrilla phase he wanted, the kind of war that had bled the Red Army, would begin sooner than he had thought. He was, therefore, en route to a high valley that he had used as a sanctuary during the war with the Soviets. Because of the steep, straight cliff walls on either side, it was hard for aircraft or satellites to see what was going on in the valley. The thin air at 13,000 feet made it impossible for some helicopters to operate up there. The many small caves in the rock wall provided natural rooms. The nearby, undemarcated border with Pakistan allowed for resupply from friendly tribes there, if necessary. No doubt bin Laden felt safe in Tora Bora. Then the B-52s came.

Afghans told the Americans where bin Laden had gone. Though it was difficult to quickly send large numbers of U.S. forces to such a high and remote location, a handful of CIA officers and U.S. Special Forces ventured onto the moonlike terrain. They called in air strikes of a magnitude that the Red Army had never visited on Afghanistan. They also called for U.S. forces to block the exits out of the area.[31] High on a mountain in Afghanistan, listening to the voice of Osama bin Laden on a tactical radio nearby, that handful of Americans knew that what they were doing was the reason the United States had attacked Afghanistan, to try to capture the al Qaeda leadership, the people who had attacked America on 9/11. Bin Laden was apologizing to his men over the walkie-talkie, sounding as if he knew it would soon be over.

U.S. CENTCOM never sent troops in to get him, despite the request of the CIA officers on the scene, and relied instead upon Afghans to go down into the valley.[32] The Afghans were apparently then bought off by bin Laden, allowing him, together with a small group, probably including his deputy Ayman al-Zawahiri, to walk out of Afghanistan.[33]

As the small al Qaeda remnants moved down into Pakistan, there was no blocking force to catch them. General Musharraf had offered to move forces from their confrontation with India, across the country to the Afghan border. Meeting with General Tommy Franks and U.S. Ambassador Wendy Chamberlin in Islamabad, Musharraf said all he needed to get his troops there in time to block al Qaeda forces from entering Pakistan was some U.S. airlift. Franks never sent the aircraft.

Osama bin Laden had sucked the United States into Afghanistan, but it had not worked the way he wanted. They had almost destroyed him. Had Franks sent the U.S. Rangers up to Tora Bora as requested by the CIA team on bin Laden's trail, had he sent Musharraf the C-130s he needed to move the blocking force, al Qaeda might have been destroyed, bin Laden killed. But Franks had failed to understand that destroying al Qaeda was his primary mission. He was busy occupying Afghanistan. So bin Laden escaped. Behind him, he left in ruins his base, which in Arabic is *al-qaeda*, but he and his movement would be back.

DEVOLUTION (2003–2005)

What happened to bin Laden after that is conjecture. He issued a videotaped message in which one arm appeared injured.[34] U.S. intelligence continued to claim publicly that bin Laden was in Pakistan, somewhere in the wild northwest region that was technically Pakistani territory, but had never really been under any central government's control.

In fact, the United States lost the trail of bin Laden almost immediately. It is just as likely in my mind that he eventually slipped out of Pakistan altogether, perhaps returning to his family's roots in the equally wild Wadi Doan region of Yemen's Hadhramaut. Perhaps with that same thought, by November 2002 the United States was flying Predators over that section of Yemen, looking for al Qaeda leaders. One armed Predator tracked Abu Ali al-Harithi near Marib, fired its Hellfire, and killed him and five other al Qaeda terrorists (including an American).[35] Although bin Laden and his deputy had slipped through the U.S. noose, the CIA was encouraged that it was doing well in tracking down many of the so-called high-value targets (HVTs) on its most-wanted list of al Qaeda.

By March 2002 it had located Abu Zubayda, the director of al Qaeda operations. He had been high on the list of targets for two years and had narrowly escaped before. On the first anniversary of the 9/11 attacks, Ramzi bin al-Shibh was arrested. He had been part of the 9/11 cell in Germany, had earlier been involved in the *Cole* bombing, and after 9/11 had planned an attack on a synagogue in Tunisia that killed 18. Six months later, Khalid Sheik Mohammed, the "mastermind" of

9/11, the man from the Qatar Water Department, was finally apprehended. As an independent operator, he had planned and carried out more terrorist attacks than anyone in al Qaeda, but had formally joined the group only in 1999 after getting bin Laden's approval for the plan that turned into 9/11. (The CIA had not believed that Khalid Sheik Mohammed was a significant terrorist until its investigation of 9/11 revealed his role.)

All three of those HVTs were taken in Pakistan, not in the wilds of the northwest, but in major cities: Zubayda in Faisalabad, al-Shibh in Karachi, and Khalid Sheik Mohammed in Rawalpindi. They were apprehended by Pakistani authorities, assisted by American intelligence leads.

Perhaps as part of their continuity of operations plan, bin Laden and his deputy, al-Zawahiri, split up, with the latter staying on in northwest Pakistan to mislead the Americans and lay the groundwork for the guerrilla war in Afghanistan. Press reports seem to indicate that al-Zawahiri narrowly escaped air strikes in the Pakistani border region in 2006.[36]

Their continuity plan seems to have been built around the national or regional chapters that al Qaeda had developed during the 1990s. Leaders of these groups had been brought to Afghanistan to be interviewed and indoctrinated. Foot soldiers had been trained at the Afghan camps. Funds were made available to get the groups into action. Three examples of these groups are Abu Sayyaf, an al Qaeda affiliate in the Philippines; the Salafist Group for Preaching and Combat (GSPC)—which in 2006 changed its name to al Qaeda in the Lands of the Islamic Maghreb—in Algeria; and Jemma Islamiya (JI) in Indonesia.[37]

Prior to 9/11 the management of al Qaeda had resided in a *shura,* or council, chaired by bin Laden, in Afghanistan. It was that shura that had reviewed planned attacks, asking questions, sending people back for more detailed work, choosing when and where attacks would occur. By early 2002, the members of that council had dispersed. Some were dead. A few were under "house arrest" in Iran. Others were in hiding in various parts of Pakistan and perhaps elsewhere. The decisions about attacks devolved to the local groups. What happened next is best illustrated by the Jemma Islamiya in Indonesia. The goal of JI is to create a single Muslim religious government, a caliphate, that will govern parts of Thailand and the Philippines, as well as all of Indonesia and Malaysia.

Jemma Islamiya's leader was Riduan Isamuddin, also known as Hambali. He was close to al Qaeda, although not a member per se. He had, however, attended the January 2000 meetings of al Qaeda in Kuala Lumpur at which the *Cole* and 9/11 attacks were planned.[38] To advise and assist JI, al Qaeda dispatched a Kuwaiti, Omar al-Faruq, to the region in 1995. To celebrate Christmas 2000, al-Faruq staged attacks on Christian churches in Indonesia, killing eighteen. He then planned an attack on the U.S. Embassy in Jakarta, but the U.S. Ambassador, Robert Gelbard, demanded and got stepped-up protection from Indonesian authorities and even persuaded a doubting State Department. Al-Faruq planned simultaneous attacks in Malaysia, Singapore, the Philippines, and Indonesia. He was arrested in 2002 before his wave of simultaneous attacks could be put together.[39] (Taken to the secret U.S. prison at Bagram, Afghanistan, he somehow managed to escape from that high-security facility in 2005 and made it to Iraq, where he showed up fighting in Basra in 2006. He was shot and killed there by British forces.)

With al-Faruq in custody, Hambali went ahead with his own attacks in October 2002, in Bali.[40] There were more than five hundred casualties, more than two hundred fatalities. Many were Australian tourists. Ten months later, JI attacked the JW Marriott Hotel in Jakarta, killing eighteen.[41] Later in the year, Hambali was arrested while planning attacks in Thailand.[42]

What was happening in south-east Asia was similar to what was going on throughout the Middle East and Europe. The al Qaeda affiliates, inspired by 9/11 and no longer under any control from the al Qaeda shura, went on the attack. Major terrorist attacks took place in Saudi Arabia, Spain, Morocco, Turkey, and elsewhere. Al Qaeda–related attacks doubled in the three years after 9/11 compared to the three years prior.[43]

Much as Che Guevara had become a powerful symbol of Communist revolution in Latin America, even when he was on the run and had only a few people under his command, al Qaeda and bin Laden had ceased to be operational threats (at least for a time) but were inspiring symbols. Che's appeal continued strong after his death and I assumed that bin Laden's would as well. To some extent, then, there seemed to be only one difference between bin Laden alive and afraid to communicate or bin Laden dead and still a potent symbol: his death would have provided some comfort to many of the families and friends of those killed in his attacks, including me.

I described the al Qaeda phenomenon in this initial post 9/11 period by talking about two geometric shapes, a triangle and a circle. The triangle was a hierarchical pyramid of terror groups that had al Qaeda at the top prior to 9/11. The attacks in Afghanistan and the arrests in Pakistan had loped off the top of the triangle, causing the supporting blocks to fall away and operate on their own. It was clearly good news that we had damaged al Qaeda. What was not good news was the increase in attacks and the devolution to regional groups.

The circle was the Islamic world of 1.3 billion Muslims. They were the target of al Qaeda's propaganda. The terrorists' goal was to convince as many of that population as possible to overthrow existing governments in places such as Egypt, Saudi Arabia, and Morocco, and replace them with theocracies. Ultimately, al Qaeda wanted to unite all of these theocracies into one new caliphate, reuniting the Muslim world as it had been under the Prophet. Others talked about then spreading Islam to all of the world, creating a global caliphate. Inside that Islamic circle in 2001, al Qaeda was just a small dot, a pinpoint of a few tens of thousands inside that large circle of 1.3 billion Muslims. But there was a second, somewhat larger inner circle of those who agreed with al Qaeda's goals. The elusive Muslim Brotherhood, which did not itself engage in terrorism, was aligned with many of al Qaeda's goals.[44] The Brotherhood had been around since the 1920s and was very strong in Egypt. It and similar groups in Pakistan and elsewhere probably numbered in the tens of millions, maybe hundreds of millions.

Bin Laden had hoped that 9/11 would suck the Americans into a draining war in Afghanistan and opposition to that U.S. war would expand the size of both the terrorist and supporters circles. That had not happened and some Islamic extremists, including one of his sons, were criticizing bin Laden for the 9/11 attacks.[45] We were about to fix his problems for him.

THE SILVER PLATTER (2003–2006)

To this day I am still not sure whether any of the Bush national security team really thought about invading Iraq in terms of the near-term effect it would have on terrorism. They focused on some distant future Middle East without terrorism, a future that would somehow evolve from the forces we let loose by invading Iraq. How one would get from the present day of the invasion and occupation to that glorious future was not discussed in any detail. There was also little talk about the terrorism that would be fueled by the invasion in the near term.

The Bush administration did talk about Iraq's previous role in terrorism to justify the invasion, implying that with Saddam gone that terrorist support would go away. But there really was not much of an Iraqi role in terrorism and the Bush team knew it. They knew early on that there was no real connection between Iraq and al Qaeda, despite Vice President Cheney's continued references to some fictitious meeting between a 9/11 hijacker and an Iraqi in the Czech Republic. U.S. intelligence and law enforcement experts could not have been more clear or definitive that there had been no such meeting and there was no operational relationship between al Qaeda and Iraq. (In March, 2008 after reviewing 600,000 captured Iraqi documents, the Pentagon came to the same conclusion.)[46] Administration officials publicly noted some other terrorist connections, but in a way that sounded as if they were not convinced themselves: the aging terrorist loner Abu Nidal had retired to Iraq, the Iraqi Baath Party was giving stipends to the families of Palestinian suicide bombers. The truth was that there were three terrorist groups of any significance in Iraq in 2002 and only one of them was in areas controlled by the Saddam regime.

- The Mujahedeen-e-Khalq (MEK) group was in an area controlled by Baghdad. Its goal was to overthrow the Tehran government, the government that President Bush had said was part of an "axis of evil."

- The Kurdish Kurdistan Worker's Party (PKK) in the north, beyond Saddam's control, had threatened Turkey, but had

temporarily quieted down after an appeal from its captured
leader, Abdullah Ocalan.

- Ansar Al Islam was also in the Kurdish north, beyond Saddam's
  control, but it had support from Iran. Iranian artillery supported the Ansar camps just over the Iranian border inside
  Iraq when other Kurdish groups tried to attack Ansar.[47] This
  group became interesting after the U.S. invasion of Iraq because it provided an infrastructure for a major part of the resistance, as we shall see.[48]

To understand how small Iraq's role was in supporting terrorism, one
only had to compare it to the extensive, active support of terrorist
groups by Iran or Syria. So the Bush administration knew it was not
ending a major problem of state-sponsored terrorism by invading Iraq.

Sometimes, however, Bush officials talked about terrorism and the
invasion of Iraq in a different, less precise way. Using almost identical
words, several of the Bush inner circle talked on separate occasions
about what they had learned on 9/11: that the regimes in the Middle
East were so dysfunctional that their societies bred people capable of
flying airplanes into buildings. After invading Iraq, they implied, we
would set up an example of a rational society where no one would ever
think about such heinous acts, where hatred would not be taught in
schools. Then, after we installed it in Iraq, this rational society movement would somehow spread across the Islamic world.

The first time I heard this line of thought it was being said publicly
by Condi Rice. I was chilled to the bone. Nothing a National Security
Advisor could have said would have filled me with more fear for my
country. It sounded as if she actually meant it and that it reflected
a major motivation for the Iraq invasion, a motivation shared in the
political groupthink of Bush-Cheney-Rumsfeld-Rice. If they really
thought that way—and I was afraid they did—the Bush team was
dangerously naive and was about to cause thousands of people to die
on the basis of some half-baked messianic theory. There were people in
the United States who had driven a truck bomb into a federal building
containing a day care center in Oklahoma; did that mean America was

a dysfunctional society in need of a military makeover? Our schools may not have explicitly taught hatred, but it was certainly practiced in many of them and schools were the scenes of repeated shoot-outs and massacres; should somebody invade us to change our society? More important, how was this going to work exactly? How did you get from the U.S. Army driving tanks into Baghdad to someone changing what was taught in schools in the place where the hijackers had come from, which by the way was not Iraq but Saudi Arabia?

When I heard the National Security Advisor try out that theory publicly, I had a quick flashback to my "exit interview" in January 2003 with Condi Rice and her deputy, Steve Hadley (who later succeeded her as National Security Advisor). I had said that I regretted that it looked as if the administration was going ahead with the invasion, despite Iraq's new cooperation with the United Nations; one could never know what would happen when you let loose the dogs of war, but I felt sure that the invasion would fuel terrorism; but if the invasion could not be stopped, at least the U.S. presence could be short and not turn into an occupation. Then I noted that there were signs that some in the Pentagon wanted a long occupation to change Iraqi society. I had just learned that the Pentagon was planning to buy new textbooks for Iraq's schools, books that did not teach hatred; this was a sign that we were biting off much more than we could handle.[49] A U.S. occupation would inflame the Arab world. Did they know about this sort of planning at the Pentagon? Rice and Hadley exchanged a glance. Yes, Hadley admitted, they knew.

That seems to have been the plan, to the extent that there was one, about how invading Iraq would stop terrorism. The next generation of Muslims would be taught using textbooks from Texas. A Texas textbook company really was printing the volumes. Western-style democracy, planted with a bayonet, would grow in the sands of the Arab world like kudzu in a Carolina August. The effects of the invasion on the Islamist terrorist movements were somehow overlooked or written off in the Bush administration's calculus about what might happen. Actually, the effects were immediate and overwhelming.

Within Iraq, the Baathist regime had laid plans for a resistance movement.[50] It had done a Lessons Learned study after its first defeat by the U.S. Army. Saddam knew that he could not defeat the United States in a conventional war. The Iraqis had studied how the Vietnamese had won and, so, had planned an insurgency. Saddam had put aside caches of money and arms to fuel the insurgency and he planned to use both military personnel and the criminals and fanatics in the Fedayeen movement as the irregulars. What he had not planned was that there would be other insurgents.

The Ansar Al Islam group in the north had become home to a Jordanian terrorist freelancer named Ahmad Fadeel al-Nazal al-Khalayleh.[51] He used a nom de guerre derived from the name of the poor village he came from in Jordan. He called himself al-Zarqawi. He was poorly educated and had been jailed in Jordan for rape and for terrorist acts. When he got out he had gone to Afghanistan. He rejected the controlled hierarchy of al Qaeda. He wanted to lead his own group, to be his own bin Laden. When it was clear that the United States would invade Iraq, he began to recruit from the global Islamist network. Even before the U.S. invasion, Saudis and Egyptians responded. Some foot soldiers who had been scattered from al Qaeda camps in Afghanistan came. Al-Zarqawi called his new organization "The Monotheism and Jihad Group."[52] In Washington, where such terrorist groups were now considered fair game to be attacked militarily, the Pentagon proposed air strikes on al-Zarqawi's camps prior to the full-scale attack on Iraq. Word came back from the White House to wait until the invasion. Al-Zarqawi was spared to kill Americans.[53]

Before the U.S. invasion, much of his group dispersed and went to ground around the country. Within months of the U.S. invasion, the group was staging attacks. Over the next four years, they were responsible for the most spectacular and politically important terrorist attacks, including one that drove the United Nations out of Iraq, one that drove the International Red Cross and other nongovernmental groups out, and the attack on the Golden Mosque in Samarra that initiated widespread Shia-Sunni kidnappings and murders.[54] Al-Zarqawi linked up with former Saddam regime elements for some operations.

For bin Laden and al-Zawahiri, wherever they were, al-Zarqawi posed both a challenge and an opportunity. The challenge was that he was getting more attention than they were and some of their former foot soldiers were now his. They were also disturbed by the vicious nature of some of his attacks and his blatant attempts to whip up Muslim-on-Muslim violence by attacking Shias. He could give terrorism a bad name. The opportunity, however, was to rebuild the al Qaeda brand, to do to the U.S. Army in Iraq what al Qaeda had intended to do to it in Afghanistan, and perhaps to cross-fertilize the resistance in Iraq with the stuttering Taliban resistance in Afghanistan. If the U.S. military could be drained by two wars in Islamic countries, perhaps al Qaeda would gain its goal: making it so painful and costly that the American people would get out of the countries of the Muslim world. With the Americans gone, bin Laden and al-Zawahiri believed, moderate regimes would collapse and be replaced by their caliphate.

Bin Laden and al-Zawahiri entered into negotiations with al-Zarqawi. Money was no doubt part of the talks. Eventually, in October 2004, they reached some agreement, including al-Zarqawi's publicly offering his loyalty to bin Laden. The text of the announcement from al-Zarqawi's group suggests what was going on:

> Numerous messages were passed between [al-Zarqawi] . . . and the al-Qaeda brotherhood over the past eight months, establishing a dialogue between them. No sooner had the calls been cut off than God chose to restore them, and our most generous brothers in al-Qaeda came to understand the strategy of the [al-Zarqawi] organization . . . and their hearts warmed to its methods and overall mission.
>
> Let it be known that al-Tawhid wal-Jihad [the al-Zarqawi group] pledges both its leaders and its soldiers to the mujahid commander, Sheikh "Osama bin Laden" (in word and in deed) and to jihad. . . . For what a fine commander you are to the armies of Islam, against the inveterate infidels and apostates![55]

After that announcement, the group altered its name slightly, dropping the reference to "Monotheism" and adding the use of the word "base." The best translation is something like "Organization of Jihad's Base in the Country of the Two Rivers." From that Western media began calling it "al Qaeda in Iraq." Later, President Bush would note that "al Qaeda in Iraq is part of al Qaeda"[56] and he would claim, "We are fighting in Iraq the people who attacked us on 9/11, al Qaeda."[57] Well, not exactly. We were mainly fighting Iraqis.

In fact, although they staged the most influential attacks, al Qaeda in Iraq (mostly Iraqi with some foreign members) made up about 10 percent of the insurgents in Iraq, according to the U.S. military, and only 1 percent of detainees in U.S. custody in 2007 were foreigners.[58] But as Peter Bergen and Paul Cruickshank noted, foreign extremists carrying out suicide bombings have played a disproportionately large role in throwing Iraq further into chaos than have other players in the insurgency (they cite figures from a University of Missouri scholar that as of mid-October 2007, 864 suicide bombings in Iraq since the invasion had killed more than 10,000 Iraqis).[59] That said, most of the fighters opposing the U.S. presence were Iraqis, either Sunni or Shia, who seemed chiefly motivated by a desire to get the United States out of their country. Many of the Shias received arms, training, and other support not from al Qaeda but from Iran.[60] The presence of the U.S. troops united the foreign fighters, the Baathists, the Shias, and Iran in a common goal, bleeding America on the battlefield. From time to time, these three unlikely partners cooperated operationally in various combinations.[61]

A few foreign fighters came to Iraq as they had done in the past to Bosnia, Chechnya, and Afghanistan when those nations had wars going on. They would come for a few months to earn their stripes, kill some of the enemy, learn techniques, meet comrades. Some would die, others would be captured. Some would return home to form cells or go on to other battlefields. By 2006 techniques that had worked in Iraq, lessons learned about the U.S. military, started making it from Iraq to Afghanistan.[62]

In cybercafés in Pakistan, in radical mosques in Europe, in their homes in Saudi Arabia or Indonesia, throughout the Islamic world, young Muslims were logging on and surfing through literally thousands of web sites devoted to jihad, to al Qaeda and bin Laden, to the ideology of the Muslim Brotherhood and the violent Islamist extremist philosophers. On these sites they watched videos of Americans in Iraq, occupying the former seat of the caliphate, breaking into homes, abusing prisoners at Abu Ghraib, devastating cities like Fallujah. They saw the suffering of the Iraqi people, millions turned into refugees, a people unemployed, with less electricity and running water than under the Saddam-era sanctions. But they also saw videos of American vehicles being destroyed and U.S. soldiers dying from sniper attacks, all to the musical accompaniment of rousing, inspiring songs of jihad. The attacks on 9/11 proved that Islamists could beat the Americans in a battle. Now they were defeating them again in a war. It was exciting, the Islamist extremists' cause looked like the wave of the future, and it looked like justice after years of what they were told had been Western disrespect and injustice toward Islam.

It was powerful propaganda. As one moderate Arab father told me, "Even one of my sons could fall for that." While in America, polls were showing that many people now drew a distinction between terrorism and Iraq.[63] On the internet and in the minds of many Islamic youths, the "war on terror" and the war in Iraq were coming together as one, and it looked like something to be part of.

In 2002 bin Laden and al-Zawahiri had cause to be dejected. The people of Afghanistan had rejected the closest thing to a caliphate that existed in the world and embraced the Americans. Al Qaeda's camps there were in ruins. Many of al Qaeda's leaders had been captured or killed; others had been dispersed. Affiliated groups were staging attacks, but often the attacks alienated people. The groups were not able to connect violent acts with a larger, appealing political agenda. The plan to suck the Americans into a costly war in Afghanistan had apparently failed. The 9/11 attacks had not stimulated the spontaneous rising up of Muslims throughout the world in one great wave against the Westerners and their moderate Muslim governments. Indeed, many in the Muslim world had rejected the slaughter of innocents that had taken place on 9/11. Then in 2003 the United States invaded and occupied Iraq, giving the al Qaeda movement a second chance, delivered on a silver platter.

The United States' failures in this phase of dealing with terrorism were obvious: not realistically assessing the chances of an Iraq occupation succeeding compared to other, less desirable possible outcomes;

not having a detailed plan for the postcombat phase of operations; not considering the unintended consequences of the occupation; not calculating the opportunity costs of Iraq vis-à-vis going after al Qaeda in Afghanistan and elsewhere. In short, the terrorism policy became, as Thomas Ricks called the Iraq policy in his devastatingly effective book, a fiasco, complete and utter.[64]

REGENERATION (2006–2008)

For the last few years, the blogosphere has been alive with talk of al Qaeda 2.0, a Web-enabled movement that has empowered the fringes of the Muslim diaspora to carry out attacks on their own.[65] In al Qaeda 2.0, the organization served to inspire and provided online support in the form of terrorist how-to guides, but it was assumed that the United States had at least succeeded in destroying al Qaeda's operational capability.

While the last few years have seen many deadly terrorist attacks, the al Qaeda 2.0 model has not succeeded in pulling off any "spectaculars" and law enforcement agencies in the United States and Europe have been highly successful in stopping attacks by sympathetic amateurs. Then, because of Iraq, we created a new generation of battle-tested terrorists and allowed the core of al Qaeda to establish real-world training bases and networks once again, this time in Pakistan.

In 2007 Homeland Security Secretary Michael Chertoff spoke of a "nervous summer." The secretary told the nation he had a "gut-feeling" that a major new attack was in the works. What I think he meant was that there was no specific intelligence that an attack was imminent, but all the signs pointed in that direction. Because the United States got bogged down in Iraq and distracted from the fight in Afghanistan, the central apparatus of al Qaeda had been able to regroup and then regenerate. It became an organization capable of training large numbers of terrorists and of planning major operations of the scale and caliber of 9/11—from Pakistan.[66] This depressing fact is detailed in declassified points from a National Intelligence Estimate produced in 2007.[67] A central theme is that al Qaeda will remain the most serious terrorist threat to the U.S. homeland for at least the next three years and that the threat has increased because al Qaeda—with the help of Pakistani allies—has created a safe haven for itself along the Afghanistan/ Pakistan border. Al Qaeda is now both a broad popular movement that inspires individuals and groups to act on their own and it is a training and operational entity. What we face now is a hybrid of al Qaeda 1.0 and al Qaeda 2.0, what some lacking creativity have labeled al Qaeda 3.0.

Al Qaeda has made a resurgence, and it can be directly attributed to the U.S. government collectively taking its eye off the ball. Iraq has been an all-consuming focus for the Bush administration, and no one at top levels of government paid adequate attention as al Qaeda rebuilt itself in Pakistan in 2006. From Pakistan, al Qaeda's media committee has issued statements in greatly increased numbers, pushing again and again an image of al Qaeda strength and successes by the group in an effort to win the battle of perception in the Muslim world.[68] Unfortunately, one of the strongest arrows in its quiver of arguments—that the U.S. presence in Iraq is an invasion of Muslim land that must be combated—is hard to counter and has resonated with thousands of youths in the Muslim world. As a result, the United States and the West have been losing the propaganda war.

The United States has also severely underresourced its military and nation-building efforts in Afghanistan, allowing al Qaeda and its ally the Taliban to regroup and expand their efforts. My friends Peter Bergen and Bruce Riedel have accurately analyzed the results. As Peter Bergen noted, "Afghanistan should have been a demonstration project of American resolve and American compassion . . . [but] you get what you pay for, and, today, Afghanistan resembles nothing so much as Iraq in the fall of 2003, when the descent into chaos began."[69] Bruce Riedel notes that by 2006 the Taliban was capable of launching major offensives and even attempted to retake the city of Kandahar.[70] He pointed out that al Qaeda has aided the Taliban effort greatly, as it brought the tactics of suicide bombings and IEDs proven on the battlefields of Iraq to Afghanistan. The Taliban staged more than three times as many attacks in 2006 as it did in 2005, nearly 5,500 in all.[71]

In Iraq, though al-Zarqawi is now dead, the forces he helped to set into motion will continue for years to come. He established a pipeline to bring sympathizers to the al Qaeda movement to fight in Iraq, primarily through Syria, from across the Middle East and the Muslim diaspora. That pipeline can flow two ways. Those who survive and gain experience will return to their home countries battle-tested and ready to wreak havoc. They will be joined by a new cadre of recruits trained by al Qaeda in its new bases in Pakistan. Some of those trainees may make a beeline for Great Britain.

Because of colonial ties, our allies in the United Kingdom are likely to be especially vulnerable. Hundreds of thousands of Pakistani immigrants and native-born British citizens with ties to Pakistan travel there every year and some undoubtedly venture to the Hindu Kush to be trained by al Qaeda.[71] The director of MI5 in Great Britain noted that it is monitoring more than two hundred networks of South Asian Muslims in Great Britain. These networks have been responsible for thirty attempted attacks in Great Britain since 2001. With the Visa Waiver Program, members of these networks who are British citizens can be on a plane and in this country with almost no prior notice to U.S. immigration and intelligence agencies.

The gains al Qaeda has made because of our fool's errand in Iraq are summed up well by Bruce Riedel:

- Al Qaeda today is a global operation.

- It has a well-oiled propaganda machine based in Pakistan, a secondary but independent base in Iraq, and an expanding reach in Europe.

- Its leadership is intact.

- Its decentralized command-and-control structure has allowed it to survive the loss of key operatives such as al-Zarqawi.

- Its Taliban allies are making a comeback in Afghanistan, and it is certain to get a big boost there if NATO pulls out.

And, he points out, "It will also claim a victory when U.S. forces start withdrawing from Iraq," even though doing so is in our best interests.

In its next phase, al Qaeda is likely to stage a series of attacks in Europe, while building its network and operational bases in failing and weak states with Islamic populations in South Asia, the Middle East, and Africa. By Riedel's estimate, fertile ground for recruiting and the opportunity to establish new bases exist in Lebanon, Yemen, Bangladesh, Somalia, and Algeria, among others.

RETURNING TO THE REAL PROBLEM (2008–)

In 2004, when the Iraq War had broad popular support in America, I argued against it in speeches across the country and in a chapter of *Against All Enemies* called "Right War, Wrong War." The Right War was the one against al Qaeda. We need to return to it. Thus far, we have failed to defeat the al Qaeda movement because we have applied solutions that have exacerbated the problem. We have misdiagnosed and misconceived the problem. There are five things that we need to unlearn:

- We are *not* in a war on terrorism, we are engaged in a struggle with violent Islamist extremists who employ terrorism and other tools in their effort to evict Americans from Muslim nations, to overthrow moderate governments, and to establish their own theocracies.

- Al Qaeda is *not* the only problem, they are key parts of a violent Islamist extremist movement that involves other groups and individuals, including both terrorist groups and supporting nonterrorist organizations that do ideological indoctrination and fund raising.

- This struggle is *not* primarily a military matter. Law enforcement and intelligence organizations are more crucial to dealing with the terrorists. Foreign Service officers and nongovernmental organizations will play a large role in dealing with the nonterrorist ideological groups supporting the al Qaeda movement. There is a role for the U.S. military, but with the exception of

Afghanistan, once we depart Iraq, the military role should be largely a Special Forces mission.

- Most people who support or join the al Qaeda movement do *not* do so because they are poor or uneducated, although the movement does seek to provide services to the needy in some countries in order to recruit. The chief motivations among al Qaeda followers are religious and cultural. People fall for the teachings that the United States, and the West in general, disrespect Islam, colonized the Islamic countries, and are now seeking to control them indirectly through apostate regimes, robbing the Muslim nations of their natural riches and preventing an Islamic renaissance. They believe that the United States and the West are irreligious and seek to spread perverted values, and that only by strict adherence to extreme versions of Islam can the Muslim world regain its strength and defeat the West.

- Western-style democracy is *not* antimatter to al Qaeda. Indeed, the al Qaeda movement and other radical groups, including Shia Islamists, have repeatedly demonstrated an ability to use elections to take over. The Bush administration insisted on immediate elections in Palestine and got Hamas, which is a terrorist organization. In Lebanon, Hezbollah, an Iranian-inspired terrorist group, has done well in elections. (Both Hamas and Hezbollah also have political and social service organizations, and neither is part of the al Qaeda movement.) In Egypt, the Muslim Brotherhood came in second to the ruling party and gained legitimacy and many seats in the legislature. In Algeria, an Islamist extremist party supported by terrorists won a national election, only to be checked by a military coup. The Algerian experience led to the saying "One man, one vote, one time," meaning that once in power the Islamists would put a halt to free elections.

Democracy, as we know it, is far more than elections. It is built on an edifice of institutions including an educational system, a free press, and civil society organizations. Distribute ballots and purple ink in some societies where there has been no real political opposition except the underground Islamist movement hiding in mosques, and the result will be that al Qaeda–like movements will be elected. If parachuting in ballot boxes does not work, how can we stop the al Qaeda movement? We can capture and kill terrorists forever, and we will have to, unless we have a comprehensive strategy that combines smart police and intelligence work with policies that counter the appeal of the al Qaeda movement.

For Americans to conceive of how we can possibly deal with the terrorist and ideological threat from al Qaeda the organization and the broader movement, I have found it helpful to use an analogy from recent U.S. history, a story where we succeeded. No analogy is fully apt, but in this analogy the goal and the three paths to it are similar to what we must do now.

The story is of how the conservative Republican President Ronald Reagan faced resurgent communism in 1980. He specified the goal, which seemed incredibly optimistic at the time. The goal was the rollback of communism, followed by its elimination or at least reduction to so small a nub that it would never bother us again. The three paths were *defensive* (saying we would develop Star Wars and, more immediately, strengthening NATO so that it could stop an attack in Europe), *offensive* (giving our friends around the world the capability to fight insurgencies and counterinsurgencies), and *ideological* (demonstrating to people in the third world and in Communist countries that the Marxist ideology was flawed). Put aside the arguments over Reagan's role and opinions about why the Cold War ended as it did. The point is that we now must take action to strengthen our defenses against terrorism, go on the offense to capture or kill the al Qaeda terrorists, and win the ideological struggle by showing the Muslim world that al Qaeda is wrong. I will talk about defensive measures in the next chapter. Here I want to look at what we can do to increase the effectiveness of the offense and, more important, what we can do on the ideological level.

IDEOLOGY: DRYING UP SUPPORT

The United States alone cannot change the mind of a twenty-year-old in a cybercafé in Karachi or a twenty-five-year-old in Riyadh who has only ever studied Koranic verses and the Hadith. The governments and nongovernmental institutions in their countries, their mosques, media, and associations, will have the largest effect on them. But there are things the United States can do to help, both by changing what we are doing and by initiating new activities.

To be blunt, much of what we need to do to dry up support for al Qaeda is to stop doing some of the stupid things we have been doing. We need to get out of Iraq, and we need to stop treating the Israeli-Palestinian peace process like something that we do only to buy off Tony Blair or create a photo opportunity in the last year of an eight-year presidency. We should withdraw major combat units from Iraq and se-riously engage in an Israeli-Palestinian peace process, not to appease anyone but because it is objectively in U.S. national security interests.

The U.S. military occupation of Iraq and our plans for permanent bases there proves to many Muslims that the al Qaeda movement is right, that America does want to punish, suppress, debase, and rob Is-lamic nations. As long as that occupation continues, our efforts to dry up support for the al Qaeda movement will be largely in vain. That might be a price worth paying for a short period if, by being there, we were doing some countervailing good. We aren't.

As we think about how to withdraw, we must not stay on seeking the perfect withdrawal plan or thinking that just a few more months of a large U.S. presence will do the trick. There are no good near-term outcomes in Iraq because the three factions there (Shia, Sunni, and Kurd) are likely to continue to engage in a bloody, violent, vicious pro-cess of ethnic cleansing and determining the distribution of power. We can seek to minimize the violence and to pressure the country's neigh-bors (Turkey, Saudi Arabia, and Iran) not to worsen the situation by their interventions, but keeping large numbers of U.S. combat troops in Iraq longer will not change the outcome. The presence of U.S. troops is doing nothing to alter the ethnic hatred that will lead to some unknown level of catharsis when the U.S. troops depart. It is not buying time during which the factions are undergoing therapy.

Major U.S. combat units can bring relative security to an area while they are present, but insufficient progress is being made in creating a multifactional national Iraqi Army or police to replace them. Thus, if we keep U.S. forces securing areas until they can be replaced by competent Iraqi forces, we will stay on forever waiting for the Godot Brigade to show up. We should not allow the incompetence of the Iraqis or the failures of the U.S. training program to hold U.S. forces in Iraq as, in effect, hostages.

U.S. national interests in Iraq center on preventing that country from becoming now what President Bush said in early 2003 it already was (he was wrong then): a major sanctuary for terrorists who threaten America. Our invasion did cause foreign terrorists to go there, but many have been captured or killed or have departed. It is likely that all three of the major Iraqi factions will eject terrorists from their areas of control once the United States departs. Already Sunni tribal leaders have begun to hunt down "al Qaeda" foreign fighters.[73]

If any area of Iraq does become a temporary sanctuary for terrorists and the Iraqis do not deal with it, the United States should. Although major U.S. combat units should be withdrawn from Iraq over the next eighteen months, to deal with residual terrorism we should maintain Special Forces and air forces for a period in neighboring countries such as Kuwait. We will also need a substantial defense capability for our enormous embassy and aid mission. But by rectifying our error in occupying Iraq in conjunction with other initiatives, a new American President could begin to contribute to drying up support for al Qaeda. Withdrawal of major U.S. combat units from Iraq is the sine qua non for defeating the broader al Qaeda movement.

For a long time al Qaeda did not talk much about the Palestinian problem or the Occupied Territories. It seemed to take the unacceptability of Israel as something that any good Muslim understood, and so it concentrated its propaganda on the misdeeds of the United States and the "apostate" regimes in Saudi Arabia, Egypt, and elsewhere. If the Palestinians and the Israelis reached a final agreement and all held hands and sang "Kumbaya," al Qaeda would still preach death to America. Nonetheless, for many in the Islamic world the suffering of the Palestinian people and the injustice of the occupation provide another reason to abandon support for moderate governments and transfer allegiance to violent Islamist extremists.

If the security of the state of Israel depended upon continuing the occupation, the effect that occupation had on support for the al Qaeda movement might not matter to America. The continued occupation, however, is injurious to Israel's long-term security interests, as Israeli patriots like the great Yitzhak Rabin have understood for some time. America's failure seriously to address the Palestinian issue for the first several years of the Bush administration contributed to the conditions that resulted in a terrorist organization, Hamas, taking control of Gaza.

There is seldom ever a good time to begin a major international peace initiative with the Palestinians and Israelis, the window after the first Gulf War being the exception. There are always reasons to wait. Both Clinton and Bush waited until too late in their terms, Clinton with Camp David and Bush with Annapolis, both in the last year of eight-year presidencies. For the next American President, the best time to begin would be January 21, 2009.

In the inaugural address, the new President should, in speaking to the foreign audience, make clear that the United States is not at war with Islam; America respects Islam as one of the world's great religions and one of its great historic cultures; Islam is one of the fastest-growing religions in the United States, where it is welcomed and where American Muslims worship in freedom. The United States does not seek to dictate to nations in the Muslim world, but to partner with them in mutual respect for our combined prosperity.

That and related messages must find their way into Muslim societies, but not in the ham-fisted, blunderbuss way we have done in the "Battle of Ideas," one battle in the "Global War on Terrorism," or GWOT, as it is known in the Pentagon. To win that battle, the U.S. government has spent millions of dollars creating an Arabic-language satellite television news channel no one watches and an Arabic-language music radio channel that people tune out when it broadcasts news.[74]

Changing Muslims' minds about the al Qaeda movement is not the same as selling toothpaste, Madison Avenue nothwithstanding. We need to act quietly, behind the scenes, with Muslim partners to find out what has already worked to diminish the appeal of the al Qaeda movement. Then we need, just as quietly, to encourage the greater use of those successful techniques. One technique, as suggested by Dan Byman in his excellent analysis *The Five Front War*, is going negative: Publicizing what the al Qaeda movement has done that is abhorrent to most Muslims.[75]

Some nations have required those who preach in mosques to be licensed and have refused to give permits to those who teach hatred or who distort the teachings of the Prophet. Some have used imams and religious scholars to argue in newspaper columns, at conferences, and on web sites against the ideology of hatred and violence. These techniques have also proved effective with al Qaeda prisoners, some of whom have been successfully released under supervision and surveillance. Student groups that stand *for* something, and against al Qaeda's violence, are a necessary element.

Finding that something to be for is key. I don't know the origin of the saying "You can't beat something with nothing," but I do know its validity. Imams can teach that Muslims should be for the true Islam, which stresses charity, abhors violence against innocents, and prohibits suicide. In addition to the true religion, however, many people, and especially the young, want to see a vision for "a future better than the past." That vision may have to be crafted country by country by charismatic leaders who can speak to national aspirations. Behind the scenes, consultants can help develop that vision, but it must be based on real programs for change, or else the vision will only create worse problems by falsely raising expectations.

In wealthy Muslim countries that vision is easier to craft and indeed has often already been designed by national leaders. Successful national visions will not abandon cultural traditions or fully embrace a McWorld view of globalization. In nations such as Jordan, Morocco, Pakistan, and Egypt with teeming slums, more resources will be required to create a realistic future vision. Europe and the United States should partner with wealthy Muslim nations to help fund programs tied to creating that positive vision of the future without fear, progress without hatred. There has to be early, visible progress tied to the vision.

THE OFFENSIVE: POLICING WITHOUT REPRESSION

Not only must the United States stop doing stupid things, Islamic governments must, too. In addition to providing the alternative vision, the key to moderate governments overcoming the appeal of al Qaeda is for them to stop being seen as engaging in repressive tactics. It is a standard insurgent and terrorist goal to provoke security forces into a highly visible campaign of repression. Such repression alienates the people, thus producing more recruits for the terrorist movement.

Torture, disappearances, brutality, disrespectful searches, police arrogance, and other overtly repressive tactics are the fuel that terrorism needs. All too often, untrained police operating in societies without democratic traditions play right into the hands of the terrorists. I have long recommended to my students that they view the movie *The Battle of Algiers* so that they will fully grasp this point. In the film the French counterterrorism forces find and kill all of the leaders of a terrorist group, but they do so in such a repressive a way that they generate another, much stronger enemy among the people.

The analogy in America is with community policing. Experts in policing such as James Q. Wilson advocated abandoning the tactic of putting fear into a neighborhood by hitting rebellious youth with billy clubs and replacing such techniques with dialogue so that a policeman knows the people in the community and tries to help them.[76] They, in turn, then help the police to identify troublemakers, arrest them, and remove them from the community. Community policing also seeks to improve the living conditions in a neighborhood, including by enforcing violations against those who degrade those conditions. Applying this technique to terrorism, security services should abandon heavy-handed police tactics and reach out into communities in which terrorists might live or recruit. They should partner with the communities, helping with problems and seeking to learn about the presence of violent Islamist extremists.

Security services in most countries need to be retrained and re-equipped. They need to be taught interrogation techniques that work successfully without torture. Many need modern surveillance and data-mining technologies. Applying community policing techniques to security efforts also requires support. That is the kind of program the U.S. State Department could expand, developing and providing training and financial support through its growing international police assistance program.

Governments threatened by the al Qaeda movement and its propaganda must walk a fine line between prohibiting terrorist front groups or precursors like the Muslim Brotherhood, yet allowing for some debate and dissent. In many nations where there has been no democratic tradition, the movement to a full democracy must be gradual, but there must be some signs of movement to an open and consultative process of governance building on local traditions. Corruption and cronyism are corrosive of popular support and are quickly seized upon by al Qaeda as a further example of the "apostate" nature of the existing government.

LOCALIZING THE SOLUTION SETS

Defeating the al Qaeda movement will also require the United States and its partners to develop a country-by-country strategy or a series of regional approaches. There are common elements in the al Qaeda movement throughout the Muslim world, but also important regional differences. Four areas require particular focus and sustained high-level attention, as does Europe (which I discuss in the next chapter).

PAKISTAN-AFGHANISTAN

The struggle in these two countries cannot be separated into two distinct efforts. As long as Pakistan permits or cannot stop its territory from being used to support the Taliban's renewed war inside Afghanistan, our efforts to support the Kabul government will fail. The problem is that the Pakistani military has not really ever abandoned its creation, the Taliban. The military has long believed that it needs a friendly government in Afghanistan as part of its strategy for dealing with India as a potential enemy. It does not want India to be able to pressure it from both sides by making a partnership with Afghanistan, and it seeks to have "strategic depth," friendly territory in which to have some forces fall back in case of a war with India. This Pakistani belief has to be addressed squarely and the military convinced to crack down aggressively on the Taliban. The Pakistanis' challenge is all the more difficult because the powerful intelligence service—staffed primarily by members of the Army on detail—contains jihadist sympathizers.[77] The effort will also require serious sustained funding of the new U.S. aid program targeted at the Pakistani northwest territories, where the Taliban and al Qaeda are often welcomed by the local tribes.[78]

On the Afghan side of the border, the United States and NATO must accept the need for a long-term security stabilization force presence combined with significantly increased development aid and reconstruction programs. As my friend, the former presidential envoy to Afghanistan, Ambassador James Dobbins, has repeatedly noted, the United States has provided far fewer aid dollars per capita in Afghanistan than have been targeted at any other recent postconflict reconstruction program (in Iraq, Bosnia, Haiti, etc.).[79] By the beginning of 2008, it was clear that the effort to rebuild Afghanistan had not only been underresourced, it was failing. On one day, January 31, three independent studies were released in Washington calling for increased efforts to rebuild Afghanistan, to prevent it from once again being a failed state and terrorist haven. Former Marine Commandant Jim Jones and former U.N. Ambassador Tom Pickering called for conceptually decoupling the Afghan mission from the Iraqi War and an end to attempts to do the Afghan effort with a "light footprint." The Atlantic Council study called the current situation there a "security stalemate" and said Afghanistan was being "dangerously neglected . . . in a Washington transfixed by Iraq." The National Defense University report said failure in Afghanistan might be worse than failure in Iraq. It pointed a finger at the drug trade as the underlying source of revenue for the insurgents.[80]

The largest source of income in Afghanistan today does come from growing poppies to supply the illegal narcotics industry. The Taliban and other destabilizing elements benefit from this illicit traffic. If we believe in stabilizing Afghanistan, we need farmers to grow something else, even if it means we overpay for it. Or we can buy their poppies. Until and unless we crack the heroin trade, Afghanistan will not achieve stability. We need to forget about traditional economics and cost-effectiveness in this instance and do what we do for American farmers: give them subsidies to grow something else. Otherwise we risk Afghanistan's becoming a failed state and home to terrorists once again.

TURKEY

Our NATO ally is one of the few majority Muslim states to have had success with democracy and a secular approach to governance. But the secular appeal of the nation's brilliant founder, Mustafa Kemal (Atatürk), is diminishing with time. Islamism is on the rise and creeping into politics and government, thus far without violence.[81] Tens of thousands of citizens have also marched in the streets in favor of secular government, so there is a real potential for discord. Europe has teased Turkey with the prospect of joining the European Union, but the racism of many people in EU member states and their fear of Turkey's economic competitiveness will probably prevent Turkey's membership. The rejection could strengthen the antisecularists. What happens in Iraq could also drive Turkey away from the United States. The Kurds may be our only friends in Iraq, but we need to understand that Turkey is far more important to the United States. We will soon need actively to broker an arrangement between the Kurds and Turkey, but when we do we need to remember which bilateral relationship has greater value: Turkey. For if the European Union and the United States both abandon Turkey at a time of rising Islamism, the al Qaeda ideological movement will find a fertile breeding ground and the model of a modern, moderate, democratic Muslim state will fail.

SAUDI ARABIA

Our friends in the Kingdom are partially to blame for the al Qaeda movement, which seeks to overthrow their government. Their government funded mosques and schools and imams throughout the Muslim world on condition that they teach a brand of Islam (Wahhabism) that is only slightly removed from the al Qaeda ideology. It funded Islamic charities that al Qaeda used as front organizations. Before 9/11, its cooperation against al Qaeda was tepid. Even after 9/11, it was less then enthusiastic until al Qaeda began bombing within hearing range of the royal family. Saudi Arabia today remains a brittle society, filled with a growing population (75 percent are under thirty years old) whose religiously focused education poorly equips them to create a modern economy (unemployment among young adults is nearly 30 percent).[82] The restrictions on women's role in the society and the dreadful education system continue despite promises of change. One Saudi professional told me that his family and those of many of his friends live in Dubai, "where my children can go to a real school and their mother can drive them there." He sees them on the weekends when he flies in from the Kingdom. The popular perception continues that the country is run as though it were the private property of one corrupt family. Al Qaeda unfortunately offers an alternative.

IRAN

The longest-running and most effective supporter of terrorists is not al Qaeda but the Iranian Revolutionary Guard and its Qods (Jerusalem) Force.[83] They created, trained, and equipped Hezbollah terrorists in

Lebanon beginning more than twenty-five years ago. They attacked Jewish centers in Argentina and the U.S. Air Force housing complex at Khobar, Saudi Arabia. During the 1990s, they facilitated both the Egyptian Islamic Jihad, which merged with al Qaeda, and occasionally helped al Qaeda itself. There is no doubt in my mind that they have trained and equipped groups in Iraq that have attacked American forces there, introducing small numbers of highly sophisticated explosive formed projectiles. They may be engaged in similar activity now in Afghanistan.[84] The United States and its allies, including the Sunni Arab states, need to engage in an ongoing intelligence and counterterrorism effort to counter and roll back the influence of Qods Force. At the same time, Americans need to understand better what may motivate the Iranian leadership to permit the Qods Force's activities.

From the Iranian leadership's perspective, the United States invaded the nations on Iran's east and west and threatened it as part of an "axis of evil." Moreover, there have been reports of U.S., Israeli, and British covert action inside Iran in the Azeri, Baluchi, and Arab regions.[85] If the Iranian leaders think the United States is trying to destabilize their nation, turning up the heat in Iraq and Afghanistan would be a logical response. Because it may be difficult and somewhat irrelevant to determine who started the increased tensions, whose covert action program came first, it is at least worth trying seriously to find a negotiated way of having both sides back down, as the Baker-Hamilton Iraq Study Group proposed. If the United States were to engage in overt military activity, such as bombing targets in Iran, we would launch a cycle of retaliation, which would severely damage our interests. There is no reason to believe that the "endgame" of that cycle would be good for the United States and many reasons to think it would be a disaster for us. We would also unite the Iranian nation behind its current President and indefinitely defer the day a more rational regime comes to power. An American bombing campaign against Iran would please two people most: Iranian President Mahmoud Ahmadinejad and American Vice President Dick Cheney. That fact alone should give us pause.

FROM FAILURE TO SUCCESS AGAINST AL QAEDA

The United States is not about to be invaded or occupied by al Qaeda. Nor need it face a series of repeated attacks like 9/11 if we take the right steps. We do not have to oversell the problem posed by al Qaeda to stress its importance. America does face many challenges: economic, environmental, and security problems. But defeating the al Qaeda ideological movement is one of our most important priorities. It will take time, significant resources, creativity, and sustained attention. Until we can reduce the threat of the al Qaeda movement to that of an ideological fossil, some of the most important regions of the world will be in turmoil and more innocent people will die. We could have done a lot by now to achieve that goal, but it is not too late to start again and this time to fight the right struggle.

Six

HOMELAND SECURITY

Americans differ widely over what roles they want their national government to perform, but all agree that it should at least protect them from violent attacks by terrorists in the United States. Few missions are as fundamental, and few have seen such managerial morass.

"Yeah, creating a huge new department, especially now, would be a big mistake," Tom Ridge said, agreeing with me, as we sat in his small, windowless office in the West Wing of the White House in December 2001. He had resigned as the popular governor of Pennsylvania weeks before, after having his arm twisted by the Bush administration to become the first Assistant to the President for Homeland Security. The tall, square-jawed Vietnam veteran had been recruited following the 9/11 attacks to give a reassuring public face to new defensive measures against terrorism. Ridge was right, but, dutiful soldier that he was, when his arm was twisted a second time, he ended up presiding over the bureaucratic kludge that became best known for color-coded security alerts. After he left as the first Secretary of the Department of

Homeland Security, his successor presided over the most obvious domestic failure of the national government in generations, the response to Hurricane Katrina.

You could almost hear the nation speak with one voice as we watched our fellow citizens being ignored and degraded in the wake of the storm called Katrina. We said, "Enough. This is not acceptable. Not in our country." David Broder, the nation's preeminent reporter on politics, said that the Bush presidency ended right then. People who had given Bush the benefit of the doubt on Iraq and terrorism lost all faith in the administration. When Bush spoke in a well-lit photo opportunity speech in the ruins of New Orleans a few days after the disaster, few believed his promises. The President's popularity dropped to the low thirties. I understood the public reaction. Watching the federal government's response to Katrina made me bitterly angry, reminding me of the fury I had felt as a teenager when I stood in front of a television to learn that yet another assassination had occurred. Only this time I knew why it had happened. People I knew and had worked with had taken a well-run Federal Emergency Management Agency (FEMA), politicized it, and buried it in a bureaucratic nightmare they called the Department of Homeland Security.

The creation and subsequent dysfunction of the Department of Homeland Security is revealing of many of the reasons why the U.S. government so often fails at national security. For several years, over two administrations of different political parties, people who were engaged in federal management and national security tried to resist a politically motivated drive to be seen to "do something" about security through bureaucratic reorganization. When, after 9/11, that drive became irresistible, the chief criteria in designing and managing the major new government enterprise were appearance and politics, not problem solving. The largest federal department created in more than fifty years was slammed together with insufficient resources and regulatory powers. Worse yet, far from recruiting the best managers that government and industry could assemble, it was laced with political hacks and contractors to a degree never before seen in any federal agency. The chance to create a model of modern government management to tackle a major problem had degenerated into television comedians joking about duct tape. They also joked about the appropriateness of the site chosen for the department's new headquarters. In 2011, the Department of Homeland Security will consolidate its more than sixty Washington, D.C., offices onto the grounds of St. Elizabeth's Hospital, an insane asylum that holds the distinction of being one of the first federally funded mental hospitals in the country.[1]

This is the story of a bad idea, poorly executed, how it happened, and why it failed. Our subject is also what we should be seeking for security inside the United States and how we might best achieve it.

THE KLUDGE COMETH

Washington is a city of myths. One of my favorites is usually told by someone who wishes to appear erudite and steeped in the classics, seeing the connections between the original Rome on the Tiber and the new Rome on the Potomac. Such a sage will quote Petronius Arbiter as saying almost two thousand years ago, "We trained hard . . . but it seemed that every time we were beginning to form up into teams, we would be reorganized. I was to learn later in life that we tend to meet any new situation by reorganizing; and a wonderful method it can be for creating the illusion of progress while producing confusion, inefficiency, and demoralization." Alas, Petronius never wrote that and it is not etched on a ruin atop Rome's Capitoline Hill, but the frequency with which it is quoted in Washington suggests that it should be chiseled into a marble wall on Washington's Capitol Hill. Had it been, perhaps the reorganizational imperative could have been resisted. But Americans have a table-of-organization mentality, and their first inclination is to address a new problem by adding boxes to charts and then moving the boxes around.

CLINTON TRIES COORDINATION

In my observation of the federal government, creating new organizations generally diverts the attention of personnel who should be working on the substance of the issue to instead spend time on the administrative demands of creating a new nest. For the same reason, detaching boxes from one department and attaching them to another is as dangerous a practice as human organ transplant. It can and sometimes must be done, but it risks the health of the patient and should be done only rarely and when absolutely necessary. The history of last half century of people playing with the federal organizational chart indicates that the box-moving, box-building approach to addressing substantive problems has often produced suboptimal results.

Thirty years after its creation in the 1960s, the Department of Transportation adopted the slogan "One DOT" as part of an effort to finally create synergy and connectivity among the independent fiefdoms that were its components. The Department of Energy, which never really jelled after its creation in the 1970s, underwent major redesign in the last decade with the removal of its largest components into a largely independent National Nuclear Security Administration. The Department of Defense was created in 1947, but the power of its predecessors (Department of the Army and Department of the Navy) was whittled back only somewhat in the early 1960s and a little more in the mid-1980s (as discussed in chapter 3). Sometimes an issue comes along that is so new that none of the existing agencies can handle it well, such as space exploration. The Army and Navy both wanted the mission, but President Eisenhower thought they did not work well with the emerging civilian technology engineering community and space would not have been the central focus of the military services. A separate space agency, the National Aeronautics and Space Administration (NASA), made sense.[2]

There are occasionally bad bureaucratic marriages that need to end in divorce. Sometimes the culture or personality of a department is immutable and that personality has irreconcilable differences with that of one of its components. Placing a large number of federal law enforcement officers in the Treasury Department never seemed to make sense. No Secretary of the Treasury was ever chosen with his law enforcement background in mind, nor did any Secretary ever spend much if any time on those Treasury law enforcement agencies. Then one day Secretary Lloyd Bentsen was told that one of his law enforcement agencies, the ATF (an organization whose very name suggests a problem: the Bureau of Alcohol, Tobacco and Firearms) had created a disaster at the farm compound of a religious extremist group outside (appropriately enough) Waco, Texas, not too far from Crawford. Poor Bentsen had probably never really focused until then on the fact that he had more federal law enforcement agents working for him than the FBI Director had.[3] In 2003, as part of the bill that created the homeland security reshuffle, ATF was transferred to the Justice Department, in which the FBI, the narcotics agents (Drug Enforcement Administration, or DEA), and the U.S. Marshals were already located.

There are always a lot of organizational structures in government that do not seem to make sense. As a rule, federal managers need to overcome their urges to clean up these historical anomalies. The engineer in Jimmy Carter drove him to want to create a more sensible executive branch organizational chart. He asked Congress for sweeping powers to jigger agencies and departments, but was refused. Moving agencies from one department to another could mean reducing the scope and power of the congressional committees that oversee those agencies and their budgets, something that usually requires a great deal of time to accomplish and usually ends in failure.

It was with this attitude toward federal management that in the mid-1990s I approached the related problems of terrorism, domestic security, weapons of mass destruction, and mass-casualty disasters. Those issues were in the forefront of my mind and, more importantly, Bill Clinton's because of three events in 1993 (the shooting at CIA headquarters, the World Trade Center bombing, and the failed attempts to blow up New York City landmarks), three in 1995 (the attempted attack on U.S. passenger aircraft in the Pacific, the use of sarin nerve gas on the Tokyo subway, and the Oklahoma City federal building bombing), and two more in 1996 (the crash of TWA flight 800 and the Atlanta Centennial Olympic Park bombing). These were disparate events caused by Middle Eastern terrorists, right-wing Americans, Japanese cultists, and faulty aircraft wiring, but they seemed indicative of larger problems that could occur in a world of globalization.

Rather than creating a new department, we tried to make the existing departments work on the newly important issues. In three Presidential Decision Directives in 1995 and 1998, President Clinton clearly articulated a policy and a new, high priority for terrorism, homeland security, and WMD defense.[4] The directives also spelled out which agency was in charge of what and created coordination and oversight mechanisms within the executive branch. During the five years beginning in 1996, Clinton increased resources for these programs by more than 50 percent.[5] A new program began funding state and local homeland security efforts, multidepartment joint terrorism task forces were assigned to more than two dozen cities, a mechanism was created to manage "national special security events," medicines and vaccinations were procured to deal with chemical and biological attacks, new laws were passed to strengthen the FBI's ability to combat terrorism, and the FBI counterterrorism budget was increased by 400 percent.[6]

To make clear the authority of the White House oversight mechanism, Clinton changed my title from Special Assistant to the President (which I kind of liked) to National Coordinator for Security and Counterterrorism (which was a mouthful). The media instantly dubbed the job "Terrorism Czar." The problem with the media's shorthand was that, in addition to the fact that the last real czar had been killed in 1917, the National Coordinator did not have czarist authority to hire, fire, move money, or order things to happen. Instead I persuaded, embarrassed, created consensus, or invoked higher authorities.

Clinton talked a lot publicly about terrorism and what he was doing about it. One result of the events of the mid-1990s and Clinton's response was an increased focus on terrorism by think tanks and several commissions. Typically, they wanted Clinton to do more, to publish a policy or strategy (although most critics never made clear what was wrong with the policy he had created), and to move organizational boxes around from department to department. Some wanted an entirely new department.[7] Clinton resisted the organizational approach, although his administration did create a Counterterrorism Center in the CIA and a National Domestic Preparedness Office in Justice.

THE OTHER CHENEY TASK FORCE

By not pursuing an organizational approach, Clinton disappointed the think tanks and commissions. They expected the new Bush administration to see things their way. It didn't. Terrorism and homeland security were not Bush priorities when the new President came into office, and the Bush administration certainly was not about to expend time, energy, and political capital on a major governmental reorganization to deal with these issues.

Those who wanted one big new department published intentionally confusing wire diagram charts purportedly explaining the way things worked, but really designed to make it seem as though there were too many departments with some domestic security– or terrorism-related mission. They urged every congressional committee with oversight of one of the relevant agencies to hold a hearing and ask each cabinet member to explain his or her role in counterterrorism. The newly appointed Bush cabinet members were not happy with the thought of testifying, so to stave off the hearings I suggested that the White House announce that the Vice President would chair a task force to examine any organizational changes that might be needed on terrorism and homeland security. Combined with the announcement was a request that the hearings be canceled. They were.[8]

Called before one of the commissions trying to create a superdepartment, I was asked why I opposed the idea. I enumerated four major objections:

- First, for fifty years the National Security Council had been coordinating a host of departments and agencies related to national security. We had never found it necessary or prudent to place them all into one organization. Coordination was preferable.

- Second, the primary missions of the organizations proposed for merger were vastly different from one another and had little to do with counterterrorism or domestic security. FEMA was designed to handle hurricanes. Customs and the Coast Guard had important missions in the area of counternarcotics.

- Third, agencies that did have important domestic counterterrorism roles would still be excluded from the superdepartment. FBI would still be in Justice. The work on biochemical vaccines and related medical issues would still be in the Pentagon and the Health and Human Services (HHS) department. So agencies that had little to do with domestic security would be forced to merge, and those that had important responsibilities regarding it would be left out.

- Fourth, all of this merger activity would divert us from the important substantive work that needed to be done.

Cheney's task force never met; indeed, it never really existed. Admiral Steve Abbott and a few staffers began to study the issue for the Vice President. Cheney was busy with another task force, one on U.S. energy policy. In consultation with oil company CEOs, the Vice President, somewhat secretly, created an energy policy and proposed legislation. Immediately following 9/11, President Bush appointed Tom Ridge to coordinate homeland security issues from the White House. Even after 9/11, the coordination strategy had won out over the box-building organizational imperative, at least for a while.

THE LIEBERMAN ACT

Following Ridge's appointment to the White House and with his enthusiastic support, the White House repeatedly stated its opposition to the idea of creating a new superdepartment to bring together all of the agencies and offices working on homeland security. The Congress had passed the USA PATRIOT Act, which had been quickly cut and pasted together after 9/11, but the members wanted to do more, to be seen addressing the problems highlighted by the attacks. Senator Joseph Lieberman, then a Democrat, had just lost to Cheney in the 2000 election, in which the two men had been their parties' nominees for Vice President. Lieberman wanted to show up the Bush administration by doing more in the wake of 9/11 than the President had done. He pushed his legislation to create the superdepartment. It gained traction in both the House and the Senate, and, because no one wanted to vote against a security bill after 9/11, it also drew support from among Republicans. The White House Office of Legislative Affairs did a head count and determined that the Lieberman bill could pass both houses. If it did, Bush would be placed in the politically untenable position of using his first veto to stop a homeland security law, which would probably be labeled the Lieberman Act by the media. Abruptly, President Bush reversed his position and announced as his own idea a Department of Homeland Security.

While the Congress waited for the administration to present draft legislation, the Lieberman bill continued to kick along. One provision that had been added by the Congress was to create a domestic intelligence function within the new department, to conduct analysis of the terrorism threat within the country. The idea of the homeland security department doing something related to, well, homeland security seemed to make at least as much sense as giving it responsibility for dealing with hurricanes, drug running, and counterfeiting, as the administration was proposing. The CIA Director and FBI Director, however, saw the intelligence function in the new department as a threat to their turf. In a rare joint proposal, they persuaded the President to act before the law was passed and create a new Terrorist Threat Integration Center (TTIC), staffed by both the CIA and the FBI, to do what the Congress thought the new department's intelligence entity might do.[9] Neither the CIA nor the FBI eliminated its own counterterrorism centers, they just added a new one, and they made sure before the Homeland Security Act was even passed that what it required in the way of intelligence analysis would never happen.

By the time the legislation passed, the new department had ripped agencies from Defense, Commerce, Justice, Treasury, Transportation, and the General Services Administration, then added in independent organizations to create a bureaucracy outsized only by the Defense Department. Although he opposed the idea of the new department and did not want to be stuck running it, Ridge was cajoled into being the first Secretary. Nonetheless, he was allowed little role in designing a quick transition to the new department. Pulling it together were the White House Chief of Staff, Andrew Card, who had other pressing responsibilities, and the White House personnel chief, Clay Johnson, who had gone to prep school and college with Bush.

Card and Johnson had four overriding interests. First, they wanted to cut the funds available to the new department from the sum of the combined budgets. Second, they wanted to avoid having career experts play a major role in the new department and instead install as many political appointees as possible. Third, they sought to reduce the role of federal employees' organized labor groups in the component agencies. Finally, they wanted the merger to occur quickly and more or less simultaneously.

As soon as it was obvious that a big new federal department was going to be created, the major Defense Department contractors and systems integrators saw a new opportunity, or perhaps a new prey. The contractors are known as "Beltway bandits," because of their elaborate corporate facilities in the Washington suburbs along the Beltway highway and because of their frequent cost overruns on DOD contracts. Suddenly former government officials working for the big contractors were asking to see me and anyone else they knew at the White House. Their purpose was always the same. They had come to explain that they were now the vice president for homeland security of their company. I asked one such visitor, whom I had known for years, "What the hell do you know about homeland security?" He laughed and admitted, "Nothing, but neither does anyone else." Trickling down from the new federal department, scores of homeland security offices cropped up quickly in the Washington area corporations and then in state and city governments. Universities suddenly had courses and research centers on homeland security, and they were seeking federal grants.

Meanwhile, the leadership of the new department was struggling to get it off the ground. Card and Johnson's insistence on making the new department not just budget-neutral but budget-negative had prevented the creation of new, integrated management systems. In their talking points, homeland security was the major priority of the administration, but in their actions they looked to it as an area in which to reduce spending. The unprecedented level of reliance on people without prior federal government experience created what one department transition team member called "the blind leading the blind in wheel-spinning contests."[10] Nonetheless, the department came into existence not in stages but in a big bang. Before too long, members of Congress and the media realized that it was a big bust.

MISSIONS NEVER ACCOMPLISHED

From the beginning the Bush White House saw homeland security as a political exercise. It had acquiesced in the creation of the huge new department, although it disdained big federal agencies, to avoid a political defeat by Democrats in the Congress. In numerous meetings Card, Johnson, and other senior White House staff expressed their belief that there were so many security vulnerabilities in the United States that they could "spend the entire gross national product" on addressing them. In fact, they didn't intend to spend even as much as the twenty-two component agencies had spent the year before they were merged into the new department.[11] For an administration that touted achieving homeland security as one of its greatest accomplishments, the gap between rhetoric and practice was enormous.

Instead of setting out to secure the nation against terrorism by reducing risks and vulnerabilities at home, their strategy was to deflect specific criticism by pointing to the new offices that they had created to address the vulnerabilities, programs that they had started, studies that were under way. Indeed, the White House and the management of the new department had no goals or end state that they were trying to achieve by a certain time. The result was a lot of program starts without program completions, studies without implementation—in short, half measures and continuing vulnerabilities.

Perhaps the best two illustrations of this "not results-oriented" focus are aviation security and weapons of mass destruction protection.

EVEN AIRCRAFT ARE STILL NOT SECURE

It was the inadequacy of aviation security that allowed the 9/11 hijackers to stage the attacks that, in the end, resulted in the new Department of Homeland Security. Nonetheless, creating a highly secure airline system was not a goal. Even now, in 2008, we have not reduced well-known vulnerabilities in our commercial aviation system. Think about what happens when you go to the airport.

First, you stand in a long line to go through a passenger screening process. At some point someone asks for your driver's license or passport. This person was until 2008 a minimum-wage employee hired by the airline or airport who would not have known if you had made the license on your home printer. There are ways of verifying the authenticity of driver's licenses, but they did not use them. This step of requiring a photo identification, which caused many to mislay their license, is largely useless. A Registered Traveler program has been planned for several years. Under that program, frequent flyers could pay for a biometric smart card and volunteer information about themselves for a background check. These prescreened passengers could then go through a smart card turnstile, allowing the security personnel to concentrate on others. With the exception of a handful of experimental installations, the long-discussed Registered Traveler program had not taken off for years.[12]

Second, you are asked to walk through a magnetometer that detects metal. At only a handful of checkpoints around the country are you also asked to walk through an explosives trace machine, which blows air on you, recovers it, and analyzes the particles for indications that you have been handling bomb-making material. Moreover, if you know you have been near such material, it is usually easy enough to select a security line that does not have the so-called puffer machine. Despite the ineffectiveness of these current methods, DHS's efforts to develop new noninvasive body imaging scanners have been slow and paltry. DHS called the development program the "Manhattan II Project" because it was aimed at getting "revolutionary" new technologies deployed on a crash basis. Yet the program spent only $6 million in its first two years (as compared to 1 percent of U.S. GDP for the real

Manhattan Project) and has failed to deploy any new technologies beyond a handful of product demonstrations. In 2003, the research and development budget of the Transportation Security Administration (TSA) was cut by half to meet other priorities.[13]

Third, while you are arguing with a screener about how much toothpaste you can take on the aircraft, your checked bags are being examined for explosives by a system thrown together as a temporary placeholder after 9/11. The TSA quickly installed 1,600 explosives detection systems (EDSs) at the four hundred airports around the country. Most of these were temporarily placed in the lobbies of airports. Where space was constrained and there was no room for the EDS, the TSA used 7,200 explosives trace detection systems, a less reliable method of detecting explosives. The DHS plan was to achieve better operational security, faster and more accurate screening, and reduce personnel requirements by placing new EDS systems "in line" with the conveyor belts that make up airport baggage-handling systems. Moving these systems out of the lobbies and building them into the airport infrastructure would save taxpayers money ($1.3 billion over seven years, according to a 2005 estimate) while providing better service and security. Yet, under current TSA plans, "optimal baggage-screening systems" will not be in place until 2024, more than two decades after 9/11.[14]

Fourth, as you pad shoeless across the tiles, airport workers are loading your plane with cargo. Chances were no one has looked at what is in most of the cargo. The Homeland Security Department actually resisted efforts to have cargo screened, offering instead a Known Shipper Program. Under that program, big cargo consolidators would pledge that they would accept cargo only from reliable sources. They, not the government, would screen anything suspicious.[15] Finally, in 2007, Congress required that cargo be 100 percent screened. Unfortunately, TSA's answer was a voluntary program relying on shipping companies.[16] (The same thing took place with seaborne shipping containers. The department resisted 100 percent screening and offered a half measure involving known shippers. Congress in 2007 mandated full inspection of shipping containers, which has not yet been implemented.)

Fifth, as the aircraft is finally lifting off from the airport, there might be someone in a parking lot a mile away who is taking a small tube out of his car and placing it on his shoulder. He could aim the tube at your aircraft and launch a missile that would seek the aircraft and explode on contact with it. Far-fetched? President Bush's second homeland security advisor, General John Gordon (USAF), didn't think it was an unrealistic threat. Gordon, a lanky nuclear physics expert with thick glasses, is one of the few men not a pilot who have made it to four-star general rank in the Air Force. He had served on the NSC staff under Bush 41, been the number two person at the CIA, and the founding director of the National Nuclear Security Agency. Soft-spoken and understated, Gordon was adamant about doing something to address "the Stinger threat." He asked that a program be developed to protect aircraft because at least thirty-five civilian aircraft have been attacked using MANPADS (man-portable air defense systems such as the Stinger missile, which can be carried and fired by a single individual). There are an estimated half million such missiles, some of which have sold on the black market for as little as $5,000.[17] To demonstrate how small and easily handled they are, I once carried one into the office of Secretary of State Lawrence Eagleburger (Larry wanted to keep it, saying there were some people whose aircraft he wanted to shoot down). In response to Gordon, the Homeland department created yet another new office, which then made grants to aerospace companies to study the problem. Companies concluded that placing a protective device on each large passenger aircraft in the United States was feasible and could be done for roughly $1 million per aircraft. Despite estimates that a shoot-down would cost the U.S. economy upward of half a trillion dollars,[18] the billion dollar price tag for the first thousand aircraft was too much.[19] So no U.S. passenger aircraft have the device, except some government ones, such as Air Force One.

Sixth, as your flight moves over the United States, at some point the pilot will likely need to visit the toilet. When he does, a flight attendant will be stationed to block anyone from trying to rush the open cockpit door. A few flight attendants have volunteered for courses in unarmed combat, but most are unlikely to be able to resist a hijacker who had been selected and trained to overcome the crew. The pilots' association has requested that a strong door be mounted on larger aircraft in the first-class cabin, to shut off the forward toilet and the area around it when the cockpit door is opened. The pilots' request for this protection has fallen on deaf ears.[20]

Is U.S. commercial aviation safer today than it was on 9/11? Yes, it is, much safer. The use of trained government employees to do the screening of passengers and carry-on and the creation of a dedicated organization (the Transportation Security Administration) for that purpose have made air travel significantly safer. But we know that there are still important vulnerabilities and that terrorists know that too, and we also know how to plug the remaining holes. Instead of doing so, the Homeland department and White House staff have refused to set a standard for aviation security or to develop a timeline for achieving that standard. Indeed, they have developed plans to reduce the TSA and have tried to give screening at some airports back to private companies.[21]

WMDs IN AMERICA?

Given both the rhetoric of the administration and the objective threat, one might also have assumed that protecting the homeland from terrorists with weapons of mass destruction would have been high on the list of things to do after 9/11. Unfortunately, it suffered a similar fate as aviation security.

Shortly after 9/11, anthrax attacks occurred in New York and Washington, D.C., using letter packages sent to U.S. senators and leading journalists. Panic ensued in both cities and in the U.S. mail system. Thousands of people throughout the country reported finding suspicious "white powder," which almost always turned out to be Cremora or sugar. Nonetheless, evacuations and disruptions were widespread. I remember the look of frustration on President Bush's face as we met in the Oval Office to design a response to the anthrax scare. The solution, he was told, would take a while. We needed vaccines and broad-spectrum antibiotics that could effectively counter likely bioweapons.

With much publicity and the personal involvement of Vice President Cheney, Project BioShield was started to develop new vaccines and treatments for diseases that could be used as bioweapons, including anthrax, botulism, the Ebola virus, and smallpox.[22] The program has generated few new medicines. The new anthrax vaccine, originally the highest priority of the program, has not gotten out of the lab. A single vendor, VaxGen, which had never produced an FDA-approved drug, was selected to make the new vaccine in November 2004. Two years later, the Department of Health and Human Services terminated the contract for failure to meet key milestones.[23] Another Project BioShield effort, a treatment program for radiological and nuclear incidents, was canceled in March 2007 for failing to yield results.[24] Michael Greenberger, the director of the University of Maryland's Center for Health and Homeland Security, explained that "the inept implementation of the program has led the best brains and the best scientists to give up, to look elsewhere or devote their resources to medical initiatives that are not focused on biodefense."[25] (The FBI was unable to prove what individual or group had conducted the anthrax attacks. Although it leaked information to the press indicating that it suspected a former biodefense researcher, they never had enough proof even to indict him.[26])

If somebody started mailing anthrax around the country again in 2008 and President Bush again summoned his senior staff into the Oval Office to discuss a response, he would find, just as he did in 2001, that there is no new vaccine and no new medication to deal with the issue.

Unfortunately, progress has been equally limited in the most frightening terrorist scenario, one involving nuclear material. Before reviewing what the government has and has not done, it's helpful to recall what the nuclear terrorism problem is. It involves two kinds of possible terrorist attacks. The most damaging scenario would be if a terrorist group obtained a nuclear weapon or weapons-grade nuclear material made by a nation-state, through either theft or the involvement of a nuclear weapons–possessing country. The second possibility is that terrorists will mix nuclear or radiological material into a conventional explosion, creating a so-called dirty bomb. The significance of such a radiological dispersal device (RDD) would depend upon what specific radiological material was used and how much of it there was. Depending upon the input, the result could range from a largely propaganda and psychological effect to something resembling the long-term effects of a nuclear weapon.

Consider the first possibility, a nuclear weapon. During the Cold War, when I was studying nuclear weapons at MIT, we were given a non-electronic calculator to determine the effects of a nuclear weapon blast. It was a series of circles on top of one another like a round slide ruler. By spinning them to adjust the variables, you could learn how big a hole would be created and how many people would die. It seemed to be a useful skill during the Cold War. All we need to know now is that if a nuclear weapon were to go off in any American city, the casualties would make 9/11 look small. Depending upon the size of the weapon, an area from several square blocks to several square miles could be incinerated. In the ring around the blast, "the living would envy the dead." Horrific burns and blindness would be combined with high levels of radioactive poisoning. Fires would be raging. First responders would not just be overwhelmed, they would be crippled. The electromagnetic pulse set off by the weapon would fry the circuitry of radios and vehicles for miles beyond the blast area. Fire trucks and ambulances would be immobilized and their ability to communicate destroyed. When a rescue and recovery could eventually get under way, the first task would be to determining a "no-go zone" inside which the radiation levels were too high for rescuers to enter. Next would come triage, i.e., deciding which of the dying outside the "no-go zone" would have to be left to die. A cloud would be carried by the wind, dropping highly radioactive material on surrounding areas. For several miles the material dropped would pose the risk of radioactive poisoning at potentially lethal levels, so-called "nonprompt deaths" from cancer. We came face-to-face with these awful facts in several exercises I ran from the White House in the late 1990s.

If the weapon went off in almost any large American city, it could eliminate national assets that would be difficult and time-consuming to replace. The government in Washington and the financial and market centers of New York and Chicago are the obvious examples, but many cities provide unique functions to the national economy. The effect on the American economy, both direct and psychological, would be profound. Nuclear weapon forensics might identify the origin of the weapon, probably producing political pressure to respond in kind to the nation whose sloppy security or complicity made the attack possible.

A radiological dispersal device would be less destructive, but could have significant effects depending upon the material involved. Medical waste from X-ray or cancer treatment machines would register as radioactive and cause a panic, but would pose only a limited health problem. Enriched material such as the waste from a nuclear power plant could cause high levels of non-prompt fatalities. A trailer truck filled with conventional explosives of the type used in the Oklahoma City attack and involving containers of nuclear waste could create an explosion so large and radioactive that it might initially look as if a nuclear weapon had gone off. There would be no electromagnetic pulse effect, but the "no-go" hot zone problem could occur.

The perhaps 50,000 nuclear weapons in the world are well guarded and accounted for. A cooperative program with Russia sponsored by Senators Richard Lugar and Sam Nunn helped to account for, lock down, or destroy many of the weapons of the former Soviet Union after the Cold War. Yet even in the U.S. nuclear weapons program, mistakes are made. In the summer of 2007, for instance, several nuclear weapons were, without permission or authority, removed from storage at a U.S. Air Force base in North Dakota. They were mistaken for inert "dummy" weapons and flown to Louisiana. It took many hours before they were discovered to be missing, and then the discovery was made by the Air Force staff in Louisiana, not the staff missing the weapons in North Dakota.[27] This incident rekindled the fear that in one of the nuclear weapons countries, some unit's commanding officer might intentionally doctor paperwork, allowing 0.01 percent of the world's nuclear weapons stockpile to go missing. That could be as many as five bombs.

In addition to the weapons of the first six nuclear weapons states, there are the less well known stockpiles of India, Pakistan, and North Korea. And there is reason for concern about a possible nuclear weapons program in Iran. While the first six states are highly unlikely to ever intentionally allow one of their nuclear weapons to get into the hands of terrorists, we have less reason to be sure about Pakistan, North

Korea, and Iran. Pakistan has already allowed its nuclear weapons laboratory to export both the know-how and the parts necessary to make a weapon (the government denies it knew about the activity and claims it was just the rogue lab director).[28] North Korea has already propped up its economy by selling counterfeit U.S. dollars, heroin, and SCUD missiles.[29] And Iran, which has talked openly about eliminating Israel, has very close ties to the Hezbollah terrorist group on Israel's border.

If the possibility of a nuclear weapon being smuggled into a U.S. city is less than zero, the chances of a radiological dispersal device going off are considerably higher. Small amounts of radiological material are in use with little security or accounting at universities, hospitals, and major construction sites. Large amounts of highly radioactive material are stored under guard at nuclear reactors, but the material is usually in used fuel rods and could not really be stolen (although there is the risk of an explosion in the storage area dispersing material). Unfortunately, powdered material from processed fuel rods is stacked by the ton in several countries, often without adequate accounting or security. One of my colleagues at Harvard's Kennedy School of Government, Graham Allison, has waged a campaign to address the security of this material, as has a private group called the Nuclear Threat Initiative, led by former senator Sam Nunn. These considerations are well-known to al Qaeda and other terrorists. We have known for some time that al Qaeda has been seeking to acquire a nuclear weapon or radiological material.[30] Al Qaeda has been the victim of scams, but so far no one seems to have sold it a bomb or the makings of an RDD. Yet.

The United States' effort to deal with this threat has largely focused on catching a nuclear or radiological weapon already in the hands of terrorists. To address this problem, Homeland Security created another office, this one known as the Domestic Nuclear Detection Office (DNDO), which is planning to spend more than a billion dollars installing new "nuke detectors" at entrances to the United States and on key roads and bridges. Unfortunately, the experiments conducted thus far show that it is very common to get false positives (bananas and kitchen countertops look a lot like nuclear material to the detectors) and false negatives (nuclear material can be shielded to fool the detectors). The Government Accountability Office (GAO) and congressional committees have argued with Homeland Security about the accuracy and utility of the detectors selected by the Detection Office. The GAO videotaped its own staff walking across the Canadian border carrying material with radioactive signatures, undetected.[31]

Moreover, no one is really sure what to do if a detector establishes that a nuclear weapon has just passed over a bridge going into a major city. In the weeks after 9/11, a suspicious freighter was stopped on the high seas and inspected by the U.S. Coast Guard. A nuclear detector system indicated that there might be a radiation source on board. In the absence of any procedure at that point, an amazing thing happened: the ship was directed to a Manhattan pier for further inspection. When the NSC staff learned that the suspect ship was tied up near Wall Street, the ship was moved outside New York City and an inspection determined the alarm was a false positive. (The Coast Guard now keeps suspect ships away from target areas.) Who is going to evacuate a city based on an alarm from systems that are frequently wrong?

A nuclear/radiological weapon in the hands of a terrorist is admittedly the hardest of the homeland security problems to solve. It is the classic case of low probability and high impact. Usually such low/high cases get few resources. Yet in this case the probability is high enough and the impact would be so very significant that something must be done. Trying to detect weapons with existing technology should be part of the solution, but only a small part. Funds for detection should be largely dedicated to creating better technologies. Most of our effort, however, should be focused on securing and eliminating existing sources of highly radioactive material worldwide. We should be engaged in a Herculean effort.

In the United States, that would mean shutting down some unnecessary nuclear research reactors at universities, better securing radiological material at medical centers and construction projects, and screening who has access. It would also mean improving security at U.S. reactors, where nuclear waste is stored. The Nuclear Regulatory Commission (NRC) has a record of limiting the security obligations of the power plant companies to limit costs to the power companies. NRC has ruled out certain attack scenarios in what it calls the Design Basis Threat, the types of presumed attacks that the power companies' security guards need to be able to counter or the design of the facilities needs to be able to prevent.

The greatest threat from enriched nuclear material is, however, overseas, where hundreds of tons are inadequately secured. We are slowly making progress in securing such material in Russia, but elsewhere there are few security upgrades going on. Most nations reject the idea of a U.S. security audit. A U.S. President should make this the focus of a major global initiative involving the United Nations and its International Atomic Energy Agency (IAEA). We should be willing to fund much of the effort to put international guards and advanced security systems on these stockpiles as a stopgap and then proceed to destroy them in an international crash program. Such a program would be expensive and we may have to pay more than our fair share, but we are the most likely target of an RDD made from this highly radioactive material and the cost of securing it would be a small fraction of the cost to us of a successful RDD.

A TENDENCY TO GET INCOMPLETES

In addition to failing at the obvious homeland security goals of securing transportation after the 9/11 attacks and addressing the highest risks posed by weapons of mass destruction, the new department seemed unable to complete almost any major program. Despite creating new offices and coming up with names for projects, the department's ability to manage major contracts to successful conclusion seems almost nonexistent. Some examples:

- *Rail security:* Subways or similar commuter rail systems have been struck by terrorists in Moscow, Paris, London, Tokyo, Mumbai, Madrid, and elsewhere. Despite that warning, efforts to improve security on Amtrak, subways, and commuter rail systems have been limited. Well after aviation security had gotten to the point that I could not carry a nail file onto a plane, I was shocked to find that I could carry my gun onto

Amtrak's Acela Express high-speed train with no one noticing (I had, at the time, the status of a Special Deputy U.S. Marshal so that I was authorized to carry a gun across state lines). The TSA and its parent department have not established a clear goal of what kind of security upgrades the nation should install on its rails, what trains would be covered, or when a given level of protection would be achieved. What they did establish was that they did not want to spend much money on it. When asked to explain why the department spent one penny on rail security for every nine dollars it spent on aviation security, the second person to head the department, Secretary Michael Chertoff, explained, "The truth of the matter is, a fully loaded airplane with jet fuel, a commercial airliner, has the capacity to kill 3,000 people. A bomb in a subway car may kill [only] thirty people."[32] Of course, if thirty people or so *were* killed in the New York, Boston, or Philadelphia subway, tens of millions of Americans would stay off commuter rail systems and the economy would be damaged. After thirty people or so are killed by a bomb on a U.S. train, we can be sure that there will then be an extensive and expensive rail security program.

- *Project Safecom,* to provide emergency responders with secure, interoperable communications, did not start to fund procurements until seven years after 9/11, but funds are still lacking to support many major metropolitan areas.[33] The director of the program, David Boyd, actually had the audacity to tell Congress that under DHS plans, first responders will not have a national interoperable system until 2023, more than two decades after firefighters lost their lives in the World Trade Center because of poor communications systems.[34]

- *Project U.S.-VISIT* was designed to use a biometrics system to track when foreign nationals enter and depart the United States, as required by law. However, the contractor, Accenture, created a system that tracks only their arrivals, thus making it impossible to known when someone has illegally overstayed.[35]

- *Project SBInet* is supposed to create a "virtual fence" along the six thousand miles of U.S. land borders, but the contractor, Boeing, experienced "software integration problems" and fell behind schedule on the more modest goal of monitoring twenty-eight miles in Arizona.[36]

- *Project Deepwater* is meant to replace the Coast Guard's decrepit fleet of cutters and aircraft, most of which are facing block obsolescence and lack all but the most basic sensors. The first "new cutters" delivered were actually old cutters extended in length, which made the ships so unseaworthy that they had to be abandoned. The first new-construction cutter employed a composite material rather than structural steel, apparently because the lead contractor, Northrop Grumman, had composite materials factory standing idle. Maritime architects believe the ship will have to be restricted in its activities and the cutter design altered for future ships.[37]

On the sixth anniversary of the 9/11 attacks, the independent GAO found that the largest department merger in recent history had failed. It concluded that only 78 of 171 objectives set by Congress and the President had been met even though the new department had spent over $241 billion. Five of 24 criteria for emergency preparedness had been met, but it had failed to implement a national response plan or develop a program to improve emergency radio communications. One of six science and technology goals, such as developing research and development plans and assessing emerging threats, had been met. Two of 15 computer integration targets had been met. Thirteen of 50 transportation security goals set after 9/11 were still unmet six years on.[38] The department's own reporting on its management was equally scathing as recently as January 2008.[39]

The problem was not just with the new department, but with the various federal regulatory authorities. Just as Homeland Security had avoided strong regulations on container shipping and the NRC had rejected higher security standards proposals for nuclear power plants, securing chemical plants and train cars with highly toxic chemicals and gas had been delayed years and watered down, so as not to cause the chemical companies and railroads additional expense. Imposition of serious security standards on electric power companies had been delayed by the Federal Energy Regulatory Commission and security requirements for internet service providers had been dodged by the Federal Communications Commission. The regulators had preferred to suggest more modest and voluntary security standards on the industries they can regulate. In sum, Homeland Security measures in the wake of 9/11 seemed to be characterized by creating a program to address an issue, not solving problems or truly reducing vulnerabilities.

OF PORK AND POLITICS

The job of reducing vulnerabilities and mitigating the effects of disasters that do occur is not just a matter of federal agencies. As implied by the slightly Orwellian name "Homeland," the task of domestic security involves local and state governments. All too often, however, the implementation of homeland security has degenerated into unfocused, often dubious spending at the state and local level. The local agencies that could write up the complicated grant proposals best were often rewarded with federal funds, rather than funds going to some predetermined set of national goals. Thus, there have occurred infamous examples of Federal pork such as air-conditioned garbage trucks and bullet-proof vests for police dogs. Congressmen, sniffing bacon, sought funds for "homeland security centers" at local colleges or gimmicky mobile interagency command posts to coordinate field personnel who still lacked basic equipment and training.

The politics of homeland security has also involved federal officials using the domestic terrorism threat to advance their own political purposes and erode civil liberties. Moreover, security issues have been confusingly intertwined with natural disaster responses, to the detriment of both capabilities.

THE CLOSEST GOVERNMENTS

State and local governments have a major role in achieving domestic security and response capability, but they have not been orchestrated in a way that allows them to achieve their maximum contribution. Those governments can help inventory some of the vulnerabilities and monitor the mitigation of those risks. They can use local law enforcement agencies to detect unusual activity and reach out to ethnic groups and other communities. If a disaster occurs, it is state and local governments that will provide most of the response capability.

A systematic approach would have begun with a national consensus among experts about the programs and goals that should be achieved in various sizes of metropolitan areas. Plans for the 150 largest metropolitan areas would cover 70 percent of Americans.[40] We could then calculate how much that effort would cost and agree on how many years we could afford to wait to achieve each of those goals. Then funds could be appropriated to accomplish the agreed-upon goals by the specified times. What would that look like? At a high level of aggregation, here is an example of what each Metropolitan Area Security Plan should include:

TRANSPORTATION

- Installing intelligent video security systems at all rail and subway stations in three years

- Conducting security awareness campaigns and upgrading public address systems on public transportation systems within one year

- Initiating random security checks on rail and subway systems within one year

- Achieving a standard level of uniformed, K-9, and plainclothes police officers at rail and subway stations within one year

- Upgrading communications and rescue capability for rail and subway systems, including tunnels, to a standard level within three years

- Establishing an operational evacuation system for cities and neighborhoods within two years

LAW ENFORCEMENT

- Creating and training a local police counterterrorism unit with community outreach and civilian oversight within one year; adding needed officers to the force

- Developing local law enforcement intelligence capabilities to bring community policing activities and national counterterrorism efforts together

- Creating a secure communications system within two years

FIRST RESPONDERS

- Creating a reliable, interoperable metropolitan communications system, including state and federal agencies, within three years

- Achieving an agreed-upon level of training and equipping for first responder capability to deal with chemical, biological, and radiological incidents within three years

- Achieving a standard level of heavy rescue capability within two years

MEDICAL

- Achieving a surge ability to perform a given level of emergency medical treatment, including for mass trauma, burns, and WMD-related incidents, within three years

- For a given ratio to the population, developing the capability to add and staff additional patient beds in the event of a mass-casualty or pandemic event within three years

RISK REDUCTION

- Identifying and mitigating vulnerabilities at chemical plants, chemical railcar sidings, radiological material facilities, tunnels, bridges, arenas, and stadiums to national levels within three years

OTHER

- Creating and testing local government crisis management and incident response systems to a national standard within one year

- Establishing intelligent video security systems for key neighborhoods and infrastructures, with appropriate civil liberties and privacy safeguards within two years

- Establishing effective public communications systems (including public address, reverse 911, e-mail) within two years

- Conducting training exercises to a national standard within two years

This concept looks at each metropolitan area holistically, determining what the area needs. The federal government, working together with metropolitan area councils and the states, could then decide what county, city, or town agency would be assigned the capability on behalf of the entire region. Experts could add to or subtract from such a list of national goals. We could determine how much it would cost to carry out the entire effort nationwide in three years or five. If it were too expensive given other priorities, some items could be stretched out. We could decide that some metropolitan areas would be given priority. If some metropolitan areas had unique requirements, they could have substituted programs. In short, we could determine what was needed to achieve a given level of enhanced domestic security nationwide, how much we were willing to pay for it, and how long we wanted to take. Then we could set out to achieve it. Instead, Congress and the Homeland Security Department together have simply given funds to the states (which gave some of the money to the cities and counties) with the broadest and vaguest of guidelines. More than $20 billion has been granted through these programs through 2007, and it has been doled out using an unusual formula so that every state gets a good amount of money, despite the low population densities in many states.[41]

The result is that seven years after 9/11 no metropolitan area has all of the capabilities listed above, and most have few. Some scattershot progress has been made, but there has also been waste. Things that should have been low on priority lists or not there at all have been procured all across the country. Many police and fire departments have large new mobile command centers, sort of big bookmobile-style trucks with satellite dishes. At any multijurisdictional incident these behemoths cluster together and provide a convenient backdrop for local television live shots. States now have Intelligence Fusion Centers that look a lot like the War Room in Cheyenne Mountain, with lots of big screens and computer monitors and televisions tuned to the FOX News channel. Most of these centers are given precious little intelligence information to fuse, and, when they do have information, they duplicate the work of the Joint Terrorism Task Forces, chaired by the local FBI.[42] In short, with new pork-barrel spending available, it has been a happy time: for congressmen, who proudly announce the grants they wrestle out of Washington; for vendors, who have seen their sales soar; for police and fire departments, which get to show off their new trucks and gear. Yet there is still no plan that will get us to a specific level of improved domestic security by a certain date. Most metropolitan areas are still riddled with vulnerabilities a terrorist could use to cause mass casualties, and most could still not deal adequately with such an event.

POLITICAL USES OF THE TERRORIST THREAT

We should hardly be surprised that the new Department of Homeland Security has become a major dispenser of pork. Who can really object to something called "homeland security" spending? Do you want the terrorists to succeed? Moreover, the newly created department has been salted with more political appointees per capita than any other department in the federal government. Some excuse this as a necessity, since they claim there was little expertise on this new issue available in the government. There were, however, several generally well run agencies swept up into the new department that were staffed by career federal workers with considerable skills and experience. For example, both the Coast Guard and the Secret Service, two of the most effective government agencies, were assigned to the new department. Their management staffers, all with decades of experience, could have made the new department work. Instead, the White House saw the new department as a way to reward all those campaign workers who still did not have that brief government job they wanted for their résumés.

Staffing the department and dispensing its funds politically was in keeping with the attitude of White House officials toward the entire issue of terrorism and homeland security. It was an opportunity to reap political benefits. Beginning in the 2002 congressional election and notably in the 2004 presidential election, a message crafted by White House strategist Karl Rove was played out across the country: run on terrorism as the issue, claim Democrats are soft on terrorism, use it in fund raising, remind people of the threat.

According to Rove, "Liberals saw the savagery of the 9/11 attacks and wanted to prepare indictments and offer therapy and understanding for our attackers."[43] Conservatives "saw the savagery of 9/11 and the attacks and prepared for war."[44] Rove claimed that groups linked to the Democratic Party had made the mistake of calling for "moderation and restraint" after the terrorist attacks. White House Press Secretary Scott McClellan claimed, "Democrats have a pre-9/11 view of the world."[45] Republican Party Chairman Kenneth Mehlman accused Democrats of wanting to weaken antiterrorism laws.[46]

Vice President Cheney claimed in 2004, "It's absolutely essential

that eight weeks from today, on Nov. 2, we make the right choice, because if we make the wrong choice then the danger is that we'll get hit
again and we'll be hit in a way that will be devastating from the stand-
point of the United States."[47] In 2006 he asserted that a Democrat's
victory in a Senate race might encourage "the al-Qaida types" who
want to "break the will of the American people in terms of our ability
to stay in the fight and complete the task." He claimed that Democrats
want to "retreat behind our oceans and not be actively engaged in this
conflict."[48]

In the days before the 2006 election, President Bush described the
Democratic approach as "The terrorists win and America loses."[49] The
theme continued into the 2008 presidential campaign, with Rudy
Giuliani saying, "The Democrats do not understand the full nature
and scope of the terrorist war against us" and claiming that if the Democrats are elected there would be another 9/11.[50]

Not content to wave the bloody shirt in campaign rhetoric, the Attorney General and White House staff repeatedly pushed for the national alert level to be raised. Television news and daily papers ran
boxes showing the alert color level rising from dangerous yellow to
threatening orange. After leaving office, Homeland Secretary Tom
Ridge admitted that he had disagreed with those announcements. He
had been outvoted in White House meetings and then forced to put
his own personal credibility behind the warnings. On one occasion,
however, a threat alert had been issued by Attorney General John
Ashcroft and FBI Director Robert Mueller without consulting with
Ridge. "More often than not we were the least inclined to raise it. . . .
Sometimes we disagreed with the intelligence assessment. Sometimes
we thought even if the intelligence was good, you don't necessarily put
the country on (alert). . . . There were times when some people were
really aggressive about raising it, and we said, 'For that?'"[51] The day
after John Kerry's 2004 nomination acceptance speech, the threat level
was raised to orange for New York and Washington, D.C., because of
al Qaeda surveillance of financial institutions. Later it became clear
that the surveillance had taken place three years earlier. Intelligence
community officials reportedly complained to the press that some information behind a threat announcement had come from a source who

was lying.[52] Even with that knowledge, the alert stayed at orange for more than three months, until eight days after the election was over.[53]

After a while the color codes and Cassandra-like threats grew old. Late-night television comedians ridiculed the color codes and the Department of Homeland Security's campaign to have all Americans build an emergency kit including rolls of duct tape. Eventually, the use of color-coded alerts was restricted, but the damage was done. Many Americans thought threats of terrorism in the United States were something used to scare them to vote a certain way. The image of the new department was tainted, and the credibility of the government was again damaged.

FIXING FAILURE

The merger that formed the department created in 2003, at one stroke, the second-largest department in the federal government. By 2007 it had more than 200,000 employees and a budget of $44 billion a year. Riddled with inexperienced political appointees and private sector contractors doing jobs typically performed by career staff, the department ranked thirty-sixth out of thirty-six federal agencies in a survey done by the White House Office of Management and Budget on a "results-oriented performance culture index." Had there been a poll of public trust in federal agencies, it might have been rated similarly following the Katrina response nightmare and the widely perceived politicization of the department's color-coded terror alerts.

There are, serving in the new department, thousands of Coast Guard and Secret Service personnel who are career employees of two of the best organizations in the federal government. Many of the other component agencies also have talented and dedicated staff, but they have been placed in an organization that was misconceived, designed to satisfy a political concern, and not crafted by federal organizational or management experts. One of the few things that went right for the embattled employees of the department was that the President withdrew the nomination of Bernard Kerik to be its Secretary after a week's public scrutiny revealed ethical and legal questions about the man suggested by Rudy Giuliani.

So we are faced with a situation in which many people believe that the government has overstated the terrorist threat for political purposes and perhaps because of the tendency of some to create a Big Brother–like, all-knowing security state. Yet there is still a violent extremist Islamist threat, and according to senior U.S. intelligence officials, that threat still targets the United States and is capable of carrying out attacks here. We have created a megadepartment to reduce our vulnerabilities, but the merger of twenty-two organizations simultaneously has not gone well. We still have many vulnerabilities to terrorist attacks. In its rush to show strength, the government has unnecessarily infringed on human rights abroad and civil liberties at home and thereby reduced our support abroad and undercut unity at home. What do we do now?

We need to start again. We need to try to put the real threat in perspective. We must admit, as New York Mayor Michael Bloomberg did after a plot to attack a fuel tank at Kennedy Airport had been over-hyped, that in the United States you stand a greater chance, based on previous data, of being hit by lightning than by terrorists.[54] But we must also understand that there are people trying to do us harm and we have a lot of vulnerabilities that they could use to do so. Therefore, we need clear goals about reducing those vulnerabilities and countering the threats. And we need to organize our government to be efficient and effective in support of these efforts, while resisting the temptation to politicize the issues and agencies.

As discussed in chapter 5, "Terrorism," we need to dry up support for the violent Islamist extremists working with other governments, while capturing and killing terrorists. We should create a serious, well-funded international effort to secure radioactive material worldwide in order to address the worst possible terrorist threat. In the United States, we should undo the bureaucratic mess made by creating the Department of Homeland Security and the numerous terrorism-related centers scattered around Washington, D.C. Here is how I would do that.

FORM FOLLOWS FUNCTION

In the private sector, three-quarters of megamergers in the United States fail.[55] When they do succeed, eventually market forces often dictate a breakup. Chrysler's being broken back off from Daimler is the latest example. Unfortunately, there are no market forces in government. So someone has to say "This isn't working" and propose a fix. As much as I think bureaucratic reorganizations are usually a mistake, when mistakes have been made through reorganization, you are sometimes right to reorganize to undo the mistake. The simplest approach here is not to try to place everything related to terrorism or "homeland security" into one department. The 2003 reorganization had that as a goal, but it created a department too big for anyone to manage, and even then it failed to bring in key components related to terrorism and homeland security in the FBI, the Justice Department, the Department of Health and Human Services, and other agencies. It was a bad idea. Having the person who worries about hurricane response also worry about people slipping across our border never made sense. The organizing principle should be consolidating around the functions the agencies perform.

The next President should split the department into three entities organized by the functions they are meant to perform:

- Screening and security for things and people on the move

- Mitigating and responding to emergencies

- Intelligence about security threats in the United States (mainly of foreign origin)

All three resulting agencies should be nonpartisan. People who have held elective offices or senior positions in political parties in the past five years should be ineligible for appointment or hiring. The number of noncareer "political appointee" positions should be limited to a percentage less than the average in other agencies. Hiring rules should be adapted to make it easy for nonpartisan experts to serve in noncareer positions for a few years. The three functional agencies would be organized along these lines:

- First, screening and security for people and things in motion is what the Coast Guard, Immigration and Customs Enforcement (ICE), the Border agency, and Transportation Security do. They are all uniformed federal officers preventing people or contraband from going where they are prohibited. Putting them all in one department together would give the cabinet member who ran them all a single focus. There could be economies of scale and joint activities. It would also be a large department, about 140,000 employees, but it would not have the size or diversity of Homeland. We could call it the Department of Border and Transportation Security, BTS.

- Second, mitigating and responding to emergencies is essentially the mission of the Federal Emergency Management Agency (FEMA). It worked well when it was an independent federal agency in the 1990s and it should be separate again. After Katrina, Congress tried a half-baked compromise that left FEMA in the Homeland Security Department but gave its leader some sort of direct-report status to the President. That sort of indecision just fuzzes up and complicates the problem. FEMA should be made fully independent and given the grant programs to build response capability and mitigate risks. FEMA has long had a close relationship with state and local emergency and first responder agencies, and under the nonpartisan leadership of James Lee Witt in the 1990s, it worked well. Planning for the transition should start after the end of the next hurricane season, with the new structure going into effect either before the start of or after the end of the following season.

- Third, intelligence about security threats in the United States is something that the person in charge of intelligence should run. Congress wisely created a Director of National Intelligence (DNI) and made most of the intelligence agencies report to that office: the CIA, NSA, NRO, NGIA, etc., and the National Counterterrorism Center (NCTC). I talked in chapter 4 about how to strengthen the DNI's control over those agencies by transferring some of them out of the Pentagon. Another thing that needs to be done with the DNI is to clear up the relationship with the FBI. The current plan is that the FBI sort of reports to the DNI on some issues but really to the Attorney General, who runs the Justice Department. Clearing up this ambiguity and the role of domestic intelligence in the United States is important because we need to have clear responsibility and accountability, not confusion about who is doing what. Thus, I would transfer the National Security Division of the FBI out and have it report to the Director of National Intelligence.

The idea of moving national security out of the FBI has been kicking around Washington for most of this decade, usually called "the MI5" proposal by advocates such as Judge Richard Posner. MI5 was the World War II name of a British domestic security organization that is now called the British Security Service (BSS). The BSS is like similar organizations in Canada, Australia, Germany, and several other successful democracies that are not anything like police states. These agencies do not generally have police powers and are not staffed by policemen. They are investigative agencies that think about and look for signs of security problems at home. They look for spies and terrorists, and when they find them, they call the cops.

In the United States, we have given this job to the cops, the federal all-purpose criminal police agency, the FBI. Along with bank robberies, corporate fraud, illegal drugs, civil rights violations, organized crime, and a host of other criminal activities, FBI agents are supposed to understand Islamist threats and Chinese industrial espionage. Few objective people familiar with the FBI's performance think they do a good job on Islamist threats or Chinese espionage. For example, *The Washington Post* reported in 2006 that "five years after Arab terrorists attacked the United States, only 33 FBI agents have even a limited proficiency in Arabic, and none of them work in the sections of the bureau that coordinate investigations of international terrorism, according to new FBI statistics. Counting agents who know only a handful of Arabic words—including those who scored zero on a standard proficiency test—just 1 percent of the FBI's 12,000 agents have any familiarity with the language."[56]

I originally opposed ripping this part of the FBI out and giving the task to a new agency on my usual grounds that reorganizations are too disruptive. I was also concerned that the FBI would actively try to undermine any new agency that it perceived as having "stolen" its turf. I suggested instead that the national security functions be strengthened and given a separate status with the FBI. The Silberman-Robb Commission on intelligence made a similar proposal, that the FBI administratively house a National Security Service. The President approved that recommendation. The FBI implemented that decision merely by changing the sign on the door and name of its existing National Security Division to the National Security Branch of the FBI.

Despite FBI Director Robert Mueller's insistence that he could make it work and that terrorism would be the number one focus of the FBI after 9/11, the division saw repeated leadership changes in the role of assistant director for counterterrorism:

Dale Watson: December 1999–September 2002

Pasquale D'Amuro: November 2002–July 2003

Larry Mefford: July 2003–October 2003

John Pistole: December 2003–October 2004

Gary Bald: October 2004–December 2004

Willie Hulon: December 2004–June 2006

Joseph Billy: June 2006–[57]

All of these officials were FBI agents who had two decades' experience in arresting criminals. To respond to criticism that the terrorism and intelligence problem needed intelligence analysts who were not chosen and evaluated by their ability to use guns, perform on physical fitness ranges, or make arrests of criminals, Mueller recruited a senior analyst from NSA to run an intelligence division, Maureen Baginski. She left the FBI shortly after taking the job, when her position was reorganized into nonexistence.[58] The counterterrorism analysts who had been hired complained that they were not taken seriously in the FBI because they did not carry a gun and a badge. One analyst, Melanie Sisson of *The Washington Post*, wrote of the FBI's "second class citizens":

> A system in which analysts are not guaranteed access to investigative information, one in which they must ask to be given the intelligence they were hired to assess, marginalizes analysts professionally and demoralizes them personally. It is a circumstance that not only breeds frustration and dissatisfaction but, by tacitly condoning the perception that analysis is of secondary importance to the FBI, perpetuates the bureau's traditional "cop culture" . . . analysts were being assigned to escort duty, collecting trash and answering telephones—and they were leaving in droves.[59]

The depth of the FBI's real focus on terrorism is exemplified by the curriculum at its academy at the Quantico, Virginia, Marine base. New agents are given 5 percent of the curriculum on terrorism and one hour on Islam. The evidence of its ability to adapt to the needs of counterterrorism is most famously demonstrated by its Virtual Case File program, meant to allow agents and analysts to share information among FBI offices in cities across the country. Though the Bureau spent more than $200 million, it could not create a functioning system. As discussed in chapter 4, the National Security Division's record on counterintelligence is equally dismal, only there its failures go back for decades. If ever there were a case of a function trapped inside an agency that cannot or will not let that function be performed well, it is the national security function within the FBI.

What we need to create over time is a civilian research and intelligence organization with skilled, career analysts who look for signs of terrorists and spies in the United States. They need to be truly integrated into the intelligence community run by the DNI. And they would need active, independent oversight to prevent any abuses of civil liberties or privacy rights. (The 9/11 Commission called for an independent Civil Liberties Protection Board. The President opposed the idea. Congress created one anyway, but the President appointed its members and it has been silent as our civil liberties have been eroded in the last few years.)

The Secret Service, which is the most misnamed of federal organizations (its police cars actually say "Secret Service" on their doors, a source of amusement to Europeans visiting Washington), is now housed in Homeland Security. Its chief function is physical protection of the President, foreign diplomats in the United States, and some senior U.S. government officials. It does prevention, using intelligence about threats. Secret Service also has an important legacy mission of tracking counterfeit U.S. currency, which is now manufactured and circulated mainly overseas. The Secret Service, too, should report to the DNI. With its reassignment, the name Homeland Security, with its Himmleresque overtones, could pass into history and a more modest, functionally aligned series of agencies could do a better job on their important core missions.

HOMEGROWN THREATS?

The politically timed color-coded alerts and the duct tape were not the only reasons that many Americans doubted the credibility of the government on the issue of the terrorist threat. Part of the problem lay outside the new department because, despite all of the pre-9/11 commissions and studies that stated that we should put all of the counterterrorism effort into one big department, in many ways the frontline agency on the domestic terrorism risk is not Homeland Security. It is the Justice Department and its FBI.

In addition to the problems of the new department, we began to be aware by 2004 that many of the much-ballyhooed terrorism arrests and prosecutions were exaggerated. And there had been no second wave of attacks in the United States. Such circumstances can create complacency, even if there still is a real threat.

ROUND UP UNUSUAL SUSPECTS

The arrests in the United States happened because after 9/11 the Attorney General had issued instructions to each of the ninety-four U.S. Attorneys, the federal prosecutors scattered around the country, to make terrorism their first priority. The FBI Director had given similar directions to the fifty-six FBI Field Offices. Such guidance cannot be faulted, but the result was that many U.S. Attorneys, supported by FBI agents, stretched hard to find someone to arrest for terrorism. When they found what they thought was terrorism, the Justice Department usually made major media announcements about plots having been foiled. The Attorney General, John Ashcroft and later Alberto Gonzales, would stand in front of a sea of flags, surrounded by FBI agents. The arrests strengthened the fears of terrorism being whipped up by Karl Rove and his band. Later, in many cases, we learned that there had been less to these cases than had originally seemed.

For example, in Lodi, California, several men were accused of plotting terrorist activities. When the case settled down, five of the men were charged only with immigration violations. Another man, an ice cream truck driver, was accused of lying to the FBI to protect his son. His son, who did go to a camp in Pakistan, seems to have done so at the behest of an FBI informant who was trying to create a terrorist offense and who was paid $200,000 to do so by the FBI. The son was given twenty-four years in prison.[60] In a similar case, the FBI and Justice announced that they had foiled a plot to blow up the Sears Tower in Chicago. The plot involved seven men in the Liberty City area of Miami. Later it emerged that the FBI had sent another informant into a local African-American club or gang and promised members money if they joined al Qaeda. He then gave them a camera and told them to photograph buildings that they could blow up, including the Sears Tower. The only weapon they possessed was one handgun. The jury in the case was not persuaded there was a real terrorist threat.[61] In a case in Pittsburgh, eighteen men were arrested. Most were Iraqi. Attorney General Ashcroft announced the arrests, discussing crop dusters with biological weapons. The charges, however, were that the men were using false information in seeking licenses to drive trucks with hazardous material. Images of trailer trucks turned into chemical weapons were conjured up. Later it emerged that the Iraqis had fled Saddam Hussein's repressive regime and were not actually seeking hazardous material licenses. There was never any connection to crop dusters. The men were convicted of dealing in false identity documents, but the judge in the case made a point of saying that it was not a terrorist conviction.[62]

In the greatest travesty of justice, José Padilla, an American citizen, was arrested in Chicago and accused in a dramatic press conference of plotting a radioactive bomb attack. The Defense Department, hitherto not involved in domestic law enforcement, declared him to be an enemy of the United States and put him in a military jail without a lawyer or a hearing, indeed without formal charges. Years later, when his case was on the way to the Supreme Court, the Defense Department gave him back to the Justice Department, which finally indicted him. He was not indicted for anything related to a radioactive bomb, but for applying to attend an al Qaeda terrorism training course and, by inference, conspiring to commit murder. And for that, he was convicted.[63]

All told, the Justice Department announced the arrests of 330 individuals for terrorism-related offenses in the three years after 9/11, according to a *Washington Post* investigation. Eighty percent were not convicted of a crime, and 90 percent were not convicted of a terrorism-related crime.[64] One man, Hassan Nasrallah of Dearborn, Michigan, appears to have been arrested because he has the same name as the head of Hezbollah in Lebanon. When they learned he was not *the* Hassan Nasrallah, the FBI searched for something to charge him with and he was eventually convicted on a credit card–related crime.[65] Overall, the federal government has had a 29 percent conviction rate in terrorism cases, compared with 92 percent for general federal felonies, according to a study conducted by the Center on Law and Security at New York University Law School. Pre-9/11, federal prosecutors in Manhattan successfully tried and convicted more than thirty terrorists in six major trials.[66]

There were, of course, real terrorists. Richard Reid did try to blow up an aircraft he was flying on by lighting explosives in his running shoe. Al Qaeda did send people to examine the possibility of making attacks on the Brooklyn Bridge and other targets. Men who had bomb-making skills and ties to Algerian terrorists and al Qaeda were arrested in Toronto. An al Qaeda cell in Britain was planning to bomb American airliners. Hamas, Hezbollah, and Palestinian Islamic Jihad supporters were identified in the United States, many involved in illegal fund raising.

What is striking, however, is the absence since 9/11 of any identified, credible plot to stage attacks in this country that has really gotten very far along. Much of what was uncovered is what the FBI admits was "aspirational, not operational."[67] Or it was in Canada or Britain, with the hope of attacking in the United States. And, thankfully, there have been no actual attacks in the United States as of this writing. Why?

FBI, homeland security, police, and intelligence officers I have asked say in private that they really do not know. As one official told me, "We've been overdue for a long time, and there is frankly not much stopping them." They offer a laundry list of potential explanations for the lack of a second wave of attacks:

- There is a perception in al Qaeda and related groups that security in the United States is tighter than it is.

- It has become very hard to get a visa to enter the United States if you are from a "country of concern."

- The U.S. invasion of Afghanistan and the arrests of senior al Qaeda officials in Pakistan disrupted "al Qaeda Central" for several years after 2001–2002, and the regional affiliated groups focused on attacking governments in their own countries.

- It has been easier to stage attacks in Europe, Asia, and the Middle East, where there is the support of indigenous radicalized Islamists.

- Most American Muslims enjoy religious freedom and economic opportunity in the United States and do not wish to have them threatened by stimulating a harsher crackdown on the Islamic community here; thus, they do not form terrorist cells here.

Two themes that emerge from those explanations are that (a) there is no permanent bar to successful terrorist operations in the United States and (b) there is the belief or assumption among these officials that a terrorist attack in the United States would likely be performed, as was the case with the 9/11 attack, by people living outside the country who come here for the purpose of engaging in terrorism.

No experts I talked with believe that security measures taken since 9/11 have made it very difficult to commit a terrorist act in the United States. Guns of all sorts are easily available here, as are the necessary ingredients for truck bombs. Brian Ross of ABC News sent college students around Virginia and North Carolina easily amassing, no questions asked, enough of the right kind of fertilizer to create a huge explosion.[68] The joke among some law enforcement officials is that if you want to get a terrorist into the United States, you need only wrap him in a ton of cocaine. Hundreds of tons of cocaine enter the United States annually despite Customs, Coast Guard, and Border Patrol efforts, as do hundreds of thousands of illegal immigrants. Although we tend to think of those border crossers as Mexicans, the Border Patrol has created a new acronym for a new class of people whom they are increasingly finding illegally crossing the border. The acronym is OTM, for Other Than Mexicans. Among the OTMs caught every year are Iraqis, Palestinians, Pakistanis, and Yemenis. Our refusal to give most people from those countries a visa does not prevent some from coming here.

Sometimes what seems to be a "homeland security" issue is also something else, and sometimes what seems to be the incompetence of the Department of Homeland Security is actually a function of exogenous variables and economic interests. I discussed how aviation security is not being done as well as it could be, in part because of the aviation industry's fear of adding a few more dollars to the cost of tickets (even though the Greyhound bus and Amtrak rail alternatives to flying are usually much less attractive). I think a similar set of economic interests is at play behind the apparent inability of the department's ICE and Border Patrol to deal with illegal immigration.

The fact that so-called OTM illegal immigrants from countries with strong Islamist terrorist organizations are regularly arrested attempting to cross our borders should give us pause. It is apparently not, however, sufficient motivation for a national consensus to secure our borders. The lack of consensus seems to pit two factions against each other: those who want to enforce our border and immigration laws vigorously and those who want to grant so-called amnesty to the millions of illegal immigrants and migrant workers. I think, however, that another reason little is being done to secure our borders is the influence of those who want neither a secure border nor "amnesty."

We have accepted insecure borders not because it would be impossible to provide a high level of security along the southern border, but because there is another issue involved that is more important for a lot of people. That issue is cheap labor. Some sectors of our economy function only by employing illegal immigrants, who, because they are here in violation of immigration laws, cannot organize and seek higher wages or demand benefits. In addition to vocal advocates of enforcement and strong supporters of regularizing the status of illegal immigrants, there is a quiet but influential group of people who like things just the way they are: with a large pool of low-wage workers who are largely powerless to improve their wages and conditions. Some industries in the United States have relatively low production costs today compared to what they would have if their workers' status were regularized and they were then free to demand more. Though the status quo may be good for their narrow economic interests, it is not in our national security interest.

From a security perspective, however, the answer is clear: the U.S. government should have a system to decide what foreign nationals enter the United States, should know what they are doing when they are in this country to ensure that it conforms with the reason they were admitted, and should know when they leave. We have none of that now. Millions of people enter without permission or enter legally under one status and then stay longer than authorized or do something other than what they were admitted to do. And we have no system in place to know when foreign nationals leave, despite Congress having mandated the creation of one.

Simply creating an enforcement system, however, is both infeasible and self-defeating. An enforcement-only approach implicitly means tens of thousands of federal agents rounding up millions of people and then moving them hundreds of miles against their will to the borders in a scene reminiscent of Josef Stalin's mass relocation of ethnic groups from one end of the Soviet Union to the other. And if we did that, in violation of what I hope is our own national sense of ethics and morality, we would suddenly find that the U.S. economy was so hugely understaffed that effectively it could not function.

Thus, while the details may be contentious, the broad outlines of what we should do seem obvious: First, place sufficient personnel and sensors on the southern border to prevent most illegal immigration. Second, register the existing illegal aliens. Third, determine which of those registered should be given migrant worker status, which should be put on a path for citizenship, and which should be deported. Fourth, then engage in workplace enforcement. Finally, establish a system to indicate whether legal visitors (students and tourists, for example) leave when their visas expire. Though these five tasks are sometimes portrayed as impossible, I believe they are all doable by a competent national government.

The series of terrorist acts in Europe by people who were born or grew up in the country they attacked has led to a new focus on the possibility of so-called homegrown terrorists in the United States. Typically, that phrase has meant the possibility of terrorists arising out of the American Muslim community. In fact, so far, the biggest homegrown terrorists in the United States have been the Christians Timothy McVeigh and Terry Nichols.

One of the reasons the counterterrorism community focuses on the threat from a terrorist group infiltrating the United States again is that American Muslims are generally assumed to be unlikely terrorists. In almost all cases, that assumption is valid. Most U.S. Muslims are patriotic Americans, although many have problems with aspects of U.S. foreign policy, just as I do. Muslims and Arabs in America are also diverse. Many U.S. Muslims are not Arabs (they are a mix of Persians, Turks, and Asians), and many American Arabs are not Muslims (they are Lebanese or Egyptian Christians).

It would take only a handful of anti-American Islamists to stage a major attack in the United States in the name of al Qaeda, with or without any direct link to that terrorist group abroad. And there are Muslims in the United States who are not successful, or who are not integrated into our society, who have only recently immigrated, who feel alienated and discriminated against, or who simply are irate at what they believe are the anti-Islamic policies of the U.S. government in Iraq and elsewhere. The same propaganda that the al Qaeda movement uses so successfully elsewhere can have an appeal to some Muslims living in the United States. It can come from sermons by imams in radical mosques, or more likely in discussion groups after prayer services when possible FBI informants have left. Radicalization can come from watching videotapes on the internet or from taking trips abroad. Law enforcement authorities fear that Islamist radicalization may be taking place in U.S. prisons.

The fear among counterterrorism security experts such New York Police Department Deputy Commissioner David Cohen is that there might well be sleeper cells in the United States now or in the near future and "the FBI would never know it." Cohen, a thirty-year CIA veteran, ran all human intelligence (spies) for the Agency before going to the NYPD. He and other experts believe that the fact that many of the FBI's terrorism-related arrests in the United States have been exaggerated does not mean that there is no threat in the United States. It may just mean that the FBI cannot find it and is forced to come up with thinly justified terrorism arrests to respond to the Attorney General's desire for prosecutions. Cohen and his boss, Ray Kelly, the long-serving New York police commissioner, believe that they cannot rely on the FBI or the Department of Homeland Security to protect New York from terrorism. "They didn't do so well at it the last few times," Cohen deadpanned to me during a rare lunch for him outside One Police Plaza in New York City.

So Ray Kelly and Dave Cohen have created their own counterterrorism capability in the New York City police. They have developed their own sources of information and have trained their own analysts. Two of those analysts, Mitchel Silber and Arvin Bhatt, authored a well-researched 2007 study on Islamist radicalization that makes a strong

case that the ideological and political circumstances are such that
homegrown terrorist cells are a real possibility in the United States.[69]
Such cells could be created by a handful of people without direct contacts outside this country, radicalized in large part by information obtained on the internet. The two key ingredients, they argue, drawing
on examples in Europe and Australia, are an ideological leader in the
cell and an operational planner. The process from moving from radical
discussion to a cell forming and staging an attack may take two to four
years, they note, but it could be done with very few external indicators.
If the cell maintains tight operational security, the only people who
may catch a whiff of what is being planned are people in their community who become aware of the depth of the cell members' radical
transformation and suspicious or secretive activity.

That fact places a premium on local law enforcement or the FBI's
having good relations with members of the various Muslim communities. The NYPD works hard at trying to maintain such relations. In so
doing it is paralleling what British authorities have done in the wake of a
half-dozen real terrorist plots and attacks in the United Kingdom. Civil
and police officials have structured a program in London and the other
major cities to engage in dialogue with Muslim groups, not just about
terrorism but about their concerns generally, identifying their complaints,
and trying to make them feel more a part of the fabric of Britain.

Outside New York City and a similar effort by the Los Angeles police chief William Bratton, there are few examples in the United States
of the use of "community policing" practices, which have been so successful in reducing crime, being applied to monitor for nascent terrorists. But Michael Sheehan, "Cohen's partner in crime," according to
Commissioner Kelly, thinks the model could work elsewhere. Sheehan
was the NYPD's assistant commissioner for counterterrorism. He argues that the threat of al Qaeda–like groups staging attacks in the
United States is real and needs a more professional approach than the
federal agencies have accorded it so far. But, he adds, "we also need to
stop terrorizing ourselves." In his 2008 book *Crush the Cell,* Sheehan
argues that much of the counterterrorism security measures the public
sees are little more than inconveniences, both to the public and to any
serious terrorists.

THE EUROPEAN EXPERIENCE

If Americans have begun to doubt whether there is a serious terrorism risk in the United States, for Europeans there is little question. Since 9/11, Madrid had its 3/11 train bombings in 2004, with more than 1,500 casualties. London had its 7/7 subway bombings in 2005, followed by an attempted copycat attack two weeks later. The British also foiled attacks planned on U.S. aircraft in 2006 and experienced partially successful car bombs in 2007. Italy broke up terrorist cells in 2003 and 2004. Germany, where the 9/11 cell was formed, narrowly avoided a series of bombs on trains in 2006. A major attack in Barcelona was averted early in 2008. Tensions with radical Islamists have caused incidents involving the Netherlands and Denmark, while in France full-scale riots by Islamic youths broke out in 2006. Many of the terrorist cells and attacks involved radicalized Muslims who had spent their lives peacefully in Europe; some had been born there, many had families, most had good jobs, few were thought to be a risk.

Most of western Europe has in the last few years come face-to-face with questions that have shocked and disturbed the generally peaceful countries there. The questions are basic: What does it mean to be Dutch or British? How can people who have grown up in these societies turn against them and kill their fellow citizens? Do the liberal traditions of religious tolerance and openness to refugees still work when people use them to create religiously intolerant and closed communities within the country, communities that reject integration and demand separatism? Although western Europe is nominally Christian in tradition, in practice it is secular and largely without religion. Can it accept a growing Muslim community that demands to be different, to apply customs and even laws at odds with European beliefs? For many European countries with little or no population growth in recent years, the high rate of Muslim births is seen as a threat that in the not-too-distant future demographics may make their nations very different places.

European security experts, politicians, and sociologists are seized with the issue of European Muslim integration. They are also not completely detached observers. On this issue Americans can be slightly more objective. One of the leading American analysts of this problem is a longtime colleague of mine in the White House and State Department, Steven Simon. Simon is at work on *Europe's Fate,* his third book collaboration with another former colleague, Daniel Benjamin. Their earlier works, *The Age of Sacred Terrorism* and *The Next Attack,* have publicly established what I knew from working with them in the White House, their mastery of the terrorism topic. It was easy to be a detached observer sitting with Simon on the broad porch of the farmhouse he and his wife, Virginia Liberatore, had painstakingly restored in the foothills of the Shenandoahs. Inside, a sea of books was stacked and shelved in a large library decorated with prints, carpets, and lamps from souks and bazaars across the Islamic world. "The U.S. is a nation of immigrants used to ethnic neighborhoods and organizations. Most European countries have been pretty homogeneous until recently," he told me. "The result is that the Muslim communities are less welcomed in much of Europe, and that produces a climate in which Islamist radicalization is much more likely."

For Europe, these issues are both immediate and long term. Moreover, at some level they are almost existential, for they go to the heart of what the European Union will be in the twenty-first century. One thing it will likely not be is a union involving Turkey. Democratic, moderate Turkey, with a tradition of separating mosque and state going back to Atatürk in the 1920s, has tried for years to join the European Union. For years it has been told that it was on a track to acceptance, if only it would do this or that. Now, with the growing fear of Islamization in Europe, the chances of the rest of Europe welcoming in the Islamic democracy seem almost nil. Rejected by the West, Turkey will seek ties elsewhere, probably with its Arab and Persian neighbors. The secular traditions of twentieth-century Turkey are now eroding in the twenty-first century.

For the United States, what is happening in Europe creates both obvious long-term implications and immediate security concerns. Citizens of the twenty-seven European Union countries can travel to the United States without prior notice and without a visa. It is not hard to imagine a scenario in which a radicalized Islamist living in and perhaps born in Britain, for example, travels to Pakistan for ideological instruction and terrorist weapons training. Some involved in the attacks in the United Kingdom in the last few years have done just that. Knowing that British authorities may be attempting to track the many young men who travel to Pakistan and return to the United Kingdom (a subset of the estimated 400,000 British visits to Pakistan annually), maybe our hypothetical suspect books his trip from Manchester or Birmingham only to Dubai, to shop and do other tourist activities in that amazing city. Once in Dubai, however, he buys a new ticket to Pakistan and goes to a camp in the northwest territories where al Qaeda and the Taliban have set up training facilities. After getting his training and an assignment, he returns to Dubai. At the British consulate, he says his passport was stolen. He is given a new passport, without any sign on it that he visited Pakistan, and returns to England. A few weeks later, he flies from London to Boston or Chicago. His name is sent ahead to U.S. authorities, along with the names of all passengers, but he is on no watch list and raises no flag. He needs no visa to enter the United States, so there is no reason to reject his visit. U.S. immigration authorities see no indication on his passport that he has been to Pakistan, so there is no chance he will be pulled aside for secondary screening and questioning.

Within an hour after arriving, he is downtown and perhaps off to meet with others who have taken a similar path. Their next step may be to buy guns or fertilizer that can be used as explosives, both easy things to do in America.

Even if we were to disbelieve the possibility of a handful of homegrown Americans becoming so radicalized by Islamist propaganda that they become terrorists, the evidence is clear that such conversion into terrorists has taken place repeatedly in Europe. And little or nothing could stop a European homegrown terrorist trained at a Pakistani al Qaeda camp from coming here. As the CIA Director noted in April 2008, they would probably not raise suspicion if they stood in the immigration line at Dulles airport.

LAND OF SWEET LIBERTIES

It is scenarios like that, perhaps, that cause some people to think that we need wiretaps without warrants and other infringements of traditional American civil liberties. The possibility that we have homegrown terrorists causes some to think we need to deal with the current terrorist threat differently than we have other security and law enforcement challenges we have faced. It is the fear of another 9/11 that justifies, in some minds, torturing suspected terrorists in camps in legal no-man's-lands like U.S. military enclaves in Cuba, Afghanistan, and Iraq.

I deeply disagree. Torture and warrantless wiretaps are unnecessary. They also erode the support we need abroad and the unity we need at home to overcome the threat from violent Islamist extremists. Most important, they are steps in the wrong direction, steps a little closer to the horrors that humans can engage in when rights are eroded.

Experts have known for decades that torture draws unreliable information from its victims and that other methods have good track records in producing cooperation and information from suspects and prisoners. We know of specific examples where tortured prisoners have provided false information, such as the erroneous report that Iraq trained al Qaeda terrorists in the use of weapons of mass destruction.[70]

The belief that Americans have used torture in Abu Ghraib and other U.S. military camps in Iraq, Afghanistan, and Cuba has convinced many in the Islamic world that we do disrespect Muslims. It has helped some to justify terrorist tactics and support for al Qaeda and similar groups. It has convinced many that we are hypocrites when we talk about human rights and democracy.

I have long believed that the U.S. Bill of Rights and the U.N. Universal Declaration of Human Rights are among the few membranes, the thin tissues, that separate humanity from another descent into the kind of world that only a few decades ago saw many millions of people degraded and industrially disposed of in the horror camps of Nazi Germany and the Communist Soviet Union. It is in humanity's genes and makeup that people can engage in such atrocities. And many people have done so.

We need to hold the line well this side of the police state, far from

the torture chamber. Yet the U.S. Justice Department originated a ruling that the only torture that was out of bounds was that which caused
pain equivalent to organ failure.[71] Anything else done by Americans
was permissible, as long as it was not done in the United States. The
Vice President of the United States drove to the Congress to lobby
members to permit what he euphemistically called "alternative interrogation techniques." It is hard to believe. You want to think it's all a
bad dream, but it's not. You thought America was a force in the world
against this sort of thing, not a nation that would actually engage in
it. Thankfully, for a while we had John McCain as our conscience.
McCain, who was repeatedly tortured, was there to remind us of what
it means to be Americans, what it is that we stand for in this world, and
who we are not. Unfortunately, he later voted against a legislated ban
on waterboarding by the CIA.

Warrantless wiretaps are far less heinous, but an equally unacceptable step toward a police state. I spent many days struggling to get
wiretaps on terrorists. I thought that many of the Justice Department
rules about wiretapping terrorists were unfounded impediments to
achieving security. The "Chinese wall" that prevented information obtained in intelligence wiretaps from being given to criminal investigators was wrong. The ban on listening to foreigners' communications
originating and terminating outside the United States but transiting
our switches was foolish. Requiring a different wiretap warrant every
time a suspect changed telephones was absurd. The Foreign Intelligence Surveillance Act (FISA), which regulates security-related wiretaps, needed updating. But we should not have ignored it.

Remarkably, the former White House General Counsel and then
Attorney General Alberto Gonzalez explained that the reason the administration did not originally try to amend the FISA was a belief that
Congress would not have approved the needed changes.[72] So instead,
he just violated the law under the specious reasoning that the President
had inherent authority to do so in the national interest and that the
congressional authorization to fight in Afghanistan somehow implied
authority to violate the FISA law. One senator asked that if the President had inherent authority to break that law, what other laws did he
have the authority to break? There was no answer.[73]

In my personal experience, the need for getting a FISA warrant never held up surveillance. The FISA judges were willing to hold hearings at any hour of the day or night if they were told that there was an emergency. Moreover, in an extreme emergency the wiretap could be initiated first and the warrant sought after the fact. During the millennium alert period in late 1999, we persuaded the FISA court to process a record number of FISA warrants expeditiously. The need for active judicial oversight of intelligence wiretaps is clear: the FBI abuses its power. The Justice Department and its component, the FBI, admit this. The Justice Department's Inspector General cited hundreds of cases where the FBI acquired records of innocent U.S. citizens without a warrant by, essentially, knowingly misstating facts.[74]

The word *rendition* has become associated with kidnapping people and throwing them into some third-country jail cell, torturing them, and never giving them a trial or any due process. Yet before 9/11, I orchestrated renditions (overseas arrests and subsequent movement out of the country) and extraordinary renditions (those where we acted without the knowledge of the country in which the suspect was captured) without throwing out the U.S. legal system. Terrorist suspects who were subject to these renditions were almost all returned to the United States, read their rights, given defense counsel, prosecuted in criminal courts, and convicted. The United States could have handled cases of rendition after 9/11 as we had done earlier. It would have been burdensome, cumbersome, slow. It would have required an infusion of new resources into the justice system. But it would have been consistent with our principles and laws. We would have been acting in the way Americans used to act, morally, leading the world by example, in a way that differentiates us.

People throughout the world knew at one point that the United States stood for something. Even if they disagreed with us on some things, they respected us for our principles. When we criticized others for violating the Universal Declaration of Human Rights, people knew that we had worked hard to overcome our flaws with regard to slavery and racial discrimination. The world knew that it was the government in Washington that fought against those in our country who still tried to violate human rights on the basis of race. It gave us a strength in the world beyond our military might and economic prowess. What we did in violating human rights in the fight against terrorists showed us to the world as hypocrites, and we lost that strength. After 9/11, the United States also abandoned the oldest protection in the Anglo-American legal system, the concept of habeas corpus. This abandonment of legal tradition allows prisoners to be held by U.S. officials indefinitely, without charges, and without any really impartial review of evidence against them.

Congress has been a party to these erosions of our legal system and civil liberties. When finally it forced the administration to amend the relevant laws instead of just ignoring them, it gave the Attorney General decision-making authority in place of judges' control over wiretaps. Congress further agreed to abandon habeas corpus when it came to some detained terrorist suspects, including those in the United States.

The disregard of civil liberties, human rights, international law, privacy rights, and due process clearly and repeatedly demonstrated by the U.S. government after 9/11 has made it almost impossible for the American people to join in a consensus with their Congress and government to do some of the sensible things that should be done to enhance security and fight crime. After the government has done all that it has to ignore and violate rights in the name of the Global War on Terrorism, there is a significant element in our nation, composed of both right-wing and left-wing citizens, who oppose the notions of government-issued identity cards or the increase in video surveillance systems in public places. I understand their trepidation, but I hope that we can engage in a national dialogue that can create a consensus to use those two security and anticrime tools with appropriate safeguards. Toward that end, let's take a look at both issues.

OVERCOMING THE BIG BROTHER

About ID cards, the issue is not really whether we should have government-issued IDs, it is whether we should have ones that work. We have government-issued identification cards today, but they are easily forged and counterfeited. Look at your Social Security card. One made on your home computer's color printer would look more official. Or consider the state-issued driver's license that you present when going through airport security. There was until 2008 no attempt at airports to verify license authenticity (although some states have added "black-light visible only" symbols, which the bouncers at bars in college neighborhoods use to verify that driver's licenses are real when they are checking proof of age). There are internet sites that offer phony driver's licenses for a small fee. In any city, you could probably get a phony ID with less than half a day's effort.

Fake IDs are used for far more than just underage drinking. They are part of a multibillion-dollar problem of fraud and identity theft in the United States. Companies that are victimized by that fraud pass the cost on to us, the consumers. The cost of verifiable IDs would be far less. Moreover, verifiable IDs would allow us to be sure we know who is working at airports and other sensitive facilities. The technology exists today to produce relatively inexpensive ID cards that would have three elements on them that would make them impossible to counterfeit. First, they would include an encrypted signature from the issuing authority that card-reading devices could scan and determine if the card had definitely been issued by the Division of Motor Vehicles or whatever agency was involved. Second, the card would carry biometric data such as a fingerprint, handprint, or iris scan that would be uniquely associated with the card carrier. Third, the card would include an encrypted PIN, perhaps a seven-digit number (which should be easy enough to remember since we remember our ten-digit telephone numbers). Handheld or kiosk card readers could verify the authenticity of the card, compare its biometric information to that of the person carrying it, and verify the PIN. These card reader machines could go online periodically to get updates on newly issued cards or cards that have been canceled because the owner died or was determined to have engaged in fraud when applying for the card.

I arrived at Dubai airport recently and waited in the long line at the immigration booth, something I also do whenever I return to the United States from a foreign trip. However, in Dubai, citizens and long-term visitors do not stand in line. They move to kiosks, slide their smart ID into a reader, punch in a PIN, have their iris scanned, and enter the country in less than a minute. Last year, that system caught more than twenty thousand people trying to enter that country using an assumed identity. Such systems are in place in many countries, adding to convenience and enhancing security, but not in the United States.

In 2005 Congress passed the REAL ID Act, requiring states to issue driver's licenses that (a) can be easily authenticated, for example through encryption and biometrics, and (b) are issued only after a background check has been performed to verify that the applicant is who he or she claims to be. States have revolted against implementing the REAL ID Act because the federal government refuses to pay for the cost of its implementation. Other critics see it as an infringement of civil liberties or a potential source of abuse, perhaps part of some Orwellian system to track where everybody is at all times. And many critics see it as part of an anti–illegal immigrant enforcement effort. Earlier in this chapter I discussed the need for both enforcement of our immigration laws and a regularized program for migrant workers. We can address the other two concerns about the REAL ID Act by federally funding the costs of implementation and by limiting the places and functions that can require someone to produce a government-issued ID. Congress could also restrict who could collect and store data drawn from uses of the new driver's licenses. If we could regain sufficient public trust in government after all of the erosions of rights in the last decade, an active Civil Liberties and Privacy Protection Agency could regulate, provide oversight, and enforce such limitations of the use of the IDs.

The issues with video surveillance are similar. Some people object to the idea that they may be subject to video surveillance. Once again, such concerns, as with government-issued IDs, misconstrue the problem. The issue is not whether we are subject to such surveillance but whether the surveillance that already goes on extensively is sufficiently effective to bother doing and whether there are safeguards to prevent its abuse. Most of us who drive on interstate highways, take trains or subways, use airports, or visit banks, grocery stores, or shopping malls are subject to video surveillance now. Cameras are everywhere. When a crime occurs, police can obtain videotapes and try to determine who committed the crime. In some sense, however, by then it is too late. Moreover, when the criminal is identified, that person can and will often be seen by many more cameras without being apprehended through the use of those cameras. Part of the reason for the cameras' limited value is that there are so many of them that it would take thousands of people to watch them all and those people would soon suffer from their eyes glazing over. In short, we have now all the loss of privacy associated with cameras without the deterrent effect and with little of the crime-stopping capability they could bring.

What most camera systems lack today are (1) regulation to protect privacy, (2) software to determine in real time that a crime is happening or a terrorist attack is about to occur, and (3) networking to determine that the person or vehicle being filmed is already wanted for a crime. Existing technology can, however, allow a digital or analog video stream from thousands of cameras to be analyzed in real time by software that can identify numerous behaviors such as someone pulling out a gun, breaking a window, driving in a prohibited area, or leaving a suspicious package in a public space. The software can locate stolen cars by reading license plate numbers. The experience of installing city government run–camera networks in several urban areas suggests that citizens approve of the systems. Indeed, nearby neighborhoods have asked to have the networks expanded so that they too can be covered. Statistics seem to show clearly that crime decreases in areas covered, although some critics have dissented from that analysis.

I spent some time in Baltimore, examining its camera system. There public acceptance has been enhanced by having the cameras run by a civilian agency, not the police, and having software installed that blocks the cameras from looking at certain zones, such as into the windows of private residences. Having groups like the local chapter of the American Civil Liberties Union involved in drawing up the rules and safeguards and assisting in the design of oversight procedures and protections is also important to the public's confidence that such a system will not be misused.

Security measures and technologies are not inherently good or evil; it is how they are applied and what oversight is employed to limit the potential for abuse that determines whether they are enhancements worth pursuing or too risky. Stripping away the overheated politicization of the debate about these kinds of security measures and rebuilding trust in government would allow us to take another look at some of these kinds of useful security measures, which have been stalled or underutilized in many places.

Every new President has a year or so when he or she can get things done more easily than later on, because of the fresh mandate from the people. The next President could undo the damage created by the advent and early operations of the Department of Homeland Security and take the needed measures to reduce our domestic security vulnerabilities. The specific agenda should include:

- Maintaining an active and positive outreach program to the U.S. Muslim community to ensure that it is not the victim of discrimination or religious intolerance and to work with it to prevent violent Islamist extremists from acting within the United States

- Realigning the Homeland Security Department into a Border and Transportation Security Department, a completely independent FEMA with grant programs authority for vulnerability reduction and emergency response, and a Domestic Security Research agency reporting to the Director of National Intelligence

- Specifying vulnerability reduction and capacity enhancement program goals in detail, including for each of the 157 metropolitan areas, and developing three- and five-year plans to fund them

- Re-creating trust and overcoming suspicion about domestic security programs by establishing an active Civil Liberties and Privacy Rights Commission, led by nationally respected leaders

- Initiating a well-funded, short-completion-time international program to account for and secure radiological material, particularly highly enriched and high-contamination materials

- Completing the efforts to achieve a highly secure aviation system and achieve specific goals for rail and subway transit security

- Brokering the necessary compromise to secure the borders, create a migrant worker program, place some currently illegal migrants on the path to citizenship, and establish a secure credentialing system including civil liberties and privacy protections

Finally, we must also take action to limit the outsourcing of critical government functions to hired contractors, and we must hold the contractors we do hire to much higher standards. Many of the failures highlighted in this chapter have been on programs where the DHS has done little more than phone in the orders for border fences, immigration security, and Coast Guard cutters. With $15 billion of DHS's $40 billion budget going to contractors, the need to examine their role is clear. As Congressman Henry Waxman put it, "There's the mindset that the government can do no good and the private sector can do no wrong. I think we have to get a better balance, and if we're going to contract out, we have to have better oversight."[75]

It is a lot to do, especially since the President will be simultaneously addressing a host of other demanding issues, including the recession, withdrawal from Iraq, countering violent Islamist extremism, addressing Iranian subversion, responding to global warming, and solving the U.S. health care crisis. Some people will be satisfied to live with the suboptimal, dysfunctional domestic security system that the new President will inherit. However, having a risk management system that itself is at a high risk of failure is not prudent. We are, after all, talking about our security in our country, one place where we should insist that the government not fail us again.

SEVEN

ENERGY

I'm not sure I can land down there, sir. The fires are everywhere, and the smoke is so thick. I mean, it looks like what Hell must be like," the young Air Force captain explained to me. He had come back from the cockpit of the Gulfstream to try to dissuade me from landing at Kuwait International Airport. It was shortly after the liberation of Kuwait by American and coalition forces in 1991. Saddam Hussein had ordered the retreating Iraqi Army to set the Kuwaiti oil wells on fire, and the resulting blazes were causing smoke to billow across the devastated landscape. Kuwait was covered in a thick, black, oily cloud. "I'm afraid we might get some of the oil in those clouds sucked into our engines, sir. We might also land and not be able to take off again if the wind shifts."

"You're the aircraft commander, you make the call," I told the pilot, who looked as if he were about nineteen (he was probably ten years older). "But I'm on a mission to meet with the members of the Kuwaiti government who have managed to get back in. Can you descend out over the gulf, where it's still clear, and then sneak in under the cloud, so you don't have to fly through it?" Reluctantly, the captain took us in under the cloud and landed at the battle-torn terminal. Every window was shot out, every wall bullet-pocked. A major tank duel between U.S. and Iraqi armor had taken place at and around the airport. When we stepped out of the aircraft, I had the sensation that we had landed on another planet. The sky was filled horizon to horizon by a very low, churning, blue-black cloud. It was shortly before noon, and it was darker than any night I had ever seen. A few portable spotlights lit the tarmac. And then there was the noise, one sound coming from all directions, guttural and rushing, the sound of hundreds of fires in the wells. It was Dante's *Inferno* come to life. And it was all about oil. Or was it?

Just as that day in Kuwait is seared in my memory, we have a national memory of those events and a shared belief that the national security concern about energy is that we need to keep oil out of the hands of our enemies. That may be the least of our worries.

In that Middle East war, and in the current one, part of the rationale for going to war was the notion that we need to secure sources of oil. It is a simple argument for the public to latch onto and it is largely wrong. Neither war was really about oil and fighting a war tends to disrupt, not improve, the flow of oil. As I write this in March of 2008, five years into the war in Iraq, oil is hovering above $100 a barrel. If the war was started to secure a cheap source of oil, we have done a heck of a job. Yet based on the false notion that we fight wars over oil, calls are now getting louder for the United States to achieve "energy independence," something a parade of Presidents over the last thirty years have pledged to do and then failed to achieve. In a global economy, achieving independence on anything is an unrealistic goal. Pursuing it will be costly in terms of dollars, will do nothing to improve our national security, and will distract us from the real threat to our national security that stems from our energy policies: climate change.

Prior to 9/11, I was incredibly frustrated because I could see a "clear and present danger" to the United States but, despite my warnings and those of others, the U.S. government remained complacent until it was too late. The result was the death of three thousand innocent people in one day of attacks on two iconic American symbols. As horrendous as that was, it may someday seem less significant than the deaths from floods, the forced migration of millions, the spread of diseases, the dust bowls that were once fertile lands, all of which may be the result of the climate change that we are causing. And, as with 9/11, we were warned, told for years that climate change was happening. Those like Al Gore who told us what was coming were not merely ignored, they were mocked. Imagine their frustration. During critical years when something might have been done to stop climate change, we not only failed to act, we made it worse. When most of the world united to address the problem, the United States rejected the approach and failed to offer an effective alternative.

The "know-nothings" of climate change have contended for years that the science of climate change was uncertain or that global warming may actually be a good thing on balance. They were right about one thing, that there is uncertainty: we are uncertain about whether we have already passed the point of no return, whether cataclysmic climate change is now inevitable. On the chance that it is not too late to mitigate the damage, to make it less bad than it might otherwise be, we should embark on a national emergency program to reduce carbon emissions. Instead, today, our government continues to fail on the conjoined issues of energy policy and climate change. We are misdiagnosing the national security issues associated with oil, and we are far from a national emergency effort on climate change. We have a muddled, leaderless effort that will not significantly reduce carbon emissions in the foreseeable future. Future generations will likely regard the last decade's activity, or lack of it, on climate change as the most important failure of government in human history. And the failure continues.

THE OIL MYTHS

Our energy policies have been contributing to climate change, but our national debate and discussion on energy policy have instead for several decades misdiagnosed the problems, focusing alternately on the need to secure oil flows from the Middle East and to achieve energy independence at home. Leaders of significant stature have contributed.

- Consider President Richard Nixon, who launched Project Independence in the 1974 State of the Union speech, saying, "Let this be our national goal: At the end of this decade, in the year 1980, the United States will not be dependent on any other country for the energy we need to provide our jobs, to heat our homes, and to keep our transportation moving."[1] We failed to achieve that deadline, but did not freeze or become immobilized. The economy continued to grow.

- Or take his successor twice removed, Ronald Reagan, who explained his military intervention in Lebanon by referring to oil. Lebanon had no oil. But for Ronald Reagan and a lot of Americans, the entire Middle East was about oil.

- Reagan's Vice President went on to become the forty-first President and invaded Kuwait to evict Iraqi forces. His esteemed Secretary of State explained the need for that action in one word: "jobs."[2] James A. Baker III and his flacks later elaborated on that, contending that Iraq's occupation of Kuwait might lead to a shortage of oil for America, leading to a loss of jobs. Yet in 1991 only a small fraction of U.S. oil came from the Middle East.

- Following 9/11, President Bush 43 called, in a State of the Union address, for "energy independence." Despite that goal, he then invaded Iraq.[3]

- The revered former chairman of the Federal Reserve Board, Alan Greenspan, explained the invasion of Iraq as being "largely about oil."[4]

By 2007 a strange-bedfellows amalgam of left and right in America was demanding changes in U.S. energy policy because our oil imports fund terrorism. Former CIA Director James Woolsey claimed, "We're sending [what we pay for oil] . . . in part to Saudi Arabia and the states of the gulf...which have wealthy families that support the Wahabi's ... and run the Madrasis ... to teach the Pakistani boys to be suicide bombers. This is the only war we've ever fought, besides the civil war, where we pay for both sides."[5]

ENERGY INDEPENDENCE AND DRINKING OIL

As the autumn of 1990 came on in Washington, I was getting the reputation of being one of the leading "hawks" in the State Department, advocating that the United States go to war to liberate Kuwait. An excellent intelligence analyst with whom I had worked the preceding four years asked to come see me privately. He closed the door to my office, sat down, and fumbled with his pipe (it was pre–smoking ban). "You really think we should go to war?" I said I did. "You know Saddam will export the oil from Kuwait, just like the Kuwaitis did. We don't need to go in to get it. He'll sell it and oil is fungible. As long as it's sold into the market, we're okay." He relit the pipe. "Saddam just wants the money that comes from selling oil. He can't drink oil."

"I know, although it's an interesting image, him downing a can of WD-40," I replied. "I think we need to evict him from Kuwait because we can't allow nations to go around invading each other with thousands of tanks and annexing territory by force. It didn't work out well when we let nations do that kind of thing in the 1930s and '40s." In 1990, we did not really think that Saddam had grabbed Kuwait and its oil only to keep that oil off the market. He wanted the money that selling the oil would bring to rebuild his country from the Eight-Year War with Iran.

Bob Gates was Deputy National Security Advisor at the time; a year later he would become Director of Central Intelligence; and in 2006 he would replace Donald Rumsfeld as Secretary of Defense. Apparently, he shared my view about the role of oil in the first Gulf War and, disagreeing with Chairman Greenspan, thinks oil is not the reason for the second war with Iraq, either. Gates told ABC News, "I have a lot of respect for Mr. Greenspan. I've known him a long time, and I disagree. I know the same allegation was made about the Gulf War in 1991, and I just don't believe it's true. . . . It's about aggressive dictators. After all, Saddam Hussein launched wars against several of his neighbors. He was trying to develop weapons of mass destruction, certainly when we went in, in 1991. . . . So I think what we were going after was an aggressive dictator who was a destabilizing force in the entire region."[6]

I had an opportunity to watch, admittedly in horror, as Gates's predecessor advocated going to war with Iraq in 2001. He did not mention oil. There were many motivations among the circle of national security experts, the inappropriately named Vulcans, who counseled President Bush after 9/11 and advocated going to war with Iraq. Vice President Cheney, who played a key role in shaping the President's thinking on the subject, probably did think about oil. I know he was concerned at the time about the long-term stability of Saudi Arabia and saw Iraq as an alternative in the role of "oil-rich U.S. ally." Bush and his Vulcans were, however, at least as focused on the need to stop schools from "teaching people it's okay to fly airplanes into buildings" (although there was never any evidence of such a curriculum in Iraq) and the requirement to create democracy in the Middle East (although elections in the region tend to bring radical Islamists to power). My belief has always been that Bush personally went to war chiefly to prove that the United States was undeterred by 9/11, that we could take combat casualties without running away, and that we could beat up the region's biggest bully. Not because of the oil. Though Bush promised that revenue from oil would pay for the war, the war actually decreased Iraqi oil exports (the insurgency kept blowing up the oil infrastructure) and increased the United States' oil demand (the U.S. Army's operation tempo pushed up its oil and gas needs significantly).

The popular impression in the United States is that we are dependent on Middle East oil and we have to keep "bad guys" from controlling that oil. This impression is misinformed. First, the top two sources of petroleum being imported into the United States are nations in the Western Hemisphere, Canada and Mexico. Of the top fifteen nations that are sources of U.S. petroleum imports, a dozen are not in the Middle East.[7] Second, the idea that nations with oil would withhold it from the world market is about as likely as it was that Saddam Hussein would drink WD-40. That fear stems from memories of 1973, when Arab states briefly withheld oil exports to the United States to protest Israeli actions. In addition to the United States' having diversified its sources of supply since 1973, there are other reasons why producers will not stop producing. Most of the world's oil-exporting nations need the income they derive from selling petroleum and would face significant, perhaps regime-threatening, internal dissent if that income ceased. They could, of course, conspire to raise the price of oil. In fact, arguably, they already have. Oil was at seventy dollars a barrel in 2006 without a U.S. economic downturn. In 2007 oil went well over ninety dollars a barrel, yet the larger threat to the U.S. economy came from unregulated bankers who had pushed low-interest mortgages on customers they knew not to be creditworthy.

Thirty years ago President Jimmy Carter put on a cardigan and told the nation to turn down the thermostat. Laughable as this piece of theater may have been, the reforms he set into motion during the oil embargo of the 1970s greatly improved the stability of our energy market. The Carter-era policy changes successfully shifted our electricity generation from burning oil to burning domestic coal and natural gas. This act eliminated a major component of our dependence on foreign oil. Today, contrary to popular belief, we burn almost no oil to generate electricity in the United States.

In a global economy in which most nations need a diversity of types of energy for electricity production, transportation, and industrial applications, no major nation is energy-independent because no nation can produce the variety of energy sources it needs more cheaply than it can acquire some of it on the world market. Although I would not recommend turning to oil companies for information on this issue, what the U.S. oil giant Chevron says in its ad campaign is true: "There are 193 countries in the world. None of them are energy independent." The ad goes on to point out in a small graphic that Saudi Arabia, the world's largest oil producer, imports gasoline, as do Norway, the United Arab Emirates, and Nigeria. Russia and Norway also import electricity and coal; Russia and the UAE both import natural gas. If these major oil export countries are not energy-independent, how can the United States hope to be?

Some U.S. oil companies have encouraged efforts to reduce our "dependence upon foreign oil," but they did so as part of efforts to reduce their taxes and increase their profitability. They successfully sought federal tax credits for increased oil exploration and production within the United States. While that might have sounded good initially, what it really means is that U.S. taxpayers are paying for some of the domestic-source oil when they pay their income taxes and when the Treasury then pays the interest on the national debt. Seeking to increase domestic sources of oil supply when the market price of foreign supply is cheaper is not good public policy. Neither is fooling ourselves by thinking that we can obtain "energy independence." We should instead be seeking energy source diversity. Daniel Yergin, the author of the best-selling *The Prize: The Epic Quest for Oil, Money, and Power* and the founder of Cambridge Energy Research Associates, is fond of a quote by Winston Churchill. When, as First Lord of the Admiralty, Winston Churchill oversaw the conversion of the British fleet from Welsh coal to Arab crude, he responded to concerns over the dependence the move would create by declaring, "Safety and certainty in oil lie in variety and variety alone." Yergin likes the quote because it perfectly articulates what has stood as the fundamental principle of energy security: diversification of supply.[8]

Europe has recently learned this lesson the hard way. The European Union has grown overly reliant on natural gas to meet its energy needs and overly reliant on Russia for its supply of that natural gas. Half of the European Union's gas comes from Russia, and some members are totally dependent on it. In the winter of 2007, Russia flexed its energy muscles by shutting down exports to Ukraine, causing a gas shortage across Europe. The situation is similar to the United States' dependence on Arab oil in the late 1970s. Europe is also taking a similar approach to addressing its problem. Rather than investing in futile attempts to increase its own production, the European Union is frantically building new means to import gas from other markets. Liquid natural gas (LNG) import terminals are being built along the coast from Italy to Poland.

THE TERRORIST TRAP

A former CIA Director, Secretary of the Navy, and the Ambassador who almost single-handedly created limits on armies and air forces in Europe during the last days of the Cold War, Jim Woolsey is now the nation's most passionate advocate for plug-in hybrid cars and alternative fuels. Woolsey argues that by using gasoline we draw ourselves into Middle Eastern wars and fund al Qaeda.

But the leader of al Qaeda has publicly urged his followers to blow up oil facilities, not just in Iraq but throughout the Arab world. So concerned are the Saudis about al Qaeda attacks on their oil infrastructure that Aramco, the Saudi state oil company, is engaged in what the head of the company's security operations told me was a $3 billion security upgrade. An attempted attack on the large Abqaiq refinery complex in Saudi Arabia was in fact perpetrated by al Qaeda. Blowing up Arab-owned facilities is probably not what you would do if you were a terrorist group getting your money from that oil. Of course, it is not bin Laden who is getting the money when Saudi Arabia sells oil. In fact, the beneficiary of oil sales by Aramco is the government of Saudi Arabia. Al Qaeda's original rationale and raison d'être was to destroy the Saudi government. There were repeated attacks in Saudi Arabia by al Qaeda after 9/11, triggering a major crackdown on al Qaeda sympathizers in the Kingdom. The Saudi government is run by the royal family, most of whom would be beheaded in Riyadh's "chop chop" square if al Qaeda came to power.

It is certainly true that al Qaeda took advantage of Saudi government–funded charities, but terrorists have also taken advantage of cigarette sales and credit card fraud to fund their activities. Reducing our use of Saudi oil because of the misuses of Saudi charities by al Qaeda makes about as much sense as banning cigarette sales or credit card use to stop al Qaeda. At least one of those ideas, banning cigarettes, would be a worthy goal if it could be achieved, but not because of al Qaeda. Plug-in hybrid cars are also a very good idea, but also not because of al Qaeda. Is the only way we think we can get people's attention and get them to do something in the post-9/11 world to scare them with the bin Laden boogeyman?

Woolsey is also concerned that our energy infrastructure is fragile and susceptible to terrorist attacks that could bring our nation to its knees. He argues that we need to move to a distributed system of generating power and move away from nuclear power completely. Proponents of this view look at Iraq and suggest that the attacks there show what terrorists can do to a nation's energy infrastructure. In all, there have been nearly 500 attacks on energy assets in Iraq, including oil wells, pipelines, refineries, and storage tanks, as well as energy company personnel since 2003.[9] In 2005 the attacks caused a 5 percent drop from the previous year's production levels. At 2 million barrels per day, Iraqi oil production is well shy of the prewar target of 3 million barrels per day.[10] Even with a 12,000-man security force dedicated to protecting the nation's oil infrastructure, 4,000 miles of pipelines have a lot of targets of opportunity. In a country that generates most of its electricity from burning oil, these attacks have not just hurt the country's finances. An attack on an oil pipeline north of Baghdad shut down the supply of fuel to the Bayji electric power station, taking out 10 percent of the nation's electricity-generating capacity.[11]

While it is true that Iraq has become a terrorist haven, with on-the-job training for terrorists to learn how to successfully attack energy infrastructure, we should not overhype the threat to our domestic energy infrastructure from a possible Iraqi blowback. The attacks in Iraq demonstrate just how hard it is to disable oil production, refinement, and distribution. Despite five hundred attacks over a five-year period, oil production in Iraq has finally managed a modest growth over prewar levels. Certainly it has been harmful to Iraq, but this sustained campaign was not able to achieve a complete shutdown or catastrophic result. Nor could it be replicated here. The assets are too many and the would-be terrorists too few for such widespread attacks to become commonplace.

The U.S. petroleum infrastructure is a complex system of production, importation, refinement, and distribution. There are no single nodes that can be used to bring the whole system crashing to a halt and leave consumers without gasoline at the pumps. There are more than 300,000 inland oil and gas production sites and 4,000 offshore platforms. Oil and gas shipped from overseas by tanker is brought in at 96 receiving ports. There are 153 oil refineries and 600 gas processing plants. There are 160,000 miles of crude oil pipelines and 95,000 miles of pipelines that carry refined products, 7,500 bulk storage facilities, and 1,400 product distribution terminals. There are 278,000 miles of natural gas pipelines and four LNG import terminals.[12] Approximately 50,000 trips are made each day by gasoline tankers. There are 170,000 service stations spread across America.[13]

This large a system with this much redundancy does not mean we are immune from attacks that could create temporary and localized disruptions, but it does mean we can bounce back rather quickly. As one former security executive at a major U.S. oil company put it to me, "Terrorists attack pipelines in the U.S. all the time—we call them backhoes."

Before 9/11, multinational oil companies had spent decades fending off local rebels and terrorist groups in the Middle East, South America, and Southeast Asia. The facility security programs of U.S. oil companies were well developed, employing former intelligence and military personnel in large numbers to deal with threats that ranged from kidnapping and extortion to rocket-propelled grenade attacks. After 9/11, the industry made heavy investments in security domestically, borrowing from the models developed overseas and employing many of the same measures. At a facility level, companies have developed and tested models for identifying critical assets and have taken appropriate measures to secure them.

While terrorists may not be able to disrupt our energy infrastructure in any significant way, they could turn parts of it into weapons, much as was done with airplanes on 9/11. On that day, one of the first things I did as crisis manager in the White House was order the closure of Boston Harbor for fear that a follow-on attack might target the liquid natural gas terminal on the Mystic River. Were such an attack to be successful, it would incinerate much of downtown Boston. In the years since leaving government, I have successfully helped stop an LNG terminal from being built in downtown Providence and unsuccessfully helped an energy company try to build facilities in places where attacks would harm few, if any, people.

There are some things we should do to address concerns over dangerous energy infrastructure in the United States. Nuclear plants should be designed to withstand aircraft impacts, and the design basis standard for a likely terrorist attack should be raised. It may be time to transfer responsibilities for protecting nuclear plants from the private sector to a government agency, if only to allay fears that security is weak, and allow more plants to be built. The highly toxic chemicals used in the oil-refining process can and should be replaced with less toxic ones as almost two-thirds of the refineries in this country have done. We need to move away from oil if for no other reason than that burning it the way we do is contributing to a global cataclysm. That ought to be enough motivation. That ought to be our focus, not made-up terrorism fears.

CLIMATE CHANGE IS THE ENERGY NATIONAL SECURITY CRISIS

I cannot think about the climate change problem without the lyrics of Buffalo Springfield wafting through my brain: "Something's happening here . . . what it is ain't exactly clear. . . . What a field day for the heat . . . I think it's time we stop . . ." Something is definitely happening here, and it is becoming increasingly clear what it is. We are experiencing climate change caused by increased carbon emissions into the atmosphere. That is the conclusion of the world's scientists, assembled by the United Nations through its Intergovernmental Panel on Climate Change (IPCC). The few legitimate scientists with relevant academic specialties who disagree with this basic finding are about as numerous as the few psychiatrists who believe in alien abductions. What will happen as a result of the climate change is that sea levels will rise, long-term droughts will hit now-fertile areas, tropical diseases will spread into temperate zones, millions of people will have to move, and our nation's wealth will be redirected into dealing with these dislocations. It has already begun and is noticeable.

What "ain't exactly clear" is how fast the various changes will develop and whether they can be slowed down or stopped. Because we do not have that precise knowledge, we seem to think it is acceptable to do little or nothing. If, however, we were told that a terrorist group was going to attack New York City or Florida sometime in the next few decades with a weapon that would flood the areas and make them uninhabitable, we would not hesitate to begin acting now. Yet climate change may have a greater effect in this century than any combination of major terrorist attacks or wars, causing population centers to disappear, millions of people to move, and the global balance of power to shift away from the United States.

The United Nations' IPCC estimates that sea levels will likely rise by two feet by the end of the century.[14] Add in the fact that the Greenland ice cap and the similar sheet in the western Antarctic have begun moving off the land and into the sea, where they are now melting, and that sea level rise could be much greater. How much the ice caps of Greenland and western Antarctica will add to the sea level rise is debated, but it could possibly double the effect of thermal warming sea rise in this century.[15] Yet even a far less dramatic rise in sea level would still be devastating.

Studies on the impact of even just a two-foot rise in sea level suggest devastating consequences including the destruction of many coastal cities and critical transportation hubs including ports and airports. One author of a multi-agency report on the impact of climate change concluded that the United States would be forced to build a massive system of coastal armor or "accept the need for strategic retreat."[16]

What all of that means is perhaps best brought home by imagining a tsunami headed for Manhattan (Boston, Miami, San Francisco, etc.). The only differences are that this tsunami is very, very slow and when the wave comes in, it will not go back out, as traditional tsunamis do. And this tsunami happens simultaneously with the creation of inland dust bowls. Think of the depopulation of Oklahoma in the 1930s as depicted in *The Grapes of Wrath*. Millions of people would leave the coastal areas, while millions more would leave the dried-up countryside. As I measured the fall in my well water level in the summer of 2007 and nearby wells gave out altogether, it became easier for me to imagine. The sustained multiyear drought in the southeastern United States was evident on my little Virginia farm. Without moisture, our hay did not grow. The price of the hay that was available quadrupled in our local market, making it impossible for local farmers to feed their animals. They were forced to sell off cattle and other livestock. It's already happening, and it's hitting home.

I have never really understood why some national security experts willingly accept the need to act on the basis of unquantifiable and remote threats from terrorists or the ballistic missiles of countries that do not yet have long-range systems, but at the same time ridicule the need to act against a threat that almost all reputable scientists say is real. In his book *The One Percent Doctrine*, Ron Suskind tells the tale of Vice President Cheney's being willing to wage a fierce (and counterproductive, the way he waged it) war against Iraq and terrorism if there were just a 1 percent possibility of a terrorist nuclear weapon going off in the United States, perhaps destroying New York, on some unknown day in the future. "The United States must act now as if it were a certainty." [17] Well, there is a far greater risk than 1 percent of destruction occurring in all of our coastal cities over the lifetime of children alive today, not because of an enemy, but because of our own and other nations ignoring climate change.

Slowly, national security professionals are beginning to realize that climate change is likely to have a significant and negative security impact. Congress forced the Director of National Intelligence to agree that a National Intelligence Estimate (NIE) on the security risks to the United States as a result of climate change must be prepared. One government-sponsored security think tank, the CNA Corporation, led by Robert Murray, got almost a two-year jump on the NIE process by assembling a panel of recently retired admirals and generals chaired by the former head of the U.S. Army, General Gordon Sullivan. Sullivan dealt directly with the issue of things that "ain't exactly clear." He compared the climate change issue to other national security issues: "We never have 100 percent certainty. We never have it. If you wait until you have 100 percent certainty, something bad is going to happen." [18] His report envisions a loss of coastal military bases due to the sea level rising, beginning with Diego Garcia, our Indian Ocean base. It discusses how forced migrations will trigger wars and resource battles and how spreading tropical diseases will enfeeble populations.

The Sullivan panel concluded that "climate change poses a serious threat to America's national security" and noted that it "has the potential to disrupt our way of life and force changes in how we keep ourselves safe and secure by adding a new hostile and stressing factor to the national and international security environment." [19] They recommended that the United States "should commit to a stronger national and international role to help stabilize climate changes at levels that will avoid significant disruption to global security and stability." [20] The problem, of course, is that we do not really know what level of reduction of carbon emissions globally would stabilize the environment. Nor do we know what inevitable forces we have already put into play. The rational and prudent response is, therefore, to reduce carbon emissions significantly now, rather than waiting around for some future technological miracle. The costs of overreacting pale against the costs of underreacting. Thus the urgent question that should shape a national emergency program is, What can we do right away and over the next very few years?

USING THE TOOLS WE HAVE

Although the United States did not join the 1997 international agreement (the Kyoto Accord) to reduce carbon emissions, most of the rest of the world did sign up. The agreement assigned carbon emission targets to nations, reductions that they were to achieve by 2012. A decade later, few nations had achieved their targets. Other, so-called developing nations such as China and India were exempt from the requirement for reductions. They had experienced dramatic increases in carbon emissions.

Opponents of the Kyoto Accord feared that it would cause the United States and other advanced technological societies to reduce their gross national product in order to achieve reduction levels, with a resulting diminution in our standard of living. They were concerned that while we were doing that, China would take advantage of our restraint, do so much damage to the environment that it would more than offset our sacrifice, and gain relative to us in both economic and military strength.

While there were problems with the critics' logic (they generally suggested that we do nothing), they did have two valid points. First, it is unrealistic to assume that we are going to get the American people to reduce their standard of living voluntarily. Second, it does not make a lot of sense to increase our cost of production or reduce our standard of living to deal with climate change while we let China, India, and other so-called developing countries increase their carbon emissions at a rate that far offsets any reductions we might achieve. What the opponents did not say, however, is that those two objections could be addressed by effective U.S. government regulation.

NOT REDUCING OUR STANDARDS

The critics of Kyoto understood how to appeal to Americans. All they had to say was that we are not going to lower our standards of living to satisfy some U.N. agency. Putting aside such propagandistic appeals, reducing our contribution to global carbon emissions does have to be done in a way that deals with the reality that Americans are, as a nation, unlikely to take sufficient individual actions on a voluntary basis to reduce their personal carbon footprints, the amount of carbon emissions they generate.

While I was researching this chapter, I interviewed a Washington-based energy expert. After we discussed global climate change, I asked him if he would be taking the Metro subway back to Virginia. He sheepishly said that he never takes the train, he drives his sport-utility vehicle. That admission led me to ask him a series of what turned out to be embarrassing questions about his personal energy savings activity. My energy expert friend is really no different from most of us. We are concerned about climate change, but we do little about it personally. Or we do guilt alleviation. I bought a TerraPass for $150 from an organization that said it would take actions (such as paving over methane-emitting landfills) that would compensate for some of the carbon emissions I generated by flying on average once a week. The truth is that most Americans are not going to travel less, they are not going to use mass transit a lot more than they do now, they are not going to sit around in darkened, chilly, or hot homes or make other sacrifices in order to stave off the threat of climatic disaster that will probably fully occur only after they die of natural causes. To date, however, most efforts to combat global warming have focused on this kind of behavior change. The results have been less than stellar.

The Kyoto Accord sought to reduce global emissions of carbon to the 1990 level by 2012, but many developed nations have failed to meet their targeted carbon reductions through the use of energy conservation strategies. Despite the refusal of the Bush administration to ratify the protocol, more than four hundred cities and towns in the United States with a combined population of 55 million have pledged to cut their emissions to meet America's Kyoto goals as part of the Mayors Climate Protection Agreement. Progress after two years is not encouraging. The Institute for Self-Reliance sampled eight cities in the program and concluded that few, if any, would meet the goals and most improvements would be negligible.[21]

In Japan, the country that hosted the Kyoto meeting, sincere efforts have been made to conserve energy, including through the government's "Cool Biz" program. Cool Biz's goal was to encourage businessmen to leave their suits and ties at home so that office workers could function with less air-conditioning. Thermostats in all government buildings were then allowed to fluctuate to as high as 82 degrees. Most Japanese companies followed suit. Japanese office workers now sweat through "a kind of hell" during the warm summer months. The joke is that the only way this policy will reduce carbon emissions significantly will be if the hot working conditions cause a decrease in productivity and the lower economic activity translates to lower emissions. So far, that hasn't happened. Under the Kyoto Accord, Japan pledged to cut emissions back to 6 percent below the 1990 level. Instead, emissions have grown to 8 percent above the 1990 level. The Cool Biz effort has saved only about one-tenth of 1 percent.[22]

Results from the United States show that we are unlikely to fully adopt the recommended measures to use less energy. What the results from Japan suggest is that even if we do adopt them, using less energy that is still produced by carbon-emitting sources can have only a limited effect on the problem. The good news is that we may not have to give up as much as we have been led to believe in order to be part of a society that emits a lot less carbon than we do today.

NOT LESS ENERGY, MORE CLEAN ENERGY

The counterintuitive thing about climate change is that dealing with it will require us, at least in the foreseeable future, to generate more energy, not less. Most of our carbon emissions come from vehicles and power plants. Plug-in hybrid cars (Jim Woolsey's answer to Osama bin Laden) are the best midterm bet to achieve cleaner-emission cars, but they will add greatly to the power that must be generated and moved on the electrical grid. Even without plug-ins, electricity needs will rise.

Desalinization, turning ocean water into something we can drink or at least water our plants with, will increasingly be needed to deal with droughts in California, the American Southwest, and possibly the Southeast. Desalinization requires a lot of electricity. If we later move to hydrogen as a power source, electricity will be needed to create that gas in a usable form. The increasing summertime heat and the longer summers will mean more demand for air-conditioning. Moreover, our growing economy and increasing use of technology will continue to add power demands.

Thus, the rate of electricity demand is, all things being equal, going to go up significantly. That could mean, if we do nothing new, a big increase in U.S. carbon emissions at a time when we need to decrease them. So we have to do something new. First, we have to slow the rate of increased electricity demand by regulations that will shift us to more efficient electrical energy devices. Second, we have to shift current electricity production to cleaner methods and then significantly increase zero-carbon electrical production.

As Professor Evar Neding has so convincingly pointed out, reducing the rate of increase in energy needs from 5 percent a year to 2.5 percent a year has the same effect as doubling the supply.[23] How can we reduce the rate of increase without lowering our standard of living? We must shift rapidly to devices that use less electricity to achieve the same results, i.e., encourage electrical energy efficiency. While Americans will not conserve energy by sitting in overly hot or chilly homes, they will gladly buy new products. New products can, if required by law and regulation and incentivized by tax credits, use energy much more efficiently. For example, switching from incandescent lightbulbs to LED lamps will produce the same brightness for 5 percent of the electricity (and they need to be replaced only every few decades). We would realize 25 percent estimated potential savings in national electricity generation requirements for lighting by 2025 through government requiring LED lamps in new construction. Other energy efficiencies are also possible, if required and/or incentivized by government regulations.

In order to lower carbon emissions from electrical production we must look beyond the popular but impractical alternatives of wind and solar energy. Neither wind nor solar can provide for the base load. Because they are not available 24/7, they are only good as supplements for peak usage periods. To produce the quantities of energy we need produced in a clean way, we will have to come to terms with two industries that are not traditionally thought of as green: nuclear and coal.

Nuclear power lacks grassroots political backers, but it is the only large-scale, always-on power source that does not produce carbon. Adding a lot of nuclear power plants is not a popular idea, I know. The two famous nuclear power plant accidents (Chernobyl and the much less damaging Three Mile Island) have left us with a fear of disaster. We also associate nuclear power plants with highly destructive nuclear weapons. There is also a justifiable concern that nuclear power plants create poisonous by-products that we do not have a system to deal with. The truth is, however, that hundreds of nuclear power plants have been running safely for decades with far fewer casualties than are caused by other power-generating systems. France derives 80 percent of its power from nuclear plants and is set to increase that percentage over the coming decade.[24] Nuclear energy has provided the power source for most of the U.S. Navy without a single significant incident in more than sixty years. If nuclear power can be made safe enough to use on a moving aircraft carrier loaded with bombs and likely to be attacked in battle, it can be made safe enough when built on land in your community.

New nuclear plant designs greatly lessen the already very low chances of accidents, and some new reactor systems address concerns about the use of their by-products in weapons programs. Nuclear waste could be stored in highly secure and survivable facilities on the plants' grounds. Solar, wind, and other renewable forms of energy should continue to be pursued, but in the next decade they cannot begin to approach the capacity that could be added by bringing several dozen nuclear power plants online.

To expand the number of privately owned nuclear power plants in the United States at the rate needed, we will need to take a number of steps.

- First, to get enough qualified operators in short order, we will have to turn to a government program for help. The U.S. Navy has trained most of the managers of our nuclear power reactors, because most of them learned their trade in the highly demanding program created by Admiral Hyman Rickover, a program that has successfully run hundreds of nuclear reactors on submarines, aircraft carriers, and cruisers. The standards and techniques used in that program have a proven track record. Rather than asking industry to try to replicate it, we should ask the Navy to allow civilians into the Rickover program.

- Second, we will have to create an effective program to deal with the NIMBY (Not In My Back Yard) and NOPE (Not On Planet Earth) problems. Thus far, the nuclear industry has dealt with this problem by planning to build most new units on existing plant sites. Of the thirty-three applications the Nuclear Regulatory Commission has received to build new reactors, all but ten have been at existing plants.[25] Congress should consider giving the NRC the same overriding authority to site nuclear plants that the Federal Energy Regulatory Commission (FERC) has to site liquid natural gas facilities. Congress should also consider allowing plants to be built on military bases closed in the downsizing process.

- Third, if for no other reason than to allay the public's fears, security at nuclear plants should be taken over by the federal government. Under the current arrangement, the NRC regulates security at nuclear plants, setting standards for pay, training, and capability for private sector guards. Though this arrangement could serve as a model for security in other industries, security at nuclear plants is too important and too easily used as an argument against building new plants. Putting security under some federal entity could help to dampen fears. The costs should be charged to the utilities as a fee.

For coal, we need to make serious near-term investments to make carbon capture and sequestration a commercial reality, and then we must require that these systems be installed in all existing plants and any new ones that are built. This can be done through a cap-and-trade system, which many economists advocate, or through outright regulation. In either case, meeting our energy demands and preventing global warming will require that we use coal and make it clean. Today, 50 percent of electricity generated in the United States comes from coal.[26] The 1,500 coal plants in the United States are not all going to be shuttered. Politics alone will not let that happen. The powerful senators from coal states such as West Virginia and Montana will not let emissions reductions go into effect if they mean that coal will stop being mined. The United States, India, and China all have huge coal reserves and relatively little oil or natural gas. This resource is not going to go unexploited.

In order to allow coal to be part of the climate change solution, technologies to prevent the carbon produced by burning coal from escaping into the atmosphere must be developed and installed at existing and newly constructed plants. Two technologies hold promise: underground sequestration and algae. Challenges exist for both. Gases trapped underground may not stay there. Algae, which can photosynthesize a steady diet of carbon dioxide, will eventually release the carbon they store back into the atmosphere, either when the algae die and decay or when biofuels produced from the algae are burned. Yet in burning biofuels produced from the algae, we will get twice the energy that was produced by the coal with half the equivalent carbon output.

But what about China? Won't it still be adding a coal-powered electricity plant a week? Sure, if we let them. Fortunately China has a dependency. It's called the U.S. market. We can and should create a tariff (free marketers beware!) system that adds import duties on products made using dirty, carbon-emitting power sources in countries that are not reducing their overall carbon emissions. To do that, we will have to be on that path ourselves and we may have to modify the World Trade Organization rules, but the Europeans would be so relieved to see us doing something about climate change that they might actually agree with us on this issue. The money generated by the tariff could be used to further reduce our own carbon emissions (and those of truly poor countries). The tariff might, coincidentally, make Chinese goods less competitive for a while. (Too bad.) I suspect, however, that given Chinese ingenuity and industriousness, they too will move quickly to low-carbon emissions if forced to by U.S. government regulations.

To summarize, we can get there in the United States, but only by government regulation and action: (1) reducing the rate of increase in our energy requirements through regulations requiring the widespread and rapid deployment of more energy-efficient devices; (2) requiring power plants and vehicles to achieve the highest possible levels of clean energy production with existing technology, and (3) instituting tax incentives and regulations to shift us to plug-in hybrid cars and many nuclear power plants using new technology. Those nuclear power plants would be heavily regulated for safety and security, and their staffs would be trained by the highly successful government training program for reactor operators. At the same time, the government would be funding research on the next step, which would come later, a new generation of solar energy, hydrogen cells and batteries, non-corn-based ethanol and other biofuels, and maybe advanced technologies such as systems that capture the carbon from coal-fired power plants (carbon capture sequestration).

That is what a national emergency program could look like, involving regulations by a series of regulatory agencies that have not done much in the way of regulating in the last eight years: the Environmental Protection Agency, the Federal Energy Regulatory Commission, the Nuclear Regulatory Commission, the office of the U.S. Trade Representative, the Office of Management and Budget, and other regulatory arms of the U.S. government, along with training by the U.S. Navy and research at the Energy Department's network of national laboratories such as Sandia, Livermore, Los Alamos, and Idaho National Laboratory. Such a national emergency effort would make both antigovernment, antiregulation, unconstrained free-market conservatives and anti–nuclear power, proconservation liberals very upset. For the sake of the planet, they need to get over their ideological hangups and we need to get on with it.

ACTING IN TIME

Government is not an inherently dirty word; neither is *regulation*. Sometimes government fails you because it does not act. Sometimes it must intervene when there is market failure. The markets and the economy failed in 1929, in part because of insufficient regulation. If it had not been for government regulation and targeted investment then, the economy, the nation, and millions of people would have suffered for decades. We face a far greater risk now, a risk of drought, disease, and coastal city flooding that will create multiple New Orleans–Katrina migrations. Or we could act, increasing electricity production with carbon sequestration and nuclear power, moving to hybrid plug-in cars that use a variety of liquid fuels as backup sources of power. And we could condition our trade with China and other developing countries on their taking steps to reduce their adverse contributions to climate change. In the process, we could create technologies and companies that would stimulate economic growth in this country. Thus, if government chooses to act, there will be winners and losers. If we do nothing or try to solve the wrong problems, there will be a lot more losers, and America itself will be one of them.

EIGHT

INTO CYBERSPACE

We had been in the Situation Room most of the day, getting reports from government agencies and internet information technology (IT) companies as they tracked the spread of a worm in cyberspace. From tens of thousands of computers infected, the toll had steadily risen to hundreds of thousands of devices around the country that had secretly been penetrated and taken over without their operators' knowing. The question was why. Was this just someone seeing how many computers he could compromise, was he going to steal all the information of value on them, or was there something more sophisticated coming? Around four in the afternoon we got the answer. A team had captured the hidden application that was being placed on the computers, but it was encrypted. With help from the government, they had broken into the applet (small computer program or application) and read its instructions.[1]

"So that's the good news, we know what it's going to do," a computer security specialist told me, his voice coming from one of eight television monitors on the wall in the wood-paneled videoconference room. "The bad news is that all of the infected computers are going to simultaneously bombard one site with messages at eight o'clock tonight, thereby knocking that site off the internet."

"Oh, great, they couldn't just have a little sign pop up and say, 'We hacked your computer?'" Paul Kurtz responded with the microphone off. Paul was part of the team at the National Security Council that worked on security crises of all sorts. He would later become Special Assistant for Homeland Security to President Bush and then later join me as a partner in my consulting firm.

I was beginning to realize that I would have to go upstairs after this meeting and give the bad news to the National Security Advisor or someone else in the new Bush administration White House hierarchy. I wasn't too sure that they would understand the implications of what was happening. It was July 2001, and they seemed in general to focus only on what they liked to work on: China, Russia, Iraq.

"But the really bad news for you, Dick, is that the internet site that all the flood of pings will be flowing to is . . . yours, the White House."

"Well, knocking the White House site off the internet mainly means that kids can't take the White House tour as seen through the eyes of Barney the dog," I replied.

"It's worse, though," the voice from the screen added. "By having so much internet traffic moving toward one location on the internet, the flood will overwhelm routers along the way, stopping traffic from getting to other sites as well. Could jam up sites that are critical to things working, like banks, airlines, you name it. It's serious. The name we are using for the worm is Code Red."

"Oh, shit!" Kurtz blurted out, this time with the microphone open.

The government and IT company experts suggested two alternatives. First, we could call all the major internet carriers (then MCI, AT&T, Level 3, and a few others) and tell them that they should reset their routers so that any traffic going to the White House Internet Protocol address (the IP address is something that looks like a long phone number) should be "blackholed," meaning that internet traffic would just die. Second, we could work with a company called Akamai to replicate the White House public web site on thousands of computers all over the world. Then we would send out a readdressal notice on the internet to send all White House–bound traffic to the nearest Akamai server. There were so many of those servers that no amount of traffic could take them down.

We moved on to the operations floor area of the Situation Room and began calling the network operation centers (NOCs) for the internet service providers (ISPs), asking to speak to the chief watch officer at every NOC. I heard Paul get through to MCI. "Hi, I'm Paul Kurtz calling from the White House Situation Room. We would like you to blackhole all traffic headed to the White House IP address beginning before eight o'clock tonight." There were IT companies around the table with us, but they were software and hardware companies, not the internet service providers that ran the fiber-optic networks on which the internet ran.

Kurtz paused, and his face turned into a scowl. "No, really. Really, I am from the White House. Look, call the White House and ask for me. . . . It's 202-456-1414. Well, if you don't believe me look it up or call Information, you're a phone company aren't you?" Later we would ensure that there were established channels for the federal government to speak at any time, day or night, to the right people at the internet providers, a two-way street so that they could also tell us when something was going wrong in cyberspace.

Well before eight that night, we convinced major ISPs that we had the authority to ask for this unusual move of killing all internet traffic bound to the White House. At eight, a then-unprecedented flood of internet traffic moved from hundreds of thousands of computers onto phone lines and then to the nearest connection to the fiber-optic lines that are the internet. In hundreds of buildings around the country where the phone lines end and the packets of data are switched onto the internet, so-called edge servers read the destination for which the packets were intended, the White House, and dropped the packets into oblivion. It was like a thousand little waves cresting against sea walls and falling back without ever coming together to create a tsunami. We dodged the bullet that night, but there have been other cyber attacks that hit their targets in cyberspace and resulted in billions of dollars in losses, millions of identities stolen, terabytes of secrets taken, and general disruption of governments, corporations, and individuals' lives.

Failures or pending failures are usually evident before a big disaster thrusts the issue into the klieg light of public attention. Often when an issue does take center stage after a major event, it becomes clear that miniature versions of the big failure had been going on for some time. In other cases, there is no major event, but the weight of individual incidents becomes so large that the issue takes on crisis proportions and becomes a focus of national attention.

One type of failure in national security is the inability to adapt to new technologies and new threats, such as the U.S. Navy in the 1930s, clinging to the battleship as the centerpiece of Pacific strategy while the possible future enemy was developing aircraft carriers that could sink battleships. Do we today have vulnerabilities to new weapons, as the French did to the British archers so disastrously at Agincourt six hundred years ago? (France may have suffered as many as 10,000 casualties to the Britain's 100 that day.)

UNINTENDED CONSEQUENCES AT THE DAWN

Dealing with problems in cyberspace was new to the White House and to America in general in the 1990s. The origins of my concern with security in cyberspace began with the bombing of Oklahoma City's Alfred P. Murrah Federal Building in 1995. An enormous bomb had completely devastated the building and much of the neighborhood. When the crisis management response was over, we began thinking about how easy it had been for the bombers to buy the materials to make that huge bomb. If people could turn Ryder trucks into block-busting bombs, what else could they blow up: the Capitol, the White House, the New York Stock Exchange? President Bill Clinton seemed to obsess over the question. The result was a special presidential commission on the security of important facilities, or, as it unfortunately became known, critical infrastructure protection.

The commission surprised us by coming back with a report that did not focus on the vulnerability of key buildings around the country but instead on the security problems in the new phenomenon of cyber-space.[2]

Computers had been around since ENIAC was turned on at the University of Pennsylvania in February 1946 and drew so much electricity that most of the lights in West Philadelphia dimmed. They had been networked since at least 1965, when a computer at MIT connected to a West Coast computer. By the 1980s, with Defense Department funds, a computer-routing language and system was created so that large numbers of computers could be connected across the country. It was still seen as a way of linking up research facilities, mainly at universities, but the users started to see other things that could be done, such as sending little messages back and forth to one another. The National Science Foundation (NSF) then took over responsibility from the Pentagon for the development of the network. Early in the 1990s, Congress authorized NSF to allow some major telephone companies to connect into this computer network and offer access to commercial companies and even to private individuals. (Al Gore was, in fact, a key player in that congressional decision.) Thus, the internet was born.[3]

That's when, I would contend, the information technology (IT) revolution began. It was at least as profound as the industrial revolution that had happened two hundred years earlier. The industrial revolution was, however, more easily observed. In the late 1700s, big brick buildings went up on the banks of rivers. Smoke poured out of their stacks, dulling the skies. People packed up from their tiny farm patches in the countryside and moved to the new jobs in the cities, creating slums and overburdening city services, spending long days in terrible working conditions for little pay. Social disruption grew to social conflict, as crime rose in the cities and labor tried to organize. Meanwhile, the factories were turning out an immense variety of items in what were then enormous, unprecedented numbers. Our societies were fundamentally changed in the later half of the 1700s and the first half of the 1800s by that industrial revolution.

When the internet started clicking away, the change took place much faster, more quietly, and less obviously. Many people thought at first it was about e-mail and later about buying books online and having them shipped to your home. One of the more surprising early phenomena was the rise of numerous pay-for-access web sites; they were usually pornographic sites, but they proved that people would pay money to get onto a web site. While the public was growing aware of the new things you could do with a computer in your office or home, major corporations were seeing something else: a much cheaper way to conduct intracompany and intercompany communications among employees and, more importantly, machine to machine. Without any real national plan, banks, airlines, electric power companies, pipelines, and a variety of other kinds of enterprises began connecting their control systems by using the internet. Previously they had used expensive leased telephone lines or physically shipped computer tapes around. With the internet, the cost of connectivity and doing business plummeted and productivity rose. The effects were soon visible in the national economy, and an era of expanded prosperity began.

Unfortunately, this was all happening on the system that the Pentagon and NSF had created to connect university-based researchers. Nobody had thought back then that the professors would abuse the system, try to get into sites where they didn't belong, or steal data from one another. Certainly, they wouldn't intentionally do anything to damage the network. Thus the system was designed without some fundamental protections. Unfortunately, it turned out that it was relatively easy to pretend you were somebody else and send messages in that person's name or do things on the network that would be traced back to somebody else. It was also pretty simple to get onto parts of the network where you had no business being and, while there, change things. You could even leave funny little messages saying that you had been there, maybe alter and deface the web site. What was worse, the entire system for addressing messages and then switching them through the network of routers and servers to the right computer was designed without any notion that someone would want to damage it or alter it without authorization. One MIT student tried to forward his e-mail from campus to his mother's house in Florida during spring break and made a mistake that sent all e-mail intended for MIT to a little ISP in Florida. The servers of that ISP crashed, and people at MIT started wondering why they were not getting any e-mail. Oops.

As the internet took off in popularity in the mid-1990s, so did its problems. People could send you e-mail even if you didn't know them. They could attach small pieces of computer code that would take over your computer and crash it, or open up "back doors" to let people into your computer without your knowing it. They could then install programs to record every key stroke you typed, identify when you typed something that looked like a password or a credit card number, and send that information off to another computer without your even knowing it. Even if you were smart and refused to open e-mail from strangers, they could plant a virtual listening device on the ethernet line that your cable or telephone company used in your neighborhood to connect you to the internet. People could use automated systems to take over thousands of computers and make them "zombies." Thousands of zombies working together were called "botnets" or robot networks. They could all flood a web site or could all try to collect credit card data or other information. If someone traced the attack back, it might well turn out to be some grandmother's computer that had stolen the credit card information without her even knowing it was doing so.

We as a nation had created a technological marvel that was accelerating our economy. We had also, without thinking seriously about it, taken all of the things that mattered in a company or government agency and opened them up, connected them to to the world. Sure, there were software and hardware devices called firewalls that people were busily installing to act as guards at our cyberdoorways, but it was becoming pretty obvious that serious players and even high school kids were getting around the guards. Once a government agency, public utility, bank, or other company connected to the internet, criminals and spies could surf in, gain access to the internal network and crash it, or steal valuable information, or cause control systems to go crazy. As the presidential commission reported this new problem to the White House in 1997, we began to worry about the fact that places like the Pentagon were connected to the internet.

CODE NAMES FOR VULNERABILITY

Working with a few people in the Pentagon and with the permission of the Secretary of Defense, we ran an exercise in 1997 called Eligible Receiver under joint White House and DOD supervision.[4] Using a small team, mainly from the National Security Agency, the exercise began on a Monday to attempt to probe the Defense Department's networks from the internet, without the benefit of any insider knowledge. The hope was that by the end of the week, the team might have found a way into some network, so that we could prove that even the Pentagon was vulnerable. By Wednesday, the team reported that they were inside not just some Pentagon network, but the Joint Chiefs' command system. Moreover, they could alter messages going out from the Pentagon. I asked to stop the exercise right away.

Deputy Secretary of Defense John Hamre later reflected on the exercise, noting, "What Eligible Receiver really demonstrated was the real lack of consciousness about cyber warfare. I mean, really, the first three days of Eligible Receiver, nobody believed we were under cyber attack."[5] After the exercise, Hamre ordered the military departments immediately to procure and install intrusion detection systems (IDS), new computer hardware and software that sat on the edge of a network's connection with the internet to see if anyone was trying to get in without permission. Within weeks the IDS were installed and turned on. They immediately showed that thousands of attempted illegal penetrations of DOD networks were going on every day.

One general was irate with the result and complained, "Before we had these IDS, we were never attacked. Now that we got them on the network, people are hitting our nets every day thousands of times, trying to get in! And some of them are getting in!" Aside from the fact that he was confusing cause and effect, the general was right: people were getting in. One holiday weekend President Clinton ordered Air Force and Navy assets to deploy to the Arab Gulf to threaten Iraq, which was refusing to allow U.N. inspectors access. As this buildup was getting ready, we became aware that someone had penetrated the Air Force logistics systems at many of the bases involved. Suspicions rose that Iraq was engaged in cyberwarfare. We feared that when troops opened the cases being sent to the Gulf, they would find sneakers and not missiles. I went to the headquarters of the Defense Information Systems Agency (DISA) on a hill above the Pentagon surrounded by Arlington Cemetery and interstate highways. There, in a network operation center, a team worked for hours contacting the Air Force bases. All the bases insisted that their networks were untouched. Frustrated DISA experts told the base computer staffs where in the computer files to look and ordered them to do so immediately. Slowly, the bases began to report back unauthorized activity throughout their networks. Late into the night, with the help of computer companies and the FBI, the culprits were identified. Two were in California and another was, in fact, in the Middle East. They were three teenagers, one of whom was in Israel. The two Californians were arrested by the FBI. The Israeli got a slap on the wrist, became a national celebrity, and helped defend Israeli networks in the cyberwar with the Palestinians.[6] The FBI gave the case a name, Solar Sunrise.

Not all the penetrations of government networks were as easily investigated. The PBS series *Frontline* reported about Moonlight Maze, ". . . a highly classified incident in which U.S. officials accidentally discovered a pattern of probing of computer systems at the Pentagon, NASA, Energy Department, private universities, and research labs that had begun in March 1998 and had been going on for nearly two years."[7] The hackers had gone through thousands of files in a highly systematic manner, gaining access to files that included "maps of military installations, troop configurations and military hardware designs." The identity of the perpetrators was never discovered. "The Defense Department traced the trail back to a mainframe computer in the former Soviet Union, but the sponsor of the attacks is unknown and Russia denies any involvement. Moonlight Maze is still being actively investigated by U.S. intelligence."

Later *The Washington Post* reported on a similar multiyear series of attacks in 2003–2005 on the Defense Department, Energy Department, and corporate networks that it said had been given the government code name Titan Rain. The *Post* quoted sources as speculating that the attacks were from China.[8] In 2007, another *Washington Post* report quoted Major General William Lord, a senior Pentagon cyberwarrior, as saying that China had downloaded "10 to 20 terabytes of data" from the Pentagon's network. "They are looking for your identity so they can get into the network as you. There is a nation-state threat by the Chinese."[9] A 2007 Defense Science Board report on the "Mission Impact of Foreign Influence on DoD Software" concluded that "DoD does not fully know when or where intruders may have already gained access."[10]

Eligible Receiver, Solar Sunrise, Code Red, Moonlight Maze, and Titan Rain took place over eight years during which the extent of the problem of cybersecurity was slowly becoming apparent to government and industry. More than any of those incidents, however, what focused attention on how reliant we were on fragile software and hardware was the beginning of the new millennium.

THE MISSING-DIGIT SCARE

As the century was coming to a close, a drumbeat from computer scientists started to gain volume. They said there was a little problem. When computer code was first developed, a convention or habit developed that dates were always written with just two digits, as in 99 for 1999. When 2000 rolled around, they explained, some computers would think it was 1900 or not know what to think about the date at all. "So what?" was the response of most of us when we heard this for the first time. "Well, nobody knows. Some computers are likely to shut down. Others may wipe out data records. You could have electrical grids shutting off, elevators stopping, respirators and other medical devices going screwy, credit cards rejected all over the world," John Koskenin explained. He was the number three person in the White House Office of Management and Budget and the person stuck with getting all of the government's computers fixed before the century ended. Tall, bald, and soft-spoken, Koskenin gave off an aura of neatness, even meticulousness, but he was presiding over a mess.

The mess soon got an acronym, Y2K, for the year 2000. Koskenin found a champion in the junior senator from Utah, a somewhat taller and balder fellow named Robert Bennett. Bennett had some experience in the private sector and with things that were unusual. He had founded the company that sold the Franklin Planner systems and before that had been press secretary for someone he never saw, a reclusive billionaire with whom he communicated by slipping things under the door of a hotel penthouse in Las Vegas. Bennett and Koskenin made a team. Bennett would convince the Senate leadership to fund an urgent effort to fix government computers. Koskenin would make sure the money was well spent and that things were fixed in time. Together they would appeal to the private sector to change corporate computers in time, too, because it would do little good if the government's computers were all humming along while everybody else's died.

Koskenin asked me to join him in the Y2K effort because he was concerned that there would be security problems as a result of systems shutting down or people taking the opportunity of Y2K to add Trojan horses or trapdoors to computer code, attacking systems in ways that made it look like a Y2K-related failure. I was concerned that al Qaeda might pick the Y2K New Year period for more conventional attacks, using truck bombs or worse, but I saw the potential for a new types of security risk in the Y2K computer problem as well.

Billions of dollars were spent around the world fixing government and private computers, changing the software before 99 became 00. When the New Year came, there were few problems. Koskenin said that the paucity of computer failures was because of the Herculean effort that had been made to fix things. Critics and skeptics said that the problem was never going to be as bad as it had been painted and had served largely to get business for IT companies.[11]

What had happened, however, was that for the first time the leaders of Congress, the government, and industry were forced to think about what would happen if computers did not work. The country would come to a grinding halt. Without airline reservation systems working, perfectly good airplanes would stand idle. (Later Delta, Air Canada, United, Northwest, and Comair would each independently experience incidents when just that happened, grounding thousands of flights.) Without computer networks running, ATC cannot control air traffic. (Thousands of flights were diverted or grounded in 2007 when the

Memphis Center's network went down.[12]) Even hospitals would have to close their operating rooms and send patients home when their computers crashed (as later happened at Boston's Beth Israel Deaconess Medical Center[13]). In sector after sector, it came as a shock to senior managers that there really was no manual way of running things anymore. Try to find a manual typewriter anywhere and you see a metaphor for the problem. The nation had quickly become totally dependent upon computers and networks, and they were, well, not exactly secure.

WHAT'S THE PROBLEM, AND HOW BAD IS IT?

Perhaps because the computer security or IT security problem was sometimes given the misnomer of "cyberterrorism," I was asked by President Bill Clinton to figure out what the problem was and what to do about it. Early in 2000, a series of malicious internet floods hit several popular online commerce sites, including eBay, Yahoo!, and Amazon, knocking them off the internet by pinging their web sites several times a second.[14] I saw an opportunity to bring people together to talk about the fundamental insecurity of the internet. Clinton agreed with my suggestion that we hold the first White House cybersecurity summit. Days later e-commerce and computer industry CEOs from Silicon Valley, cabinet members, government and university experts, and a self-described hacker known only as Mudge walked into the Cabinet Room in the West Wing.

They agreed on a few things right away. There was definitely a big problem, and neither the government nor industry could solve it by themselves. It would take a public-private partnership. They also agreed that there were some technical solutions that most companies and government agencies had not yet installed. There was no one "silver bullet" solution; rather, multilayered defenses were needed on networks. As soon as the defenses were in place, however, people were finding new ways around them. It was an arms race that the offense was winning, and it was going to take constant attention. When it came to explaining why it was possible to get into computers and networks that were supposed to be restricted, the computer company executives were quiet. Mudge, a fellow with a beard, earring, and Jesus-like shoulder-length hair, explained it rather simply: "Software is millions of lines of instructions written in one of the computer code languages. People write them sloppily. Nobody checks them for mistakes before they get sold. Some of those mistakes allow you to get in where you shouldn't or get control of systems or turn off the defenses or pretend to be somebody else. Most of the problem is just bad computer code. And the rest is bad configuration. People install software and hardware improperly, or various pieces of software or hardware weren't designed to work together and when you put them together they create a seam or a crack." Nobody disagreed.

The meeting agreed that there should be a national plan to create and implement the public-private partnership. I was asked to pull it together. As we were filing out of the West Wing onto the North Lawn, the press swooped in and asked for comments. Spotting the guy with the shoulder-length hair, the cameras soon circled around Mudge ("Hey, there's the hacker guy!"), leaving famous CEOs standing in little groups hoping some reporter would ask them something. Looking down his nose at Mudge's impromptu press conference, one CEO asked, "Who the hell invited him, anyway?"

I had. When I wanted to learn more about cyberspace in the mid-1990s, I traveled to NSA, DOD, and a number of government labs and IT companies. When I raised with them the concerns I was hearing, most of the corporate types denied that there were problems or minimized them. Their software and hardware worked just fine, they told me. On some occasions, I found myself explaining things to CEOs that I thought were pretty basic, but they did not seem to know. There was the CEO of a company that manufactured computer routers who asked me to write down the letters BGP and what it stood for (Border Gateway Protocol) because "I don't think I have ever heard of that, but if you say there is a vulnerability with it that affects our routers, I will check up on it." The BGP was the software protocol that told his routers where to send internet traffic. Using BGP, his company had made billions. The problem was that the BGP protocol could easily be spoofed, as when the MIT student had sent all of the university's e-mail to his mom. What if somebody intentionally spoofed several BGP tables on major internet routers? Internet traffic would bounce all over cyberspace, misdirected, clogging the networks. The internet could effectively crash.[15] But that was apparently nothing that the CEO of the company that made the routers needed to know about.

FUNNY PLACE FOR A FED

I was beginning to think that maybe I needed to talk to other kinds of people than the corporate officials of the companies that made the software and hardware whose defects allowed all of this malicious activity to occur. I had been to scores of information technology companies, talking with the engineers as well as the CEOs. I had been to university and government research centers and to the Defense Department and all the three-letter agencies (NSA, CIA, FBI, etc.). I had gone up and down Silicon Valley and done the Haj to Redmond, Washington. Insisting that I see the internet ("You can't *see* it, Dick, it's virtual"), my staff and I had gone to windowless buildings through which large percentages of the world's internet traffic was routed, saw where fiber-optic cable to Europe emerged from the Atlantic, eyeballed the domain name servers that translate the "www" addresses into numerics, traced the lines from the New York Stock Exchange under the streets of lower Manhattan. But there was an element missing.

Maybe I needed to talk with the hackers, since they seemed to know more about the problems with the information technology systems than the people who made and sold them. But I was a White House official, and it would not be a good reflection on the President if someone found out that I was meeting with criminals. So I asked around, carefully, "Know any hackers? Ever heard of somebody who is one?" Eventually I learned of a group in the Boston area called The L0pht (that's a zero in there), a club of hackers. I asked the FBI if it had any open cases or complaints, any investigations or reasons I should not talk with L0pht. The surprise answer came back that not only were they not a problem, but the Boston FBI office had actually asked them technical questions once or twice, maybe, off the record. (It's a good thing that I didn't know at the time that this was the same Boston FBI office that was using Irish murderers to snitch on the Italian mob.) So I asked the Boston FBI to set up a meeting, which in retrospect is probably not the best way to contact a group of hackers, but it was 1999 and I was not as sensitive to these things as I would later become.

The meeting, or maybe I should say meet, was set up not at an office somewhere but at John Harvard's Brew House, a bar off the eponymous square. I was to meet the L0pht at five and, in a bit of movie melodrama, to come alone. By five-thirty and with one Stoli on the rocks finished, I was still alone at the bar. I asked the bartender for the check, whereupon the young man next to me asked, "You were only going to wait half an hour?" That's how I met Mudge, who had been spending the preceding hour trying to spot who it was in the bar that I had brought with me. He had decided I actually did come alone. We talked for an hour at the bar. "Didn't think you'd come. Funny place for a fed." He started with definitions. "A hacker is just someone who can slice and dice computer code and take the hardware apart and put it back together better. It doesn't mean you're a criminal. We call criminals crackers, guys who crack their way into other people's computers and networks. That's illegal. But if I buy the computer or software, then I can legally dissect it . . . to make sure I know its vulnerabilities, to be safe, to fix them."

And when the L0pht found a hole in a software program, what exactly did they do next? "Well, we tell the guys that made it, give 'em a chance to fix it, to issue a software patch." And if they didn't fix it? "They usually don't. They wait til people start using the glitch to crack into systems and install Trojan horses, back doors allowing them to get in and out of networks without being seen, without having been granted access. When the software companies get enough complaints, they act, eventually." So the L0pht just sits around after being ignored by the software company? "Oh, hell, no. After a while we post the problem on a web site like Bugtraq. That usually accelerates the process of them issuing a fix, a patch." The real problem was Zero Day attacks, Mudge went on, that is, when somebody finds a vulnerability in software and uses it right away, writing an exploit code and launching a virus or worm. The threat of those no-notice attacks is that the first time you learn about the software vulnerability would be when it's being used in a widespread attack. It could take days to write a patch for the software and weeks before it was widely installed on systems around the country.

It was a fascinating hour of seeing the problems from a different perspective. And then Mudge introduced me to the six guys at the nearest table, who had been listening to our conversation. They were the L0pht. Two hours later we were in a badly beat up old car going to a warehouse. Their clubhouse was filled with what could only be described as a museum of hardware and software, complete with a jerry-rigged parallel processor pretending to be a supercomputer. Most of the hardware had been acquired by "Dumpster diving" in the parking lots of firms on Boston's beltway, Route 128. What the L0pht knew better than the FBI, NSA, or CIA was that there were very highly skilled cybercriminals around the world who traded secrets and homemade software in password-secured chat rooms, using only their "handles" as identification. These cybercriminals boasted to one another about what networks they had broken into and how. And some of the bad guys were for hire.

Want to know what your competitor is charging special customers? How about their next product release, when will it be and how does the product work? What's the secret formula, how is that pharmaceutical made, what's the schematic for that aircraft, what's the software for that new airborne radar? If you are a foreign country your intelligence service may have its own crackers, or they may rent them. If you are a foreign corporation, you may hire a business intelligence firm and not ask too many questions about how it gets its information. The people running the networks rarely know that they have been hacked into because "if you're good, if you're really good, you wipe your tracks away on your way out the back door."

I had heard the L0pht guys being quoted as saying that the internet itself could be taken down, so after a while, I asked how to do it. "Crash the DNS, mess up the BGP." When you send an e-mail out or ask your web browser to go somewhere like www.whitehouse.gov, your computer reaches out through cyberspace to the equivalent of telephone books, servers that convert those letters into IP addresses. Flood those phone books, called domain name servers, so nobody can do a lookup, and things will slow to a halt. (That happened in October 2002, but the attacker stopped after learning how much of a flood it would take to crash all of the thirteen high-level DNS servers in the world.[16] There were only thirteen because they were still the ones designated by a National Science Foundation employee when the internet started. He asked friends he knew in the DOD, universities, and companies to host the servers. They still do. Another big DNS attack took place in February 2007, testing to see what it would take to crash the system and then backing off before actually destroying it.[17])

I already knew about the Border Gateway Protocol (BGP) flaw from BBN Labs, so I tried to explain it to see if I had it right. Each site on the internet was connected to one internet service provider, such as AT&T. So if someone in China who is connected to China Telcom wants to send you an e-mail or browse to your web page, how do they know how to get to your site? Easy. AT&T isn't connected, perhaps, to China Telcom, but MCI is and AT&T "peers" with MCI, meaning it connects to it in windowless buildings called telcom hotels or internet exchanges. So AT&T sends out a list of all of the sites on its network, including your web site, and tells all the other carriers it's connected to, "If somebody asks to see Joe's web site, send the traffic to me." Then MCI tells China Telcom, "To get to Joe's web site, send the traffic to me and I will send it to AT&T." The only problem was that it was relatively easy to get into the routers that pass these BGP messages back and forth. Many of the routers were still using their factory-installed default password, which everybody seemed to know. And when you told an MCI router you were AT&T, the MCI router would believe you because there was no way to authenticate valid users from fakes.

"In a very simplified, high-level way, you're right," one of the L0pht guys agreed. So, if the internet is so fragile, why doesn't somebody take it down? "And ruin a good thing? Hell, the people who know how to do this are either working for the governments or they're crooks making money by cracking into sites all over the world. Crash the Net, you're outta business." It was well after midnight in the L0pht's warehouse, and I had a feeling that it was getting late for users of cyberspace, too. And that was all of us.

TRYING TO MAKE THE MARKET WORK

The question I kept coming back to was "What is government's role?" The U.S. government, specifically the Pentagon and National Science Foundation, had funded the creation of the internet. What responsibility did the government have for what happened after that? The universal answer I got from people outside government was "Hands off." Silicon Valley was a long way from Washington, and Redmond was even further philosophically. In the late 1990s, folks in the Valley worried about a government plan called Clipper Chip, which would have forced the use of a computer chip that the government could get a virtual key to hack into (the idea had created a firestorm, and the government had backed off),[18] and in Redmond the monofocus was the fact that the government was trying to break up Microsoft's monopoly. Lurking not far behind those concerns was the fear that governments, including states, would see the commerce now flowing on the internet and try to tax it. The IT industry had made a strong case that taxing the young internet would limit its full commercial potential, and it had won that argument so far.

"But what about security?" I asked in a series of White House town meetings on cybersecurity, open public forums I ran in Texas, Pennsylvania, California, Colorado, Massachusetts, Illinois, Arizona, Georgia, and Virginia and online. Didn't government have a role in stopping people from using the internet to steal money, industrial secrets, or national security information, from hacking into electric power grids, radars, or banks? Yes, certainly it did, everyone agreed. Government could share information about the threats. (This reaction reflects a larger and common public misunderstanding that the government has threat information that is worth sharing. In the case of IT security, the best information was with private cybersecurity companies such as

Symantec and McAfee.) Government could fund research into better defensive systems and then share the technology with the private sector, which would then sell it and make money (Government funds for research into cybersecurity are now a fraction of what they were less than a decade ago). And the government could serve as a convener, a broker to get all the concerned parties to the table to work things out: hardware manufacturers, software developers, IT security firms, internet service providers, university researchers, infrastructure owners like banks, airlines, and so on. (We did that, creating more than a dozen industry groups called Information Sharing and Analysis Centers, where industries such as banking shared best practices and information about the threats with one another and sometimes with the government.) Finally, the government could lead by example and secure its many large computer networks and databases. (Instead, according to annual report cards released by the Government Accountability Office and Congress, government agencies were typically an example of the least well secured systems.[19] A federal judge ordered the Department of Interior to disconnect from the internet because its network was so susceptible to illegal hacking that it risked exposing privacy data about citizens and specifically the Native American trust funds.[20])

What almost all of the private sector wanted to hear was that we would not solve the cybersecurity problem by issuing government regulations. If they heard that promise, they suggested, their willingness to cooperate in seeking solutions would increase. Thus, President Clinton's eventual National Plan for Information Systems Protection said the government would "eschew regulation."[21] Oddly enough, three years later President Bush's National Strategy to Secure Cyberspace pretty much said the same thing. The only time I had ever used the word *eschew* before was in quoting Mao, "Dig tunnels deeper, bury food everywhere, eschew hegemonism." (It's a good quote to describe a situation where the leadership simply tells you to do more, lots more, and not challenge the ideology.)

So the executive branch of the government stayed away from regulation, while muttering something about reconsidering that policy if there were a "market failure"—that is, if the invisible hand did not create enough economic pressure from theft and consumer complaints that the industries solved the problem themselves. But for market forces to fix the problems, there had to be economic pressures that could be applied on the people who could fix some of the problems. And the economic system was too balkanized; there was not really one monolithic IT industry that could solve the cyberinsecurity problem.

Much of the problem derived from the glitches in the operating system that almost everyone was using in his or her desktop or laptop, Microsoft's Windows. To say that there had not been a lot of quality control for security during its code development would have been a massive understatement. There seemed to be no end to the things that hackers could do to the Windows code to make it malfunction or let them in where they should not be. It got so bad that the major banks and financial institutions organized and went to Redmond, threatening to switch to open-source systems like Linux (a free alternative operating system developed by an informal network of people all over the world).[22] Microsoft promised changes, said that its new system called Longhorn (later named Vista) would be better. Work began on Longhorn in 2001, but it was not until late 2006 that it became available. Soon after Vista appeared, hackers were finding ways to make it malfunction.[23]

There were lots of problems with other companies' software, too, but the software giant could have done more to create a more secure cyberspace. As Bill Gates suggested to me in his tiny, spartan office in Redmond, the "real security problem is anonymity on the Net. And we could solve that." He was right that it was a problem and probably right that he could have created the momentum to solve it by incorporating authentication methods as the default in the Microsoft browser and e-mail programs, but he didn't. Although the company dominated the software industry worldwide and could have taken the lead in solving many of the IT security issues, it engaged in half measures. For Microsoft, which was building up an immense financial reserve from the sales of its software and games, there was no IT security crisis.

Anonymity is also something that many people find to be part of the beauty of the internet. You can go anywhere and read anything, post any comment, download any information without saying who you are. Human rights activists note that this feature of the internet has allowed people in brutal dictatorships to become active dissidents, learn what the rest of the world is like, sneak out information about the repression. Anonymity also allows fraud and facilitates illegal hacking and sexual predators. If every time you logged on you had to establish your identity in a foolproof way, then we would know it was you when you hacked your way into a bank's computer or a nuclear weapons lab. When you were in a network, you could have to go through a reliable access control system that would verify your identity before it let you get into certain files like a payroll, a school's report card grades, or the Pentagon's plans to invade Canada. These ideas are not fantasy; such access-control technology exists. Two-factor and three-factor authentication systems work, and while some can be hacked with great effort, a concerted program could make it extremely hard or impossible to defeat such security. Two-factor authentication means something more than passwords, which are notoriously unreliable. Passwords can be "sniffed" as they are sent in the clear over the internet. Cleaning crews in office buildings can easily pick up passwords during their nightly rounds by looking for yellow stickies under the mouse pads.

Authentication could be a biometric factor, such as a fingerprint or an ever-changing multidigit number on a fob, like the RSA token. A third factor could be a series of questions that only you would know the answers to and are unlikely to be in public records or your résumé (favorite color, pet's name). Data files and documents can also be encrypted so that only people on an access list can read them. Indeed, entire laptops can be encrypted so that if they are lost or stolen, no one can read your files.

Your anonymity in cyberspace today is less than you might think. Somewhere on your computer is a file filled with little applets called "cookies." Cute name, can't be bad? Well, actually cookies are often snitches that tell web sites who you are and what you do on the Net. These web sites sometimes sell this information about you to those who want to know more about you so they can sell you things you like. One firm engaged in learning about you and your surfing habits, and selling that information, just sold itself. DoubleClick was bought by Google for more than $3 billion, leading to a surmise that the absence of anonymity on the web is making some people a lot of money.[24]

If passwords can be so easily compromised, why is a password all you are using to access your bank or stock account online? Your bank has not given you a better way because it would cost it money and the current cost to the bank of online banking is very low. As one bank official told me, "Go to a teller window to do a transaction, that costs us about seven dollars when you consider the cost of the teller, the guard, the building. Do it with an ATM, and it costs us twenty-five cents. Do it online, and it costs us a penny." Banks save so much money from your using online banking that they can afford to cover the cost of criminals hacking in and stealing from your account, up to a point.

We may, however, quickly be reaching the point at which the costs of cybercrime are becoming unmanageable. Since 2005, commercial companies have lost 150 million account records, including bank information and files containing credit card numbers.[25] Americans lost at least $200 million last year to online fraud.[26] Each phishing scam (people pretending to be your bank or credit card company to get your account number and password) costs the victim an average of $1,250.[27] A 2006 FBI study placed the cost of cybercrime to corporations at $67 billion.[28] These problems not only cost us billions, but require thousands of hours of our free time and corporate productivity to fix.

The problems exist and are costing billions of dollars. The solutions exist and are available from well-established vendors. Using verifiable identification systems online, combined with encryption and access controls (software that says what privileges you have, what files you can read), would greatly reduce or eliminate spam (those annoying marketing junk e-mails), phishing, online sexual predators, fraud, identity theft, and maybe even much of the industrial and state-sponsored espionage online.

Is the invisible hand making that all happen? No, but government could. The Federal Communications Commission (FCC) could require all internet service providers to provide two levels of service. On the first or secure level, ISPs would require two- or three-factor authentication systems to get online. Some networks and web sites would allow people to connect to them only if you were originating from a secure service, thus solving most of the problems of fraud, identity theft, and espionage online. The second level of service would be anonymous. The FCC, however, is a regulatory body that does not want to regulate, at least with regard to anything related to the internet. It has bought the line that the fragile, young internet should be allowed to grow up before we subject it to the kind of regulations every other major industry has. Former FCC Chairman Michael Powell asked IT security experts from the private sector to develop voluntary security best practices for internet service providers. He said the FCC should require compliance through regulation if the voluntary approach did not work. His voluntary appeal did not work, but then Powell left the FCC.

While the executive branch was eschewing regulation, Congress and state legislatures were not.

- Buried in the Banking Modernization Act (also known as the Gramm-Leach-Bliley law, or GLB), which liberalized nationwide banking, was a provision requiring six federal banking regulators to audit financial institutions for cybersecurity. The regulators have created some standards, but have not taken steps that would deal a serious blow to online fraud and theft.[29]

- Part of the Health Insurance Portability and Accountability Act (HIPAA) requires doctors, dentists, clinics, hospitals, insurance companies, and others to have cybersecurity measures to protect patients' data. There is no regular auditing to see that they comply.[30]

- After the collapse of Enron and its accounting firm Arthur Andersen, Congress passed the Sarbanes-Oxley Act (SOx), which led to regulations that require audits for cybersecurity in companies whose stock is publicly traded.[31]

- California's legislature (S. 1386) required that any company doing business with anyone in California (that's almost every major company) be required to tell all customers if someone has hacked into the company's network and may have stolen customer data such as credit card numbers, Social Security numbers, etc. Most states followed with similar laws, but Congress has been unable to agree on a national standard.[32]

Thus, there is a crazy-quilt hodgepodge of government regulation now, but it has been largely unsuccessful at dealing with the epidemic of hacking, identity theft, data loss, fraud, and espionage. And there is no one in charge. The position I once held as Special Advisor to the President for cyberspace security, chair of a governmentwide coordination mechanism, is no more. The highest-ranking official in the government charged with defending America's cyberspace is buried levels down in the Department of Homeland Security, with no authority and few resources.

TEACHING CYBERSECURITY

One of the reasons that many large corporations, government agencies, and universities suffer from insecure networks is the paucity of IT security personnel to configure and manage systems. In most places the chief information officer (CIO) is not trained or certified in IT security. The person responsible for MIT's networks' IT security complained to me that most people getting an undergraduate or graduate degree in computer science at MIT had never taken a single semester's course on security. I was startled by that fact, but found that it was true in almost all the major universities' computer science programs.

If it is hard for companies to find certified IT security professionals, it is even more difficult for government agencies, which typically pay such employees less than they would earn in the private sector. I explained this problem to Attorney General Janet Reno one day, and she immediately shot back, "Then why don't you create a ROTC-like program? Pay college kids tuition if they will study IT security and then come to work in the government." It was one of those rare really good ideas about how to make government work better. But such ideas are seldom tried.

In this instance, though, with the help of the National Science

Foundation, the National Security Agency, and the Office of Personnel Management, the Clinton administration created a scholarship for service program called Cyber Corps.[33] Beginning at colleges such as Idaho State University, Tulsa University, and James Madison University, the computer science departments have given nineteen-year-olds a concentration on IT security and the federal government has paid for it. Now more than eighty colleges are taking part and dozens of federal agencies have young, highly trained computer security specialists. The graduates usually have a two-year obligation to work for the federal government to "pay back" their scholarships. Many stay on after their required work period is over rather than going to a more lucrative position in the private sector because, as one young woman told me, "I'd rather be serving my country. And I can do that in cyberspace."

CYBERTERRORISM? CYBERWAR?

While criminals are making billions of dollars on identity theft and fraud online and foreign corporations and governments are engaged in espionage, the media likes to focus on "cyberterrorism" and wonder about "cyberwarfare." What do those terms mean, and are the phenomena they describe real?

Use of cyberspace by terrorist groups is extensive, but it does not directly cause things to blow up. They use it not as an avenue of attack to bring down infrastructures, at least not yet, but rather to convey their propaganda and to recruit. Thousands of web sites are filled with compelling videos and documents from violent Islamist extremists. These web sites promote or facilitate donations and perhaps trips to places where training and indoctrination occur. Terrorists probably also use web sites and e-mails to communicate, although they also seem to assume that any electronic medium may be monitored.[34] Australian investigators think that the cell that conducted the Bali bombings in 2002 (killing 202 people and wounding more than 200) may have funded their preparations by using online fraud and identity theft.[35]

Cyberwarfare has thus far apparently been limited to simple hacking. When China and Taiwan have a spat, there is often a fair amount of defacing of web sites (replacing what should be on the web page with something less flattering) and denial-of-service attacks (the floods of messages that overwhelm servers and knock sites offline).[36] In 2007 the problems of tiny Estonia seemed to be a possible case of low-level cyberwar. The Estonians had had the temerity to move a giant statue put up during the Cold War by the Soviet Red Army to honor itself. Known in Tallinn as "the only Russian solider who did not rape in 1945," it was seen by Estonians, not as a symbol of their 1945 liberation, but as a testament to their 1945–1990 oppression and occupation. When it was moved, Estonia's networks and web sites were assaulted with defacements and denial-of-service attacks that went on for weeks. The attacks were easily traceable to Russia, where the government said it must be private citizens doing it and added that it was incapable of doing anything to stop them. (Oh, so limited are the enforcement capabilities of the KGB's successors under Putin.)[37]

Cyberwarfare, however, may be grander stuff than what we saw going on in Estonia and Taiwan. A possible window into the potential of cyberwarfare may have been opened when Israel flew F-16s and F-15s into Syria in 2007. News reports indicate that Syria's expensive Russian radar and apparently never saw the attack. *Aviation Week* magazine suggested that a cyberwarfare capability similar to a U.S. program known as Suter could have allowed the attackers to take over the defense's radar screens and eliminate any indications of the attacking aircraft.[38] It could be simlar to the scene in the movie *Ocean's 11* where the hacker replaces a video feed of a vault looking nice and safe while the vault is actually in the hands of the gang.

Around the same time as the Israeli attack on Syria, *USA Today* and CNN reported that U.S. government researchers had experimented with a way of damaging electric power generators by hacking from the internet into the internal network running the Supervisory Control and Data Acquisition (SCADA) software that controls the generator. Spin a big electric power generator at the wrong speed, and it can go crashing off its moorings and break apart.[39] Theoretically, one could also try the *Ocean's 11* technique on a section of a power grid. If you could get into the grid's SCADA system, you could perhaps send instructions to transformers and switches that would trigger a blackout, while all the while the control room's dials would show that things were normal. But how could you get into such a network? I am tempted to say let me count the ways, but I will merely note that some power grids actually send SCADA commands via radio. Almost no utility companies use encryption or authentication on their networks, so that if you can get in, you can issue instructions. Guides to the software used on SCADA systems are not hard to get. A handful of SCADA software systems are used around the world.

In January 2008 we saw the first hints that this threat had gone from theory to reality. A CIA spokesman told an audience at a summit on SCADA security that a series of attacks had occurred against foreign utilities involving intrusions through the internet, followed by extortion demands. The CIA spokesperson said that "in at least one case, the disruption caused a power outage affecting multiple cities. We do not know who executed these attacks or why, but *all* involved intrusions through the internet."[40]

The Federal Energy Regulatory Commission (FERC) has considered imposing high security standards on power grid companies, but the companies have resisted because it would cost them a lot to implement. Of course, they could pass the costs on to consumers and, if every power company were required to do it, the regulations would not give competitive advantage to some firms. But federal regulations are just such a bad idea these days. True, they do prevent us from eating meat with *E. coli* or having our babies lick lead paint off toys, but more federal rules just do not fit well with the prevalent economic ideology that eschews regulation.

In the absence of effective federal regulation to create security on the power grid, could a future enemy nation actually black out parts of the country? In 2008 the U.S. Air Force began a recruiting compaign with an ad that read "Sometimes a blackout is a blackout. In the future, it could by a cyperattack."

More broadly, could a nation attack us in cyberspace and have a real effect beyond defacing web pages and jamming up internet sites? The potential present and future culprit most often identified as a possible cyberwarrior is China. In 1999 two Chinese Army colonels published a book called *Unrestricted Warfare,* noting how China could use computer network attacks to cripple the United States.[41] Was it just an idea, or have the Chinese developed the idea into a capability? In 2007 a Pentagon report revealed this about the Chinese People's Liberation Army (PLA) and its computer network operations (CNO):

> The PLA sees CNO as critical to achieving "electromagnetic dominance" early in a conflict. Although there is no evidence of a formal Chinese CNO doctrine, PLA theorists have coined the term "Integrated Network Electronic Warfare" to . . . disrupt . . . network information systems. The PLA has established information warfare units to develop viruses to attack enemy computer systems and networks, and tactics and measures to protect friendly computer systems and networks. In 2005, the PLA began to incorporate offensive CNO into its exercises, primarily in first strikes against enemy networks.[42]

The Pentagon should know something about Chinese hacking capability. In 2007, according to press reports, the PLA hacked into the Pentagon and all the way to Secretary of Defense Robert Gates's office. According to one account, the system that was attacked carried only unclassified traffic, but that is the system that would be used to mobilize the logistics for any major U.S. military activity:

> When suspected Chinese hackers penetrated the Pentagon this summer, reports downplayed the cyberattack. The hackers hit a secure Pentagon system known as NIPRNet—but it only carries unclassified information. . . . NIPRNet [Nonclassified Internet Protocol Router Network] is crucial in the quick deployment of U.S. forces should China attack Taiwan. By crippling a Pentagon net used to call U.S. forces, China gains crucial hours and minutes in a lightning attack designed to force a Taiwan surrender.[43]

While no adversary of the United States has yet employed these kinds of tactics in a crisis, a Defense Science Board report concluded in

2007 that "it is only a matter of time before an adversary exploits this (cyber) weakness at a critical time in history."[44]

General Ed Eberhart, a four-star U.S. Air Force general, was among the first defense leaders to speak publicly about the threat of Chinese cyberwarfare back in 2001: "We see this espoused in their doctrine. . . . It concerns us when we see these capabilities out there . . . we've become so reliant on our computer systems, our information, and as we train and exercise and are involved in these contingency operations, we've come to take those capabilities . . . for granted."[45] He also acknowledged publicly that the United States also had cyberwarfare units.[46] While little is publicly known about the United States' offensive cyberwarfare capabilities, even if they were far advanced and sophisticated, the United States would suffer from a great asymmetry in any cyberwar, the enormity and vulnerability of the privately owned and operated internet infrastructure and the similarly private sector systems controlled by computer networks: banks, airlines, power grids, pipelines, telephones, and so on. The U.S. government does not have a system for defending the national economic infrastructure from cyberattack. If that infrastructure is degraded to a significant degree by cyberattack, the fact that we may then be fooling somebody else's air defense system on the other side of the globe may not make us feel a lot better.

DETERRING DETERRENCE

There was a time when we had nuclear weapons, as did our adversary, but we had not yet any highly developed strategy, theory, or doctrine about how they might be employed. Fred Kaplan documents this period in the 1950s in his book *The Wizards of Armageddon,* the story of the strategists who finally did develop strategic nuclear doctrine. Some who would be the wizards of cyberspace are attempting to import concepts and strategy from that nuclear era to this period in which we have cyberweapons, as do our potential adversaries, but we lack a conceptual framework for their use. One concept that is being much discussed is what in the nuclear era was called "mutually assured destruction," or deterrence: Can we stop a nation from attacking us in cyberspace by threatening it with destruction of its systems through cyberwar techniques?

Unfortunately, deterrence theory may be nontransferable from strategic nuclear theory to cyberwar for three reasons. First, for deterrence to work, your opponent must be significantly vulnerable to your attack. Few nations are as reliant upon cyberspace as is the United States. Some nations, China for example, might have the capability of unplugging its networks from the global internet to minimize vulnerability to external attack. Second, for the United States to adopt a deterrence strategy in cyberspace, we would have to be highly confident that if we ever "pulled the trigger," the offensive cybersystems would work. In the absence of any realistic way to test offensive cybertools on a large scale, we cannot be sure. Third, deterrence theory rests on the assumption that your opponent knows that he is vulnerable to your potential attacks and fears what you could do. There is so much secrecy about U.S. cyberwarfare capabilities that it is difficult to create a fear of them.

SECURING CYBERSPACE

Although the extent of the problem of reliance upon insecure computer systems is beginning to be understood broadly, government has yet to act decisively to address it. The National Strategy to Secure Cyberspace, signed by the President in 2003, sat gathering dust, unimplemented for four years. The public-private partnership that created the strategy withered, largely because the private sector lost faith in its partner because of the government's inaction.

Then as 2007 wore on, stories leaked that an intrusion into the network in Secretary of Defense Robert Gates's own office had been traced back to China. German Chancellor Angela Merkel's office reported her system had also been hacked by a Chinese entity. British authorities were also tracking Chinese hacking, prompting MI5 (the British Security Service) to send an advisory to the top three hundred British corporations telling them that in all probability their networks were already penetrated by China. The warning did not suggest that it was Chinese individuals, but rather the Chinese government, saying it was an "electronic attack sponsored by Chinese state organizations . . . designed to defeat best-practice IT security systems."

Private-sector IT security experts were finding evidence of Chinese hacks everywhere, including an ingenious Trojan-horse program embedded in digital picture frames sold at electronics stores across America, such as BestBuy. When you connected the digital picture frame to your computer to download your photos, the picture frame uploaded a program into your computer that disabled antivirus programs, found all of your passwords, and sent them to China. The picture frame was, of course, made in China.

The results of the investigation of the hacking into the Pentagon reportedly led Admiral Mike McConnell, the second person in the job of Director of National Intelligence, to hit the alarm bell. Rumors spread that China was well inside sensitive and classified U.S. networks, casting doubt on the Pentagon's current and future plans based on "net centric warfare." According to one U.S. Air Force officer, the new "Byzantine series (of attacks) tracks back to China."

McConnell proposed a massive new cybersecurity initiative, which President Bush signed as National Security Presidential Directive 54 on January 8, 2008. The much-needed reinvigoration of cybersecurity will reportedly channel $6 billion into government programs in 2009. The new initiative was criticized, however, because it emphasized the use of U.S. intelligence agencies to deal with the problem, a marked departure from the 2003 strategy that sought to build a public-private partnership to protect the banking and finance, transportation, electric power, oil and gas, health care, and other critical infrastructure owned and operated by private companies.[47]

For those companies to be motivated, the federal government must serve as a model, getting its own house in order. And then it must employ smart, light regulation to even the playing field, making all companies in a sector assume the additional cost and burden of compliance with cyber-security standards. Among the steps the Federal government should take, I would recommend:

- All federal government computer networks be required to employ two-factor authentication systems and anyone, including citizens, interacting with those networks be required to use authentication.

- All data files stored on federal networks, all e-mails, and all laptops, be encrypted.

- The staff of the White House Office of Management and Budget working on enforcing federal IT security be expanded from two people to something closer to two hundred, and they be given authority to order agencies to take specific actions to conform to a set of high security standards.

- Funding for unclassified IT security research be increased from the present $20 million to $200 million, consistent with recommendations of the President's own outside experts advisory panel on technology. Much of that research should focus on how to write computer code that does not contain errors (Current tools that find vulnerabilities in computer identify only about one-third of the total that are eventually found; moreover, these tools are also available to our adversaries.)[48]

The government needs to overcome its ideological aversion to regulating the internet. If ever there were a case of "market failure," it is IT security.

- The Federal Communications Commission should require internet service providers to take specific measures to reduce spam, worms, viruses, denial-of-service attacks, phishing, botnets, and other malicious activity.

- The Federal Energy Regulatory Commission should require power companies to conform to specific high standards for IT security.

- Federal bank regulators should require two-factor authentication for all online banking and stock trading.

We have to plan for the possibility that a concerted attack on the internet by a nation-state or a sophisticated nonstate actor could cause significant outages, with the result that power grids, financial networks, energy systems, transportation, and government and national security systems would be severely degraded. The government needs to develop a plan and a system in conjunction with the private sector to respond to that new kind of disaster, rapidly restoring order to cyberspace, prioritizing service restoration, and fighting off sustained attacks, including on privately owned and operated networks.

Finally, we need to think about what all of this means for our national defense. Ten years ago the U.S.S. *Yorktown,* a Navy cruiser, had to be towed back to port by a tug because the ship's main computer, controlling all of its vital systems, crashed while using a version of a widely adopted computer operating system.[49] The *Yorktown* was named after the scene of a major defeat for a proud empire. The future of the United States' defense and military capability is based upon the assumption that there is and will be a highly secure and reliable Defense Department internet, separate and walled off from the chaos in the public worldwide internet. The Pentagon buzzword is "netcentric warfare," linking everything together. We are building a twenty-first-century military that is completely dependent upon that net. Take it away, and most units will be about as useful as the French at Agincourt, as vulnerable as Achilles' heel.

When I have spoken of that concern publicly, some have suggested that I am a warmonger for raising the prospect of conflict with China. Don't I understand that our two economies are so intertwined that we will never have a war? I certainly hope that is right. I am concerned that too much talk about a future war with China may become a self-fulfilling prophecy and make an enemy where there was not one. But I am also trained to look for vulnerabilities, and I know that the computer I am writing this manuscript with was made in China, as are many of our nation's computers and the chips they run on. Whether the cyberthreat is from China or a nonstate actor, whether it is a big event or a series of constant damaging intrusions, we face a major problem and we should not think that we have seen the worst of it yet. Even without a shooting war, our economic competitive advantages are diminished by having network systems that cannot secure our proprietary data and our national security secrets. We would be fools not to take the cyber threat seriously, fools to ignore what the *Iliad* taught us about ignoring the threat from Trojan horses. But so far, your government has failed to do so.

NINE

GETTING IT RIGHT

Well, it's close enough for government work," my boss at the Pentagon said to one of the officers on our team. I was stunned. It was 1973, and I had never heard that phrase before. It flew in the face of everything I had internalized about the importance of what the government did, so I asked him what he meant. "Really, you never heard that before? It's an old phrase, at least in Washington. Government work, you know, sloppy, half-assed," the colonel explained.

I learned that most Americans do have a dim view of the efficacy of what their government does. The failures discussed in this book (and detailed further elsewhere, such as in Timothy Weiner's *Legacy of Ashes* on intelligence, Thomas Ricks's *Fiasco* on Iraq, Christopher Cooper and Robert Block's *Disaster* on Hurricane Katrina and Homeland Security) have in recent years added justification to that public impression. Deficiencies in government performance are hardly new, nor are they unique to government. Private sector disasters and underperformance are at least as common. But mistakes in national security affairs usually cost lives and have significant secondary effects in our society and around the world. We need to have and to achieve higher standards of government performance. Part of that process has to be to admit when we have overreacted, when we have thrown money and people at a problem disproportionate to what can be used effectively, and when we may have created a perpetual motion machine whose purpose has become, in part, just to stay in motion.

RIGHTSIZING THE BLOAT

It's a neighborhood with Tiffany, Hermès, and Gucci boutiques among hundreds of other stores in several sprawling shopping malls. It is also a neighborhood filled with the offices of firms with large contracts with the national security agencies and departments. Tysons Corner was the nation's first "edge city," according to Joel Garreau's seminal work on self-sufficient minicities in suburbia.[1] It is a place where one can live in a high-rise condo or town house, shop or dine in one of hundreds of choices, exercise in a variety of gyms and health clubs, watch a newly released movie in a multiplex, and work in a high-rise for any one of scores of outsourcing firms. If you live there, you never have to leave. It is, of course, slightly unreal, detached from the nearby nation's capital, indeed from the lives of most Americans. After 9/11, a huge new office building started to go up on one of the few underdeveloped streets in the edge city. Oddly, there was no sign saying what company the new complex would house.

When the outer structure of the building was complete, designers from the Walt Disney Company arrived. Disney has a large store less than a mile away (I know because I have stood in line there buying presents for a three-year-old). But these designers were not there to create a place for Princess Bride birthday parties; they had come to help build a counterterrorism command center. Jumbotrons now hang above a broad expanse with scores of workstations. It has a Hollywood feel, looking like the set for the command center in movies like *Dr. Strangelove* and *War Games*. It is also reminiscent of the network operations center for a major telephone company I visited in New Jersey. There a corporate Vice President had been candid enough to admit to me, "We spent a boatload making this place look like NASA's Mission Control, but it's just to wow the customers. It could all be done from a normal office with cubicles." Counterterrorism could all be done from a normal office, too, but the Disney-designed command room is meant to impress members of Congress and the media that the new National Counterterrorism Center (NCTC) is cutting edge. It is also extremely popular with NCTC staff and their guests when they use the Jumbo-trons to watch the Super Bowl. In case the command center did not impart its mission statement sufficiently, NCTC renamed the street outside Liberty Crossing.

The hundreds of people working for NCTC come in two flavors: first, government employees, mainly on loan from the CIA and FBI, and second, the equally numerous private contractors. "The only way you can tell the difference is the color of their badge," one person who frequented Liberty Crossing explained. (Every person in the center is required to have a plastic identification tag hanging around his or her neck or pinned onto his or her lapel.) Much of what the NCTC staff does all day is to talk with people at other terrorism centers around Washington, the largest of which is the CIA's Counterterrorism Center (CTC) about a mile away at CIA headquarters. Probably next in size is the FBI's counterterrorism center in the J. Edgar Hoover Building near the White House. These are not to be confused with the Terrorist Screening Center, for which the FBI is the executive agent, which is housed in a nondescript office tower near National Airport. Nor should one overlook the Foreign Terrorist Asset Tracking Center, which is run by the Treasury Department, or the new Intelligence Fusion Centers for counterterrorism in every state capitol, or the Joint Terrorism Task Forces now in one hundred cities, or . . .

Next to the large NCTC complex, another huge edifice is rising at Liberty Crossing. This one is to house the staff of the burgeoning Office of the Director of National Intelligence and the many contract employees supporting it. Reflecting the suburban sprawl that has de-faced northern Virginia outside Washington, the FBI is moving some things a little farther out, to Prince William County, where a building, "nicknamed 'the Taj Mahal' by some FBI officials, will feature highly finished terrazzo floors at the entrance, a soaring atrium and a giant fingerprint etched into the elevator doors. The Bureau plans to bring new counter terrorism squads to the new Prince William office and to open a language translation unit there, to help with the chronic problem of attracting Arabic speakers."[2] No doubt the terrazzo floors and the access to more distant shopping malls will help the FBI overcome its chronic inability to recruit or maintain employees with the needed linguistic capabilities.

Nearby is the first of several buildings in another CIA campus, curiously, called the Discovery Center. The building serves as an "intake center" for polygraphing, interviewing, and assigning the many new CIA employees needed to obtain the goal of doubling the staff of the Agency. Prospective employees sit awaiting their turn to have their bodies strapped to a machine whose results are not admissable in any federal court. If they were applying for a private sector job, the law in most states would prohibit an employer from screening prospective employees with a polygraph, but this is the CIA, which believes in the disproven flutter box. So they sit, perhaps in the nice new Starbucks in the center or in the lounge where all of the new flat-screen televisions are set to FOX News.

I know that good work is done at the National Counterterrorism Center, but I also know how to run counterterrorism operations and they do not require Jumbotrons or the very nice color calendar one can download from NCTC's web page, which notes for each day of the year what famous terrorist-related events took place on that day in history. "The NCTC for Kids" web page has a nice Disney quality, with a cartoon eagle and a cartoon Lady Liberty,[3] but the command center, calendar, and cartoon characters all bespeak a larger issue: bloat.

Every imaginable agency and department has asked for and received funds so that it can participate in the GWOT, Global War on Terror. They all have centers, large staffs, and support from even more staff obtained by outsourcing to private contractors. The private contractors' new offices spread down the long road to Washington's distant Dulles International Airport like the moon mission aerospace corporations spread in Houston and Los Angeles in the 1960s. The firms run lushly produced commercials on Washington television channels, with stirring music, deep-voiced announcers, and waving flags. If you live outside the National Capital Region, you may not have seen them. In one ad, a defense contractor extolls the virtues of the men and women, civilian and military, who serve as government employees. Thousands of the same firm's employees do work formerly done only by government employees. In another ad, an announcer intones in a mellifluous voice, "We never forget who we're working for," as images of soldiers flicker on screen. Whom they are working for, of course, is their stockholders, who have done very well since 9/11 as the defense, intelligence, and homeland security industry has boomed.

What federal employee or congressman will say it is too much, that we went overboard after 9/11, that we have a bloated counterterrorism bureaucracy? It is not just an issue of saving money; it is a problem of effectiveness. The terrorism bureaucracy has become so enormous that it is filled with many inexperienced staff who must spend large amounts of time dealing with one another. But it will take an unusually courageous bureaucrat to suggest this new behemoth be pared, because who will want to be blamed after the next attack that his downsizing proposal cost lives?

Nonetheless, as much as we needed commissions to call for the growth of institutions to deal with terrorism and homeland security, we now need a commission to examine whether we have overdone it to the point of creating inefficiencies from excess. When the White House and Congress realized that closing military bases was too controversial and prone to horse trading, they agreed to transfer the authority to a commission on Base Realignment and Closure (BRAC). The White House and Congress could say only yes or no to the entire package of proposed closures, thus insulating them somewhat from political pressure. It is time for a BRAC-like review of the bloated bureaucracy that has grown up in response to 9/11.

A commission should also examine the outsourcing of intelligence and national security operations to private firms. This phenomenon goes well beyond Blackwater flying armed helicopters and driving little tanks in Iraq. In recent years government agencies have seen increasingly large numbers of new "staff": employees of outsourcing firms, systems integrators, and "body shops" who do jobs in federal offices identical to the work performed by federal employees. Many of the new staff were, until recently, government employees doing very similar jobs. They were trained and given costly security clearances by the government. If they have worked for twenty years in government, they are also receiving retirement pay. One has to wonder whether the willingness of some government managers to use outsourced staff is at all shaped, even subconsciously, by the thought that they may want the option of working in such companies in the future. While there are rules that prohibit for a time the ability of federal managers to go to work for companies with which they have done business, there is nothing to stop a manager from going to work at another, similar company.

Specifically, the commission should address (1) whether such firms are more expensive or cheaper than having government employees do the work, (2) what the impediments are to having the government do the work directly and how those problems can be addressed, (3) what the inherently governmental functions are that should not be outsourced, (4) whether we need to create a level playing field by offering government managers the choice of using direct staff or contractors, rather than forcing the choice of outsourcing by the imposed ceilings on civil service personnel numbers, (5) whether we can reduce the incentive to do unnecessary outsourcing by further limiting the ability of government managers to work for outsourcing firms after they "retire," and (6) whether we should stop the revolving door of federal employees' going to work as employees of contract outsourcing firms at their former departments. These are important questions because as long as it is more attractive to work for an outsourcing firm than for the government, the quality of federal employees and of federal government activity will suffer. It is particularly important that we get those answers right when it comes to national security programs.

Getting it right in national security is not primarily a matter of making a better fighter jet or tank, not really about an improved spy satellite or a new technology for information sharing. It is fundamentally about four basic things:

- The people who work in the government on national security issues, their training and professionalization

- The degree of partisan politicization of national security and the personnel system

- Effective, analytical interagency decision making and oversight mechanisms

- Accountability, responsibility, and leadership through the use of national security program managers

The sine qua non for successful national security operations is a cadre of trained, experienced, nonpartisan career officers who can orchestrate a multiagency program. That interagency skill is rare because most national security problems require several departments to work together and most staff know well only one part of one agency. Agencies tend to see things narrowly, from the perspective of their main mission. When presented with a new challenge, most government personnel tend first to ask how it affects their organization, its budget, its turf, its reputation. Only then, if at all, do they think about the national priority. Thus, adding all agency or departmental interests together does not sum to the national interest. Political appointees in national security jobs add another consideration: How will it help or hurt their political party? Getting something new or important done well usually requires the President to empower someone or a team on behalf of the entire administration. And it usually requires bringing in an experienced person who, in addition to having interagency experience, is somewhat unconventional, a person not risk-averse or afraid of challenging assumptions, turf, or superiors. What would such people look like?

PEOPLE: CONDUCTORS OF THE ORCHESTRAS

For years, when someone at the top of the U.S. intelligence community or someone on the National Security Council staff was frustrated with or stumped by the inability of the many U.S. intelligence agencies to get something important done when it mattered, they called Charlie Allen. He is almost never described without the words "workaholic," "legendary" and "national treasure." Sometimes you also hear "contrarian" and "controversial." Tall and with a full head of gray white hair, now slightly stooped and with thick glasses, Charlie joined the CIA shortly after graduating from the University of North Carolina in 1958 (when I was in third grade), but I first met him in the 1980s when he chaired something called the Warning Committee. Every Friday he convened a small group of us, managers from around the intelligence community, in a windowless conference room in a building that had no sign, no name, on a side street a block from the White House. He would pore through snippets and reports most of us had overlooked and would pepper us with questions: Was something about to happen? How did we explain some activity he had noticed somewhere? Had we thought about this or that possibility? How could we be sure? Had we redirected a satellite, called an embassy, looked at the pictures, read the transcript? If something were about to happen, what would be the indicators? What if they didn't want us to know? At the end of the meeting, we were usually spent, but Charlie had a thorough report on "all the things that could surprise us, pop up and bite the President in the ass" in the next week and beyond. I have never seen another person who knew so much about how to get the myriad U.S. intelligence agencies to address a problem.

When in July 1990 Charlie asked to interrupt a meeting I was in so I could take a secure call from him, I was eager to hear what he had to say. "Iraq is going to launch an invasion of Kuwait in a few days, take the whole country in one fell swoop." Allen began with that, instead of hello. He was telling me that the CIA's analysis was wrong. It was not unusual for Charlie to challenge conventional thinking, nor was it surprising when he turned out to be right. Thus, a few years later when the CIA's Directorate of Operations ("the DO") claimed it never knew Osama bin Laden's location until after he had left it, in raging frustration I called Charlie. "That's bullshit. I'll find a way to pin his ass down." Later, when he came to my office claiming to have a solution, Charlie Allen unlocked his old, beaten-up leather bag and took out a picture of what looked like a remote-controlled toy airplane. "Ever hear of the Predator?" he asked. "The DO and the Air Force won't want you to fly it looking for UBL, but that's what we have to do." After a minor war with the DO, we flew the Predator and were, shortly after starting the program, looking at a live image of bin Laden walking out of a house. Concerned about the paucity of recent intelligence on the alleged Iraqi weapons of mass destruction program, Allen reportedly created a list of people living in Iraq who would probably know about the status of the WMD program. He then allegedly found Iraqis living abroad who were related to them or otherwise knew them. He arranged for the overseas Iraqis to visit their friends and, in passing, ask how their work was going. The consistent answer was that the WMD program had stopped, the weapons had been destroyed. Allen's report, which proved to be accurate, was not what the administration wanted to hear and so, was ignored.

His report to then–CIA Director Porter Goss after a fact-finding trip to Iraq in 2005 was probably also not what anyone in the White House wanted to read: there was a full-blown insurgency in Iraq, and the U.S. military and civilian leadership in Baghdad did not have a strategy for dealing with it; things were getting increasingly out of control and casualties would mount. To Allen's surprise, however, Goss did give it to the White House, and the President sent it on to the head of the U.S. civilian team in Baghdad, Ambassador John Negroponte. Unfortunately for Charlie Allen and U.S. intelligence, Negroponte retaliated for the criticism by stripping Charlie of a job when, a few months later, Negroponte was elevated to run all of U.S. intelligence. Already in his seventies, Mr. Allen accepted an offer from the Secretary of Homeland Security to make something of the then-unimportant post of Assistant Secretary for Intelligence. When we met at lunch to talk about that task, he chose a restaurant off the beaten path, in a residential neighborhood. Many of our fellow diners were ladies who looked to be Charlie's age and had probably been retired for more than a decade, as Charlie could have been. I doubt that anyone in the room knew that neat the man in the gray suit kept decades of intelligence secrets in his still lightning-fast brain. Had they been able to listen to our low conversation at the corner table, they would have heard an acronym soup and arcane references virtually impenetrable outside a small fraternity. Approaching his fiftieth year in government, Allen had no intention of slowing down. "As long as they give me hard problems and as long as I can tackle those problems, I'll keep it up." Allen smiled his Cheshire cat grin. Of course, as we have seen, having people like Charlie around does not ensure that government leaders will do the right thing, but it does increase the chances they will have the right intelligence on which to base their actions and policy choices.

As Charlie Allen has been able to bring together all of the disparate pieces of U.S. intelligence, so have a group of people been able to bring the military, defense agency, State Department, development assistance, and international organizations together to address seemingly intractable failed states. People like Bob Gelbard and Jim Dobbins had joined the Foreign Service in their twenties, and each had served in it more than thirty years. In their final dozen years of service, each had acted as presidential envoys for leaders of both parties, in places such as Haiti, Bosnia, Kosovo, Somalia, and Afghanistan. They knew from personal experience where to go in the U.S. government, other nations, the United Nations, the international financial institutions, the press, and Congress to get what they needed to solve tough, multidimensional problems.

"But can you really be nonpartisan and work for whichever party is in power, given the wide swings in ideology?" I asked Ambassador Robert Gelbard, looking out at the water through the pines, on the deck of his home in Friendship, Maine. Gelbard was educated in the New York City public schools, and went, sight unseen, to Maine's Colby College. Now in his sixties, Gelbard still seems as wired and spring-loaded as when he played basketball for Colby. "Of course you can." His answers came like machine-gun fire. "I helped formulate and implement Ronald Reagan's approach to South America and represented Bill Clinton in the Balkans. Think those two administrations were different?"

Gelbard had been a Deputy Assistant Secretary of State for Reagan and a special envoy for Clinton. His career demonstrates the breadth and scope that a career officer can develop, if he or she is in high demand. Gelbard's work had touched every continent except Antarctica. In addition to the two jobs that he had undertaken for Reagan and

Clinton, he had served the State Department as as a consul in Brazil (replacing a predecessor shot by terrorists), an economics attaché in Paris (after graduate work in economics at Harvard paid for by the State Department), director for southern African affairs during the era of U.S. sanctions on the apartheid regime, Ambassador to Bolivia, Assistant Secretary for International Law Enforcement and Counternarcotics, and Ambassador to Indonesia (sounding the alarm about the local al Qaeda affiliate prior to its wave of attacks).

"I got to work for highly talented political appointees who just wanted people who could get things done. They wanted interagency program managers," Gelbard reflected on his thirty-two-year career. What makes a good program manager? "You have to be more than just a good analyst; you need to manage money, develop friends of both parties in the Congress, work with the media, talk to the military and the intel guys in their language." The President and his White House national security staff have to be actively involved to ensure that the agencies are responsive to priority interagency goals, according to Gelbard. A major problem, Bob told me, is that "we don't train people to know about how to get all of the relevant pieces of the government working together in a concerted way toward a single goal." Trained people are not enough, however, as Gelbard and Jim Dobbins found out when their years of experience at failed states were ignored, as were their offers to work on Iraq.

The first time I had a private conversation with Ambassador James Dobbins was in 1979, and he was carefully painting a small lead toy soldier in his State Department office. On a nearby shelf were models of old warships, with delicate sails and lines. Dobbins is tall, thin, and given to double-breasted suits. He is a man of precision, so when he says "National security is too important to trust to amateurs" he has a remedy in mind. Jim calls for a "standard of professionalism for the senior officials who staff the Defense Department and other national security agencies, including the National Security Council," set down in legislation fencing off a certain percentage of key positions to experienced personnel. In the White House and State Department and overseas, Dobbins has served as Assistant Secretary of State for Europe; Special Assistant to the President for the Western Hemisphere; special adviser to the President and Secretary of State for the Balkans; Ambassador to the European Community; and the Clinton administration's special envoy for Somalia, Haiti, Bosnia, and Kosovo.

In his last role before leaving the administration for the nonprofit Rand Corporation, Jim Dobbins served as the Bush administration's special envoy for Afghanistan. His recommendations for U.S. military presence and development assistance for Afghanistan were based on successful experiences elsewhere and they were many types of what the administration finally approved. Dobbins warned that the modest investment would fail to stabilize the country and could result in a resurgent Taliban, which is exactly what happened.

Jim sees the politically based churning of senior positions in national security as handicapping the country by regularly divesting itself of institutional knowledge. "Our patronage system creates such a huge turnover of personnel. Most democratic governments, when they change administrations from one party to another, there are perhaps fifty or a hundred people who leave their office and another fifty or a hundred people come into the office. In the United States, it's a staggering number. As a result, particularly in institutions like the White House, there's virtually nobody left. The file drawers are empty, a new team comes in, and there's a process during which they learn lessons . . . often it's not so quick and it's very painful, and it's very costly." Jim would also have Congress pass an interagency version of the Goldwater-Nichols Act, which reformed the military, specifying roles and missions for key tasks such as international military and police training, humanitarian and reconstruction assistance, institution building, and democratic development.

"The military can't succeed by itself when it is in the lead . . . and in most national security operations, it isn't the lead agency," Rand Beers, my longtime colleague and close friend, said, agreeing with Gelbard and Dobbins on the need for an interagency approach run by trained and experienced nonpartisan professionals. Beers worked on the White House national security staffs for Reagan, Bush 41, Clinton, and Bush 43. We were sitting on the dock overlooking his pond in the Virginia foothills. Randy should know about the need for broad experience: he has been a Marine in Vietnam, a Foreign Service officer at NATO, a career member of the Senior Executive Service, an Assistant Secretary of State, and Special Assistant to the President for Intelligence.

"A civilian Goldwater-Nichols Act requiring that people get experience in a variety of departments and agencies is necessary, but it's also insufficient," Beers argued. In his mid-sixties but still looking like a younger Robert Redford, Randy's style is less confrontational than Dobbins's, Gelbard's, or mine. "You also need interagency planning, training, and exercises," he suggested. "We tried in PDD-56 to require all of those things to deal with these recurring, complex contingencies, but it was ignored by the next administration." Beers is talking about the Presidential Decision Directive in which Bill Clinton tried to build on the lessons learned from the successes and failures in Panama, Grenada, Somalia, Haiti, Bosnia, and Kosovo. "Something like that probably does have to be required by law to endure." Such legislation, he feels, should facilitate and give incentives for personnel who cross the divide that now separates the intelligence community and the rest of the national security bureaucracy.

"Policy makers do need to better understand the intelligence community and vice versa," Joan Dempsey insisted while stopping for scrambled eggs with me on her way from her house in Annapolis to her office in northern Virginia. Dempsey exudes a quiet sense of command. Like Beers, she understands both policy and intelligence, because, like him, she has worked in both. Joan spent years in the Pentagon, the CIA, and the White House complex and coordinated the entire intelligence community as the Deputy Director of Central Intelligence. To help her see things from all sides, she even stayed on as a midlevel officer in the Navy Reserve when her civilian rank was the equivalent of a four-star admiral. ("I think she gets special treatment when she's on duty," her husband, Jack, a navy veteran, deadpanned.) Described in one press account as "a tough, shrewd professional . . . the best 'closer' . . . someone who knew how to cut deals and get the job done," Joan Dempsey now runs intelligence analysis being done for government agencies by a large private consulting firm. "If you have policy makers who don't know how to read intelligence or who get away with cherry-picking it, who don't know how to task it, what to ask for, don't know what it can do and what it can't . . . then we're wasting billions of dollars every year."

Two of the handful of people who have worked on "both sides of the river," policy and intelligence, in recent years, Bruce Riedel and Charles Duelfer, agree with Dempsey about the need to understand, preferably from experience, both dimensions. Riedel served in White House National Security Council positions for Clinton and both Presidents Bush and also served as a Deputy Assistant Secretary of Defense in the Pentagon and at the CIA as a member of the National Intelligence Council. He was also active in the Camp David peace talks. Duelfer, who had spent years at State and the Office of Management and Budget, was running the State Department's defense trade programs when the first Iraq War broke out. He quickly became the head of the Department's Iraq War Task Force. Later he ran the U.N. Special Commission on Iraq as its deputy director. After the United States occupied Iraq, Duelfer was chosen by the CIA Director to investigate and write the definitive account of what had happened to the weapons of mass destruction. He agreed to take on the task on condition that his report would exist only in an unclassified, i.e., public, form. The subsequent Duelfer Report is the most comprehensive and detailed account available of the activities of Saddam Hussein's government before the U.S. invasion, including its bribery of U.N.-related officials. Duelfer's 2008 book tells the story of America and Iraq over more than a decade in a highly personal and readable manner.

Riedel sees defeating the resurgent al Qaeda and Taliban not just as an intelligence or military issue, but also as requiring a cross-disciplinary approach. We should "supplement a military build up (in Afghanistan) by taking the lead on a major economic reconstruction program." He notes that U.S. aid per capita in Afghanistan is "far less . . . than it has [been] to recovering states such as Bosnia." Soft-spoken and somewhat owllike in appearance, Bruce argues that one of the keys to defeating al Qaeda and the Taliban in Afghanistan is to create "a mainstream agricultural economy." Not exactly a James Bond solution coming from a thirty-year CIA man, but a realistic one.

"None of these guys had ever really spent any time in Iraq or the

region. Almost none of them even knew a real Iraqi. Incredible!"
Charles Duelfer exclaimed, sitting on my patio and reflecting on the
problems recent Iraq policy makers have had. Blond and wiry, Charlie
had stopped by my home after spending the day "relaxing" by parachuting nearby. "You can't understand these things from some think
tank or wood-paneled government office in Washington or on a whirl-
wind windshield tour," Duelfer insisted. "You got to get some of the
dirt under your fingernails." Charles got more than that when, as the
highest-ranking CIA officer in Iraq at the time, his car was attacked
and destroyed, his bodyguards in a chase vehicle killed. Crawling out
of his upside-down, burning armor-plated BMW, Duelfer had returned
fire while waiting for reinforcements. "These guys that decided to fire
all the Iraqi military, how many Iraqi military officers had they ever
talked to?" Duelfer, who had talked to many, was not consulted until
well after the Iraq disaster was developed.

Nor was Michael Sheehan, a former Green Beret who had personal
experience with failed states, civil wars, and invasions from his service
in El Salvador, Somalia, Haiti, and Bosnia. Thin and balding, he gives
off an aura of pent-up energy and is known for his iconoclastic views.
At the time the second Iraq War started, he was serving as U.N. Assistant Secretary General for Peacekeeping, one of the few Americans
in a senior position in the international organization. He had also
served on the White House National Security Council staffs for President Bush (41) and President Clinton. If there were a better résumé or
qualifications to give advice or assistance to the Bush (43) administration as it planned for and occupied Iraq, it would be hard to imagine.
"But why would they ask me anything? After all, I might disagree
with them and they would have to endure listening to a new thought."
Sheehan laughs in his sarcastic, biting style. Sheehan and I were sitting
at the bar in the basement of the Penn Club in New York City, a city
where he served as Assistant Commissioner for counterterrorism in the
New York police. "I'm Irish and I worked with cops. I feel at home in a
bar," he joked. What he would do now to improve the national security
apparatus would include creating a single, integrated nation-rebuilding
agency under the State Department, "complete with its own academy,
what the Army calls a 'schoolhouse,' to institutionalize expertise in

dealing with complex contingencies on the ground." He's skeptical about a civilian Goldwater-Nichols Act creating an integrated personnel cadre across all national security departments. "Departments will all want control of their own people. If you want to get better performance out of the national security agencies, find the good people in them and give them responsibility, give them a challenge. That will attract more good people. Keep challenging them and they will stay, and then you're institution building before you know it."

The United States will need more good people like Charlie Allen, Bob Gelbard, Joan Dempsey, Wendy Chamberlin, and the others for the indefinite future. But will it have people like them? Will such talented people in the next generation join government, and if they do, will they stay long enough to make a meaningful contribution, to develop an institutional memory? The tradition of working in one company or career for thirty years is now passé in much of the economy. Yet the biggest financial incentive the federal government gives its workers is a retirement system designed around long-term employment. To get talented, creative, agile new workers, do we need to redesign the recruitment and personnel system to allow for shorter—ten years, perhaps—careers in national security? If national security staff serve a limited career, or if they are given narrow portfolios and little training, if many of them are actually working for private companies, who will know how to conduct the interagency orchestra?

Even these career officials whom I have selected as models admit that there were skills they developed later than was ideal, that they picked up some knowledge on the fly, that there was and is no real system to teach the necessary senior management skills or to institutionalize lessons learned. Recognizing the need for some steps to increase the professionalization of the career national security cadre, the President issued an executive order on national security professional development in May 2007, creating a cabinet-level committee and asking for studies. But, as several of those I interviewed suggested, it is a law that is really needed, passed by Congress and mandating a new system that would endure beyond any one administration. The law would include:

- An interagency personnel system for career national security personnel in intelligence, homeland security, defense, and foreign affairs to ensure standards for training and to facilitate assignments among the various civilian agencies and departments; as with the Goldwater-Nichols reform of the military, assignment to some senior interagency positions would require certain prior interagency experience and training

- An integrated recruitment and entry program to make it easy for potential applicants to learn what the options are and how to apply

- Professionally developed minimum curriculum requirements for entry into the personnel system and for accomplishment at various stages in a career: entry, refresher, midcareer, senior management

- Integration and rationalization of the extensive schools, academies, and other training institutions now run separately by the various agencies and departments; this might lead to a National Security University System, with the current departmental training facilities turned into elite graduate colleges, perhaps run in association with leading universities

- Periodic testing and certification in required fields such as ethics, media relations, congressional affairs, budgeting, emerging technologies, civil liberties, and limitations of partisan activity

Who would want to undergo an open-heart operation by a doctor who was not board-certified in cardiac surgery, a process that requires regular training and recertification? Nor would we want a lawyer, accountant, dentist, financial adviser, or auto mechanic working on our affairs if he or she had not been trained and recently updated and certified. The national security affairs of the United States are at least as important as your wisdom tooth or fuel injector.

LIMITING PARTISANSHIP

Partisanship in Washington has become more acute than in earlier times, as Ron Brownstein has recently documented in a solidly researched book he subtitled "How Extreme Partisanship Has Paralyzed Washington and Polarized America." In the area of national security, extreme partisanship has seen party leaders take serious concerns about which there could be a broad national consensus and try to use them as campaign tools, wedge issues, scarecrows. Two things have resulted. First, we have been unable to develop sufficient support in this country to accomplish major national security goals. Second, much of the country no longer trusts the government on security issues, believes that it manufactures or exaggerates threats, and fears that government officials do not respect the law or the Constitution. Limiting partisanship on security issues will be difficult, but one way to move in that direction is to strengthen the role of the career professionals.

The career national security officials I discussed above were nonpartisan and had high-level multiadministration service, and interagency experience. They also had something else: invisible scars, thick skin, and backbone. Often when they served Republicans, Democrats attacked them, and vice versa. If a career civil servant first rises to a prominent position during a Republican administration, many Democrats will distrust her and even target her. The same can be said of how Republican members of Congress and the media will treat someone if he first rose to a significant position in a Democratic administration.

Instead of avoiding controversial issues, the career officials I profiled helped to manage such hot potatoes and thereby often got caught in the crossfire. Events that would have caused most people to find another way of earning a living did not dissuade them from continuing in public service. Charlie Allen was given a reprimand, largely for working to free U.S. hostages, working too closely with those involved in the Iran-contra scandal. Allen had had nothing to do with the illegality and fought the mark on his reputation, hiring a lawyer to get the reprimand removed. (The lawyer, James Woolsey, later became CIA Director and promoted Allen, as most CIA Directors have.)

Jim Dobbins was accused by a congressman of having allegedly misled him on an aspect of Haiti policy, resulting in his blocking Dobbins's subsequent nomination for any jobs requiring Senate confirmation. Jim went on to serve Clinton and Bush 41 in the Balkans and Afghanistan. When it became public knowledge that FBI Director Louis Freeh had not warned the White House about possible Chinese attempts to influence a congressional election, Freeh blamed Rand Beers of the NSC staff for not reporting it, even though Freeh's agents had instructed Beers not to share the preliminary reports. Newspaper editorials called for Beers to resign. He was later confirmed by the Senate, which found that he had acted appropriately. When I refused to apply pressure on Israel based on false reports of illegal arms transfers, an inspector general at State leaked to the press his accusation that I had failed to investigate Israeli violations, including allegedly giving Patriot missiles to China. An independent Army investigation later found no evidence of such missile transfers, congressmen attacked the inspector general in a hearing on the matter, and I went on to serve eleven years in senior positions in the White House. Nonetheless, being assailed and falsely accused on national television and in national newspapers is not the kind of perk that comes with most jobs. For senior career civil servants it often can be.

There is also a tension between civil servants and political appointees, one that I have witnessed firsthand in many administrations of both parties. Sometimes that tension can be productive; often it is not. Although this is a bit of a caricature, I think its close to the mark:

- Civil servants believe they hold the jobs they do because of relevant training and experience and as a result of a competitive selection process in which their party affiliation has not been known or considered. Political appointees may sometimes see career employees as arrogating power away from the elected representatives of the people, thinking they know better than the President and his team, resisting the change the President was given a mandate to bring about. Or they sometimes see civil servants as slothful, uninformed, unskilled, and unaccountable, protected by job tenure rules from being reassigned when they are unproductive or unresponsive.

- Political appointees believe they have their jobs because they played a role in the President's election or are part of the team the President relies upon to ensure that campaign promises are implemented and that the government runs in a manner consistent with the President's ideology and intent. Civil servants see them as partisan ideologues intent on using the government to benefit their party and its backers. Or they view them as people spending a brief period in low-paying civil servant jobs to burnish their résumés and make contacts that will benefit them financially when they quickly move on to lobbying, public relations, private equity, or law firms.

You may have surmised that as someone who spent thirty years as a career civil servant, I think highly of those who have chosen to spend most of their working lives in government. You could also assume that I think less of political appointees who are injected into positions in the bureaucracy for a few years because they are associated with the party and the group within the party that most recently won the presidential election. What I actually believe, however, is that a balance of career personnel and political appointees is needed for an American government to be responsive. Career personnel should bring the institutional memory, professional skills, and detailed knowledge of the government machinery, laws, regulations, and substantive issues. Political appointees in the right positions can serve as translators, speaking to the bureaucracy in language it will understand about what the President's broad intent is, explaining to higher-level political appointees and legislators what the bureaucracy thinks in terms those audiences will appreciate.

That healthy equilibrium has, however, been upset by the steady intrusion of political appointees into increasingly lower-level jobs in the bureaucracy and into jobs that require skills they do not have. When I was confirmed as an Assistant Secretary of State with responsibility for military-related issues and international security affairs, I had the authority to choose five direct reports with the rank of Deputy Assistant Secretary. One of them, any one, had to be a political appointee, drawn from a list approved by the political office in the White House, a list largely of people who had helped the President's campaign. "Create a portfolio for the political appointee that doesn't require any real experience in what your bureau does," I was told. Take one of my handful of senior, direct-report slots and craft a sinecure for it, to be filled by someone who was on a political list, but had no national security experience? Rather than do that, I combed the White House political list and found Sandy Martel. He had spent twenty-five years in Navy intelligence, retired the year before, and had spent that year working in President Bush 41's campaign. I was lucky; Martel was vastly experienced in national security. More typically now, assistant secretaries, the managers of government, are themselves political appointees without prior government experience, as are many of the deputies and staff. What other type of institution would populate the senior management level with people with no prior experience in the organization or even a similar organization?

In his devastating account of the United States in Iraq, *The Washington Post*'s Rajiv Chandrasekaran detailed how the staff of the American occupation administration was filled with personnel who had never before left the United States, never had a passport, never before served in the U.S. government and yet were supposed to run the Iraqi government. The primary qualification these staff had was their involvement in the President's campaign or the Republican Party machine. They did, however, go through an additional filter, one that asked them about their views on ideological issues irrelevant to their jobs in Iraq, such as their views on abortion and a woman's right to choose.

Moreover, the chaos in the U.S. Embassy apparently did not stop after the initial months and years. One of the political appointees was a former aide to Bill Frist, the Republican Majority Leader in the Senate. Manuel Miranda had been accused of involvement in hacking Democratic Senators' computer systems and left the Senate. He was later assigned to Baghdad. Yet even he found the staff sent to Baghdad with him woefully inexperienced for their jobs. Miranda wrote in February 2008, as he was leaving the embassy after a year, that "at the keystone moment that America's leaders and people were pained over the debate of our continued national sacrifice, the Baghdad Embassy was doing a bureaucratic imitation of the Keystone Cops."[4]

When the first President Bush was defeated, I was on his national security staff. During the transition, the man who would become Bill Clinton's national security advisor, Tony Lake, interviewed me about the issues I had been managing. At the end of the talk, he asked me to join his new team, and I agreed to. As I was leaving the room, I turned and said, "You forgot to ask me my party or who I voted for."

Lake looked up over his glasses and shot back, "Whom. And no, I didn't forget. I don't care. I'm hiring professionals." The law establishing the National Security Council in 1947 explicitly prohibited political activity of any type by its staff, yet in recent years there has been a political litmus test in violation of that law. One man nominated for an NSC staff position was rejected a few years ago because public voting records did not indicate that he was a registered Republican. He was, at the time of his consideration for the NSC staff job, a serving colonel in the U.S. Army and a member of its Special Forces.

In the British bureaucracy, a cabinet minister, a "junior minister," and some on their immediate office staffs are political appointees, perhaps a dozen or fewer, and the rest of the ministry (department) is staffed by career civil servants. Each department is managed by a career officer, the number three ranking person in the ministry, the permanent under secretary (unfortunately called the PUS, pronounced "pee you ess"). Most British permanent under secretaries have had more than two decades' experience in government and may have served in several different departments; they may even have already been a PUS at another ministry. They are expected to carry out the cabinet member's orders and to make the ministry work. In a similar American cabinet-level department, there could be hundreds of political appointees at all levels, many in management jobs even though they have never worked in government before or perhaps never even had a management job before. The number of political appointees decreased by 17 percent in the 1990s but is now up by 33 percent in the last seven years.[5] Political appointees have also recently been made eligible for cash awards, with some receiving as much as $25,000 on top of their salary.[6]

I think the record is fairly indisputable that national security issues have been used for partisan electoral advantage in recent years: terrorism threats have been overhyped near elections, predictions have been made about terrorist attacks occurring if the other party wins, people's patriotism has been questioned. A well-funded lobbying and campaign contribution effort by members of a small ethnic group (Armenians) bent on addressing a century-old atrocity by a long-since-dead empire (the Ottomans) has damaged relations with a crucial ally. There may be no way to restrain elected officials and party apparatchiks from engaging in such activity, even though it makes conducting national security and achieving the needed national consensus on issues far more difficult. We can hope for more courageous politicians like Senator John McCain, who in 2006 decried those in his party who were attacking Democrats as being less opposed to al Qaeda. Such candor is likely, however, to remain in short supply. Thus, perhaps the best we can do to limit the damage partisan politics can inflict on national security is not only to legislate a more professional career system for national security personnel, but also to include limits on noncareer and partisan appointees in sensitive national security positions. For example we could impose such limits as these:

- The National Security Council staff could have fifteen senior positions, Special Assistants to the President for national security affairs, who would would lead the directorates that manage interagency affairs; twelve would be drawn from career ranks, and none of the fifteen could have held electoral office or paid positions on a campaign committee or political party staff in the preceding four years.

- In the State Department, a similar percentage (less than a fifth) of Deputy Assistant Secretary, Assistant Secretary, Undersecretary, and ambassadorial posts would be available to noncareer officials and the rest would be staffed by Foreign Service and other Civil Service personnel.

- In the intelligence and law enforcement agencies, there would be a ban on partisan personnel (those who had held electoral office or paid positions on a campaign committee or political party staff in the preceding four years).

Similar limits could be devised for the Defense and Homeland Security departments. The result could be more frankness and honesty from national security officials testifying before Congress and to the public, increased use of analysis in decision making, and more talented people being willing to enter and stay in government service. Underperforming career personnel could still be reassigned or dismissed, and nonpartisan outside experts could still be brought in to national security agencies for limited appointments to reduce the risk of groupthink. But the use of the national security bureaucracy as an extension of the ruling party would have been curtailed.

THE R WORD

Part of the partisan tactic has been to attack government as a phenomenon. The Republican Ronald Reagan ran for President by attacking government. Later the Democrat Bill Clinton declared, "The era of big government is over," and reduced the number of federal employees and balanced the federal budget. George W. Bush associated himself with a particular strain of probusiness lobbyists who wanted to staff government regulatory agencies with people who did not believe the agencies they ran should do much regulating. It was consistent with his general pattern of staffing, which left important positions vacant for long periods and then filled them with people who passed various ideological and political litmus tests and scored low on professional qualifications or relevant work experience.

It is, however, their attitude toward regulation that perhaps limited the effectiveness of government the most. Asking government to work without adopting new regulations to address new problems and not enforcing existing regulations is like asking a modern military to operate without airpower. Governments can essentially do three things: they can make certain actions illegal and empower prosecutors to arrest those who engage in them, they can fund programs, and they can regulate certain activities. Doing only two of those things and abjuring the third tool in the tool kit makes it very unlikely that government will actually succeed in solving many of the problems most people want it to solve.

The distaste for regulation stems from a 1930s through 1970s era of government in which large federal regulatory agencies grew around Washington like mushrooms in compost after a summer rain. They wrote long and complicated volumes, requiring corporations to hire legions of Washington lawyers to interpret the ever-changing Delphic offerings. I first experienced this world when, as a student in college, I learned that the government was proposing to eliminate student airfares, a discount program that allowed college students like me to fly home more than once a year. I convinced my undergraduate association to petition a federal regulatory body called the Civil Aeronautics Board (CAB) to keep its hands off student airfares. Somehow, in the process, we became a "party" to an incredibly complex regulatory process through which the CAB was deciding on a Talmudically complicated system telling airlines how much they could charge for various kinds of tickets. Every day pounds of documents arrived at my college office, since the CAB required every party to paper every other party with every analysis, telephone book, and computer printout it could find. When it became obvious that this was a window into government not provided by my college courses, I decided to accept one of the invitations to attend a CAB hearing. To say that it was theater of the absurd would be an understatement. Eventually, Congress got smart and simply abolished the CAB and let airlines charge whatever they wanted to and fly pretty much wherever they wanted to. Ticket prices plummeted.

The well-deserved demise of the CAB was part of a reaction to over-regulation. Some hamhanded intrusions of the Occupational Safety and Health Administration (OSHA) also inspired widespread hatred of regulation, especially in small businesses. Much of the deregulation that took place in the 1980s and '90s made good economic sense, but it too was overdone. The pendulum swung too far in the opposite direction. Now the very idea of a new regulation is treated in many quarters as akin to apostasy.

The Homeland Security Department has run away from its role of regulating chemical plants producing lethal gas, container shipping, and cybersecurity. Such regulations could have applied equally to all companies in a vertical and not created economic advantage for some or given a boost to unregulated foreign competition. Indeed, the major chemical companies even asked to be regulated for plant security. Only the smaller independents objected. When Congress forced the Homeland Security Department to regulate chemical plants, the department dragged its feet and finally issued watered-down, ineffective rules designed more to show that it had acted than actually to solve a problem. A similar story took place with container shipping, where the world's three largest container shippers asked for security regulations, only to be rebuffed by the Homeland Security Department. In the area of cybersecurity, the Federal Communications Commission refused to regulate almost anything having to do with the internet, including security, even though Congress gave it the power to do so. The Environmental Protection Agency had to be taken to the Supreme Court by advocacy groups to get a ruling that it had the responsibility to regulate new-vehicle emissions. The Food and Drug Administration, often leaderless in recent years, has come under repeated criticism for not inspecting a wide range of poisonous products, particularly from China. This list of refusals to regulate could go on and on.

Were it not for government regulation, we would likely still be driving unsafe cars without seat belts, air bags, or crash tests; we would frequently be dangerously sick from food poisoning; and we could not trust that the medicines we take would not make us more sick. When you see a child playing with a toy, remember that it is only federal regulations that stand between that child and her licking Chinese lead paint off it and developing brain damage or learning disabilities as a result.

Not all federal regulation has to be like the old CAB and its airfare monstrosity. Smart regulation says the goals and objectives, allowing industry and academic experts to develop best practices and guidelines to get there. Smart regulation permits outside, third-party auditors to certify compliance. Smart regulation can transfer costs from the federal government's budget to the consumers of products, in essence as a user fee for guarantees of safety, security, or reliability. Running away from regulation because of some neofederalist ideology results in lead painted toys, mortgage meltdowns, and uninspected airlines.

ANALYZE THIS

"Is this the best you can do?" Henry Kissinger is said to have remarked, returning an options analysis for further work. Kissinger, then national security advisor, had not yet read the paper but knew it would come back better after the various agencies involved engaged in a redraft. As a junior staff member in the Defense Department and State Department in the 1970s, I drafted scores of analyses of nuclear arms control issues, political military strategy, and budget options. Major national security decisions in the 1970s were subject to as much analytical rigor and debate as possible. There had to be credible options, not just a single preferred course. The options had to be compared with a variety of yardsticks: feasibility, financial cost, acceptability to key allies, congressional reaction, Soviet reaction, effect on other issues. The factual basis for assertions, particularly intelligence community data, was subject to detailed review. An important decision could involve a half-dozen separate related analyses, each of which might undergo ten iterations plus review and comment from several agencies' and departments' experts. Departments routinely differed on their choice of policy options and competed to write the most compelling case for their option and against the alternative. The resulting documents were far better than most legal briefs or university debate teams' cases.

Policy analysis is now a lost art in the federal government. Gradually and steadily the use of rigorous, competitive interagency national security policy analysis withered, and it stopped altogether shortly after the end of the millennium. For the decision to go to war with Iraq in 2003, there not only was an absence of an options analysis, there was not even a cabinet-level meeting to discuss the option of invading. There are probably three reasons for the death of national security options analysis in the U.S. government. First, officials fear that the sensitive papers will leak and their deliberative process will be exposed. Second, officials like Vice President Cheney know what they want to do and believe that debate would be a waste of time. Third, there are few people in government who have ever written a rigorous analysis of options on a complex national security issue. They don't even know how.

Part of bringing increased professionalism to national security affairs must be a return to competitive analysis. National security staff should be trained to create realistic policy alternatives and compare them using the same evaluative criteria for judging each option. A President should, by national security decision directive, require the interagency system to produce such options analysis for all major decisions. The rationale for decisions, dissents, and alternatives, the weight given various considerations, the accuracy of facts, the expertise brought to bear, excursions considering unexpected results should all be transparent to decision makers. Without such information, decision makers must, by definition, make uninformed choices.

OF CZARS AND MANAGERS

"They killed the last czar and all of his family," I explained to a reporter who asked why I objected to being called the Terrorism Czar by the media after I was given the title of National Coordinator for Security and Counterterrorism in 1998. "Besides, I don't have any czarlike powers." Indeed, the departments and agencies involved in counterterrorism so feared anyone holding them accountable that they had insisted on watering down the role of the National Coordinator to the point where I could do little more than try to persuade agencies and serve up options to the cabinet-level committee and the President. The decision document creating the new title actually listed the things I could not do, which included not being able to order anyone to do anything. Nonetheless, having presidential authority to know everything about an issue ("be fully informed in a timely manner"), draw attention to problems, propose options, and suggest budget changes was useful. To have more authority, I was told, would make the White House "operational," which everyone seemed to think was somehow a bad thing for reasons that they never quite articulated.

Those who oppose the concept of White House czars are usually people who held positions in cabinet departments and agencies. They see czars as people who would try to tell them what to do. In that regard, the opponents of White House czars are right; such positions really make sense only if the czars have the authority to issue implementing instructions on behalf of a presidentially approved policy. Where the opponents are wrong is in thinking that complex, multidepartmental activities can be carried out well without a czar. Almost any significant national security issue now involves numerous departments and multiples of that number in terms of component agencies. Understanding what they are all doing, ensuring that they are all doing what the President's policy requires, creating new policy options, performing quality control oversight of decisions, and having a holistic view of an important complex issue requires a czar. Four years after invading Iraq, President Bush decided he needed a White House "war czar" to coordinate Defense, State, and the other agencies involved. He created a position in the West Wing with equivalent rank to the National Security Advisor for that purpose.

While I have been told that having "czars" is against the American tradition, it is in fact the only way in which the government has successfully tackled complex issues. Leslie Groves, Hyman Rickover, and James Webb had czarlike authority over three major government projects: the Manhattan Project to build nuclear bombs, the creation of nuclear-powered submarines (and other major Navy ships), and the Apollo mission to land humans on the moon. Each man was controversial. They also delivered what was asked of them, making the U.S. government perform well in uncharted areas fraught with risks and complexities. None of the three was really a dictator or totally without supervision. To varying degrees, they were all subject to executive branch and congressional oversight. If they failed, they would have been relieved, and they knew that. There was no doubt who was accountable for program failure, were that to occur. They were, however, given sufficient latitude to achieve results.

As a public servant, few have ever equaled Hyman Rickover, who served his nation for sixty-three years under thirteen Presidents, from Woodrow Wilson to Ronald Reagan. At the dawn of the nuclear age in the 1940s, Rickover understood better than anyone else the promise of a nuclear Navy. He also understood that for it to work, there could be no toleration of failure. One radiation leak or meltdown, and the entire program would be scrapped. So Rickover oversaw every detail of construction on every nuclear-powered vessel for more than thirty years. When a new boat (as submarines are affectionately known in the Navy) went out for sea trial, you could be sure that Hyman Rickover would be on it.

He demanded excellence from everyone around him, handpicking every single officer, and would go to somewhat unusual lengths to test them. He asked one candidate to do something to make him mad. The officer stood up, saluted, and then broke a hand-carved wooden replica of the *Nautilus* that was sitting on Rickover's desk over his knee. Rickover hired him on the spot. He told another candidate to go stand in the closet and close the door and not to come out until Rickover came to get him. Rickover then left for the day. The next morning he walked into his office, opened the closet door, and hired the young officer who had not budged all night. In the submarine community, it is widely reported that the young officer was Jimmy Carter.

Today, Rickover's influence continues to be felt as each successive admiral in charge of the nuclear Navy continues to personally select each new nuclear officer. The Navy also continues its perfect record in operating nuclear reactors after sixty years and the commissioning of two hundred nuclear-powered vessels.

In a 1982 speech at Columbia University, Rickover outlined his management philosophy in a speech titled "Doing a Job." I tried to keep his points in mind as I attempted to manage programs from the White House. They could well be applied to most national security senior management positions today:

- People, not organizations or management systems, get things done.

- Management is hard work.

- Subordinates must be given authority and responsibility early in their careers.

- Get rid of formal job descriptions and organizational charts. Define responsibilities, but define them in a general way so that people are not circumscribed.

- Complex jobs cannot be accomplished effectively with transients. Short rotations ensure inexperience and nonaccountability.

- Don't downplay problems to try to save face.

- Flatten management structures, but empower the remaining managers and hold them responsible.

- Good ideas are not adopted automatically. They must be driven into practice with courageous impatience.

- The man in charge must concern himself with details. If he does not consider them important, neither will his subordinates.

- Develop simple and direct means for finding out what subordinates are doing and what the status of projects is.

- Don't let your inbox set your priorities. Unimportant but interesting trivia pass through every office.

- Check all work through independent and impartial review. In engineering and manufacturing, industry spends large sums on quality control but the concept of impartial reviews and oversight is important in other areas also.

- Important issues should be presented in writing. Nothing sharpens the thought process like writing down one's arguments.

Alas, there are no Rickovers today. Who is accountable for destroy-ing al Qaeda? Who can we hold accountable for safeguarding the world's nuclear materials or securing aviation? What person is respon-sible for rebuilding and securing Afghanistan? Who is ensuring that we can respond effectively to a pandemic such as avian influenza? Do you know their names? I don't. If there are skilled managers willing to take on difficult, important national security challenges, we should empower them, provide them with some periodic oversight and report-ing, and hold them accountable for getting the task accomplished or for returning to the President with an explanation of what exogenous variable is preventing them from success.

THE OVERSIGHT OVERSIGHT

Are the President's policies being well implemented, are they working, are there new issues that require attention? White House staffs are too busy or too self-important to bother to know. Czars would know. And a well-designed system would cause the czars themselves to be reviewed periodically to see if their programs are meeting measurable milestones.

Under the existing model of national security governance, the only real oversight (or implementation review) that occurs is by the media and occasionally by a congressional committee backed by Congress's Government Accountability Office. The inspectors general whom Congress required to be appointed in every department are usually oc-cupied investigating fraud, corruption, personnel, or procurement abuses. Moreover, they are appointed by and leave with the President. The likelihood that the inspector general in a department will publicly criticize the department, and thereby implicitly the administration, is remote. The rare example is Clark Kent Irwin, a Texas Republican ap-pointed by Bush, who did his job at the new and bumbling Depart-ment of Homeland Security. He was not rewarded for doing so; rather, he was driven out of government. If we consider public administration to be a profession, like law or accounting or dentistry, the inspectors general should be appointed by or from a list generated by a professional committee of public administration professors and practitioners. Their term should not be coterminus with that of the administration.

Just as the interagency policy analysis system that was once run by the National Security Council staff has atrophied, so too has the NSC staff's interagency oversight function. The NSC staff was once responsible for the detailed monitoring of covert actions, which were authorized by the President on a case-by-case basis, and counterterrorism operations. In addition to those sensitive and highly secret tasks, the NSC staff once managed program and policy performance reviews, sometimes in conjunction with another White House staff, the Office of Management and Budget (OMB), to determine if the departments and agencies were implementing the President's policies well. In recent years the NSC staff has been too busy with press guidance (the daily spinning of the administration's policy to the media) and talking points (the script for the President and senior White House officials to use in meetings with department officials or visitors from other governments) to conduct oversight of the departments. To restore accountability, the work of departments, agencies, and any czars who might be created must be subjected to a regular oversight review process by the White House NSC staff.

This shift away from quality control and accountability review by the NSC staff derives from the attitude of the last two National Security Advisors, who have been less assertive than any of their predecessors, in relationship to the Pentagon, State Department, and CIA. Part of the reason for that diminution of authority was the role of the Vice President. At the beginning of the Bush 43 administration, thought was given to demoting the National Security Advisor by having Vice President Cheney chair the key operating group, the cabinet-level Principals Committee. What happened instead was that the Vice President attended the principals meetings, outranking the NSC advisor, who nominally chaired the sessions. With the Vice President's support, the Secretary of Defense instructed the Pentagon staff to ignore any attempt at oversight by the NSC staff. The interagency control system thus broke down.

Another cause of the weakened NSC system was the limited scope of interest of the National Security Advisor. During the transition period in January 2001, Dr. Rice expressed surprise to me that my office was involved in so many things that were not "foreign policy." Some of them, she suggested, would have to go. Early on in the administration, she repeatedly characterized the role of the NSC staff that she ran as coordinating "foreign policy." The 1947 law that established the NSC staff had included intelligence, defense, international economics, and domestic security in the writ of the organization. Before 9/11, the National Security Advisor had not been able to find the time for a principals meeting on terrorism, which she seemed to regard as being something different from the "foreign policy" role she preferred. After 9/11, she urged the creation of a parallel staff and advisor that would take over the NSC's domestic security coordination function. When in October 2001 there was an outbreak of anthrax attacks, Dr. Rice told the White House Chief of Staff in my presence, "I didn't take this job to work on things like that." Things like Americans getting killed. Unfortunately, the line between what is domestic national security and what is foreign national security is not a bright demarcation in the real world, not a distinction that our enemies honor. Thus, one step needed to restore the oversight function is to merge the White House Homeland Security Council staff and advisor back into the National Security Council organization.

Well after the normal dinner hour one night, a frustrated member of my staff came to me in my office at the National Security Council, steaming that the government did not work. The agencies with which he was working were "dysfunctional." He seemed genuinely surprised at my response: "The U.S. government is not designed to work. We have taken the principle of checks and balances to its illogical extreme. Americans have always distrusted government and have designed a system to so limit the bureaucracy that when it does work it is largely by accident. Only once in a while we decide something is so important that we are going to get it done." We have to decide what it is that we really need to get done and then design a system, with accountable interagency managers, with oversight, that can produce results.

INSPIRED TO PARTICIPATE

"National Security Management: Getting Stuff Done" is the name of a course I coteach with Rand Beers. (The students use another word for "stuff.") After leaving government, we were asked by Graham Allison to teach at Harvard's Kennedy School of Government. Since 2004, I have had the privilege of working there with hundreds of midcareer students from government agencies and with younger students thinking of a government career. Many in the latter group have chosen, upon completing their studies, to take jobs in the private sector. Having coffee with a group of students in the Forum, the school's meeting place and speakers' venue, I asked, "Why do people go to a school of government and then not go into government?"

"It will cost me over a hundred thousand dollars to get my MPA out of this place," one student told me frankly. "I gotta pay some of my loans off before I can even think of buying a place to live. The private sector pays better. With a government salary, after a few years I could maybe buy a town house over an hour commute from downtown Washington." It was a practical, if not inspired, response, contrasting with the motivation of some of the career government employees of an earlier generation. In Maine I had asked Bob Gelbard why he had joined the government. "It had everything to do with John Kennedy" and his call to serve the country, he said. Gelbard had gone from Colby to the Peace Corps in Bolivia, where he would, many years later, be our Ambassador. Wendy Chamberlin, also inspired by Kennedy, had joined the Peace Corps and gone to Laos, and she too, after years of service in Washington and around the world, would end up going back to her Peace Corps assignment country as the Ambassador of the United States and personal representative of the President. Like Bob Gelbard, Wendy earned a rare, second ambassadorial posting. As U.S. Ambassador to Pakistan, arriving shortly before 9/11, she helped to change the Islamabad government, which had supported the Taliban, into an ally against them. "Kennedy made public service seem so noble," she recalled, her blond hair shining even in the darkened library of the Middle East Institute in Washington, where she is now president. "I don't hear that call to national service any more," Gelbard had mused in Maine, looking out at the lobster traps. "I think I remember after 9/11 being asked to go shopping . . ."

Despite the lack of an inspiring call to service, many students and people in the private sector tried to get involved in national security after 9/11. Some had gone to the Kennedy School first for training in national security studies. From my unscientific survey, what many of them experienced was off-putting. There was no way of throwing their résumé into a central national security pool, no way of joining a national security cadre that would train them in the ways of government at the secret/top secret security clearance level. Instead, they had to contact a dozen agencies, most of which tried to match them against specific, existing job openings. They were usually told that after they applied for a job, they would need to find something else to do for up to a year while they waited to be granted a security clearance. And then there were the salaries. Contrast that with the typical experience of students going to a corporation doing work for government agencies. One of my students told me he had joined an outsourcing firm because "they said they would put me in for a government security clearance and while I waited for that they would pay me, put me in training programs, and then when I got cleared I could bid to join project teams that needed staff. I also got a hiring bonus and moving expenses, neither of which the government offered. And, of course, the starting salary was better." Another concurred but added, "I'm just not so sure I want to work in government right now. I love my country and want to serve it, but I don't support a lot of what they are doing now. I just couldn't do some of those things, be part of it."

Congress does not want any federal employee making more money than a congressman. Thus, a congressman's salary is the top salary for a senior manager and other federal managers get somewhat less. Multibillion-dollar programs have federal managers who have chosen to work for much less than they could get for doing something similar in the private sector, or perhaps they would not be competitive in a competitive environment. Singapore, seeking to have the best managers run important government programs, pays salaries more commensurate with those of major multinational corporations. Singapore has one of the best-run, most effective governments in the world. There may be some "cause and effect" involved. Someday, perhaps, some courageous President will suggest that some programs in government are so important that we should offer performance-based compensation competitive with that of industry, even if it means that people who actually manage complex things well would be paid more than the 435 members of the House of Representatives.

But sitting in the Forum, reflecting on my students' comments, I realized that as much as some of the government's national security system makes it difficult or unappealing to join, the essential element missing today is really the invitation, the challenge, the inspiration to serve. As corny or trite as it may have seemed to some in later years, what the President said in 1961 had drawn a generation of talented young people to public service like a Pied Piper. His words echo there in Cambridge in the school named for him: "Ask not . . ." Without such a new clarion appeal, backed up by serious reform of the system, many people will choose careers in finance and consulting, rather than intelligence and national security. The new presidential appeal must inspire, but it needs also to address the real barriers that keep many people away from national security service. That means acknowledging the recent disasters, the lies, the departures from our core values, and it means pledging real change so those failures will not be repeated. The call also must include promises about opportunity to participate meaningfully, in a professional career path, with training, testing, responsibility, recognition, and protection from partisan sniping. If a new President makes that call and means it, follows through, the good people will come and others will follow.

RETURNING TO GOOD GOVERNMENT

There was a government reform movement in the early twentieth century that aimed to end corruption and to professionalize civil service and public administration. It was known as the Good Government Movement, and its advocates were called Goo Goos. It's time to bring back the Goo Goos, not just to end corruption but to restore professionalism in public administration and end the practice of using government as a political whipping boy, limiting its effectiveness and then complaining about how it can't get anything done.

As you will have noted throughout the book, I have my views about what a good government should be doing on specific and important national security issues in the near term. Two factors shape how I believe we should approach those issues. First, we need to approach national security issues at home and abroad within the context of our values. When we detach ourselves to any degree from the Constitution, civil liberties, and human rights, we soon find ourselves adrift, without a compass, and engaging in counterproductive activities. Second, the threat of violent Islamist extremists is significant and we can do a much better job of countering it, but it is not an existential threat to the United States and we will do a better job of addressing it if we put it into context and do not artificially inflate the threat.

Those two parameters have driven me to make up a specific list of things we need to do:

- Abroad, we must act boldly to reestablish our moral leadership, respect for international law, and support for human rights. We must refocus our efforts on countering the violent Islamist extremists, chiefly through nonmilitary means, helping our friends whenever possible with law enforcement and intelligence and as they develop an ideological counterweight to the al Qaeda movement. A major new international effort is required to secure radiological material from falling into terrorists' hands because such weapons would make terrorism a vastly different kind of threat. If another government will not act against a violent Islamist extremist terrorist or terrorist facility, we should do so, consistent with legal standards and methods.

- At home, there are things we can and should do to reduce important security vulnerabilities, but we need to do them in ways that are consistent with our Constitution and beliefs about civil liberties. (We can also do them without all of the massive counterterrorism government-industrial complex that has grown up.) The Army must be rebuilt. Our veterans given the health care and the opportunities they need to lead successful lives after their service. We must urgently turn our technological prowess to achieving specific accomplishments in energy technology, climate change mitigation, and cyberspace security.

Wherever you stand on those issues, there is an institution-building agenda for good government in national security. It includes recruiting and training, retaining and rewarding civilian professionals the same way we have with our military. Achieving good government in national security also means depoliticizing it to the maximum extent possible. We must ask our politicians to restrain themselves from continuing to make terrorism and other national security issues into campaign tools and wedges with which to artificially divide Americans. We may have limited success with the politicians and their electoral campaigns, but we should try to keep politics out of the practice of national security by limiting the number and role of political appointees and requiring of them that they meet professional standards of qualification for the positions they would occupy.

Good government in national security also means active oversight by truly independent inspectors, by interagency policy committees, and then by informed congressional committees. Use of smart regulation and the restoration of the interagency policy analysis process are also both required if we are to restore effective national security program management. We must develop a set of specific and clear national security goals, even bold ones, empower managers to achieve them, and hold them accountable when they do not. And most important of all, our President must again make federal service a noble calling.

Off the piazza in Siena in Tuscany, two murals by Ambrogio Lorenzetti have adorned the Palazzo Pubblico since 1328. One depicts a country in which farmers cultivate rich fields, merchants sell their wares, scholars study, and the people are happy. In the other, there is obvious poverty, people are in chains, the oppression and depression are palpable. The two panels are titled "Good Government" and "Bad

Government." They knew then, in 1328, as we have relearned in recent years, that there is a direct relationship between people's security, health, prosperity, and happiness and the concerted practice of good government. If we stop denigrating government and using its instruments as partisan punching bags, if we work in a bipartisan way to rebuild our institutions of national security, your government will fail you much less; it could even make you proud of it once more.

ACKNOWLEDGMENTS

Many, many people made this volume possible and to them I give much thanks. I want to especially note five of them.

After the twenty years we've spent as a team, it is hard for me to imagine how I would function without the thoughtful support of my Executive Assistant, Beverly Roundtree-Jones.

My intellectual challenger and partner in thinking through the issues addressed in the book is Rob Knake, of Good Harbor Consulting, with whom I have co-authored several op-eds and other analyses. Knake is a star in the next generation concerned with national security who will, I hope, make government fail less in the future.

Emlian Papaduopolus, my Course Assistant at the Harvard Kennedy School of Government, provided superb research assistance, helping to keep the volume accurate and the sourcing clear. I expect you will also be hearing a great deal more about him someday soon, probably in the government of Canada.

Len Sherman, my literary agent, has now guided me through the production of four books. Without his confidence, optimism, and pestering, the two novels, *Against All Enemies,* and this volume would not have happened.

Finally, it is an immense pleasure to work with the crew at Ecco, particularly publisher Daniel Halpern. Dan has an innate sense of what will work and a velvet-glove approach to getting his way, a way that always improves the product.

2: No More Vietnams

1. During World War I, the Department of War restricted overseas military voting. Through World War II and its aftermath, military personnel deployed overseas remained somewhat disenfranchised because of cumbersome state requirements, despite legislation like the Soldier Voting Act of 1942 and the Federal Voting Assistance Act of 1955. In 1975 Congress began to tackle the procedural and state-imposed impediments to military and overseas voting with the passage of the Overseas Citizens Voting Rights Act, which was superseded in 1986 by the Uniformed and Overseas Citizens Absentee Voting Act. For a full history of military voting, see R. Michael Alvarez, Thad E. Hall, and Brian F. Roberts for the Institute of Public and International Affairs, University of Utah, "Military Voting and the Law: Procedural and Technological Solutions to the Ballot Transit Problem," March 8, 2007 (forthcoming in the *Fordham Law Review*), available at content.lib.utah.edu/cgi-bin/showfile.exe?CISOROOT=/ir-main&CISOPTR=922&filename=776.pdf and David M. Walker, "Elections: Issues Affecting Military and Overseas Absentee Voters," Testimony before the Subcommittee on Military Personnel, Committee on Armed Services, House of Representatives, U.S. Government Accountability Office, May 9, 2001.

2. For more on military voting patterns, see Benjamin Wallace-Wells, "Corps Voters," *Washington Monthly,* November 2003, and Rosa Brooks, "Weaning the Military from the GOP," *Los Angeles Times,* January 5, 2007.

3. For perspectives on the civilian-military relationship, see Michael C. Desch, *Civilian Control of the Military: The Changing Security Environment* (Baltimore: Johns Hopkins University Press, 1999), and more recently Peter D. Feaver and Christopher Gelpi, *Choosing Your Battles: American Civil-Military Relations and the Use of Force* (Princeton: Princeton University Press, 2004).

4. For a discussion of civil-military relations in Turkey, see David L. Phillips, "Turkey's Dreams of Accession," *Foreign Affairs,* September–October 2004.

5. For details on the high proportion of disadvantaged Americans in the military, see Christian G. Appy, *Working-Class War: American Combat Soldiers and Vietnam* (Chapel Hill: University of North Carolina Press, 1993).

6. Harry G. Summers, Jr., Colonel of Infantry, *On Strategy: A Critical Analysis of the Vietnam War* (New York: Presidio Press, 1982; new edition 1995).

7. H. R. McMaster, *Dereliction of Duty: Lyndon Johnson, Robert McNamara, The Joint Chiefs of Staff, and the Lies That Led to Vietnam* (New York: HarperCollins, 1997).

8. For more information on support units being reassigned, see James Kitfield, *Prodigal Soldiers* (Washington, D.C.: Brassey's, 1997), p. 441.

9. For additional reading on the creation of the "Total Force" concept, see ibid., pp. 149–150.

10. For additional reading on the Army's views on how U.S. society would react to a National Guard and reserve mobilization, see ibid., p. 441.

11. Additional details on the "Desert One" operation and its disastrous end can be found in ibid., pp. 223–226.

12. Reagan administration officials' positions on use of the military in the peacekeeping operation in Lebanon alongside Italian, French, and British forces can be found in a RAND publication on the comparison between the United States and Russia on reasons for the use of force, available at www.rand.org/pubs/conf_proceedings/ CF129/CF-129.chapter6.html.

13. More on the peacekeeping mission can be found in Kitfield, *Prodigal Soldiers,* pp. 260–263.

14. Reagan administration officials' desire to invade Grenada in order to save the students and to divert attention from the situation in Lebanon can be found in a 1996 RAND publication on the comparison between the United States and Russia on reasons for the use of force, available at www.rand.org/pubs/conf_proceedings/ CF129/CF-129.chapter8.html.

15. For more on the Grenada invasion and its mishaps, see Ronald H. Cole, "Grenada, Panama, and Haiti: Joint Operational Reform," *Joint Force Quarterly,* Spring 2003.

16. Information on how the Goldwater-Nichols Defense Reorganization Act of 1986 altered how the military operated can be found in Kitfield, *Prodigal Soldiers,* pp. 296–297. Also in James R. Locher III, *Victory on the Potomac: The Goldwater-Nichols Act Unifies the Pentagon* (College Station: Texas A&M University Press, 2002).

17. For additional information on the capture of the crew of the U.S.-flagged merchant ship *Mayaguez* by the Cambodian Khmer Rouge Navy in 1975 and the botched initial U.S. military efforts to recover the crew, see John F. Guilmartin, Jr., "The Mayaguez Incident, 12–15 May 1975: A 30-year Retrospective," *Air & Space Power Journal,* Spring 2005.

18. Information on the creation of the SEALs and Delta Force can be found in Kitfield, *Prodigal Soldiers,* p. 297.

19. The Goldwater-Nichols Defense Reorganization Act of 1986 called for, among other things, a "comprehensive description and discussion of the following: (1) the worldwide interests, goals, and objectives of the United States that are vital to the national security of the United States, (2) the foreign policy, worldwide commitments, and

national defense capabilities of the United States necessary to deter aggression and to implement the national security strategy of the United States, (3) the proposed short-term and long-term uses of the political, economic, military, and other elements of the national power of the United States to protect or promote the interests and achieve the goals and objectives referred to in paragraph (1)."

20. Commmentary on the creation of the QDR was given in a speech by Deputy Secretary of Defense John White on December 19, 1996, available at www.defenselink .mil/releases/releas.aspx?releaseid=1112.

21. A review of the Weinberger doctrine can be found in Kitfield, *Prodigal Soldiers,* p. 269.

22. Charles W. Ostrom and Robin F. Marra, "U.S. Defense Spending and the Soviet Estimate," *American Political Science Review* 80, no. 3 (September 1986): 819–842, at p. 820 and also Larry M. Bartels, "Constituency Opinion and Congressional Policy Making: Reagan Defense Buildup," *American Political Science Review* 85, no. 2 (June 1991): 457.

23. For more on the discussions on when to end the war, see Kitfield, *Prodigal Soldiers,* p. 413.

24. For a review of the Powell Doctrine, see Arnel B. Enriquez, "The U.S. National Security Strategy of 2002: A New Use-of-Force doctrine?," *Air & Space Power Journal,* Fall 2004.

25. Powell's reluctance for U.S. forces to be used in Bosnia, along with his statement on the need for 250,000 troops for the proposed operations, are discussed in Lyle J. Goldstein, "General John Shalikashvili and the Civil-Military Relations of Peacekeeping," *Armed Forces & Society: An Interdisciplinary Journal,* March 22, 2000.

26. For more on the intervention in Haiti, see Robert I. Rotberg, "Clinton Was Right," *Foreign Policy* no. 102 (Spring 1996): 135–141.

27. U.S. military activity in Somalia in 1992–1994, and General Powell's role in it, are detailed in Walter S. Poole's *The Effort to Save Somalia: August 1992–March 1994* (Washington, D.C.: Joint History Office, Office of the Chairman of the Joint Chiefs of Staff, 2005).

28. For additional reading on the "Black Hawk down" incident, see Mark Bowden, *Black Hawk Down* (New York: Penguin Books, 1999), and Janie Blankenship, "Memories of Somalia Remain Vivid," *VFW Magazine,* October 2003.

29. Shalikashvili's support for the United States' efforts in the former Yugoslavia are documented in retired General Wesley Clark's book *Waging Modern War* (New York: Public Affairs, 2001), primarily pp. 47–56. Comments made by Shalikashvili during an interview in late 1995 also demonstrate his support for involvement in Bosnia. See Jim Gamarone, "Chairman Says Service Members Aware of Need for Bosnia Force," *American Forces Press Service,* December 13, 1995. Descriptions of U.S. military activities in Bosnia are taken from a Congressional Research Service report from 2004, available at www.au.af.mil/au/awc/awcgate/crs/rl30172.htm.

30. Eric Schmitt, "Some Lawmakers Say Clinton Can Order Haiti Invasion," *The New York Times,* September 9, 1994.

31. For more information on the decision to create the international police force, see Eric Schmitt and Michael R. Gordon, "Looking Beyond an Invasion, U.S. Plans Haiti Police Force," *The New York Times,* September 11, 1994.

32. Information on PDD 56 comes from Office of the Historian, Bureau of Public Affairs, "History of the Department of State During the Clinton Presidency (1993–2001), section 03. Security Policies," available at www.state.gov/r/pa/ho/pubs/8519.htm.

33. Information on Yousef's arrest can be found in David Johnston, "February 5–11: Fighting Terrorism, World Trade Center Suspect, One of F.B.I.'s Most-Wanted, Is Captured in Pakistan," *The New York Times,* February 12, 1995.

34. The phrase "hollow army" was used to describe the current readiness crisis as early as 2004; see James Fallows, "The Hollow Army," *Atlantic Monthly,* March 2004, available at www.theatlantic.com/doc/200403/fallows. For a thorough discussion of military readiness, see Lawrence J. Korb, Peter Rundlet, Max Bergmann, Sean Duggan, and Peter Juul, "Beyond the Call of Duty: A Comprehensive Review of the Overuse of the Army in the Administration's War of Choice in Iraq," March 6, 2007, available at www.americanprogress.org/issues/2007/03/readiness_report.html.

35. For more details on U.S. payment arrears to the United Nations since the 1980s, see the United Nations Association of the United States and the Business Council for the United Nations Policy Proposal, "Paying Our Dues on Time: A Plan to Restore U.S. Financial Leadership to the UN," January 2001, available at www.unausa.org/site/pp.aspx?c=fvKRI8MPJpF&b=346037&printmode=1. Also see Barbara Crosette, "After Long Fight, UN Agrees to Cut Dues Paid by U.S.," *The New York Times,* December 23, 2000.

36. The provision of U.S. U-2 spy planes to assist the U.N. missions is covered in Tim Weiner, "U.S. Says Iraq Spied on Inspectors to Know When to Hide Weapons," *The New York Times,* November 25, 1997.

37. The history of U.S. military involvement in Macedonia as part of the United Nations Preventive Deployment Force (UNPREDEP) can be found on the Global Security Web site at www.globalsecurity.org/military/ops/able_sentry.htm.

38. For more on the Contract with America and the proposed National Security Restoration Act, see www.house.gov/house/Contract/CONTRACT.html.

39. On August 3, 2000, then-Governor George W. Bush delivered the following remarks during his nomination acceptance speech at the Republican National Convention: "Our military is low on parts, pay and morale. If called on by the commander-in-chief today, two entire divisions of the Army would have to report, 'Not ready for duty, sir' "; see www.cnn.com/ELECTION/2000/conventions/republican/transcripts/bushhtml.

40. For a thorough discussion of military morale during the Iraq War, see Korb, Rundlet, Bergmann, Duggan, and Juul, "Beyond the Call of Duty."

41. For coverage of Sestak winning his congressional race, see William Bender, "How Sestak Did It," *Delaware County Daily Times,* November 9, 2006, available at www.usna74.com/files/JoeSestak.pdf, and Susan Kuczka, "Congress Has Fewest Veterans Since WWII," *The Seattle Times,* September 16, 2007, available at http://seattle times.nwsource.com/html/politics/2003886811_vetcong16.html.

3: No More Iraqs

1. For more on Abrams's thinking on how mobilizing the National Guard and reinstating the draft would affect public opinion, see James Kitfield, *Prodigal Soldiers* (Washington, D.C.: Brassey's, 1997), pp. 149–151.

2. For a discussion of private military contractors, see P. W. Singer, "Outsourcing War," *Foreign Affairs*, March–April 2005, available at www.foreignaffairs.org/20050301 faessay84211/p-w-singer/outsourcing-war.html.

3. "Poll: 70% Believe Saddam, 9-11 link," *USA Today,* September 6, 2003, available at www.usatoday.com/news/washington/2003-09-06-poll-iraq_x.htm.

4. For additional reading on the intelligence community's role in distorting the WMD-Iraq link, see Michael Isikoff and David Corn, *Hubris* (New York: Crown, 2006), pp. 162–166.

5. For information on intelligence community findings that Iraq was not involved in the 9/11 attacks, see ibid., pp. 410–413.

6. For a review of the issue of inadequate training times for units between deployments, see Anna Badkhen, "Corners Cut in Rush to Add Troops: Shorter Training Time, Lack of Equipment Hurt Readiness, Experts Say," *San Francisco Chronicle,* February 4, 2007.

7. Zogby International poll, "Zogby Poll: 9/11 + 5 Reveals Dramatic Partisan Split: 9/11 + 5 Finds a Nation Badly Divided as GOPers Back U.S. War on Terror, Wiretapping, and Saddam's Role in 9/11; Dems, Indies Suspicious of All Three," September 5, 2006, available at www.zogby.com/news/ReadNews/dbm?ID=1169.

8. The Bush administration's ability to keep members of the House of Representatives and the Senate supportive of its Iraq strategy is reflected in Jon Cohen and Dan Balz, "Most in Poll Want War Funding Cut: Bush's Approval Rating Ties All-Time Low," *The Washington Post,* October 2, 2007.

9. Information on the reasons for Myers's selection as Chairman of the JCS taken from Michael R. Gordon and General Bernard E. Trainor, *Cobra II: The Inside Story of the Invasion and Occupation of Iraq* (New York: Pantheon, 2006), p. 502.

10. Reference to the hasty production of an invasion plan for Afghanistan is found in ibid., p. 23.

11. Commentary on Franks's campaign plan to focus on the Taliban rather than al Qaeda, and on bin Laden's escape from Tora Bora in late 2001 because of a dearth of U.S. forces fighting in the battle of Tora Bora can be found in ex-CIA operative Gary Berntsen's book (coauthored with Ralph Pezzullo) *Jawbreaker: The Attack on bin Laden and al Qaeda* (New York: Crown, 2005). Also see Sean Naylor's review of the book, "Slouching Toward Tora Bora: What Would It Really Have Taken to Catch bin Laden?," *Washington Monthly,* May 2006, available at www.washingtonmonthly.com/features/2006/0605.naylor.html.

12. CENTCOM's invasion plan for Iraq from the 1990s, titled OPLAN 1003-98 and developed by Army General Anthony Zinni, can be found in Gordon and Trainor, *Cobra II,* p. 26.

13. Franks's part in actively slimming down the planned Iraq invasion force at Rumsfeld's urging is detailed on pp. 27–37 of chap. 2 and in all of chap. 3 of Gordon and Trainor, *Cobra II.*

14. Nadia Schadlow, "War and the Art of Governance," *Parameters,* Autumn 2003, pp. 85–94, available at http://carlisle-www.army.mil/usawc/Parameters/03autumn/schadlow.htm.

15. Franks' lack of adequate planning for the postconflict phase of the invasion can be found in Thomas E. Ricks, *Fiasco* (New York: Penguin, 2006), chap. 5.

16. See, e.g., James Glanz, William J. Broad, and David E. Sanger, "Huge Cache of Explosives Vanished from Site in Iraq," *The New York Times,* October 25, 2004, available at www.nytimes.com/2004/10/25/international/middleeast/25bomb .html.

17. Shinseki's appearances before congressional committees and the reference to several "hundreds of thousands" are cited in Matthew Engel,, "Scorned General's Tactics Proved Right," *The Guardian,* March 29, 2003, available at www.guardian.co.uk/ international/story/0,3604,925140,00.html. This information is also referenced in Larry Diamond, "What Went Wrong in Iraq," *Foreign Affairs,* September–October 2004, available at www.foreignaffairs.org/20040901faessay83505/larry-diamond/ what-went-wrong-in-iraq.html.

18. A public rebuke of Shinseki's testimony on possible required postcombat troop levels came from Deputy Secretary of Defense Wolfowitz. He is quoted as saying that the suggested numbers were "wildly off the mark" in reporter Ken Guggenheim's article "Democrats Want Answers, but Pentagon Says It Doesn't Know Size of Postwar Force in Iraq," Associated Press, March 3, 2003.

19. In early November, just days before the 2006 midterm elections, President Bush supported Secretary of Defense Rumsfeld, as well as Vice President Cheney, saying "Both these men are doing fantastic jobs and I strongly them"; see "Bush Stands by His Men" (editorial), *Boston Herald,* November 3, 2006.

20. On November 8, 2006, President Bush, in an East Room press conference, delivered the following remarks: "Don Rumsfeld has been a superb leader during a time of change. Yet he also appreciates the value of bringing in a fresh perspective during a critical period in this war. . . . He likes to call it fresh eyes. . . . He and I both agreed in our meeting yesterday that it was appropriate that I accept his resignation"; see www.whitehouse.gov/news/releases/2006/11/20061108-2.html.

21. Newbold's comments can be read in his editorial "Why Iraq Was a Mistake," *Time,* April 9, 2006.

22. Michael C. Desch with other authors in "Responses: Salute and Disobey? The Civil-Military Balance, Before Iraq and After," *Foreign Affairs,* September–October 2007, p. 155; the article is a series of responses to Desch's original article titled "Bush and the Generals," *Foreign Affairs,* May–June 2007.

23. Winslow T. Wheeler and Lawrence J. Korb, "Fire the Generals!," Appendix 1 in *Military Reform: A Reference Handbook* (Westport, Conn.: Praeger Security International, 2007).

24. Ricardo S. Sanchez, quoted in Josh White, "Ex-Commander in Iraq Faults War Strategy," *The Washington Post,* October 13, 2007, available at www.washingtonpost .com/wp-dyn/content/article/2007/10/12/AR2007101202459.html.

25. Ralph Peters, "General Failure," *USA Today,* July 24, 2007, available at http://blogs .usatoday.com/oped/2007/07/general-failure.html.

26. Administration members' mistaken belief that U.S. forces would be overwhelmingly welcomed by Iraqis can be found in Isikoff and Corn, *Hubris,* p. 412.

27. Rumsfeld's rebuke can be reviewed in "Rumsfeld: Don't Call Iraqi Enemy 'Insurgents,' " Associated Press, November 29, 2005, www.msnbc.com/id/10255205/.

28. Commentary on Mattis's preparation of his marines for deployment to Anbar province can be found in Ricks, *Fiasco,* pp. 317–318.

29. A discussion of the 4th Infantry Division's tactics can be found in Ricks, *Fiasco,* pp. 232–234.

30. The quotation from Colonel Hogg is from Ricks, *Fiasco,* p. 234.

31. Rumsfeld's decision to cancel the operation when Navy SEALs were in helicopters, about to begin the operation, is found in Mark Mazzetti, "U.S. Aborted Raid on Qaeda Chiefs in Pakistan in '05," *The New York Times,* July 7, 2007.

32. Walter Pincus, "Assessments Made in 2003 Foretold Situation in Iraq: Intelligence Studies List Internal Violence, Terrorist Activity," *The Washington Post,* May 20, 2007.

33. James Dobbins, "Who Lost Iraq?," *Foreign Affairs,* September–October 2007, p. 70.

34. For example, in May 2007 President Bush said to Congress, "Why don't you just wait and see what [Petraeus] says? . . . Fund the troops, and let him come back and report to the American people"; see "Bush Stakes Iraq on General's Report: Poll Finds Americans Trust Military Commanders to Win War," *Grand Rapids* (Michigan) *Press,* September 10, 2007.

35. General David H. Petraeus Commander, Multi-National Force—Iraq, "Report to Congress on the Situation in Iraq," *Foreign Affairs,* September 10–11, 2007, available at www.foreignaffairs.house.gov/110/pet091007.pdf.

36. See https://pol.moveon.org/petraeus.html.

37. "Petraeus: I 'Don't Know' if Iraq War Makes U.S. Safer," *The Nation,* September 11, 2007, available at www.thenation.com/blogs/capitalgames?pid=231766.

38. Representative Ron Klein (D-Fla.) issued a statement on September 10, 2007, following the testimony of Ambassador Ryan Crocker, asserting that "we have no business putting the lives of our troops on the line as we wait for the Iraqi government to get their act together"; see "Klein: Iraqi Government Must Learn to Stand on Its Own," press release, September 10, 2007, available at www.house.gov/list/press/fl22_klein/petraeus.shtml.

39. Lieutenant Colonel Paul Yingling, "A Failure in Generalship," *Armed Forces Journal,* available at www.usatoday.com/news/world/iraq/2007-04-28-failure-generalship_N.htm.

40. Fred Kaplan, "Challenging the Generals," *The New York Times Magazine,* August 26, 2007.

41. Buddhika Jayamaha, Wesley D. Smith, Jeremy Roebuck, Omar Mora, Edwards Sandmeier, Yance T. Gray, and Jeremy A. Murphy, op-ed, *The New York Times,* August 19, 2007.

42. For more details, see the article by twelve former Army captains, "The Real Iraq We Knew," *Washington Post,* October 16, 2007.

43. "Soldiers in Iraq Still Buying Their Own Body Armor," Associated Press, March 26, 2004.

44. For a thorough discussion of the MRAP fiasco, see Peter Eisler, Blake Morrison, and Tom Vanden Brook, "Pentagon Balked at Pleas from Officers in Field for Safer Vehicles," *USA Today,* available at www.usatoday.com/news/military/2007-07-15-iedcover_N.htm?csp=34.

45. This is reported in Tom Vanden Brook, "Humvee Doors Can Trap Troops; Army Adjusting Combat Vehicles," *USA Today,* May 7, 2007.

46. The Joint Improvised Explosive Device Defeat Organization (JIEDDO), its budget, and some problems the office has had are found in Bob Brewn, "What's Brewin': Organizational Chaos," *Government Executive*, August 13, 2007, available at http://govexec.com/dailyfed/0807/081307bb1.htm. The Joint Improvised Explosive Device Defeat Organization (JIEDDO) Web site is www.jieddo.dod.mil/default.aspx.

47. This was reported in David Wood, "Better Armor Lacking for New Troops in Iraq," *The Baltimore Sun,* January 10, 2007.

48. Biden's quote is taken from Tom Vanden Brooks, "Corps Refused 2005 Plea for MRAP Vehicles," *USA Today,* May 23, 2007.

49. This is detailed in "Pentagon Dithering Turned U.S. Forces into Sitting Ducks," editorial, *USA Today,* July 17, 2007. Also see Eisler, Morrison, and Vanden Brook, "Pentagon Balked at Pleas."

50. The success rate of MRAPs for Marines in Iraq is detailed in "Pentagon Dithering Turned U.S. Forces into Sitting Ducks."

51. Hejlik, quoted in Vanden Brook, "Corps Refused 2005 Plea," and in "Lack of MRAPs Cost Marine Lives" by Richard Lardner, Associated Press, February 15, 2008.

52. This is detailed in "Pentagon Dithering Turned U.S. Forces into Sitting Ducks."

53. See Eisler, Morrison, and Vanden Brook, "Pentagon Balked at Pleas."

54. The push to purchase the additional MRAPs is described in Tom Vanden Brook, "Army Seeks $20B for MRAPs, but Quick Fielding Has Hurdles," *USA Today,* May 18, 2007.

55. Dana Priest and Anne Hull, "Soldiers Face Neglect, Frustration At Army's Top Medical Facility," *The Washington Post,* February 18, 2007.

56. "Serve, Support, Simplify: Report of the President's Commission on Care for America's Returning Wounded Warriors," July 2007 (the Dole-Shalala Commission), located at www.pccww.govdocs/Kit/Main_Book_CC%5BJULY26%50.pdf.

57. The extent of U.S. military involvement in Kosovo, Bosnia, and Macedonia since the early 1990s is documented in a Congressional Research Service report from 2004, available at www.au.af.mil/au/awc/awcgate/crs/rl30172.htm.

58. Hannah Fischer, Kim Klarman, and Mari-Jana Oborceanu, "American War and Military Operations Casualties: Lists and Statistics," Congressional Research Service, June 29, 2007, available at www.fas.org/sgp/crs/natsec/RL32492.pdf.

59. For a review of the Powell Doctrine, see Arnel B. Enriquez, "The U.S. National Security Strategy of 2002: A New Use-of-Force Doctrine?," *Air & Space Power Journal,* Fall 2004.

60. See Ken Guggenheim, "Democrat says Whie House pushed unverified intelligence," *Oakland Tribune,* July 18, 2003. Also see Seymour Hersh, "The Stovepipe," *The New Yorker,* October 27, 2003.

61. From Seymour M. Hersh, "Who Lied to Whom?" *The New Yorker,* March 31, 2003.

62. The administration's focus on the alleged meeting is outlined in Isikoff and Corn, *Hubris,* p. 105.

63. Commentary on the CIA's dubious view of intelligence on the alleged meeting can be found in Senator Carl Levin (D-Mich.), "New CIA Response Raises Question Again: Where Does Vice President Cheney Get His Information?," July 8, 2004,

available at www.levin.senate.gov/newsroom/supporting/2004/070804cheney.pdf. This is also discussed in Mark Hosenball, "Dems Allege Intel Community Shields White House," *Newsweek,* September 13, 2006.

64. Information detailing the alleged chemical training can be found in "Report of the Senate Select Committee on Intelligence on Postwar Findings About Iraq's WMD Programs and Links to Terrorism and How They Compare with Prewar Assessments," 109th Congress, 2nd Session, September 8, 2006, p. 13, available at http:// intelligence.senate.gov/pub109thcongress.html. This is also discussed in Isikoff and Corn, *Hubris,* p. 119.

65. Commentary on Powell's appearance before the House International Relations Committee on February 7, 2001, and his statements about Iraq can be found in Phyllis Bennis, "Some Preliminary Assessments of Powell's Iraq Trajectory," *Institute for Policy Studies,* March 13, 2001.

66. Hans Blix, *Disarming Iraq* (New York: Pantheon Books, 2004).

67. For the complete text of the September 2002 National Security Strategy of the United States of America, see www.whitehouse.gov/nsc/nss.pdf. The section on pre-emption, entitled "Strengthen Alliances to Defeat Global Terrorism and Work to Prevent Attacks Against Us and Our Friends," begins on p. 6.

68. David Stout, "Rumsfeld and Myers Dismiss Second-Guessing of War Plans," *The New York Times,* April 1, 2003.

69. For more information on the broad extent of international opposition to the war, see Elaine Sciolino, "Estranged Allies: Europe Assesses Damage to Western Relationships and Takes Steps to Rebuild," *The New York Times,* April 2, 2003; R. W. Apple, Jr., "A Nation at War: News Analysis: A New Way of Warfare Leaves Behind an Abundance of Loose Ends," *The New York Times,* April 20, 2003; Susan Sachs, "Internal Rift Dooms Arab League Plan to Help Avert a War by Pressing Iraq," *The New York Times,* March 14, 2003.

70. The level of U.S. public support for the war in early 2003 is discussed in Patrick E. Tyler and Janet Elder, "Poll Finds Most in U.S. Support Delaying a War," *The New York Times,* February 14, 2003. Also, a CBS News poll, "Poll: Losing Patience with the U.N.," March 10, 2003, showed that 66 percent of the respondents approved overall of taking military action against Iraq.

71. Poll data taken from Tyler and Elder, "Poll Finds Most in U.S. Support Delaying a War."

72. Ibid.

73. "Military Is Called Unprepared for Attack," AP, February 1, 2008.

74. For a full history of military voting, see R. Michael Alvarez, Thad E. Hall, and Brian F. Roberts for the Institute of Public and International Affairs, University of Utah, "Military Voting and the Law: Procedural and Technological Solutions to the Ballot Transit Problem," *Fordham Law Review*, March 8, 2007 available at http://law .fordham.edu/publications/articles/400flspub8745.pdf, and David M. Walker, "Elections: Issues Affecting Military and Overseas Absentee Voters," Testimony Before the Subcommittee on Military Personnel, Committee on Armed Services, House of Representatives, U.S. Government Accountability Office, May 9, 2001.

75. Rosa Brooks, "Weaning the Military from the GOP," *Los Angeles Times,* January 5, 2007.

76. Polling data taken from "Poll of Active Duty Military," *Military Times,* December 29, 2006. Also see Robert Hodierne, "Down on the War," *Military Times,* December 29, 2006.

4: Can We Reduce Intelligence Failures?

1. The CIA's belief that North Korea would not invade South Korea is described in Tim Weiner, *Legacy of Ashes: The History of the CIA* (New York: Doubleday, 2007), p. 52.
2. Graham's slip is detailed in Stephen Losey, "Intelligence Budget Revealed: $44 Billion," *Federal Times,* November 14, 2005.
3. Details of the TTIC's creation were found in a White House fact sheet from February 2003, available at www.fas.org/irp/news/2003/02/wh021403.html. The text of the congressional bill that authorized NCTC's creation in 2004 is available on the Library of Congress Web site at http://thomas.loc.gov/cgi-bin/bdquery/z?d108: SN02845. Details on the NCTC's creation by presidential executive order in August 2004 were found in a White House press statement from August 2004, available at www.whitehouse.gov/news/releases/2004/08/20040827-13.html.
4. For additional details on how the intelligence community is organized, with links to the sixteen members of the IC, see www.dni.gov.
5. The text of UNSCOM's reports to the U.N. Security Council on its activities in Iraq from 1991 to 1999 is available on the Federation of American Scientists' Web site at www.fas.org/news/un/iraq/s/index.html. For a review of the total numbers of Iraqi chemical and biological weapons destroyed by UNSCOM, see Steve Bowman, "Iraqi Chemical & Biological Weapons (BW) Capabilities," Congressional Research Service report, September 4, 1998, http://digital.library.unt.edu/govdocs/crs/permalink/meta-crs-8635:1.
6. For a review of UNSCOM's discovery of Iraq's nuclear weapons development program, see David Albright and Robert Kelley, "Has Iraq Come Clean at Last?," *Bulletin of the Atomic Scientists,* November–December 1995. For details on Iraq's efforts to produce a nuclear weapon after invading Kuwait, see David Albright, Frans Berkhout, and William Walker, *Plutonium and Highly Enriched Uranium 1996: World Inventories, Capabilities and Policies* (Oxford, England: Oxford University Press, 1996), pp. 344–349.
7. For details of Soviet scientist Kanatjin Alibekov's defection and his statements about the Soviet biological weapons program, see Tim Weiner, "Soviet Defector Warns of Biological Weapons," *The New York Times,* February 25, 1998.
8. A review of the U.N.'s Biological Weapons Convention and recent efforts to improve its capabilities can be found in "New Unit Created to Help World's Efforts Against Biological Weapon Threat," States News Service, August 20, 2007, which includes a press release from the United Nations' Biological Weapons Convention Implementation Support Unit.
9. Details of the Saudi-Chinese missile deal and how the United States was initially unaware of its existence can be found in Jim Mann, "U.S. Caught Napping by Sino-Soviet Missile Deal," *Los Angeles Times,* May 4, 1988; also see Elaine Sciolino, "Chinese Missiles Sold in Mideast Worrying Schultz," *The New York Times,* July 16, 1988.
10. Information on the NSA intercepts is available in the "Findings and Conclusions"

section of the declassified Congressional Joint Inquiry into the September 11, 2001, attacks report, issued December 10, 2002, and available at www.globalsecurity.org/ intell/library/congress/2002_rpt/intelfindings.pdf.

11. Bin Laden's apparent policy of not using telephones after a newspaper article was written about his phone conversations is described in Daniel Benjamin and Steven Simon, *The Age of Sacred Terror* (New York: Random House, 2002).

12. Weiner, *Legacy of Ashes.*

13. The American al Qaeda member Adam Gadahn's meetings with Osama bin Laden and other top al Qaeda leaders is detailed in Greg Krikorian and H. G. Reza, "O. C. Man Rises in al Qaeda; 'Azzam the American,' or Adam Gadahn, Has Moved from Translator to Propagandist," *Los Angeles Times*, October 8, 2006.

14. Beirut station chief Bill Buckley's death is discussed in Greg Miller, "CIA Values Show in Stand on Detainees," *Los Angeles Times,* September 24, 2006. Buckley's kidnapping, torture, and killing are also discussed in Weiner, *Legacy of Ashes,* pp. 393–398.

15. For details on Freddie Scappaticci, who worked for the British Army, infiltrated himself into the leadership of the IRA, and was involved in multiple killings, see Rosie Cowan and Nick Hopkins, "British Army Spy at Heart of IRA Death Squad Unmasked," *The Guardian,* May 12, 2003.

16. A review of the weak CIA presence in Somalia during Operation Restore Hope, 1992–1993, is discussed in Weiner, *Legacy of Ashes,* pp. 441–442.

17. For additional details of Reuel Marc Gerecht's suggested changes to improve the CIA and the National Clandestine Service (NCS), see his article "A New Clandestine Service: A Case for Creative Destruction" in *The Future of American Intelligence,* ed. Peter Berkowitz (Stanford: Hoover Institution Press, 2005).

18. See Greg Miller, "CIA's Ambitious Post-9/11 Spy Plan Crumbles," *The Los Angeles Times,* February 17, 2008.

19. For a review of the forged documents and their origin, see Laura Rozen, "The Italian Job; if Anything, a Visit to Rome Only Deepens the Niger Forgeries Mystery," *The American Prospect,* March 2006.

20. For a history of the CIA's difficulty operating in Cuba, see Pablo Bachelet, "Experts: U.S. Spies Are Often in the Dark on Cuba," *The Miami Herald,* April 8, 2007.

21. For additional information on the German intelligence service's claim that its source Curveball was lying and the CIA knew it, see Bob Drogin and John Goetz, "Germany Warned U.S. on Faulty Intel; Claims by Informant Misstated, They Say," *Chicago Tribune,* November 20, 2005.

22. A full transcript of Powell's speech to the United Nations is available at www.cnn .com/2003/U.S./02/05/sprj.irq.powell.transcript/.

23. See Douglas Jehl, "Report Warned Bush Team About Intelligence Suspicions," *The New York Times,* November 6, 2005, available at www.nytimes.com/2005/11/06/ politics/06intel.html.

24. Al-Libi's interrogation by Egyptian intelligence is reported in Michael Hirsh, John Barry, and Daniel Klaidman, "A Tortured Debate," *Newsweek,* June 21, 2004.

25. The CIA report that al Qaeda never received WMD training from Iraq is detailed in David Ensor, "Prewar CIA Report Doubted Claim That al Qaeda Sought WMD in

Iraq," CNN, November 11, 2005, available at www.cnn.com/2005/US/11/10/iraq-intel/index.html.

26. For details on Chang's story and the successful efforts by the Reagan administration to get Taiwan to shut down its nuclear research program, see Stephen Engelberg and Michael R. Gordon, "Taipei Halts Work on Secret Plant to Make Nuclear Bomb Ingredient," *The New York Times,* March 23, 1988. Also see Weiner, *Legacy of Ashes,* pp. 418–419. Also see William Burr, "The Taiwanese Nuclear Case: Lessons for Today," *Carnegie Endowment Proliferation Analysis,* August 9, 2007.

27. Penkovsky's intelligence on Cuba and its use by President Kennedy are detailed in Tennant H. Bagley, *Spy Wars* (New Haven, Conn.: Yale University Press, 2007), p. 52. His execution is detailed in Weiner, *Legacy of Ashes,* p. 232.

28. Additional information on Gordievsky's inside information on the KGB's views about the West can be found in Oleg Gordievsky and Christopher Allen, *KGB: The Inside Story of Its Foreign Operations from Lenin to Gorbachev* (London: Hodder & Stoughton, 1990), *The KGB* (New York: HarperCollins, 1990), and *Instructions from the Centre: Top Secret Files on KGB Foreign Operations 1975–85* (London: Hodder & Stoughton, 1991).

29. Details on Nosenko's claims about access to the KGB Kennedy assassin Lee Harvey Oswald file and his detention by the CIA are detailed in Weiner, *Legacy of Ashes,* pp. 232–233.

30. For details on Bagley's assertion that Nosenko was a double agent, see Bagley, *Spy Wars,* chap. 16. For additional information on the CIA's belief that Nosenko was a double agent, see Weiner, *Legacy of Ashes,* p. 231.

31. Details on bin Laden's escape from Tora Bora can be found in "Into Thin Air," *Newsweek* Special Report, September 3, 2007.

32. For additional insights into the U.S. intelligence community, see Michael Turner, *Why Secret Intelligence Fails* (Dulles, Va.: Potomac Books, 2005). His list of intelligence failures as well as successes is on p. 27 of that book.

33. 9/11 Commission testimonies are available at www.9-11commission.gov/report/index.htm.

34. Hayden's commentary on the average work experience of CIA employees is detailed in Walter Pincus, "CIA Morale on Hayden's Menu," *The Washington Post,* May 18, 2006.

35. Lowenthal's comments on how open source needs a greater place in the intelligence community can be found in Scott Shane, "No Snooping Necessary: U.S. to Collect Data from Open Sources," *International Herald Tribune,* November 9, 2005.

36. For details, see David Ignatius, *Agents of Innocence* (New York: Norton, 1997).

37. For additional reading on the need for the inclusion of more open-source intelligence, see Stephen C. Mercado, "Reexamining the Distinction Between Open Information and Secrets," *Studies in Intelligence* 49, no. 2 (2005).

38. For details on the failed FIA program and the NRO's massive funding losses as a result, see Philip Taubman, "In Death of Spy Satellite Program, Lofty Plans and Unrealistic Bids," *The New York Times,* November 11, 2007.

39. For the full story, see Sebastian Abbot, "The Outsourcing of U.S. Intelligence Analysis: Will It Make Us More or Less Secure?," News21 Initiative, available at http://newsinitiative.org/story/2006/07/28/the_outsourcing_of_u_s_intelligence.

40. This quote was taken from R. J. Hillhouse, "Outsourcing Intelligence," *The Nation,* July 24, 2007.

41. For more information on the growth of private contractors in the intelligence community post-9/11, see Tim Shorrock, "The Spy Who Billed Me," *Mother Jones,* January–February 2005.

42. The CIA's decision to cut 10 percent of its contractors at some future date was reported in Patrick Radden Keefe, "Rent-a-Spy," *International Herald Tribune,* June 27, 2007.

43. "Declassified Key Judgments of the Iraq WMD" (National Intelligence Estimate) is available at www.fas.org/irp/cia/product/iraq-wmd.html.

44. The SSCI report is available at the National Security Archive, www.gwu.edu/ ~nsarchiv/NSAEBB/NSAEBB129/senateiraqreport.pdf.

45. A full transcript of Hussein Kamal's 1995 interview with UNSCOM and IAEA chief inspectors, including his statements that Iraq had destroyed its WMD stockpiles, is available at www.globalsecurity.org/wmd/library/news/iraq/un/unscom-iaea_ kamal-brief.htm.

46. Quote taken from a Carl Ford interview on PBS's *Frontline* show titled "The Dark Side," January 10, 2006.

47. For additional details on Makhtab Al Khidmat and its presence in the United States, see *The 9/11 Commission Report,* pp. 56, 58–59; also see my book *Against All Enemies* (New York: Free Press, 2004), p. 79.

48. Commentary on al Qaeda's use of hawallahs can be found in Rohan Gunaratna, *Inside Al-Qaeda: Global Network of Terror* (New York: Berkley Books, 2002), p. 17.

49. For more details on Emerson's work, see www.investigativeproject.org.

50. Details on the activities of Feith's Office of Special Plans can be found in Julian Borger's article "The Spies Who Pushed for War," *The Guardian,* July 17, 2003, available at www.guardian.co.uk/Iraq/Story/0,2763,999737,00.html.

51. Additional details on Bolton and his critics can be found in Barbara Slavin, "Critic Says Bolton a 'Kiss-Up, Kick-Down Sort of Guy,' " *USA Today,* April 12, 2005.

52. A review of Goss's actions as director of the CIA and how they weakened the agency can be found in Kevin Drum, "The Death of Policy," *Washington Monthly,* May 7, 2006.

53. The 9/11 Commission recommendations can be read at www.9-11commission.gov.

54. For additional details on the tensions between the office of the DNI and Secretary Rumsfeld, and on the law that created the DNI, which left much of the intelligence community under the Secretary of Defense, see Daniel Eisenberg, "Bush's New Intelligence Czar," *Time,* February 20, 2005.

55. For a review of the bipartisan criticism of Negroponte, see Scott Shane, "In New Job, Spymaster Draws Bipartisan Criticism", *The New York Times,* April 20, 2006.

56. For additional details on the CIA's Operation Phoenix in Vietnam, see Stuart A. Herrington, *Stalking the Vietcong: A Personal Account* (Novato, Calif.: Presidio Press, 2004).

57. Casey's actions to roll back communism are detailed in Weiner, *Legacy of Ashes,* pp. 375–387.

58. For additional details on ex–CIA employees' involvement in the Watergate scandal, see Tim Weiner, "E. Howard Hunt, Agent Who Organized Botched Watergate Break-In, Dies at 88," *The New York Times,* January 24, 2007.

59. Pavitt's reluctance to go after bin Laden is reviewed in Chitra Ragavan, "Clinton, Bush, and the Hunt for bin Laden," *U.S. News & World Report,* September 29, 2006.

60. The full article this quote was taken from is available at www.fas.org/irp/eprint/snyder/covertaction.htm.

61. For additional information on the 118 cases of indictments or prosecutions for espionage, see Michelle K. Van Cleave, *Counterintelligence and National Strategy* (Washington, D.C.: National Defense University Press, 2007), p. 24, available at www.ndu.edu/inss/books/2007/SNSEE.pdf.

62. For a discussion of William Kampiles's selling of satellite information and other cases of espionage during the Cold War up to 1985, see Evan Thomas, "Why the Ship of State Leaks," *Time,* June 17, 1985.

63. For a review of Department of State employee Geneva Jones's espionage for Liberian rebels and her arrest, see Stephen Labaton, "U.S. Charges 2 With Espionage for Liberia Rebels," *The New York Times,* August 5, 1993.

64. For details on the Felix Bloch investigation, see David Wise, "The Felix Bloch Affair," *The New York Times,* May 13, 1990.

65. For a review of Wen Ho Lee's arrest and subsequent release, and the settlement of his lawsuit against the government, see Paul Farhi, "U.S., Media Settle with Wen Ho Lee," *The Washington Post,* June 3, 2006.

66. For additional details on Talal Chahine and his sister-in-law Nada Prouty's illegal activities, see Grant Ross, "Former FBI, CIA Agent Pleads Guilty to Computer Crime," IDG News Service, November 13, 2007; and Joby Warrick and Dan Eggen, "Ex–FBI Employee's Case Raises New Security Concerns: Sham Marriage Led to U.S. Citizenship," *The Washington Post,* November 14, 2007.

67. For more information on the Office of the National Counterintelligence Executive, see www.ncix.gov.

5: Terrorism

1. Al Qaeda and other jihadists' use of perceived injustices to and humiliation of Muslims to justify their actions against the West and the Bush administration's mishandled response to the "war on terror" are documented in Philip H. Gordon, *Winning the Right War: The Path to Security for America and the World* (New York: Times Books, 2007), chap. 1.

2. For additional reading on Sunni Islamic extremists'—including al Qaeda's—motivations, beliefs, and goals, see Jessica Stern, *Terror in the Name of God: Why Religious Militants Kill* (New York: HarperCollins, 2003); Rohan Gunaratna, *Inside al Qaeda: Global Network of Terror* (New York: Berkley Books, 2002); Peter L. Bergen, *The Osama bin Laden I Know* (New York: Free Press, 2006); and Mark Danner, "Taking Stock of the Forever War," *The New York Times,* September 11, 2005.

3. For details on al Qaeda's role in these attacks, see *The 9/11 Commission Report,* pp. 59–63, available at www.9-11commission.gov/report/index.htm.

4. The creation of Alec Station in northern Virginia is discussed in Lawrence Wright, *The Looming Tower: Al-Qaeda and the Road to 9/11* (New York: Alfred A. Knopf, 2006), pp. 3–6.

5. For a full review of al Qaeda's activities and setbacks in Bosnia, see Evan Kohlmann, *Al-Qaida's Jihad in Europe: The Afghan-Bosnian Network* (Oxford, England: Berg Publishers, 2004).

6. For additional information on the Clinton administration's actions to boost terrorism preparedness in 1995, see my book *Against All Enemies* (New York: Free Press, 2004), pp. 97–99 and 155.

7. For a detailed discussion of the attacks, see Stansfield Turner, *Terrorism and Democracy* (Boston: Houghton Mifflin, 1991), pp. 161–176.

8. Buckley's kidnapping, torture, and killing are also discussed in Tim Weiner, *Legacy of Ashes: The History of the CIA* (New York: Doubleday, 2007), pp. 393–398. Higgins's capture and killing are detailed in "Blame Hezbollah," *The New York Times,* August 1, 1989.

9. For an account of the TWA flight 847 hijacking and the killing of Stethem, see Turner, *Terrorism and Democracy,* pp. 188–191.

10. For additional information on the Khobar Towers attacks by Saudi Hezbollah with Iranian government support, see Scott Shane, "Iranian Force, Focus of U.S., Still a Mystery," *The New York Times,* February 17, 2007.

11. Additional information on Bahrain's claims against Iran can be found in Department of State, *Patterns of Global Terrorism 1996,* available at www.fas.org/irp/threat/terror_96/middle.html.

12. Tenet's statement that the CIA was "at war with Al-Qaeda" can be found in Mark Stout and Mark Mazzetti, "Tenet's CIA Unprepared for Qaeda Threat, Report Says," *The New York Times,* August 21, 2007.

13. For a thorough review of Clinton administration actions against al Qaeda after the 1998 embassy bombings, including bombing al Qaeda camps in Afghanistan, authorizing CIA covert action, arresting al Qaeda operatives, and obtaining U.N. sanctions on the Taliban, see *The 9/11 Commission Report,* chapters 4 and 6.

14. Information on the United States' warnings to the Taliban that it would be attacked following any future al Qaeda attack on the United States is available in *The 9/11 Commission Report,* p. 121.

15. For a complete review of the attack on the U.S.S. *Cole,* see Raphael Perl and Ronald O'Rourke, "Terrorist Attack on USS *Cole*: Background and Issues for Congress," Congressional Research Service, January 30, 2001, available at www.gwu.edu/~nsarchiv/NSAEBB/NSAEBB55/crs20010130.pdf.

16. For information on congressional opposition to the proposed antiterrorism legislation, see Clarke, *Against All Enemies,* pp. 98–99.

17. For details on Cheney's opposition to U.S. sanctions against Iran and other countries hostile to the United States during the 1990s, see Christopher Marquis, "The 2000 Campaign: The Record; Over the Years, Cheney Opposed U.S. Sanctions," *The New York Times,* July 27, 2000.

18. See Philip Shenan, *The Commission: The Uncensored History of the 9/11 Investigation* (New York: Grand Central Publishing, 2008).

19. For details of the Bush administration's inaction, see *The 9/11 Commission Report.*

20. For details on Midhar and Hamzi's movements and FBI and CIA actions on their activities, see *The 9/11 Commission Report.*

21. For details on the Helgerson Report, see Douglas Jehl, "Report Warned CIA on Tactics in Interrogation," *The New York Times,* November 9, 2005. The full text of the report is available at www.cia.gov/library/reports/Executive%20Summary_OIG%20Report.pdf.

22. Senator Graham's assertion and his discussion of the joint committee can be found in statements he made on February 2, 2004, available at www.fas.org/irp/congress/2004_cr/graham020204.html.

23. For information about the conspiracy theory concerning how the "Blind Sheik" got a visa at the U.S. Embassy in Khartoum, Sudan, in 1990, and evidence that apparently debunks the conspiracy theory, see Fred Burton, "Consequences of the Blind Sheikh's Eventual Death," *Stratfor,* December 20, 2006.

24. See James Dobbins, "Who Lost Iraq?," *Foreign Affairs,* September–October 2007, p. 71. For additional commentary on the administration's missteps against al Qaeda, see Peter Bergen, "War of Error: How Osama bin Laden Beat George W. Bush," *The New Republic,* October 22, 2007.

25. Information on bin Laden's desire for a U.S. invasion of Muslim lands so that al Qaeda could fight and defeat the United States is detailed in an August 24, 2007, ABC News interview with Abdul Bari Atwan in an article titled "Bin Laden Wanted U.S. to Invade Iraq, Author Says." Bari Atwan, the author of *The Secret History of al Qaeda* (Berkeley: University of California Press, 2006), describes his face-to-face interviews with bin Laden in 1996, during which bin Laden stated that he was actively working to push the United States to invade Muslim lands.

26. For more information on the CIA's successful support of the Northern Alliance to defeat the Taliban, see Weiner, *Legacy of Ashes,* pp. 482–485.

27. Details on the fight for and capture of Kabul can be found in Gary C. Schroen, *First In: An Insider's Account of How the CIA Spearheaded the War on Terror in Afghanistan* (New York: Ballantine Books, 2005), pp. 323–351. Also see Gary Berntsen and Ralph Pezzullo, *Jawbreaker: The Attack on bin Laden and Al-Qaeda: A Personal Account by the CIA's Key Field Commander* (New York: Three Rivers Press, 2005), chap. 10.

28. For commentary on Atef's death and the loss of other high-level al Qaeda members in late 2001 to early 2002, see Gunaratna, *Inside al Qaeda,* pp. 302–305.

29. The evacuation of Pakistani officials from Kunduz can be found in Berntsen and Pezzullo, *Jawbreaker,* p. 241.

30. For details on Pakistan's aid to the Taliban, see Bruce Riedel, "Al Qaeda Strikes Back," *Foreign Affairs,* May–June 2007, pp. 25–26.

31. Details of CIA requests for U.S. forces to block al Qaeda's escape from Tora Bora, and on bin Laden's use of radios to direct al Qaeda members during the battle, can be found in Bergen, "War of Error."

32. Criticism of relying solely on Afghan troops at the battle of Tora Bora, and Defense Secretary Rumsfeld's defense of this decision, can be found in Thom Shanker, "A Nation Challenged: Tactics; Rumsfeld Defends Strategy Used in Tora Bora Last Year," *The New York Times,* April 18, 2002.

33. Details on bin Laden's escape from Tora Bora can be found in "Into Thin Air," *News-*

week Special Report, September 3, 2007. Also see Schroen, *First In,* p. 359, and Berntsen and Pezzullo, *Jawbreaker,* pp. 299–300 and 305–308.

34. For details on how bin Laden was injured during the battle of Tora Bora, see Bergen, "War of Error."

35. For details on the killing of al-Harithi in Yemen and on the use of the Predator to target other al Qaeda members, see Dana Priest, "Surveillance Operation in Pakistan Located and Killed al Qaeda Official," *The Washington Post,* May 15, 2005.

36. In a video in early 2006, al-Zawahiri stated that America had missed him in an air strike in Pakistan. For details, see David Ensor, "Al Qaeda's No. 2 Taunts U.S. in New Video," CNN, January 31, 2006.

37. For additional information on the three groups, see Department of State, "Country Reports on Terrorism 2006," available at www.state.gov/s/ct/rls/crt/2006/.

38. For additional information on Hambali's interactions with 9/11 and U.S.S. *Cole* plotters, see "Malaysian Militants Linked with Al-Qaida, Paper Says," *Asian Political News,* January 14, 2002.

39. Faruq's activities are detailed in "Confessions of an Al-Qaeda Terrorist," *Time,* September 15, 2002.

40. For additional details on the 2002 Bali bombing, see Wayan Juniartha, "Indonesia: BaliTV Airs 2002 Bombing Documentary," *The Jakarta Post,* October 11, 2007, available at www.asiamedia.ucla.edu/article.asp?parentid=79738.

41. For details of the August 2003 bombing in Jakarta and the subsequent arrests of Jemmah Islamiya operatives, see "Marriott Blast Suspects Named," Associated Press, August 19, 2003, available at www.cnn.com/2003/WORLD/asiapcf/southeast/08/19/indonesia.arrests.names/.

42. For commentary on Hambali's life and arrest, see Baradan Kuppusamy, "Hambali: The Driven Man," *Asia Times Online,* August 19, 2003, available at www.atimes.com/atimes/Southeast_Asia/EH19Ae06.html.

43. Commentary on increased jihadist attack levels since 9/11 are found in Bergen, "War of Error," and Riedel, "Al Qaeda Strikes Back."

44. For details on the Muslim Brotherhood's goals being similar to those of al Qaeda, see Daniel Benjamin and Steven Simon, *The Age of Sacred Terror* (New York: Random House, 2002).

45. For information on Omar bin Laden's criticism of his father for conducting the 9/11 attacks, see Bergen, "War of Error."

46. This is discussed in Mark Hosenball, "Dems Allege Intel Community Shields White House," *Newsweek,* September 13, 2006. Additional information on Cheney's focus on the alleged meeting can be found in Michael Isikoff and David Corn, *Hubris* (New York: Crown, 2006), p. 105.

47. Additional information on Ansar Al Islam's presence in northern Iraq, its al Qaeda ties, and Iranian aid provided to the group can be found in Scott Peterson, "The Rise and Fall of Ansar Al-Islam," *The Christian Science Monitor,* October 16, 2003.

48. For details on the terror groups MEK, PKK, and Ansar Al Islam, see Department of State, "Country Reports on Terrorism 2006," available at www.state.gov/s/ct/rls/crt/2006/. More information on Ansar Al Sunnah's activities prior to and after the invasion in 2003 can be found in the Department of State's "Patterns of Global Ter-

rorism" for 2002 and 2003, available at www.state.gov/s/ct/rls/crt/2002/ and www
.state.gov/s/ct/rls/crt/2003/, respectively.

49. The provision of new textbooks to Iraq's Ministry of Education in 2003 is detailed in Gail Russell Chaddock, "Next, Iraq's Cultural Regime Change," *The Christian Science Monitor,* April 21, 2003.

50. Details on the Iraqi government's preparation for an insurgency is found in Edward T. Pound, "Seeds of Chaos," *U.S. News & World Report,* December 20, 2004.

51. Details on al-Zarqawi's life and his creation of several terror organizations, including in Iraq, can be found in Jean-Charles Brisard and Damien Martinez, *Zarqawi: The New Face of al Qaeda* (New York: Other Press, 2005).

52. For a life history of al-Zarqawi and information about the organizations he created before and after the 2003 invasion of Iraq, see ibid.

53. The Bush administration's decision not to strike al-Zarqawi-affiliated camps in northern Iraq before the 2003 invasion is detailed in Jim Miklaszewski, "Avoiding Attacking Suspected Terrorist Mastermind," MSNBC Interactive, March 2, 2004, available at www.msnbc.msn.com/id/4431601/.

54. Al-Zarqawi's organization al Qaeda in Iraq, its role in the Samarra attack, and the widespread sectarian violence that followed it can be found in Bill Nichols and Steve Komarow, "Sectarian Unrest Will Test Iraq's Security Forces," *USA Today,* February 23, 2006.

55. The text of al-Zarqawi's pledge of loyalty to bin Laden is available on the Jamestown Foundation's Web site at www.jamestown.org/publications_details.php?volume_id=400&issue_id=3179&article_id=2369020.

56. The quote was taken from a speech by Bush on July 24, 2007, at Charleston Air Force Base, available at www.whitehouse.gov/news/releases/2007/07/print/20070724-3.html.

57. The quote was taken from a speech by Bush on June 28, 2007, at the U.S. Naval Academy, available at www.whitehouse.gov/news/releases/2007/06/20070628-14.html.

58. For an analysis of AQI's size within the Iraqi insurgency and the range of size estimates among U.S. government agencies, see Andrew Tilghman, "The Myth of AQI," *Washington Monthly,* October 2007.

59. See Peter Bergen and Paul Cruickshank, "Al Qaeda in Iraq: Self-Fulfilling Prophecy," *Mother Jones,* October 31, 2007, available at www.motherjones.com/news/feature/2007/11/iraq-war-Al-qaeda-extended.html.

60. Additional details on Iran's training of Iraqi Shia and the United States' efforts against it can be found in Robin Wright, "U.S. Starts a Push for Tighter Sanctions on Iran," *The Washington Post,* September 13, 2007.

61. For information on Iran's provision of support to Sunni insurgents in Iraq, see Sudarsan Raghavan, "Iran Giving Arms to Iraq's Sunnis, U.S. Military Says," *The Washington Post,* April 12, 2007. For instances of Iraqi Shia and Sunni fighters cooperating against U.S. forces, see Jeffrey Gettleman and James Risen, "The Struggle for Iraq: Alliances; Ex-rivals Uniting," *The New York Times,* April 9, 2004.

62. For additional information on the shift in tactics from Iraq to Afghanistan, see Department of State Acting Coordinator for Counterterrorism Frank Urbancic's com-

ments in Scott Shane, "Terrorist Attacks in Iraq and Afghanistan Rose Sharply Last Year, State Department Says," *The New York Times,* May 1, 2007.

63. In a Penn, Schoen & Berland Associates, LLC, poll published in July 2007 titled "American Public Opinion Toward Foreign Policy," 56 percent of those polled believed the war in Iraq was distracting the United States from fighting the War on Terror, and 67 percent believed the Iraq War to be creating, rather than eliminating, terrorists.

64. See Thomas E. Ricks, *Fiasco: The American Military Adventure in Iraq* (New York: Penguin Press, 2006).

65. For additional information on al Qaeda and Islamic extremists' use of the internet for training and propaganda, see Nadya Labi, "Jihad 2.0," *The Atlantic Monthly,* July–August 2006. Also see "Jihad Online: The Changing Role of the Internet," *Jane's Intelligence Review,* August 2007.

66. For details on U.S. intelligence community views that al Qaeda is resurgent in Pakistan, see Mark Mazzetti and David Rhode, "Terror Officials See al Qaeda Chiefs Regaining Power," *The New York Times,* February 19, 2007.

67. A full text of the declassified judgments from the Homeland National Intelligence Estimate is available at www.dni.gov/press_releases/20070717_release.pdf.

68. An analysis of al Qaeda's use of media statements for propaganda from the 1990s to 2007 can be found in Christopher M. Blanchard, "Al Qaeda: Statements and Evolving Ideology," Congressional Research Service, January 24, 2007, available at www.fas.org/sgp/crs/terror/RL32759.pdf.

69. Quote taken from Bergen, "War of Error."

70. Riedel's article "Al Qaeda Strikes Back," *Foreign Affairs,* May–June 2007, p. 29, is available at www.foreignaffairs.org/20070501faessay86304/bruce-riedel/Al-qaeda-strikes-back.html.

71. A discussion of the Taliban's resurgence in Afghanistan and its increased attacks in 2006 can be found in Riedel, "Al Qaeda Strikes Back."

72. For additional information on the annual travel of British citizens to Pakistan and on British citizens' ability to travel to the United States without a visa, see Jane Perlez, "U.S. Seeks Closing of Visa Loophole for Britons," *The New York Times,* May 2, 2007.

73. For additional details on Sunni insurgents turning to fight against al Qaeda in Iraq, see Richard A. Oppel, "Sunni Fighters Battle al Qaeda in Baghdad," *The New York Times,* June 1, 2007; Thomas E. Ricks and Karen DeYoung, "Al Qaeda in Iraq Reported Crippled," *The Washington Post,* October 15, 2007; and Bergen and Cruickshank, "Al Qaeda in Iraq: Self-Fulfilling Prophecy."

74. Details on U.S. propaganda efforts with Muslims through TV and radio were highlighted in a *Foreign Policy* interview with Mouafac Harb, the director of news for the U.S.-funded Alhurra news channel; see the May–June 2004 issue of *Foreign Policy,* p. 16.

75. See Daniel Byman, *The Five Front War: The Better Way to Fight Global Jihad* (Hoboken, N.J.: Wiley, 2008).

76. For a more in-depth review of Wilson's ideas on policing, see James Q. Wilson and George L. Kelling, "Broken Windows," *The Atlantic,* March 1982, available at www.theatlantic.com/ideastour/archive/windows.mhtml.

77. For details on Pakistan's long-standing ties with the Taliban and on jihadist sympathies in the Army and intelligence service, see Zahid Hussain, *Frontline Pakistan: The Struggle with Militant Islam* (New York: Columbia University Press, 2007).

78. For details on increases in U.S. aid to Pakistan, the Northwest Frontier Province, and the Federally Aministered Tribal Areas since 2001, see Lisa Curtis, "U.S. Aid to Pakistan: Countering Extremism Through Education Reform," lecture at the Heritage Foundation, May 9, 2007, available at www.heritage.org/Research/Asiaand thePacific/hl1029.cfm.

79. For additional information on Dobbins's statement that the international community hasn't provided enough aid to Afghanistan, see his statement before the Senate Foreign Relations Committee in 2007, available at www.senate.gov/~foreign/testi mony/2007/DobbinsTestimony070308.pdf.

80. "Study: Afghanistan Could Fail as a State," by Anne Flaherty (AP), January 29, 2008; *The Search for Security in Post-Taliban Afghanistan,* Cyrus Hodes and Mark Sedra, I.I.S.S., 2007, Adelphi Paper 391, chap. 3: "The Opium Trade."

81. For a review of the rise of political Islam in Turkey in recent years, see Hassan Nafaa, "A New Turkey," *Al-Ahram Weekly Online,* September 6–12, 2007.

82. Details on Saudi Arabia's economic and demographic situation were taken from Dana Moss and Zvika Krieger, "A Tipping Point in Saudi Arabia," *The Christian Science Monitor,* August 15, 2007.

83. For a review of the government of Iran's foreign policy, internal politics, anti-U.S. rhetoric, and support for terrorism since the 1970s, see Ray Tayekh, *Hidden Iran: Paradox and Power in the Islamic Republic* (New York: Times Books, 2006).

84. For details on the capture of Iranian arms being shipped to the Taliban in Afghanistan, see Robin Wright, "Iranian Arms Destined for Taliban Seized in Afghanistan," *The Washington Post,* September 16, 2007.

85. For details on probable U.S. covert action programs aimed at Iran, see Brian Ross and Richard Esposito, "Bush Authorizes Covert Action Against Iran," ABC News, May 23, 2007, available at http://blogs.abcnews.com/theblotter/2007/05/bush_ authorizes.html.

6: Homeland Security

1. Michael Hampton, "Homeland Security to Move into Loony Bin," *Homeland Stupidity,* March 20, 2007, available at www.homelandstupidity.us/2007/03/20/home land-security-to-move-into-loony-bin/.

2. Elements of the Naval Research Laboratory and the Army Ballistic Missile Agency were pulled into the new entity. For a detailed history of NASA's early years, see Piers Bizony's excellent *The Man Who Ran the Moon* (New York: Thunder's Mouth Press, 2007), which details the bureaucratic battles of James Webb, NASA's administrator under Presidents Kennedy and Johnson.

3. In 1993, in addition to the ATF, the Secretary of the Treasury had under his control the U.S. Secret Service, which protects the President and fights counterfeiting, and the U.S. Customs Service, an agency whose revenue-generating role has steadily decreased while its law enforcement role has grown exponentially with the War on Drugs and now terrorism. The Secret Service and Customs were transferred to the new Department of Homeland Security in 2003.

4. PDD-39, in 1995, outlined "United States Policy on Counterterrorism"; PDDs 62 and 63, in 1998, covered "Protection Against Unconventional Threats to the Homeland and Americans Overseas" and "Critical Infrastructure Protection," respectively. The Federation of American Scientists (FAS) keeps an archive of all presidential decision documents at www.fas.org/irp/offdocs/pdd/index.html.

5. For FY 1997, the General Accounting Office estimated total spending on counterterrorism at $7 billion; see "Combating Terrorism: Spending on Governmentwide Programs Requires Better Management and Coordination" (Letter Report, 12/01/97, GAO/NSIAD-98-39), available at www.fas.org/irp/gao/nsiad98039.htm. The FY 2001 budget enacted by President Clinton pre-9/11 topped $9.69 billion; see "Annual Report to Congress on Combating Terrorism," p. 100, available at www.whitehouse.gov/omb/legislative/nsd_annual_report2001.pdf.

6. President Clinton increased the FBI's counterterrorism budget from $78.5 million in 1993 to $301.2 million in 1999. "The Threat to the United States Posed by Terrorists," Statement for the Record of Louis J. Freeh, Director, Federal Bureau of Investigation, Before the United States Senate Committee on Appropriations Subcommittee for the Departments of Commerce, Justice, and State, the Judiciary, and Related Agencies, February 4, 1999.

7. These commissions included the U.S. Commission on National Security in the 21st Century, known as the Hart-Rudman Commission after the two chairs, former senators Gary Hart and Warren Rudman; the National Commission on Terrorism, known as the Bremer Commission after its chair, Ambassador Paul Bremer, and the Advisory Panel to Assess Domestic Response Capabilities for Terrorism Involving Weapons of Mass Destruction, known as the Gilmore Commission after its chair, Governor James Gilmore of Virginia.

8. Joshua Micah Marshall, "Vice Grip: Dick Cheney Is a Man of Principles. Disastrous Principles," *Washington Monthly,* January–February 2003.

9. Richard A. Best, "Homeland Security: Intelligence Report," Congressional Research Service, February 23, 2004.

10. Alasdair Roberts, "The War We Deserve," *Foreign Policy,* November–December 2007, p. 5.

11. The proposal was sold to Congress and the American people as "revenue neutral"; Press Briefing by Ari Fleischer Aboard Air Force One, The White House, June 11, 2002.

12. Roger Yu, "Trusted Traveler Programs Grow," *USA Today,* April 30, 2007.

13. Roberts, "The War We Deserve," p. 4.

14. "Aviation Security: TSA Has Strengthened Efforts to Plan for the Optimal Deployment of Checked Baggage Screening Systems, but Funding Uncertainties Remain," GAO-06-875T, June 29, 2006.

15. Bart Elias, "Air Cargo Security," CRS Report for Congress, July 30, 2007.

16. The legislation provides a process whereby airports can be exempted from the requirements. See H.R. 1, p. 214.

17. Christopher Bolkom et al., "Homeland Security: Protecting Airliners from Terrorist Missiles," CRS Report for Congress, November 3, 2003.

18. Peter Gordon, James E. Moore II, Ji Young Park, and Harry W. Richardson, "The

Economic Impacts of a Terrorist Attack on the U.S. Commercial Aviation System," *Risk Analysis* 27, no. 3, 2007.

19. "Protecting Civil Transports from Stingers," *Airport Security Report,* August 15, 2007.

20. "Secondary Flight Deck Barriers and Flight Deck Access Procedures," Air Line Pilots Association International White Paper, July 2007, available at www.alpa.org/ DesktopModules/ALPA_Documents/ALPA_DocumentsView.aspx?itemid=9153& ModuleId=1316&Tabid=256.

21. "Aviation Security: TSA's Staffing Allocation Model Is Useful for Allocating Staff Among Airports, but Its Assumptions Should Be Systematically Reassessed," GAO Report to Congressional Committees, GAO-07-229, February 2007.

22. Eric Lipton, "Bid to Stockpile Bioterror Drugs Stymied by Setbacks," *The New York Times,* September 18, 2006.

23. Frank Gottron, "Project BioShield: Purposes and Authorities," CRS Report for Congress, updated June 12, 2007.

24. Breanne Wagner, "Germ Warfare: Agencies Scramble to Create Vaccine Market," *National Defense* 91, no. 643 (June 1, 2007).

25. Lipton, "Bid to Stockpile Bioterror Drugs Stymied by Setbacks."

26. Allan Lengel, "Little Progress In FBI Probe of Anthrax Attacks," *The Washington Post,* September 16, 2005.

27. "Air Force Investigates Mistaken Transport of Nuclear Warheads," CNN, September 6, 2007.

28. William Langewiesche, "The Wrath of Khan," *The Atlantic Monthly,* November 2005.

29. For an interesting take on the North Korea situation, see Jasper Becker, *Rogue Regime: Kim Jong Il and the Looming Threat of North Korea* (New York: Oxford University Press, 2006).

30. Graham Allison's excellent *Nuclear Terrorism: The Ultimate Preventable Catastrophe* (New York: Henry Holt, 2004), provides an overview of al Qaeda's attempts to acquire nuclear weapons as well as its motivations to do so.

31. David de Sola, "Government Investigators Smuggled Radioactive Materials into U.S.," CNN, March 27, 2006.

32. Eric Lipton, "Senators Clash on Security Cost," *The New York Times,* July 15, 2005. Between 2001 and 2005, the federal government allotted $250 million for transit security, compared with $15 billion for aviation security.

33. Six years after 9/11, most city police agencies and fire departments still lack the necessary equipment to be able to communicate effectively during a large-scale disaster. The GAO summed up the state of play in the title of its April 2007 report, "First Responders: Much Work Remains to Improve Communications Interoperability," GAO-07-301 April 2, 2007. The report found that the DHS had not used a strategic approach to guide investments in interoperable communications. No national plan has been developed to coordinate investments across states, and the DHS has no plans to ensure that grant requests are in line with DHS or state-level interoperable strategies.

34. Statement of David G. Boyd, Ph.D., Director, Office for Interoperability and Com-

patibility, Department of Homeland Security, before the Senate Committee on Commerce, Science, and Transportation, September 29, 2005.

35. A law requiring the U.S. government to track foreign visitors' entrances into and exits from the country has been on the books since 1996. More than a decade later, this goal remains elusive. In 2003, the Department of Homeland Security issued a multibillion-dollar contract to the consulting technology firm Accenture to create U.S.-VISIT, a biometric enabled entry-exit system. Poor management and poor technology performance have constantly plagued the program. In June 2007 the GAO issued its ninth report in a scathing series on the program, titled "Prospects for Biometric U.S.-VISIT Exit Capability Remain Unclear." The report notes that after $1.3 billion spent over four years, DHS has "delivered essentially one-half of U.S.-VISIT" because it has created a capability to record entries but not exits. The report cites "weaknesses in how DHS is managing U.S.-VISIT in general" and repeats recommendations made in the previous eight reports to improve management. See Statement of Randolph C. Hite, Director Information Technology Architecture and Systems Issues, Government Accountability Office, "Homeland Security: Prospects for Biometric U.S.-VISIT Exit Capability Remain Unclear," Testimony before the Subcommittee on Border, Maritime, and Global Counterterrorism, Committee on Homeland Security, House of Representatives, GAO-07-1044T, June 28, 2007.

36. "Secure Border Initiative: Observations on Selected Aspects of SBInet Program Implementation," Statement of Richard M. Stana, Director, Homeland Security and Justice Issues, GAO-08-131T, October 24, 2007.

37. "Challenges Affecting Deepwater Asset Deployment and Management and Efforts to Address Them," Government Accountability Office, GAO-07-874, June 2007.

38. Statement of David M. Walker, Comptroller General of the United States, "Department of Homeland Security: Progress Report on Implementation of Mission and Management Functions," Testimony before the Committee on Homeland Security and Governmental Affairs, U.S. Senate, GAO-07-1081T, September 6, 2007.

39. "Major Management Challenges Facing the Department of Homeland Security," DHS Inspector General Report OIG-08-11, January 2008.

40. According to the 2000 Census, the combined population of the 150 largest Metropolitan Statistical Areas is 195,459,136 people. The 2000 Census put the U.S. population at 281,421,906. See "Current Lists of Metropolitan and Micropolitan Statistical Areas and Definitions, U.S. Census Bureau," available at www.census.gov/population/www/estimates/metrodef.html.

41. Remarks by Secretary Michael Chertoff at a Press Conference on the Fiscal Year 2007 Homeland Security Grant Program, January 5, 2007.

42. Todd Masse et al., "Fusion Centers: Issues and Options for Congress," CRS Report for Congress, July 2007.

43. Patrick D. Healy, "Rove Criticizes Liberals on 9/11," *The New York Times,* June 23, 2005.

44. Ibid.

45. David Jackson, "White House Steps Up Defense of Domestic Spying," *USA Today,* January 22, 2006.

46. Martiga Lohn, "RNC Chief Faults Democratic Leaders on Terrorism," *The Washington Post*, August 5, 2006.

47. "Cheney: Wrong Vote Invites Attack," CBS News, September 8, 2004.

48. Interview of the Vice President by Wire Service Reporters, The White House, August 9, 2006.

49. Michael Abramowitz, "Bush Says 'America Loses' Under Democrats," *The Washington Post*, October 31, 2006.

50. Marc Santora, "Giuliani Broadens His Message on Terrorism," *The New York Times*, April 26, 2007.

51. Mimi Hall, "Ridge Reveals Clashes on Alerts," *USA Today*, May 10, 2005.

52. Sidney Blumenthal, "What the Terror Alerts Really Tell Us," *The Guardian*, August 5, 2004.

53. The White House maintains a "Chronology of Changes to the Homeland Security Advisory System," at www.dhs.gov/xabout/history/editorial_0844.shtm.

54. "Bloomberg on JFK Plot: 'Stop Worrying, Get a Life,' " CBS News, June 5, 2007.

55. Amie J. Devero, "Look Beyond the Deal," *MWORLD*, Spring 2004.

56. Dan Eggen, "FBI Agents Still Lacking Arabic Skills," *The Washington Post*, October 11, 2006.

57. Scott Shane and Lowell Bergman, "F.B.I. Struggling to Reinvent Itself to Fight Terror," *The New York Times*, October 10, 2006.

58. Ibid.

59. Melanie Sisson, "The FBI's Second Class Citizens," *The Washington Post*, December 31, 2005.

60. The case is recounted in detail in *Frontline*'s "The Enemy Within," aired in October 2006 and available online at www.pbs.org/wgbh/pages/frontline/enemywithin/.

61. Abby Goodnough, "Trial Starts for Men in Plot to Destroy Sears Tower," *The New York Times*, October 3, 2007.

62. Jerry Markon, "The Terrorism Case That Wasn't—and Still Is," *The Washington Post*, June 12, 2005.

63. "Padilla Convicted in Terrorism Case," ABC News, August 16, 2007.

64. Dan Eggen and Julie Tate, "U.S. Campaign Produces Few Convictions on Terrorism Charges," *The Washington Post*, June 12, 2005.

65. Ibid.

66. Adam Liptak and Leslie Eaton, "Financing Mistrial Adds to U.S. Missteps in Terror Prosecutions," *The New York Times*, October 24, 2007.

67. Scott Shane, "Scale and Detail of Plane Scheme Recall al Qaeda," *The New York Times*, August 11, 2006.

68. "Half Ton of Bomb Material Stored a Few Miles from the White House," ABC News, September 8, 2006.

69. The study, "Radicalization in the West: The Homegrown Threat," NYPD, 2007, is available at sethgodin.typepad.com/seths_blog/files/NYPD_Report-Radicalization _in_the_West.pdf.

70. Ibn al-Shaykh al-Libi was transferred by U.S. officials into Egyptian custody in 2002, and his statements extracted through torture were used by the Bush administration as evidence that Iraq had trained al Qaeda operatives in the use of WMDs.

Mark Mazzetti, "Questions Raised About Bush's Primary Claims in Defense of Secret Detention System," *The New York Times,* September 8, 2006.

71. Mike Allen and Dana Priest, "Memo on Torture Draws Focus to Bush," *The Washington Post,* June 9, 2004.

72. Press Briefing by Attorney General Alberto Gonzales and General Michael Hayden, Principal Deputy Director for National Intelligence, December 19, 2005.

73. Emily Bazelon, "Cowardly Lions: Congress Talks Tough to Gonzales—and Then Turns and Runs," *Slate,* February 6, 2006.

74. Dan Eggen, "FBI Found to Misuse Security Letters," *The Washington Post,* March 14, 2008.

75. Rob Margetta, "Homeland Security for Hire," *CQ Weekly,* November 12, 2007.

7: Energy

1. Ronald Bailey, "Energy Independence: The Ever-Receding Mirage: 30 years of Presidential Futility and Failure," *Reason Magazine,* July 21, 2004.

2. Thomas L. Friedman, "Mideast Tensions; U.S. Jobs at Stake in Gulf, Baker Says," *The New York Times,* November 14, 1990.

3. 2003 State of the Union Address, www.whitehouse.gov/news/releases/2003/01/20030128-19.html.

4. Peter Beaumont and Joanna Walters, "Greenspan Admits Iraq Was About Oil, as Deaths Put at 1.2m," *The Observer,* September 16, 2007.

5. Erik Rosales, "Former CIA Director: Kick Oil Addiction," ABC7, February 16, 2007, available at abclocal.go.com/kgo/story?section=politics&id=5043508.

6. Quoted on ABC News, *This Week,* September 16, 2007.

7. For 2006, the top countries from which the United States imports oil are, in order, Canada, Mexico, Saudi Arabia, Venezuela, Nigeria, Algeria, Iraq, Angola, Russia, the Virgin Islands, Ecuador, the United Kingdom, Norway, Brazil, and Kuwait. See "U.S. Imports by Country of Origin 2006," available at tonto.eia.doe.gov/dnav/pet/pet_move_impcus_a2_nus_ep00_im0_mbbl_a.htm.

8. Daniel Yergin, "Energy Security and Markets," *Goldman Sachs World Oil Supply Panel,* 2005, p. 52.

9. Iraq Pipeline Watch: Attack on Iraqi Pipelines, Oil Installations, and Oil Personnel, 2003–2005, Institute for the Analysis of Global Security, www.iags.org/iraqipipeline watch.com.

10. Iraq: Country Analysis Breif, Energy Information Administration, August 2007, www.eia,doe.gov/emeu/cabs/Iraq/Oil.html.

11. John C. K. Daly, "The Threat to Iraqi Oil," *Terrorism Monitor,* no. 12, June 17, 2004.

12. The National Strategy for the Physical Protection of Critical Infrastructures and Key Assets, The White House, February 2003, p. 9.

13. "Truck Driver Plot, Schumer to Warn That the 3.5 Million Trucks Going Through Cap Region Pose Major Terrorist Threat," Charles Schumer Senate Office, June 23, 2007.

14. Climate Change 2007 Synthesis Report, Summary for Policy Makers, An Assessment of the Intergovernmental Panel on Climate Change, November, 2007, p. 8.

15. Bea Csatho, et al., "Intermittent Thinning of Jakobshaun Island, West Greenland, Since the Little Ice Age," *Journal of Glaciology* 54, no. 184, 2008.

16. Cornelia Dean, "Government Reports Warn Planners on Sea-Rise Threat to U.S. Coast," *New York Times,* March 12, 2008.

17. Ron Suskind, *The One Percent Doctrine* (New York: Simon & Schuster, 2006).

18. *National Security and the Threat of Climate Change* (Alexandria, Va.: CNA Corporation, 2007), p. 10.

19. Ibid., p. 44.

20. Ibid., p. 46.

21. Alex Nussbaum, "Few Keep Vow to Cut Pollution; Towns Stymied in the War with Global Warming," *The Record,* March 11, 2007.

22. David Kestenbaum, "Japan Trades in Suits, Cuts Carbon Emissions," NPR Morning Edition, October 2, 2007, www.npr.org.

23. Evar D. Nering, "The Mirage of a Growing Fuel Supply," *The New York Times,* June 4, 2001.

24. Eleanor Beardsley, "France Presses Ahead with Nuclear Power," NPR News, may 1, 2006.

25. Expected New Nuclear Power Plant Applications, updated February 27, 2008, www .nrc.gov/reactors/new-licensing/new-licensing-files/expected-new-rx-applications .pdf.

26. U.S. Electric Power Industry Net Generation, 2006, Energy Information Administration.

8: Into Cyberspace

1. The best analysis of the Code Red worm and its implications can be found in the GAO report "Information Security: Code Red, Code Red II, and SirCam Attacks Highlight Need for Proactive Measures," Statement of Keith A. Rhodes, Chief Technologist, Before the Subcommittee on Government Efficiency, Financial Management, and Intergovernmental Relations, Committee on Government Reform, House of Representatives, GAO-01-1073T, August 29, 2001.

2. The final report of the commission is available at chnm.gmu.edu/cipdigitalarchive/ files/5_CriticalFoundationsPCCIP.pdf.

3. The best and shortest history of the internet was written by nine people who were responsible for its creation; see Barry M. Leiner, Vinton G. Cerf, David D. Clark, Robert E. Kahn, Leonard Kleinrock, Daniel C. Lynch, Jon Postel, Larry G. Roberts, and Stephen Wolff, "A Brief History of the Internet," Internet Society, December 10, 2003, available at www.isoc.org/internet/history/brief.shtml.

4. *Frontline*'s "Cyberwar!" series described the program: "Eligible Receiver is the code name of a 1997 internal exercise initiated by the Department of Defense. A 'red team' of hackers from the National Security Agency (NSA) was organized to infiltrate the Pentagon systems. The red team was only allowed to use publicly available computer equipment and hacking software. Although many details about Eligible Receiver are still classified, it is known that the red team was able to infiltrate and take control of the Pacific command center computers, as well as power grids and 911 systems in nine major U.S. cities."

5. Interview with John Hamre, for *Frontline*'s "Cyberwar!," February 18, 2003, available at www.pbs.org/wgbh/pages/frontline/shows/cyberwar/interviews/hamre .html.

6. Kevin Poulsen, "Solar Sunrise Hacker Joins Mid-East Cyber-war," *The Register,* November 21, 2001, available at www.theregister.co.uk/2000/11/21/solar_sunrise_ hacker_joins_mideast/.

7. *Frontline*'s full description of the Moonlight Maze incident along with interviews and video files is available at www.pbs.org/wgbh/pages/frontline/shows/cyberwar/ warnings/.

8. Bradley Graham, "Hackers Attack via Chinese Web Sites; U.S. Agencies' Networks Are Among Targets," *The Washington Post,* August 25, 2005.

9. Ellen Nakashima and Brian Krebs, "Contractor Blamed in DHS Data Breaches," *The Washington Post,* September 24, 2007.

10. "Report of the Defense Science Board Task Force on Mission Impact of Foreign Influence on DoD Software," Office of the Under Secretary of Defense for Acquisition, Technology, and Logistics, September 2007, p. vii.

11. American RadioWorks' series *The Surprising Legacy of Y2K,* by Chris Farrell, Ochen Kaylan, and Catherine Winter, details the history of Y2K and looks at its lasting effects.

12. Woody Baird, "Failure of Memphis Air Traffic Control Communications Examined," Associated Press, October 15, 2007.

13. Peter Kilbridge, "Computer Crash—Lessons from a System Failure," *The New England Journal of Medicine* 348, no. 10 (March 6, 2003): 881–882.

14. "Cyber-attacks Batter Web Heavyweights; Strikes on eBay, Amazon, Cnn.com follow Monday Yahoo! Attack," CNN, February 9, 2000, available at http://archives .cnn.com/2000/TECH/computing/02/09/cyber.attacks.01/index.html.

15. John Leyden, "Want to Know How to Crash the Internet?" *The Register,* May 11, 2001.

16. Will Knight, "Internet's Foundations Shaken by Attack," *NewScientistTech,* October 23, 2002.

17. Joris Evers, "Internet Backbone at Center of Suspected Attack," *ZDNet News,* February 7, 2007.

18. The Electronic Privacy Information Center maintains an archive on the Clipper Chip program; see www.epic.org/crypto/clipper/.

19. The 2006 Federal Computer Security Report Card gave an overall grade of C– to the twenty-four federal agencies included in the survey; see http://republicans.oversight. house.gov/Media/PDFs/FY06FISMA.pdf. *Computerworld* provides a concise summary of the House Committee on Government Reform report cards for federal IT security at www.computerworld.com/securitytopics/security/story/0,10801,109609, 00.html.

20. Amelia Gruber, "Judge Severs Interior Department Web Connections Again," *Government Executive,* March 16, 2004.

21. "Defending America's Cyberspace: National Plan for Information Systems Protection (Version 1.0), An Invitation to a Dialogue," White House, 2000, p. v.

22. Peter Galli, "Microsoft Sees Open-Source Threat Looming Ever Larger," *eWeek,* September 5, 2004.

23. Ryan Naraine, "Vista Security Woes," *PC World,* April 27, 2007.

24. David A. Utter, "Analysts: Privacy Won't Stop Google, DoubleClick," www.web
pronews.com/insiderreports/2007/10/11/analysts-privacy-wont-stop-google-
doubleclick.

25. Ryan Blitstein, "Ghosts in the Browser, Part II: How Well Are We Protecting Ourselves?" *The Mercury News,* November 12, 2007.

26. Ryan Blitstein, "Ghosts in the Browser, Part I: How Online Crooks Put Us All at
Risk," *The Mercury News,* November 9, 2007.

27. Ibid.

28. Ibid.

29. An overview of the Gramm-Leach-Bliley data security requirements is available at
www.netapp.com/ftp/GLBA-decru-compliance.pdf.

30. The Cyber Security Industry Alliance (CSIA) provides a concise FAQ of HIPAA's IT
security requirements at www.csialliance.org/issues/hipaa/.

31. The SANS Institute provides an overview of cybersecurity requirements that stem
from the Sarbanes-Oxley legislation; see Gregg Stults, "An Overview of Sarbanes-
Oxley for the Information Security Professional," May 9, 2004, available at www
.sans.org/reading_room/whitepapers/legal/1426.php.

32. Neil Roiter, "Flurry of State Disclosure Laws Creates Confusion for CISOs," *Information Security Magazine,* February 5, 2007. The text of the California bill is
available at http://info.sen.ca.gov/pub/01-02/bill/sen/sb_1351-1400/sb_1386_bill_
20020830_enrolled.pdf.

33. More information about the Cyber Corps program is available at www.usdoj.gov/
jmd/ocio/cybercorps.htm.

34. Steve Coll and Susan B. Glasser, "Terrorists Turn to the Web as Base of Operations,"
The Washington Post, August 7, 2005.

35. Clay Wilson, "Emerging Terrorist Capabilities for Cyber Conflict Against the
Homeland," Congressional Research Service, November 1, 2005, p. 3.

36. Connie Ling, " 'Virtual' War over Words," *Asian Wall Street Journal,* August 16,
1999.

37. Joshua Davis, "Hackers Take Down the Most Wired Country in Europe," *Wired,*
August 21, 2007.

38. David A. Fulghum, "Why Syria's Air Defenses Failed to Detect Israelis," *Aviation
Week,* October 3, 2007.

39. Kim Zetter, "Simulated Cyberattack Shows Hackers Blasting Away at the Power
Grid," *Wired,* September 26, 2007.

40. "CIA Confirms Cyber Attack Caused Multi-City Power Outage," *SANS Flash*, January 18, 2008, http://www.sans.org/newsletters/newsbites/newsbites.php?vol=10&
issue=5.

41. "Annual Report to Congress: Military Power of the People's Republic of China
2007," Office of the Secretary of Defense, p. 22, available at www.defenselink.mil/
pubs/pdfs/070523-China-Military-Power-final.pdf.

42. Ibid.

43. Robert Marquand and Ben Arnoldy, "China Emerges as Leader in Cyberwarfare,"
The Christian Science Monitor, September 14, 2007.

44. "Report of the Defense Science Board Task Force on Mission Impact of Foreign In-

fluence on DoD Software," Office of the Under Secretary of Defense for Acquisition, Technology, and Logistics, September 2007, p. v.

45. Bill Gertz, "Military fears attacks from cyberspace," *The Washington Times,* March 29, 2001.

46. Ibid.

47. Ellen Nakashima, "Bush Order Expands Network Monitoring," *Washington Post,* p. A3, January 26, 2008; Siobhan Gorman, "Bush Looks to Beef Up Protection Against Cyberattacks," *Wall Street Journal,* January 28, 2008; Deborah Gage, "Virus from China, the Gift that Keeps Giving," *San Francisco Chronicle,* February 15, 2008; "MI5 Alert on China's Cyberspace Spy Threat," *London Times,* December 1, 2007; Demetri Sevastopulo, "Chinese Hacked into Pentagon," *Financial Times,* September 3, 2007; Andy Greenberg and Brian Wingfield, "From China with Love," Forbes.com, February 11, 2008; "China Hacked into Pentagon Computer Network," Beijing (Agence France-Presse), September 4, 2007. "The New Espionage Threat," *BusinessWeek,* April 21, 2008.

48. "Report of the Defense Science Board Task Force on Mission Impact of Foreign Influence on DoD Software," p. ix.

49. Gregory Slabodkin, "NT Leaves Navy 'Smart Ship' dead in the water," *Government Computer News (GCN),* July 13, 1998.

9: Getting It Right

1. Joel Garreau, *Edge City: Life on the New Frontier* (New York: Anchor Press, 1992).

2. Jerry Markon, "FBI's Fairfax Agents Packing for Pr. William," *The Washington Post,* October 25, 2006.

3. See www.nctc.gov/kids/kids.html.

4. Matthew Lee, "Former Staffer Slams Diplomats in Iraq," Washington (AP), February 8, 2008; Helen Dewar, "Frist Staffer Quits over Judiciary Probe," *Washington Post,* February 6, 2004, p. A5.

5. "The Growth of Political Appointees in the Bush Administration," United States House of Representatives Committee on Government Reform—Minority Staff, Special Investigations Division, May 2006.

6. Eric Lichtblau, "Bush Restoring Cash Bonuses for Appointees," *The New York Times,* December 4, 2002.

INDEX